NOTABLE

BANGALORE VENKATA RAMAN
Editor, THE ASTROLOGICAL MAGAZINE

MOTILAL BANARSIDASS PUBLISHERS PVT. LTD.
DELHI

Fifth Edition: 1981
Sixth Edition: Delhi, 1991

ISBN: 81–208–0900–9 (Cloth)
ISBN: 81–208–0901–7 (Paper)

Also available at:
M O T I L A L   B A N A R S I D A S S
41 U.A., Bungalow Road, Jawahar Nagar, Delhi 110 007
120 Royapettah High Road, Mylapore, Madras 600 004
16 St. Mark's Road, Bangalore 560 001
Ashok Rajpath, Patna 800 004
Chowk, Varanasi 221 001

PRINTED IN INDIA
BY JAINENDRA PRAKASH JAIN AT SHRI JAINENDRA PRESS, A-45 NARAINA
INDUSTRIAL AREA, PHASE I, NEW DELHI 110 028 AND PUBLISHED BY NARENDRA
PRAKASH JAIN FOR MOTILAL BANARSIDASS PUBLISHERS PVT. LTD.,
BUNGALOW ROAD, JAWAHAR NAGAR, DELHI 110 007

CONTENTS

v

PREFACE TO THE SIXTH EDITION

This edition has been revised and some of the errors found in the previous editions corrected. The horoscopes have been revised and at places rewritten taking into account events that have occurred subsequent to the publication of the earlier editions.

Of late a doubt is being expressed in some quarters as to whether the planetary positions given in this book in respect of very ancient horoscopes, would stand the scrutiny of computer calculations.

Computers take into account astronomical formulae based upon modern observations, but the criteria for the accuracy of the planetary longitudes in respect of very ancient horoscopes cannot be the assumptions of the computer-programmes. It is essential to note the limitations of the analytical methods as well as the restricted applicability of computers when long-time effects are to be evaluated.

Suffice to say that the castings given in the book have been calculated by noted astronomers like Cyril Fagan, F.C. Dutt and L. Narain Rao both on the basis of Brown's tables an *Suryasiddhānta*.

I hope this edition of NOTABLE HOROSCOPES will be of much use to both students and savants of Astrology leading to a better appreciation of the practical aspect of Astrology.

I thank the publishers Messrs Motilal Banarsidass for bringing out this edition in an attractive form.

Bangalore
Date: 31-1-1991

B.V. RAMAN

PREFACE TO FIFTH EDITION

In the fifth edition of NOTABLE HOROSCOPES herewith presented, some of the horoscopes have been revised and re-written taking into consideration happenings in their lives subsquent to the publication of the previous edition.

The whole book has been revised and some of the errors found in the previous editions corrected.

It is hoped that this new edition of NOTABLE HORO-SCOPES will aid both the students and savants of astrology to a better appreciation of the practical aspect of the subject.

NOTABLE HOROSCOPES Volume II is under preparation. It will cover the horoscopes of Lal Bahadur Shastri, Kennedy, De Gualle, Nixon, Indira Gandhi, Morarji Desai and other notables.

Thanks are due to IBH Prakashana, Gandhinagar, Bangalore–560 009 for having brought out this edition attractively.

"Sri Rajeswari",
BANGALORE
4-7-1981

B. V. RAMAN

PREFACE TO FIRST EDITION

For some years I dealt with prominent horoscopes in THE ASTROLOGICAL MAGAZINE under the caption *Horoscope of the Month*. This feature was immensely liked. But it had to be given up for obvious reasons.

During the last three or four years repeated requests reached me from several of my readers that I should bring out a book, solely dealing with horoscopes containing notable astrological features. In response to these requests this book has been prepared. Some of the horoscopes given in this treatise have appeared in THE ASTROLOGICAL MAGAZINE, but this cannot lessen the worth of the book inasmuch as, such horoscopes have either been revised or re-written.

In the recent times, there appears to have been a great spur in astrological activity both in India and abroad and this necessarily calls for the publication of new astrological books dealing with the subject more systematically and comprehensively.

It is this fascinating quest for astrology that has made me bring out *Notable Horoscopes* and if by my humble labour I could make others take a more lively interest in this sublime science, my labours will not be in vain.

It has not been found possible to obtain the permission of all living presons whose horoscopes have been published in this book. I request them not to take offence at the comments made about them, as the discussions are essentially objective and scientific.

BANGALORE
Durmukhi
New Year's Day
12-4-1956

B. V. RAMAN

INTRODUCTION

There is an unfortunate taboo amongst a section of the so-called thinkers against discussion of beliefs concerning man's relationship with the cosmos. As a result, even in the more liberal platforms the question of planets and men seldom comes out in open. Enquiring minds who challenge established scientific beliefs mostly western oriented are viewed with suspicion. Amongst themselves astrologers are used to propound hypotheses which must run the gamut of criticism. Astrologers are not politicians whose words spoken today are gospel tomorrow and forgotten the day after. It takes time for the acceptance of astrological advances—advances made in the face of rabid, destructive and damaging criticisms of the Press and the Politician. It was thirty-five years before Newton's *Principia* was taught in his own University. Mendel, who published his theory in 1865, died in 1884 a disappointed man whose work had gone unrecognised. No wonder therefore that astrological theories, even when commonly accepted, are sometimes "challenged" by ill-informed and half-informed critics.

Astrology or Jyotisha Sastra, as developed by the Maharshis, makes a precise study of the position and inter-relation of the stars and planets. It has perceived by intuition certain facts which western science can barely demonstrate. Astrology may be considered a science of sciences in as much as it tends to give objective form to man's desire for a better knowledge of his future. As Dr. Castiglini observes in his great work *Adventures of the Mind* "modern research in radiations emitted by substances contained in the stars and revealed by the spectrum, the hypotheses that have been recently advanced concerning the relations between solar spots and extraordinary historical events, the publications by Swaboda and Fliess on the laws of septennial periods, all these lead us to think that the intuitive and profoundly human conception, deriving directly from man's immediate sensitivity to the action of the stars may have a vaster and deeper foundation of truth than was realised when this primitive idea of intercosmic solidarity seemed to be forgotten".

One cannot dismiss astrology with a contemptuous gesture by calling it a superstition. Truth, as the history of science shows, cannot be killed by giving it a bad name. On the face of it, prediction of a future event, which has not yet occurred, may appear to be impossible. As astrology has shown that 'foreknowledge' of things is possible, science must find a place for it in its purview of universe. Astrology is based upon scientific data for the horoscope is a picture of the heavens, *i.e.*, the astronomical positions of the planets with reference to the moment and the locality of one's birth. I would refer my readers to my book, "Planetary Influences on Human Affairs" for a more detailed understanding of the rationale of Astrology.

According to the sages, the horoscope indicates our past Karma—the Prarabdha portion of the Karma being our destiny in this life and that astrological predictions are only tendencies of nature on their way towards fulfilment or manifestation and one can either augment or lessen their momentum in the particular direction desired by recourse to remedial measures. Hence astrology has been fulfilling a very desirable social function.

In the study of astrology there are two factors to be considered, *viz.*, theory and practice. The theory of astrology can be studied with the aid of any standard book on the subject. In studying horoscopes, we arrive at certain inferences. And the inferences can be valid when they are justfied by the evidence given in support of them. For instance, in a given horoscope, an inference is drawn regarding longevity—this inference being justified by the evidence (combinations) given in support of it. But sometimes we may make inferences which turn out to be true though they may not be valid, *i.e.*, are not justified by the available evidence. In astrology the inference must not only be valid but also true. The study of the conditions of true inference would mean, an investigation into the truth of all possible premises—an obviously impossible task and hence the limitation of a strictly logical approach in regard to astrological prediction. Here comes the importance of intuition or judgment power in predictive astrology. Prediction implies first an analysis of the various combinations in the horoscope and second, a synthesis of a given or required event, on the basis of the analysed evidence. It is therefore no child's play to weigh and balance the relative strength of each factor and then synthesise the chart as to form a reasonable judgment of the whole. According to the great Satyacharya the astrologer must be well versed in the different branches of the subject and an adept in weighing the *pros* and *cons* of the horoscope. He must have the creative or inferential ability to interpret horoscopes and above all he must have spiritual equipment. It must be noted that in the matter of interpretation, each branch of astrology calls for its own particular technique. While the concepts of the ancient Rishis continue to form the basis, ancient, medieval and modern conditions—political, economic and social—necessitate certain modifications in judgment and application.

In the light of these introductory remarks, the indulgent readers must view my interpretation of the seventy-six charts given in *Notable Horoscopes*. It may be that some of my readers may not be inclined to agree with my interpretation of a given combination in a given chart. It does not mean, however, that my interpretation is necessarily incorrect. Taking the chart as a whole, I have endeavoured to construct the life-history of the individual in the light of the planetary patterns present in the chart thus enabling the astrological student to sort out the distinguishing or notable features of the horoscope. By the expression 'notable', as applied to this book, I mean not only noteworthy people but also horoscopes which are noteworthy in themselves as illustrating certain rare and definite combinations such as *Raja Yogas* (combinations for political power), *Parivraja Yogas* (combinations for renunciation), *Dhana Yogas* (combinations for immense wealth) and combinations which render a man great not necessarily in the public eye but by virtue of certain special qualities of head and heart, selflessness and religious discipline. The usefulness of such a discussion will not be disputed if we remember that each horoscope is illustrative of certain fundamental astrological principles which can be easily recognised thus fixing the attention of the reader and stimulating his mind for research and deep study.

The horoscopes selected cover a wide range of politicians, statesmen, saints, philosophers, scientists and public men and even maniacs and afford a unique opportunity to students of astrology to develop their "predictive sense". We now possess such a large amount of astrological information that its very immensity prevents us from using it properly. This book therefore is not intended to be a text-book. My intention has been merely to build up an intelligible synthesis of the data, which I have collected for over four decades. I have attempted to describe a large number of astrological facts in a simple manner having in view a readership consisting of the scholars as well as the laymen.

The horoscopes given in this book have been arranged chronologically. The most ancient chart, *e.g.*, that of Sri Krishna has been given first and the subsequent charts follow a strictly chronological order.

Regarding the accuracy of the birth data, two types of horoscopes can be recognised, *viz.*, the speculative and the authentic. To the former category belong the charts of Krishna, Buddha, Sankara, Christ, etc. In fixing dates of birth of these personages, due attention has been given to not only astronomical factors but also to historical, epigraphic and allied details.

It must be noted that several well-meaning Indian historians, following the footsteps of western scholars have unconsciously or deliberately ignored the most valuable documents, *viz.*, the Puranas, in assessing the age of such celebrities as Krishna, Sankara or Buddha. Even now there are some scholars whose hobby seems to be to think that the Hindus copied all their sciences, arts, literature and philosophy from the Greeks and that the antiquity of the Hindus cannot be placed before one or two thousand years B.C. Some of the modern astronomers assert with ill-founded reason that the Hindus borrowed their astronomy from the Greeks, those ignorant geniuses in astronomy who said that the Sun was a red-hot iron ball suspended in the heavens between the Peloponnesian and some other mountains. We can excuse ignorance, but we cannot show sympathy for wilful perversion of intellect.

Some Orientalists give the Puranas of Veda Vyasa the age of ten or eleven hundred A.D. They are unwilling to acknowledge the antiquity of the Hindu culture. Rev. Marshman placed the age of Ramayana after Mahabharata because he found in Ramayana, a certain verse (Ramo Bheema parakramah) in which the word Bheema (which usually means terrific) occurs which Marshman interpreted as the hero of Mahabharata and concluded thereby that Mahabharata must have taken place earlier than Ramayana. Col. Todd wished to ascribe to Krishna and other Yadavas, inheritance from Hercules, and Athri to Attrius. Other dabblers wanted to make Rama the descendant of Romulus. They would like to prove that the heroes of the Mahabharata learnt the art of fighting under Alexander of Macedonia and thus curb the pride of Indian antiquity. The mathematical absurdities were even greater and they had to open, rather very reluctantly in the beginning, their eyes to the dates given in the confounding number of inscriptions found all over India on which were given clearly information which could not be contradicted. Not being able to understand the complications of the vast knowledge of the Hindus, many of these European scholars and their blind Indian admirers found no other way than to bury them in the pits of oblivion, or mould them to fit into their ethnical grooves. The expositions on these matters so well offered by the Hindu Pandits were always matters of great difficulty to the European judges. In one single sentence some of the European investigators of Sanskrit sciences and Vedas transferred the whole lot to the regions of mythology and superstition. A huge misguided literature soon covered the face of the country—and it is current even now—in which the orientalists went on doing as much mischief to the spirit of Hindu culture and sciences as their intelligent brains allowed them to do.

Things do not seem to have improved much even after the dawn of political independence. Our angle of vision in approaching the ancient documents, such as the Puranas, has not varied even after the disappearance of the British ruel.

Some of our well meaning but misguided scholars still ignore these authentic sources, and fix up the age of Krishna and the Mahabharata in the 15th century B.C., lest they may be laughed at by their more ''enlightened'' brethren. On the basis of Mahabharata and Bhagavata, the date and time of birth of Sri Krishna can be accurately determined and we have done this (*vide* page 1) ; yet our scholars labour under the delusion that Krishna was not a historical reality and that if he were a real personality he could not have lived earlier than in the 11th century B.C. Names of the various kings and their dynasties that ruled the different parts of India from the beginning of Kali yuga upto the Christian era have been systematically dealt with in Bhavishya and other Puranas that it is a wonder how they could have been, or could be, ignored by our learned historians. Horoscopes of Krishna, Buddha, Sankara, etc., though 'speculative', have been constructed on a sound basis as the reader will be able to appreciate from the footnotes appended to each of these 'speculative horoscopes'.

So far as authentic horoscopes are concerned, the data have been secured from trustworthy sources. Some discrepancies in dates such as Samvat and Saka, Gregorian (new style) and Julian (old style) puzzled me. But I was able to overcome the difficulty with the help of friends well versed in chronology. Due thought has been given to the different kinds of calendar reckoning current in different parts of India and then the dates, given in Samavat or Saka, have been converted into their equivalent English dates. The collection of birth data for this book commenced as early as in 1930. Often, the details furnished by historians, authors and friends, either in regard to birth date or time, differed and these were subsequently compared with information unearthed from more reliable sources and then the authentic information picked up.

For instance, in the case of Aurangzeb, half-a-dozen versions were collected, but finally, the birth details, furnished by one Mr. Srikanta Sastry of Varanasi, were found to be reliable. Notwithstanding care on my part in collecting the data from reliable sources, it is left to the discretion of the reader to treat my findings as authentic or doubtful. Regarding the modern horoscopes given in this book, there is no doubt whatsoever that they can be considered as quite authentic. To a large extent, I am indebted to *American Astrology*, *Modern Astrology and Coming Events*, for data pertaining to European and American horoscopes, modern and ancient. Others who helped me in securing the data have been mentioned in the appropriate places. In any case, I will have the satisfaction of having furnished students of astrology with charts which may prove interesting subjects from the point of view of research and study.

The plan adopted by me in preparing this book is simple. First, the birth details have been mentioned in English reckoning. Then the planetary positions have been given from the first point of the Nirayana or fixed zodiac. The Ayanamsa in respect of each horoscope is appended so that one may get a Sayana chart, if he so desires. The Ayanamsa as adopted by me is 0 for 397 A.D., negative for subsequent years and positive for years prior to 397 (as applied to tropical zodiac). When the Ayanamsa is given as plus (+) it has to be deducted from the Nirayana positions to get Sayana positions. When the Ayanamsa is given without prefix it means the Ayanamsa value is to be added to the Nirayana positions to get corresponding Sayana positions. The Rasi and Navamsa diagrams, with which most of my readers should be familiar, are given according to the South Indian style and the charts are followed by the balance of Dasa. Except in two or three cases, first the "special features" of the horoscope are examined, the discussion mostly bearing on the combinations, which could have produced the native whose chart is under consideration. This is followed by the listing of important life-events in the light of the directional or Dasa influences. How a particular event could have happened under a particular Dasa and Bhukti has been clearly discussed. Finally, under 'Remarks', the horoscope is summed up, bringing out the salient combinations that have made the native what he was or is. In a sense, some sort of an astrological biography has been given enabling the student to fully appreciate the life-history in the light of the astrological factors. I am sure the book will meet with general approval in the hands of my esteemed readers.

I am fully conscious of the difficulties inherent in presenting a book of the type of *Notable Horoscopes* before a critical and discriminating public. Of course I may not have succeeded. I may not satisfy the adept because I know much less than he does. However, in order to enable one to obtain a synthentic knowledge of astrology, I feel the publication of such a book is called for, bearing in mind that an attempt, such as this, however imperfect, is better than no attempt at all.

In closing this introduction I must acknowledge my indebtedness to my friend Mr. Cyril Fagan of Dublin for his unstinting help. He has calculated for me, several of the ancient horoscopes given in this book ; in some cases, each horoscope several times.

BANGALORE
12-4-1956

B. V. RAMAN

No. I.—SRI KRISHNA

Birth Details.—*19th July 3228 B.C., at about midnight (Lat. 27° 25′ N., long. 77° 41′ E.)

Planetary Positions—The Sun 139° 48′; the Moon 47° 42′; Mars 91° 6′; Mercury 152° 48′; Jupiter 148° 54′; Venus 102° 54′; Saturn 224° 42′; Rahu 106° 24′; and Lagna 50°. Ayanamsa + 50° 40′.

		Lagna Moon			Ketu	Moon Lagna
		Mars Venus Rahu				Mars
	RASI		NAVAMSA			
Ketu		Sun Jupit.	Merc.			
	Saturn	Merc.	Jupit.	Rahu Saturn	Venus	Sun

Balance of the Moon's Dasa at birth : Years 4-2-21.

Special Features.—The Lagna is Taurus or Vrishabha, a sign of Venus, and it is occupied by the Moon and aspected

---

* Regarding the date of Sri Krishna, there is no doubt difference of opinion amongst historians who have been largely inspired and influenced by oriental scholars and their Indian followers. But if an unprejudiced study of the Puranas, Srimad Bhagavata and other records of

by Saturn making Sri Krishna extremely handsome. The dominance of the influences of the Moon and Venus, with Saturn and Mars, made the Lord's appearance, wonderfully graceful. From classical texts we gather that Sri Krishna possessed a magnetic personality, crimson cheeks, 'coral lips', a fascinating face and a sky-blue complexion—features largely due to the delicate blending of the martian, saturnine, venusian and lunar features. Lagna lord Venus is in his own navamsa. Consequently, Krishna was a master of courtesy even to the "low-born Chandalas", as the Bhagavata refers. His invincible prowess in the field of battle is brought out by the neecha-bhanga of the martial planet Mars in the 3rd or house of courage. It must be noted that he defeated mighty Sisupala and other kings and formidable foes by dint of courage, tact and resourcefulness.

Indian origin is made, interesting details regarding Krishna's birth date and time come to light. We may easily dismiss the findings of some of the modern scholars that Mahabharata took place near about 2000 B.C., that Bhagavadgita was composed in 1000 B.C. and that Krishna was a mythical person, based as such findings are on untrustworthy and one sided data and because of the fact that the great historical documents, *viz.*, the Puranas are completely ignored.

In Bhagavata, tenth skanda, third chapter, it is said that Krishna was born when the Moon was in the constellation of Prajapathi, *i.e.*, Rohini. By a careful study of the 26th sloka of first chapter, fifth amsa of Vishnupurana, it can be construed that Krishna was born on the night of Krishnashtami (8th day of dark half) in the lunar month of Sravana. Information furnished in Harivamsa (1 Part, 52nd chapter) is clear and to the point so far as the lunar day, month and time are concerned. It is said that Krishna was born on the 8th lunar day of the dark half of Sravana, in the constellation of Rohini at midnight. From

Ashtamyam Sravanemase Krishnapakshe mahatithou ;
Rohinyamardharatre cha sudnmsa udayonmukhe

The Moon, the planet of emotion, is exalted in Lagna, and unafflicted by Rahu conferring great serenity of mind, while Mercury the planet of intellect who owns the 2nd or house of speech is exalted in the 5th or house of intelligence. This is a unique combination denoting wonderful intelligence and extraordinary conversational ability. His was a giant intellect unequalled in analytic understanding. He passed through the virtues and deceptions of the thoughts of His day. He was superior to any thinker of His times. Krishna possessed an uncanny diplomacy and unbounded vision and this should be attributed to the ideal disposition of Mercury. Jupiter is in the 4th. Sri Krishna was a man of rich and responsive human sympathy but the Sun's association in his own place rendered Krishna a terror to the wicked and a friend to the wise.

Bhagavata, we can also glean (Skanda 11, Chapter VI) that Krishna lived for 125 years, Vishnupurana (Amsa 5, Chapter 37) corroborates the same in suggesting that Krishna lived for 125 years. If we again refer to Bhagavata (Skanda 11, Chapter 7) and understand the 2nd sloka clearly we can find that Kali entered (i.e. Kaliyuga began) immediately after Krishna shuffled off his mortal coil. That Kali entered on the day Krishna passed away and that Krishna was born in Yaduvamsa at the end of the Dwaparayuga of the 28th Mahayuga, i. e., the Dwapara preceding the current Kaliyuga, becomes evident by a perusal of Vishnupurana (4th and 20th Chapters and V Amsa, 23rd Chapter). Thus by placing together details taken from the most important historical and cultural documents of ancient India, viz., Srimad Bhagavata, Vishnupurana and Harivamsa, it may be clearly inferred that Sri Krishna was born at midnight, on the 8th lunar day of the cyclic year Srimukha, in the 126th year counted backwards from the date of commencement of Kaliyuga on 18-2-3102 B.C. corresponding to the 1st day of the lunar month Chaitra of the cyclic year Pramadhi. This corresponds to the midnight of 19th (20th) July 3228 B.C., and the above horoscope is cast for this date.

The 10th lord aspects the Lagna, the Atmakaraka Sun and the planet of Dharma Jupiter, in their turn aspect the 10th. Consequently He possessed a passionate zeal to safeguard *Dharma*. Krishna's birth in prison is justified by the association of the lords of Lagna (Venus) and the 12th (Mars) with Rahu. Jupiter, lord of the 11th (elder brothers and sisters), has gained 8 navamsas and is in the 9th. He is aspected by Saturn in Rasi and has joined Rahu in navamsa. It must be noted that Krishna was the 8th issue, all the elder ones having been put to death by Kamsa. Due to the exaltation of Matrukaraka Moon and the situation of Pitrukaraka Sun in his own house with Jupiter, his parents were long-lived.

Both Kalatrakaraka Venus and the 7th lord Mars together, with Rahu, explain the fact that Krishna had a number of wives. But as Venus is near Rahu and away from the sensual planet

---

In his *Royal Horoscopes*, Prof. B. Suryanarain Rao, by a careful study of the Bhagavata records, mentions that Krishna was born "in the Dwaparayuga after the lapse of 863874 years, 4 months and 22 days in the cyclic year Srimukha, on the 8th day of the dark half of the lunar month of Sravana, when the constellation Rohini ruled, at about midnight". Prof. Rao's findings may be considered as correct. But the Chart or Kundali he gives showing Saturn in Aquarius, Jupiter and Mercury in Virgo, the Sun and Venus in Leo, the Moon and Lagna in Taurus, Mars in Scorpio and Rahu in Libra does not fit in with the birth data. Mr. Cyril Fagan, to whom I am much indebted for the immense trouble he has taken to calculate some of these ancient horoscopes, informs me that by making a thorough astronomical search from 4000 B.C. to 2000 B.C., *i.e.*, for 2,000 years on either side of the traditional date of Kaliyuga he has been able to find that the position of the Sun, Jupiter and Saturn in Leo, Virgo and Aquarius respectively and Rahu in Libra could occur only in 3251 B.C., in which case, Krishna's birth should have occurred on 4-7-3251 B.C., and His death in February 3125 B C., *i.e.*, exactly 23 years before the beginning of Kaliyuga. These "justify" to some extent that Kaliyuga

Mars, His love for His wives had no taint of carnality as He was free from attachment of any kind. Though "associated with Prakriti, He was never affected by its qualities". Birth in a sign of Venus no doubt endowed him with a vital nature but it was under conscious control. Mercury, exalted in the 5th or house of children, occupies the constellation of the Sun while Jupiter Putrakaraka is in association with the Sun, with the result He had innumerable children born to Him. The 4th or house of education is considerably fortified due to the presence of Jupiter and the Sun-Jupiter occupying the constellation of Venus. It is said that Krishna became an expert in "siksha, kalpas, vedangas and all the vedas, and also in archery mimamsa, logical and six expedients of politics" and that "within 64 days and nights" He became "an expert in sixty-four forms of learning".

Important Events.—The Moon, though excellently placed, owns the 3rd while Mars, as ruling the 7th, is a definite maraka. Consequently practically throughout the Dasas of the

---

began "shortly after Krishna's death." On 4-7-3251 B C., the positions of all the planets will be as per the Kundali given by Prof. B. S. Rao, but Mercury will be in Leo and Mars in Aries. The term "shortly after" death, used by Prof. B. S. Rao, may mean a couple of days or a couple of months or even a couple of years after Krishna's death. But according to Matsya Purana (*vide* Adhyaya 271, slokas 51–52) the matter becomes quite clear when it says that the year and day on which Krishna passed away mark the commencement of Kaliyuga.

Yasmin Krishna divam jatastasminneva (hi vatsare) ;
Tadahani pratipannam Kaliyugam pramanam tasyame srunu

Without straining these authoritative quotations, we may safely assume that on the (traditional) day of Krishna's death, Kaliyuga commenced and that Krishna was born in the 126th year counted backwards from 3102 B.C. It occurs to me that the Kundali given by Prof. Rao was not probably verified as otherwise, he would have taken care to see that there was no inconsistency between the planetary positions and birth details.

Moon and Mars, which extended till the native was aged about 11 years, Krishna suffered from severe strokes of Balarishta in the sense that He faced many a crisis in His life, especially from those deputed by Kamsa to slay Him. Probably at the fag end of Kuja Dasa, Krishna put to death His maternal uncle and tyrant Kamsa. As we have already said, Mars as lord of the 7th in association with Venus, lord of the 6th (enemies), in the 3rd (an upachaya) enabled Krishna to achieve victory over His greatest enemy and thus tide over the maraka period.

His subsequent exploits in disposing off innumerable wicked kings, in saving the pious and the god-fearing from death and in trying to prevent the fatricidal war between the Kauravas and the Pandavas are a legion and students of astrology can study them in the light of the Lord's horoscope. The most important event is His part in the Mahabharata war, which took place about 3138 B.C. when Ketu Dasa was in progress in the Lord's horoscope. Ketu is in the 9th, the house of Saturn, whose results Ketu should give. Saturn is Yogakaraka and occupies the 7th having gained digbala or directional strength. Krishna's part in the Mahabharata war is well known. As charioteer to Arjuna, He remained a silent observer of the war, but directed "the movements to accomplish His final object of destroying the wicked and protecting the innocent".

Ketu is Mokshakaraka and he is in the 9th in the constellation of the Moon aspected by the martial planet Mars. And Saturn, as we have already seen, is immensely fortified. It was at the fag end of Ketu Dasa, that the immortal Bhagavadgita was taught by the Lord to Arjuna, on the battle-field, before the war commenced, when Arjuna, overcome by emotional weakness, shirked from his duty as a Kshatriya to fight for a just cause. In the remaining Dasas of Venus, the Sun and the

Moon, Krishna passed a peaceful and happy life. With the dawn
of Kuja Dasa again dissensions amongst Yadavas broke out.
Finally Krishna shuffled off His mortal coil under the same
directional influences. It will be seen that Mars as lord of the
7th is a definite maraka and he occupies the 3rd, a house of
longevity, with Rahu. In the Navamsa again Mars is in the 2nd,
a house of maraka. Consistent with the nature of Mars, Krishna
departed by being hit by an arrow. When Krishna was sitting
under an Aswatha tree in a forest, a fowler named Jara, thinking the foot of Krishna to be like the face of a deer, mistakenly
shot his arrow. According to Bhagavata, the Lord departed to
His own abode Vaikunta "in person".

Remarks.—It is impossible for ordinary mortals to evaluate
the personality of Sri Krishna—the Lord incarnate, statesman,
counsellor, diplomat, philosopher, Yogeeswara, the expounder
of the immortal Bhagavadgita, the destroyer of the wicked and
the protector of the pious. All the three important factors in His
horoscope, *viz.*, the Lagna, the Sun and the Moon have been
rendered strong. Atmakaraka Sun with the Gnanakaraka Jupiter
aspecting the 10th or Karmasthana reveals an integrated and
balanced personality. Yogakaraka Saturn is Vargottama and has
digbala. His aspecting the Sun and Jupiter and his being placed
in his own constellation are favourable factors rendering the
nativity strong and sound. Since Saturn happens to be Ayushkaraka also, his strong disposition conferred a long life of 125
years. Mercury's exaltation in a trikona—as lord of the 2nd
(speech) in the 5th (intelligence) denotes wonderful and
extraordinary intellect. It will be seen that Lagna lord Venus
is with two malefics. This combination *plus* the kendra position
of Jupiter and the Sun indicates perfection of all aspects of His
personality. He was an ideal father and an ideal son, an ideal

king, an ideal husband, an ideal statesman and an ideal teacher. He showed the way to do things, to do one's duty, by being non-attached and He illustrated this in His own life.

Whatever be the opinions of some of the modern scholars, there is no doubt that **Sri Krishna** was a historical reality. A mere literary creation cannot by any stretch of imagination move millions of human beings and bring solace to countless souls. The clue to His personality can be found in the manner the benefics and malefics are disposed in His horoscope and the spheres of influences involved. The meaning of what He did can only progressively reveal itself to the generations that follow Him. The immortal Bhagavadgita, preached by the Lord, when Arjuna became uncertain as to his duty, has inspired and influenced the moral and spiritual thought and actions of innumerable persons and offered such persons solutions to their problems according to their own stage in evolution.

No. 2.—SRI GAUTAMA BUDDHA

Birth Details.—*14th April 623 B.C. at about midday (Lat. 27° 8′ N., Long. 83° 5′ E.)

Planetary Positions.—The Sun 29° 3′ ; the Moon 200′ 45′ ; Mars 26° 54′ ; Mercury 53° 6′ ; Jupiter 11° ; Venus 6° 12′ ; Saturn 24° 36′ ; Rahu 86° 54′ ; and Lagna 116° 45′, Ayanamsa +14° 16′.

Jupiter Sun Saturn Venus Mars	Mercury	Rahu	Lagna	Moon	Venus	Rahu
		Lagna				Mercury Jupiter
	RASI			NAVAMSA		
Ketu		Moon		Sun Mars Ketu	Saturn	

Balance of Jupiter's Dasa at birth : Years 15–1–6.

Special Features.—The lord of Lagna Moon is full and occupies the sign of Venus aspected by five planets. Hence

---

*There is a difference of opinion as regards the date of birth of the Buddha. Oriental scholars "usually place it" about 563 B.C. I have carefully examined the historical and other evidences adduced by different scholars in support of their versions and have found that most of these

Lagna lord is immensely fortified. Both the Lagna and the
Lagna lord are subject to the aspect of Mars. In Navamsa,
Lagna lord Moon is in Aries. These dispositions conferred
on the Buddha, great physical beauty and a magnetic personality. Because of the aspects of Venus, Mars and Jupiter on
Lagna lord, He was handsome, fair in colour, stately to
behold and of majestic mien. Aristocrat by birth He was at
home with all—kings, princes, warriors and beggars—a characteristic largely due to birth in the constellation of Visakha.
Mercury the planet of humour is in a benefic sign, otherwise
unafflicted. The royal planet the Sun is exalted in the 10th.
Consequently, His dignity was unshakable and His humour,
invariable. The Moon, ruling mind, is no doubt aspected by
five planets, of which, the most powerful aspect is cast by
Saturn. Mars in his own sign and Saturn debility have
rendered each other's association harmless. Consequently, the
Moon's peculiar position rendered him in infinitely patient and
moved Him to anxious and puzzled reflection on the true purpose of life.

---

scholars have either deliberately ignored or unconsciously overlooked the
astronomical and traditional factors bearing on the date of Buddha's
birth. My friend, Mr. Cyrus D. F. Abayakoon of Ceylon, has furnished
me with important details as current in Ceylonese tradition. He says that
according to palm leaves in possession of certain Ceylonese Priests, the
Buddha was born in Kaliyuga 2478, on the Full Moon day of the lunar
month of Vaisakha, Tuesday, at about midday. In the sloka cited by him
the weekday is clearly given as *Kshitisutha divasa, i.e.*, Tuesday, Kaliyuga
2478, Vaisakha Sukla Purnima corresponds to 26th April 624 B.C. but
the weekday happens to be Friday. Moreover the planetary positions
obtaining on this day (the Sun $40° 36'$; the Moon $211° 48'$; Mars $141° 12'$;
Mercury $62° 24'$; Jupiter $344° 30'$; Venus $72° 48'$; Saturn $13° 6'$; Rahu
$105° 18'$) do not fit in with the great personality of the Buddha. But on

Venus, away from Mars and within close range of Jupiter, protected the Buddha from sensuous feeling and enjoyment. The 7th lord Saturn is not only neecha but is considerably afflicted by his conjunction with Mars—both occupying the 7th from Chandra Lagna. This explains the affliction of Kalatrabhava and want of happiness, in the conventional sense of the term, on this account. The lord of Lagna Moon—karaka for the mind—in the constellation of Jupiter—the divine planet—occupying the Navamsa of Mars, gave Him an iron will, a strong determination and the urge to undiscouraged action. But for such resoluteness of purpose, He would not have subjected Himself to mortification and servere forms of ascetic penances for a period of six years till He found more successful clues to understanding.

_____

the Full Moon day of Vaisakha of Kali 2479 (623 B.C.) the weekday happens to be Tuesday which confirms the traditional data. Mr. Abayakoon informs me that according to a Buddha Gaya inscription (as quoted by Mr. M.N. Sastri in his book *Lord Buddha, His Life, Teaching and Order* Buddha's death occurred in B.C 544 and that this is supported by other sources. By all accounts Buddha lived for 80 years. This means that His birth should have occurred in 624 B.C. Here I should like to caution readers that some confusion is bound to occur in reckoning B.C. years for Kaliyuga dates. There is no B.C. '0' or A.D. '0' in the Roman Calendar and in consequence all B C. datings are generally in error by one year. For example the Kaliyuga actually commenced 3101 years before Christ, but for conventional usage we would write it as 3102 B.C. As most historians and astronomers may not be aware of this, it is possible an error of one year in the B.C. datings are likely. Hence even in regard to Buddha's date of birth, an error of one year may have crept in the reckoning. Having due regard to historical, astronomical and traditional factors, I am inclined to believe that the Buddha was born on the Full Moon day of the lunar month of Vaisakha, Kali 2479, Tuesday, corresponding to 14th April 623 B.C. The horoscope of the Buddha for this

Buddha's nobility, serenity and the deep compassion He felt for all are due as much to the blessings of *Amala Yoga*, as His ascetic denial of the body's demands in extreme form are due to the presence of *Pasa Yoga*. The most formidable combinations in this horoscope refer to the 10th house or Karmasthana. The Sun lord of the 2nd, who also happens to be Atmakaraka, is elevated in the 10th. Mars as lord of the 5th with Saturn as lord of the 7th ; Mars as lord of the 10th in association with Jupiter lord of the 9th ; Venus as lord of the 4th in association with Mars as lord of the 5th ; Venus as lord of the 4th in association with Jupiter lord of the 9th—have given rise to a series of powerful Rajayogas—all converging their influences on the 10th from Lagna and the 7th from the Moon who happens to be Lagna lord.

———

date has been calculated by four independent sources, *viz.*, Mr. F.C. Dutt, Mr. Cyril Fagan, Mr. L. Narayana Rao and myself and the positions of planets arrived at, according to these four different sources, more or less tally with perhaps a slight difference of a degree or two.

Mr. Fernando of Panadura has suggested that in the Kskayar Nadi, the date of Buddha's birth has been given as "Sunday, 15th day of the first half of lunar month Vaisakha, Kaliyuga 2478, at Gh. 11—4", the Sun to Saturn, in the order of the weekdays occupying respectively, Taurus, Libra, Capricorn, Aries, Virgo, Pisces and Aquarius. It will be seen that the weekday happens to be Friday and not Sunday. Moreover the planetary positions are all incorrectly given. Hence we can safely reject this horoscope. For the information of those who may differ from my view and assume that the Buddha was born in 557 B.C. or 543 B.C. or 1887 B.C. I give the planetary positions for the Full Moon of the lunar month Vaisakha for each of these years.

10–3–1887 B.C , Tuesday at Noon.—The Sun 4° 54′ ; the Moon 178° 6′ ; Mars 358° 24′ ; Mercury 340° 30′ ; Jupiter 158° 12′ ; Venus 23° 24′ ; Saturn 46° 48′ ; and Rahu 75° 38′.

Gnanakaraka Jupiter and the philosophical planet Saturn—both together again constituting another Rajayoga—gave Him unexcelled philosophical power. He had annihilated sensuous passions and led a life of immaculate purity, results undoubtedly due to the sublime effects of Jupiter over Venus. Rahu's presence in the 12th—Mokshasthana— in the constellation of the Moon—made the Buddha a philosophic genius while His intellectual eminence is due to the Upachaya disposition of Mercury.

Important Events. — In his 16th year, Gautama was married to Yasodhara. This took place as soon as Sani Dasa commenced. Mark the fact that Saturn owns the 7th from Lagna and the 5th from Chandra Lagna with the lord of the 7th Mars and Kalatrakaraka Venus. Till the end of the sub-period of Mars in Saturn Dasa—by virtue of their position in the 7th, Gautama grew amid scenes of luxury with their constant stimulations to self-centered indulgence but always protected by His father from learning about the frustrations and sorrows of life. But as soon as Rahu Bhukti commenced—and I must emphasize here the presence of Rahu in the 12th or Mokshasthana—in His 29th year, Buddha, on the day of the birth of His son Rahula, made the great renunciation. He left His young wife and child and wandered into the forest. For six years thereafter, *i.e.*, during the sub-period of Jupiter in Saturn Dasa and the sub-period of Mercury in his own Mercury Dasa, He went through all

4-4-557 B.C., Friday at Noon.—The Sun 21°′; the Moon 197° 5′; Mars 40° 36′; Mercury 30° 36′; Jupiter 206° 12′; Venus 35°; Saturn 115° 6′; and Rahu 243° 17′.

1-4-543 B.C., Friday at Noon.—The Sun 18° 36′; the Moon 204° 51′; Mars 179° 48′; Mercury 38° 8′; Jupiter 279° 6′; Venus 335° 24′; Saturn 286° 18′; and Rahu 339° 30′.

the experiences of *Hatha Yoga* and not satisfied with
the outcome, He decided on meditation. In his 35th year, in
Mercury Dasa, Mercury Bhukti, sitting under the Bodhi tree, on
the Full Moon day of Vaisakha, He is said to have attained
enlightenment. Mercury as lord of the 12th—Mokshsathana—is
in the constellation of Lagnadhipathi. In the Navamsa he
occupies the 5th with exalted Jupiter, lord of Navamsa Lagna.
Under the same directional influences He preached His first
sermon of the "sweetly reasonable middleway" which lies
"between two extremes of sensuality and mortifications".

It was in Venus Dasa that his triumphant spiritual conquest
of the land took place, Venus is fully empowered to confer this
great Rajayoga, by virtue of his association with Jupiter.
During Venus Dasa, the Master moved from place to place
organising and spreading His doctrines and organising the
expansion of the order. As soon as Mars Bhukti in the Sun's
Dasa commenced, the Buddha was taken ill. He recovered
from His illness. At the age of 80, He passed away with the
words : "Decay is inherent in all compound things. Work out
your own salvation with diligence." Buddha's death took
place at the end of Mars Bhukti in the Sun's Dasa. It will
be seen that the Sun is a distinct maraka not only as lord of the
2nd but also as associating the lord of the 7th. The sub-lord
Mars owns the 2nd and 7th from Chandra Lagna and occupies
the 7th therefrom with the major lord. The Buddha knew
about His end which was peaceful. This is explained by the
fact that the 22nd drekkana has reference to a benefic sign.

Remarks.—Five planets in the 10th—both by Rasi and
Bhava—bring out the dynamic personality of the Buddha. The
grouping together of these five planets within an arc of twenty-
three degrees, has resulted in a number of Rajayogas as well

as Parivraja Yoga, giving us a clear insight into the real
achievements of the Master.   Buddha never preached anything
hostile to Hinduism.   He was a Hindu of Hindus. Buddhism is
not a new religion but it is just an offshoot of Hinduism, or
rather a part of Hinduism just as Saivism or Vaishnavism is.

What the Buddha has said has been mostly delivered from
the luminous and inspiring thoughts contained in the Upanishads.   Consistent with the peculiar structure of His horoscope,
the Buddha's concern was to free human life from the net of
overwrought metaphysics as much as from superfluous ritualism.

Gnanakaraka Jupiter, Mokshakaraka Saturn, and Atmakaraka the Sun in Karmasthana (10th) must suggest to any tyro
in astrology that Buddha could never have denied either God or
soul.   Buddha accepted ''as essentially sound, the concepts
of Dharma, Karma and Moksha, although after Buddha, His
disciples, indulged freely in subjecting to harsh criticism, some
of the basic doctrines of Hinduism''. Hindus acclaim the Buddha
as an Avatar of Vishnu and if at all philosophers like Sankara
have only criticised some of the Buddhistic doctrines as interpreted by subsequent Buddhist scholars, the Buddha had
always remained as sacred and sublime as any other Avatar of
Vishnu.   The goal of the Hindu was union with Brahman,
which was transformed rather than rejected by Buddha, into
Nirvana.

The fact that Buddha accepted the basic features of
Hinduism like Karma, Samsara, Moksha (or Nirvana) clearly
indicates the degree to which His thinking was embedded in
the heritage of Upanishads.   The five-planet grouping taken as
a whole constitutes *Gola Yoga*, a combination which is said to
cause great upheavals, when present in national horoscopes.
In an individual horoscope, such a yoga renders one capable of

stupendous achievement. The Buddha made available to all men the wisdom of the Maharshis, in a different garb by laying stress on practical ethical life. The Sun in this horoscope is strong *par excellence*, not only as natural Atmakaraka, but also by longitudinal position and his exalted situation must give the clue to the depth of *Atmashakti* possessed by the Buddha.

Summing up, the horoscope of the Buddha is ideally disposed bringing into relief His qualities, mental and moral, and His attainments, intellectual and spiritual. He was a pioneering lover of men and a radiant personality, arousing in His followers affectionate devotion. By His immense sacrifice and by His great renunciation He has left an indelible impression upon India and upon the teachings of India's great Maharshis.

by Jupiter and the Moon, lords of the 5th and 4th respectively
while Lagna lord Mars is equally well fortified by his disposition in the 3rd and the aspect of Jupiter. In the Navamsa
again, Lagna is aspected by Jupiter and Mars. This renders the
horoscope strong.

of yogas ......

a fairly powerful ......
still rising to ......

Alexander ......
and Indian ......
......
being bitterly ......
Rajayoga in the 7th (for ......

No. 3.—ALEXANDER THE GREAT

Birth Details.—*Born on 22nd July 356 B.C. between 10
and 12 at night. (Lat 40° 43′ N,, Long. 22° 35′ E.)

Planetary Positions.—The Sun 123° 35′ ; the Moon 208°
31′ ; Mars 86° 18′ ; Mercury 105° 31′ ; Jupiter 185° 54′ ;
Venus 126° 20′ ; Saturn 59° 54′ ; Rahu 314° 2′ ; Ketu 134°
2′ ; and Lagna 19° 31′ ; Ayanamsa + 10° 32′.

	Lagna	Saturn	Mars		Venus Sun Mars	Moon
Rahu			Merc. Rahu			
	RASI		Sun Venus Ketu		NAVAMSA	Ketu
		Moon Jupiter			Jupiter Mercury	Lagna Saturn

Balance of Jupiter's Dasa at birth :   Years 5-9-11.

Special Features.—The Lagna is Aries, a movable and
masculine sign and is rendered very strong by being aspected

*The horoscope of Alexander is of course a speculative one. The very
day he came into this world the celebrated temple of Diana at Ephesus
was burnt. According to Plutarch, Hegasias joked "that it was no wonder

2

by Jupiter and the Moon, lords of the 9th and 4th respectively
while Lagna lord Mars is equally well fortified by his disposition in the 3rd and the aspect of Jupiter. In the Navamsa
again, Lagna lord is equally well placed. This renders the
horoscope strong.

A look at the horoscope reveals the presence of a number
of yogas—the most significant ones being Amala, Parvata,
Vasumathi, Gajakesari, Mahabhagya and Parijata. It will be
seen that three benefics occupying kendras and the 6th and 8th
being free from the occupation of any planets has resulted in
a fairly powerful Parvata Yoga, the significance of which is
well known to students of astrology.

Alexander's immense physical courage, impulsive energy
and vivid imagination stand out prominent by virtue of Aries
rising as Lagna aspected by Jupiter and Lagna lord Mars
being similarly aspected by Jupiter. Mark the position of
Gajakesari in the 7th (foreign relations) house, and the Amala

---

the temple was burned, because Diana was that day employed at the
delivery of Olympias to facilitate the birth of Alexander". Plutarch further says that "Alexander was born on the sixth of Hecatombaeon which
month the Macedonians call Lous, the same day that the temple of Diana
at Ephesus was burnt__ _Just after Phillip had taken Potidae, he received
at one time, three messages, that Parmenio had overthrown the Illyrians
in a great battle, that his race-horse had won the course at the Olympic
games, and that his wife had given birth to Alexander__ _" Based on the
authority of Plutarch, my esteemed friend Mr. Cyril Fagan writes thus in
a letter addressed to me recently :—

"As the Olympic games were held every fourth year since 776 B.C.
this places 356 B.C. (—355) as the year of Alexander's birth. In that year
the sygyzy (astronomical new moon) fell on July 14 (Julian) at 6·54 p.m.
(L.M.T.) at Pella and the crescent new moon did not become visible until
sunset of July 16, when the 1st day of Lous began. Hence the 6th day of
Lous began at sunset of July 21 and ended at sunset of July 22. There is

Yoga having reference to the 10th from Chandra Lagna. His "lasting reputation even long after death" is due to his conquests and ambitions.

The 4th lord the Moon with Jupiter in the 7th richly endowed Alexander with natural abilities. He was educated by no less a person than Aristotle. The 4th is occupied by Mercury while the 4th from the Moon is aspected both by Mercury and Mars. It is alleged Alexander carried with him throughout life, a passion for Homer. Alexander's education was not merely from books. Something of the actual conditions of the world was learnt by the coming and going of envoys from many States to Greece. Consistent with martian aspect (on the 4th from the Moon) he was schooled early in war.

The 5th house is considerably afflicted as the 5th lord the Sun is with Venus in the constellation of Ketu. No child was born to him during his lifetime.

Important Events.—Alexander succeeded his father Philip II in Saturn Dasa Rahu Bhukti. Mark Saturn is lord of the 10th from Lagna and yogakaraka from Chandra Lagna, occupying as he does, benefic sign and the nakshatra of Lagna lord Mars.

---

no record of the hour of birth, but we are informed that Herostratus, in order to immortalize himself, set fire to the temple of Artemis at Ephesus on the same night that Alexander was born, therefore it is assumed that birth took place at night, *i.e.,* between sunset of July 21 and sunrise of the next day (July 22)."

Another astronmer-friend, who wishes to remain anonymous, states that a difference of one day is likely while reckoning these ancient dates and equates the 6th day of Lous with 22nd/23rd July. I am inclined to accept 22nd July. The ruling Dasa would be that of Jupiter, who for the Lagna which I have fixed as Aries or Mesha taking into consideration Alexander's meteoric rise, his military prowess and his illustrious generalship, causes a powerful Rajayoga in the seventh house, indicating his regal birth.

Under the same directions, his father died by assassination. In Rahu Bhukti (Saturn Dasa) again the newly-born son of his father by Cleopatra, and Augustus, another cousin, were put to death by Alexander. Mark the position of Jupiter in the 7th (foreign relations). Jupiter is lord of the 9th or house of fortune. It was in Jupiter Bhukti (Saturn Dasa) that Alexander marched against the army of Darius and completely overthrew it at Issus. Great spoils fell into his hands but Darius escaped. Mercury Dasa began in 331 B.C. Mercury's disposition as lord of the 9th (from Chandra Lagna) in the 10th enabled Alexander to rout Darius and sweep on to the Persian capital.

Mercury is the planet of trade and commerce. As soon as Mercury Dasa commenced, the city of Alexandria was founded at the Canopic, north of the Nile. Venus Bhukti in Mercury Dasa was of outstanding importance. Venus is lord of the 2nd and 7th and occupies the 5th with the imperial planet the Sun in Ketu's constellation. It was during Venus Bhukti that he led his army into India. Having conquered Punjab, Alexander had to return to Persia as the machine of empire there had not functioned smoothly and as his troops refused to go further. In the Sun Bhukti (Sun in Ketu's constellation) he projected the rounding off of his Asiatic dominion and was on the point of starting when at Babylon he was stricken with fever and died at the age of 32. Thus his death took place in Mercury Dasa, Moon's Bhukti. It will be seen that Mercury is lord of the 3rd and 6th and in the Navamsa has joined the 3rd in association with Jupiter who happens to be lord of 7th both from Lagna and the Chandra Lagna. The sub-lord the Moon is not only in the constellation of Jupiter who is in a maraka place, but himself occupies a marakasthana causing the death.

Remarks.—The horoscope is significant in two ways to a student of astrology. First : it is an Alpayu horoscope ; and second : it is a horoscope illustrative of certain powerful Rajayogas and a spirit of adventure. On the basis of Jaimini, the three sets of factors concerned with longevity reveal three different types and the term indicated by the sign dispositions of Lagna and Hora Lagna, *viz.*, Alpayu holds good. The Moon-Jupiter in the 7th constitutes a Rajayoga according to Jaimini. **The fact that Navamsa Lagna and Atmakaraka are in the same sign causes a powerful Rajayoga.** The position of Lagna lord Mars in an upachaya reveals that he was a great master of war. The traditional view is that he aimed at conquering the world and demanded to be worshipped as God. The position of Jupiter in the 7th from Lagna aspecting Lagna lord favours the inference that Alexander cannot be convicted of mad ambition and vain glory.

No. 4.—AUGUSTUS CAESAR

Birth Details.—*Born on 23rd September 63 B.C. at about 5-48 a.m. (Lat. 41° 53′ N., Long. 12° 28′ E.)

Planetary Positions.—The Sun 183° 25′; the Moon 303° 55′; Mars 39° 25′; Mercury 173° 25′; Jupiter 111° 25′; Venus 230° 25′; Saturn 36° 55′; Rahu 39° 25′; and Lagna 180° 30′; Ayanamsa +6° 25′.

		Mars Saturn Rahu		Mars Rahu Sat.			
Moon			Jupit.				
	RASI		Jupit. Venus	NAVAMSA			Mercury
			Merc.				
Venus Ketu	Lagna Sun			Sun Moon	Lagna	Ketu	

Balance of Mars Dasa at birth : Years 1-5-10.

Special Features.—The Lagna is Libra but the lord Venus is aspected by Mars, Saturn, Rahu and Jupiter. He was "exceptionally good looking, with very delicately modelled features, grey eyes, luminous and penetrating", a description answering to the mixed influences operating on Lagna and

---

* "A little before sunrise" according to Suetonius.

Lagna lord. Three malefics aspecting the 2nd rendered him suffer, all his life, from throat trouble. The character of Augustus was cool and cautious. The Moon is in Aquarius, a sign of calculated thinking and Venus is in the 10th from Chandra Lagna. He set himself consistently against senseless brutality to slaves. In youth he appeared cold and self-contained consistent with the nature of Rahu, whose Dasa he enjoyed till he was about 20. In a biography of Augustus published in 1903 occurs the following passage : "As he went on, there gradually awoke in him a nobler ambition, that of retiring and directing the distracted state. Neither now, nor afterwards do the most vulgar attributes of supreme power-wealth, luxury and adulation—seem to have had charms for him." While the 4th lord is no doubt afflicted, the 4th is aspected by exalted Jupiter. It is said that he was a scholar from his youth.

The 7th lord Mars as well as Kalatrakaraka Venus are both afflicted. He was married twice—the first a marriage of convenience lasting for only two years and the second marriage endured to the end of his life. The association of the 7th lord as well as Venus with Rahu confirm the slanderous talks about his second wife, narrated by Roman chroniclers. The 5th lord Saturn is equally well afflicted. He had only one daughter who disappointed him.

Mark the powerful Pancha Mahapurusha Yoga having reference to the 10th from Lagna. Aughstus "believed himself destined for a high mission, to which personal happiness, friendship, ease, common morality must all be sacrificed". Consistent with the divine nature of Jupiter who has caused Hamsa Yoga, he had the confidence that every step is divinely ordained. He was on occasions ruthless in the extreme,

probably because of the combined aspects of Mars and Saturn
on Lagna lord, who is situated in the 2nd, in the sign of Mars,
but because Jupiter also aspects Lagna lord, his inner conscience must have revolted against his own actions. As Mars
and Saturn aspect Lagna lord in the 2nd, he made use of all
competitors for power—Mark Antony, Brutus, Casius and even
Cicero—but assisting none. In the Roman world of that day
moral laxity went side by side with scepticism and neglect of
religious observances. Marriage was at a discount and birth-
rate had fallen...... the economic policy of Rome was one of
individualism and *laissez faire*".

According to classical texts, the person born in Hamsa Yoga
will be a king extolled by the good, he will possess a beautiful
body and will be of righteous disposition. Jupiter is the planet
of religion and when he is strong, the person not only becomes
religious and moral himself but will also revive true religion.

Apart from the financial and administrative reforms
introduced by Augustus which added to the comfort and happiness of innumerable lives, he achieved a diplomatic triumph by
making peace with Rome's traditional enemy Parthia, and cut
a very tangled knot without the use of the sword. Augustus
set himself to revive religion—not to stifle it. He believed
firmly in the need for a religion in the state. He succeeded to
a great extent not only in putting new life and dignity into the
impersonal state worship of Rome connected with the olympian
deities, but he also revived the simpler, truer form of religion,
known as the "religion of Numa" defined by Buchan as a
"sense of the mystery of life and the immensities which over-
shadow man, a desire to walk humbly and to propitiate the
unseen, not only by ceremonial, but by a grave and reverent
spirit" (*cf.* Hindu values).

From Chandra Lagna, a powerful Adhi Yoga operates by virtue of the position of exalted Jupiter and exalted Mercury in the 6th and 8th. Other notable yogas are Mahabhagya, Parijata and Damini. The political planet Sun is Neechabhanga. All these combinations made him not only an astute and successful intriguer, but an accomplished politician.

Important Events.—His father died in his 5th year, when he was having Rahu Dasa Jupiter Bhukti. The 9th house from the Moon is afflicted. Rahu in the 9th from the 9th lord "destroyed" father in his Dasa. In Rahu Dasa Venus Bhukti, he was elected into the pontifical college, an exceptional honour due to the blessings of the sub-lord Venus. The most important period was the year 45 B.C. (the fag end of Rahu Dasa) in which year he was made Julius Caesar's heir. Consistent with Rahu's position this inheritance was a perilous one. But he was confident in his own abilities. Libra rising with Jupiter exalted in the 10th and Lagna lord Venus being aspected by exalted Jupiter—he declared that he would undertake the obligations.

Jupiter's Dasa was the most remarkable. Jupiter's ownership of the 3rd and 6th is no doubt evil. But as a natural benefic, his exaltation in the 10th and his disposition in the 6th from the Moon (success over enemies) is unique. Jupiter's Dasa lasted from 44 B.C. to 28 B.C. And as soon as this commenced, Antonius was defeated. It was again in Jupiter's own Bhukti that a triumvirate (coalition with Antonius and Lepidus) was effected. The remaining part of Jupiter was one of struggle and encounter with increasing political chaos until peace was established in 29 B.C., just at the fag end of Jupiter's Dasa.

It will be seen that the results due to Jupiter's ownership

of the 3rd and 6th expressed themselves completely in the shape of civil war and confusion which throughout the country Octavius had to overcome. Saturn is the real yogakaraka for Libra Lagna. His Dasa being the 4th suggests *kshema* or happiness.

As soon as Saturn's Dasa commenced, Augustus was awarded the civic crown in token that he had saved and restored the republic, and he became undisputed head of the Roman world. Mercury though exalted is in the 12th or house of loss with the Sun lord of the 11th while from the Chandra Lagna the reference is to the 8th house, and consequently Mercury Dasa brought losses.

The last five years of his life (Ketu Dasa) were untroubled by war or disaster. And he died in A.D. 14 just at the fag end of Ketu Dasa, the sub-period being that of Mercury. It will be seen that Ketu is in the 8th in conjunction with Mars, a first-rate maraka, aspecting Lagna lord.

Remarks.—Augustus was the man who gave to Rome regeneration and a further life of centuries and who, by saving Rome, saved the European world of his day from disintegration. The Lagna is strong and unafflicted. Lagna lord is also rendered strong by being aspected by Jupiter who has caused Hamsa Yoga and by Saturn the yogakaraka. Jupiter's exaltation in 10th is a combination *par excellence* and a very desirable combination for a ruler who wishes to consolidate and build his country and confer happiness on his people. From the Chandra Lagna, Lagna lord Saturn occupies a kendra, aspecting the 10th with lord of the 10th. Yogakaraka Venus is also in the 10th aspected by Jupiter.

Because of these constructive yogas, his political career lasted for a long time and ended only when he was 77 years old.   Immense benefits were conferred on the country and the people owing to the unique nature of the combinations obtaining. Mark also the absence of Dwirdwadasa positions in the horoscope. As a consequence of the powerful affliction of the 5th lord Saturn, the greatest calamity he had to endure was the disgraceful conduct of his daughter Julia, whose scandalous debaucheries filled Rome with horror. Hamsa Yoga, the powerful Adhi Yoga *plus* the Parijata Yoga made him "one of the world's great men, a statesman, who conceived and carried through a scheme of political reconstruction which secured for his empire peace and tranquillity and preserved civilisation for more than two centuries", in spite of the association of Rahu, Saturn and Mars. It will be seen that this association has no reference either to the 9th or 10th.

No. 5.—SRI ADI SANKARACHARYA

Birth Details.—*Born on 25th March 44 B.C. at about noon. (Lat. 8° 29′N., Long. 76° 59′ E.)

Planetary Positions.—The Sun 8° 12′; the Moon 69° 12′; Mars 332° 36′; Mercury 24° 6′; Jupiter 303° 36′; Venus 3°; Saturn 265° 30′; Rahu 41° 18′; and Lagna 99° 22′. Ayanamsa +6° 10′.

Mars	Sun Mercury Venus	Rahu ~~Ketu~~	Moon		Venus Rahu		Sun
Jupiter			Lagna				Mars
	RASI				NAVAMSA		
Saturn	Ketu			Moon	Saturn Mercury Jupiter	Ketu	Lagna

Balance of Rahu Dasa at birth: Years 14–6–29.

Special Features.—Lagna is unafflicted both in Rasi and Navamsa while Lagna lord Moon though occupying the 12th is

---

*A learned Indian scholar who has written a book entitled *Life and Teachings of Sankaracharya* says that "in all this confusion of evidence it is safe to assume that Sankara flourished some time between the *middle of the seventh and the first quarter* of the ninth centuries". On what

rendered highly fortified, by the combined aspects of Saturn (lord of 7), Jupiter(lord of 9) , and Mars (yogakaraka). The Moon's situation in the sign of the intellectual planet Mercury who in his turn is in the 10th conferred on Sankara a magnificent intellect, penetrative mind and lofty character. His wonderful dialectic skill is due to Mercury being free from combustion. **Jupiter's aspect on the Moon denotes profound spirituality, while the martian aspect shows a vived emotional temperament which animated his philosophical expositions with matchless charm and dignity.** Vaksthanadhipati (lord of the 2nd the Sun is exalted in the 10th and in association with the intellectual and logical Mercury and the poetic Venus. The house of speech is aspected by divine Jupiter. A master of the strictest logic, yet so sweet-tongued, that he was able to convince thousands and thousands of his opponents by the sheer beauty of his speech and argument. Mark the strong disposition of Vidyasthana or house of education. The lord of the 4th is in the 10th aspecting the 4th while the Sun, Mercury and Jupiter

grounds he has come to this conclusion has not been made clear. There is no doubt confusion prevails regarding the year of Sankara's birth but much of it could have been avoided if some of these scholars had taken the trouble to carefully examine all the relevant literature bearing on Sankara's life and times, free from any prepossessions which are a concomitant of Western education. A careful study of such authorities as *Sankaravijayas* of Madhavacharya, Anandagiri and Chidvilasa, *Punyasloka Manjari* and the *Guru Porampara* list preserved in Sringeri Mutt reveals that Sankara was born definitely before Christ and not in the 7th or 8th century A.D. as oriental scholars—Indian and European—have made out. It looks as though these scholars have confused Adi Sankara with his name-sake Abhinava Sankara who was the Guru of Kamakotipeetha and the 36th in succession to Adi Sankara. This Abhinava Sankara, a very learned and pious man, was born in 788 A.D. in the cyclic year Vibhava, solar month Vrishabha, on the 10th day of the bright half. It is also aspect the 4th. The influences of the Atmakaraka Sun, Vidyakaraka Mercury, Gnanakaraka Jupiter and Kavyakaraka Venus are all focussed on the 4th ; besides the influences of the matter of fact planet Mars. The native was a prodigy and a *Sakala Sastra Parangata*, attainments possible only under very powerful yogas. How capacious his mind was and how solid and substanial were his learning, become evident in every line of his writings. Who is not moved by the animated and ecstasy-inspiring poetry characterising the Master's writings ?

Lord of the 8th Saturn in the constellation of Venus who is almost in conjunction with the Sun, lord of the 2nd, a maraka, conferred Alpayu. In the Navamsa again, the 8th house is considerably afflicted by the situation of Venus a maraka, and his association with Ketu. Added to these, the position of Lagna lord in the 12th is not favourable for long life.

Lord of the 9th (house of father) is in the 8th(12th from the 9th) and Mars a malefic occupies the 9th. Pitrukaraka Sun is subject to Papakartari Yoga and occupies the constellation of Ketu, with the result father died very early in life. Lagna lord being Matrukaraka (indicator of mother) occupying a benefic

---

said that like Adi Sankara this Abhinava Sankara also toured all over India, held discussions with learned men and conquered them intellectually. He died in A.D. 839. Almost all authorities are unanimous that Adi Sankara was born on *Vaisakha Suddha Panchami*, at midday.

Suklapaksheshu panchamyam tithyam bhaskaravasave :
Madhyanhechobhijinnama muhurta subha veekshate.

As regards the year, Sukhacharya's *Brihat Sankara Vijaya* and Chidvilasa's *Sankara Vijaya* make it clear that Sankara's birth took place in Kaliyuga 2593, Sunday, Vaisakha Sukla Panchami, in Punarvasu nakshatra, at midday, when the Sun was in Aries, the Moon in Punarvasu last quarter and when Jupiter, Saturn and Mars were in kendras, exalted or in own house, Venus was exalted and Mercury was with the Sun. This

sign and the 4th lord well placed reveals Sankara's affection to his mother. It must be noted that his conduct, even as a Sanyasi, in performing the death ceremonies of his mother, despite social taboo and opposition, brings out the moral beauty and sublimity which are to be found in the noble duty of a man having to honour the sacred memory of his mother. Mark also the disposition of the 7th lord Saturn in the 6th (12th from the 7th) and the affliction of Kalatrakaraka Venus by his presence in Ketu's constellation and subjected to Papakartari Yoga.

Jupiter in the 8th and Venus in the constellation of Mokshakaraka Ketu denotes sublimation of the sex energy and a spotless character. The 6th house in this horoscope is very significant. The 6th indicates enemies, opposition and, of course, debts and diseases. The 6th is occupied by Saturn, lord of the 7th and 8th, while the 6th lord Jupiter is in the 8th. Thus, there is Parivarthana between the 6th and 8th lords, both of whom aspect Lagna lord placed in the 12th or Mokshasthana.

---

date corresponds to 3rd April 509 B.C., the weekday being Monday. Unfortunately except in regard to the Sun and Mercury, the positions of other planets (the Sun 20°; the Moon 71° 42'; Mars 252° 18'; Mercury 7° 6'; Jupiter 225° 30'; Venus 37° 18'; Saturn 338° 12'; and Rahu 41° 18') do not tally with those suggested in the authorities. As Prof. B. Suryanarain Rao says: "According to the records of Sringeri Mutt (Guru Parampara Patti) which are well preserved and reliable", Sankara was born on the 5th day of the bright half of the lunar month of Vaisakha of the cyclic year Eswara in Vikrama 14. This corresponds to 25th March 44 B.C. I am inclined to give greater weight to the reliability of this date as it is given in the lists preserved by the Gurus of Sringeri, and consequently, there was no chance of their having been tampered with. Sankara's Guru was Govindapada, who is said to have begotten by his Kshatriya wife, the great Vikramaditya. Sankara must therefore have lived about the time of Vikramaditya.

Lagna Lord here is the Moon, karaka of the mind. These dispositions give us a clue to understand the formidable nature of the opposition and the opponents he had to face and how he was able to overcome them by calm judgment, clever argument and by his perfect familiarity with the traditional interpretation and exposition as well as his masterly insight into the philosophical lore.

Atmakaraka Sun with the intellectual planet Mercury (who owns Mokshasthana and which in turn is aspected by divine Jupiter) explains Sankara's philosophy, viz., Advaita. The world has no absolute reality, it has an apparent and relative reality. Another notable combination in this horoscope is the disposition of four planets in the 12th from the Moon in the Navamsa.

Important Events.—When Sankara was six years old, his father Sivaguru died. This happened in Rahu Dasa Mercury Bhukti. The major lord Rahu occupies a maraka place from Pitrukaraka while the sub-lord Mercury, as owning the 7th (from the 9th or Pitrusthana), occupies the 2nd from the 9th. Rahu and Mercury are Dwirdwadasa. His mother had his Upanayanam performed in the same year and then sent him for education. This took place under the same directional influences. Mark the fact that Mercury aspects the 10th or Karma sthana.

It is said that Sankara learned all the Vedas and Sastras within two or three years. This means, that his education took place and was completed in Venus Bhukti. Rahu, the major lord, being in the sign of Venus should give the results of Venus and as Venus happens to own the 4th or house of education and is in association with the intellectual planet Mercury, he becomes capable of conferring Vidya or education. Just at the fag end of Ketu Bhukti in Rahu Dasa he was ordained as a Sanyasi. Mark the fact that Rahu is in the 12th from the Moon in the constellation of the Moon who in his turn occupies the 12th from Lagna. Ketu aspects the 12th from Chandra Lagna, and occupies the constellation of Saturn, who in his turn aspects the 12th from Lagna. The chronological order of events in Sankara's life is not clearly known. But we may assume that his training in philosophy under the famous Govinda Bhagawatpada, a disciple of Gowdapada, was completed before Sankara was 15 years old, *i.e.*, before the completion of Rahu Dasa. Rahu's situation in the sign of Venus lord of the house of education, rendered Rahu capable of giving the results of Venus. Jupiter's Dasa was the most significant period in the Master's life. Jupiter is Gnanakaraka and owns a Dharmatrikona. He aspects Lagna lord occupying the 12th; the 2nd or house of speech; and the 4th or house of acquisitions— here intellectual and philosophical. Besides these, he occupies the constellation of Mars—a first-rate yogakaraka. All the results of this yogakaraka found expression in the Dasa of Jupiter. Within the sub-periods of Jupiter, Saturn and Mercury, Sankara's chief works—commentaries on the principal Upanishads, the Bhagavadgita and Brahma Sutras—were written in Varanasi where he lived for several years occasionally going to Badrinath.

Under the same planetary directions Sankara seems to have met and discussed with some of the most famous scholars of his day. It is alleged that even Vyasa, the reputed author of Brahma Sutras, came to Sankara's abode on one occasion, of course as an old man, and entered into a disputation with Sankara. His triumphal tour of the country must have commenced in Venus Bhukti, Jupiter's Dasa.

Though doing ascetic rodes, he enjoyed all the para-phernalia of royalty, which was provided to Sankara by the various kings, in recognition of his great learning and authority. These results are the blessings of Jupiter's presence in the constellation of the yogakaraka Mars.

The most pathetic part of Sankara's life must probably relate to Mars Bhukti of Jupiter's Dasa, during which his mother died. Mars aspects both Matrusthana (4th house) and Matrukaraka (Moon) while Jupiter is in a martian constellation. Sankara, as per the promise he had made to his mother when she was alive, desired to perform her obsequies himself. A Sanyasi performing the mother's ceremonies was against established practice. Sankara's relative and own people declined to help him. Unable to soften their hearts, he removed the dead body and cremated it in the backyard. Though Sankara's name had spread far and wide, he was no prophet in his own land. He died at the age of 32, in Saturn Bhukti in his own Dasa. Saturn, as owning the 7th from Lagna, occupies the 7th from Chandra Lagna and is therefore a powerful maraka.

Remarks.—It is impossible for ordinary mortals to assess the true worth and work of the great Sankara. Probably the world has not seen a like personality whose work in his all too short span of life produced marked and momentous results which have so profoundly influenced the religious, intellectual and cultural thoughts of millions of persons during the last 2000 years. There must be certain uniqueness in the horoscope of such a celebrity.

Lords of the 7th and 9th aspecting Lagna lord occupying the 12th or Mokshasthana, Atmakaraka Sun exalted in the 10th with Mercury the karaka for gnana, and Venus lord of the 4th and the house of "acquisitions" receiving the combined aspect of five planets, are all noteworthy features of no mean significance. Saturn, the planet of philosophy, occupies the constellation of Jupiter, lord of the 9th or Dharmasthana. Saturn, in a sense, is also a planet of logic. Consequently, Sankara's unflinching logic led him to the supra-rational.

He starts with the view that the essence of reality must be its absoluteness unconditioned by time, space and causality. He preached a philosophy which while satisfying the ethical and spiritual requirements of the people weaned them away from the corrupt atheistic and agnostic thoughts of the Buddhists and Jains, and the overburdened ritualism of the Mimamsakas.

In Sankara's horoscope, though Saturn and Mars aspect the Moon, there is also the neutralising effect of Jupiter's aspect. Consequently, there was a spirit of compromise characterising Sankara's preachings. He did not condemn outright the Karmakhanda practices or *bhakti* schools. Only the spirit underlying the doing of them had to become different. His is a creative horoscope. He gave a common basis to the most prevalent form of Vedic faith and reconciled them to a cardinal and co-ordinating idea.

Sankara, like every great man, was the product of his age. It was a critical period in the history of the Hindu nation. It was necessary to counteract the unwholesome sceptic influences of the agnosticism of Buddhists and establish the high value of Vedas and this task was taken up by the great Sankara. "On the strength of the eternality and infallibility of the Vedas, he had to establish that the agnostic ethics and humanitarianism of Buddhism, though very high in their then moral value, were really inferior to Vedantic ethics and Vedantic humanitarianism."

In the course of his endeavour to re-establish Hinduism unshakably on its ancient foundations Sankara worked most nobly and heroically for purity as well as unity in human life and human society. The Lagna is completely free from affliction both in Rasi and Amsa, either by aspect or association. Consequently his achievements in "strengthening the philosophical fortifications of Vedantic Hinduism are non-sectarian in character". He said that the Supreme Brahma is identical with the soul and that everything in the phenomenal universe is an illusory manifestation (maya) of that Brahma who is in fact the one and only reality.

Modern people can hardly imagine a personality such as that of Sankara. "In the course of so few years, to have nominated no less than ten great religious orders, of which four have fully retained their prestige to the present day, to have acquired such a mass of Sanskrit learning as to create a distinct philosophy and impress himself on the scholar's imagination of India in a pre-eminence" that twenty centuries "have not sufficed to shake ; to have written poems whose grandeur makes them unmistakable, even to the foreign and unlearned ear and at the same time to have lived with his disciples in all the radiant joy and simple pathos of the saints— this is a greatness that we may appreciate, but cannot understand".

No. 6.—JESUS CHRIST

Birth Details.—*Born on 25th December 7 B.C. on Friday at about 10–18 p.m. (A.V.C. 747). (Lat. 31° 43′ N., Long. 35° 13′ E.)

Planetary Positions.—The Sun 247° 59′ ; the Moon 336° 41′ ; Mars 314° 29′ ; Mercury 255° 58′ ; Jupiter 353° 17′ ; Venus 233° 1′ ; Saturn 351° 47′ ; Rahu 210° 35′ ; and Lagna 165° 29′. Ayanamsa + 5° 27′.

RASI

Saturn Moon Jupiter	Ketu		
Mars			
	RASI		
Sun Mercury	Rahu Venus	Lagna	

NAVAMSA

		Lagna	Sun
Mars			Rahu
Ketu Sat. Jupit. Venus	*NAVAMSA*		Mercury
			Moon

Balance of Saturn's Dasa at birth : Years 14–0–21.

Special Features.—The Lagna is Virgo or Kanya. Virgo representing the virgin and thus is in conformity with the belief

---

* Regarding the date of birth of Jesus, I have mostly relied upon the findings of Mr. Cyril Fagan, as given in the 1937 winter issue of *American Journal of Astrology*, wherein he has endeavoured to construct Christ's

held by Christians that Jesus was born to Virgin Mary. The Lagna is powerfully aspected by Jupiter, Mars and Saturn. Jupiter's aspect as a benefic is highly significant. Lord of Lagna Mercury is in a friendly sign with the Sun. Mercury is in Lagna in Navamsa, powerfully aspected by Jupiter who is neecha but who has obtained Neechabhanga as also by Mars. Jesus was born under the influence of Elarata so that soon after his birth himself and his mother were removed to Egypt through fear of kind Herod. Jesus grew up in extreme seclusion and this is indicated by Saturn aspecting Lagna. The house of profession from the Moon is powerfully aspected by Saturn and this shows that Jesus followed "a humble trade" (carpentry) and worked with his own hands. The presence of Ketu in the 9th from Lagna gave him Atmagnana or the knowledge of the Self and Saturn aspecting the 9th suggests that he consecrated the common lot of toil and poverty and thereby showed the intrinsic sacredness of human life. Saturn aspecting the 10th from the Moon also reveals that his followers were unlearned and

---

horoscope on the strength of the available evidence gathered from different reliable sources. In the 6th century A.D. Dionysius Exigius, the Synthian monk, fixed the "present calendar by laying down that Jesus Christ was born on 25th December 753 years from the foundation of Rome". Biblical scholars have "seriously questioned his findings. In the 2nd century St. Iranaeus and St. Tertullian fixed the date of the nativity as occurring in the 41st year of Augustus (3 B.C.)". Many methods have been adopted to arrive at the true date of Christ's birth but all attempts seem to have led to nothing but highly dubious results. The one important *data* which should guide an astrological student is the reference made to the remarkable conjunction of Jupiter and Saturn in Pisces "which must have heralded the birth of the Messiah". The Magi or the Persian astrologers were mindful of these prophecies "and were expecting the birth of the long promised Messiah". The conjunction

ignorant men chosen from the humblest of the people. The lord of Navamsa Lagna is associated with several planets especially Jupiter and Ketu suggesting his ascetic leanings. Ketu in Karakamsa with (or aspected by) Saturn made him a Tapaswi. Malefics in Karakamsa or in the 12th from Karakamsa have the power of making one renounce the world and devote himself to serving others and showing them the way to salvation. In Jesus' horoscope, Ketu and Saturn, two powerful malefics, are in Karakamsa. Atmakaraka is Jupiter and he is responsible for having caused Hamsa Yoga and Gajakesari Yoga. This is a unique combination indicating the high degree of soul-force possessed by Jesus.

His moral stability is evident not only from the fact that Venus is completely free from affliction (Rahu is 21° removed from Venus) but also by the presence of Kama Yoga. His kindness and benevolence are brought out by the presence of Pasa Yoga. A slight adaptation of the 4th stanza of Chap, XV of *Brihat Jataka* reveals the presence of Parivraja Yoga which

---

took place in 7 B.C. and this must be the year of Jesus' birth. The Magi or the Chaldean astrologers who had gathered their knowledge of the science from the Hindu sages were pastmasters in the art of divination and they were accustomed to wander to various countries and to interest themselves in renowned horoscopes. That the Magian astrologers should have been deeply interested in any sidereal phenomenon is in accordance with what we know of their studies and that a planetary combination of the rarest kind, and one which by the recognised rules of astrology was of stupendous significance actually did occur at this very epoch, we know by the independent investigations of the great Kepler who found that the conjunction had occurred in Pisces in A.V C. 747 or 7 B.C. The conjunction of planets which occurred on 17-12-1613 was followed by the appearance of a new evanescent star of the first magnitude in the foot of Ophiuchus and this attracted the notice of Kepler's pupil Brunowski.

has contributed considerably to the greatness of Jesus as a yogi.

Important Events.—We do not have many important events to illustrate. Throughout Saturn Dasa, life must have been one of poverty, toil and simplicity but it must also have been a life of exalted joy—joy born from within. At the age of 12, Joseph and Mary took Jesus to Jerusalem and there occurred the memorable incident of his temporary loss and the parents' discovery of him in the temple. This occurred in Jupiter's Bhukti in Saturn's Dasa. Both these planets have contributed to the spiritual dignity of Jesus.

Mercury's Dasa lasted till he was aged 31. Mercury is the planet of Buddhi or intelligence and it must have been during his period that Jesus underwent inner spiritual experiences and struggle so very essential for realisation of the ultimate truth. Ketu as we have seen has contributed a lot to his spiritual perfection. It was only in the beginning of Ketu Dasa that

---

From this may be inferred that the great conjunction had some bearing on the "star of the wise men". Readers will note that similar Jupiter-Saturn conjunctions have produced great teachers, *viz.*, Zoroaster and the Buddha. Such an astrological event must have naturally turned the thoughts of the Chaldean astrologers to some great birth. The traditional date of the nativity is 25th December and the planetary positions calculated to this date and the other astrological evidence present seem to leave no doubt that Jesus Christ was born on 25-12-7 B.C., and the Lagna has been fixed by taking into account (1) that Jesus was a great yogi; (2) he was born to a virgin mother; and (3) his death was due to torture. Horoscopes of great men are sometimes elusive and cannot be analysed in the light of the ordinarily known combinations. The astrologer's task is indeed stupendous because he has to sift through a large amount of confusing and contradictory evidence before he is able to hit upon the appropriate combinations.

Jesus began his preaching and delivered the "Sermon on the Mount" which hardly lasted for 3 years. Ketu is in the 9th from Lagna both in Rasi and Navamsa and occupies the Karakamsa. He was crucified in 30 A.D., at the end of Ketu Dasa. His death occurred by torture and this is shown by Saturn and Mars aspecting Lagna and both these planets aspecting the 7th from the Moon. Ketu is in the 3rd from the Moon. Venus, whose results Ketu should give, owns the 2nd house from Lagna and the 3rd and 8th from the Moon and occupies the 3rd thus causing maraka.

Remarks.—Whether Jesus Christ was a historical reality on only a mythological figure, the teaching ascribed to him has seized the imagination of all mankind excepting of course the Hindus and Buddhists to whom the principles of morality preached by Christ contain nothing new and are merely ordinary rules of conduct with which every Hindu is expected to be acquainted. Christ's teachings cannot make an appeal to a cultured people like the Hindus whose philosophical and ethical achievements as revealed by the writings of the great Vyasa, Sankara, Ramanuja and others stand alone as embodying grand truths ever discovered by mankind.

Yet, Christ's achievements were remarkable. Jesus is alleged to have learnt yoga in Hindustan. He gave a moral system to the inhabitants of the Western hemisphere who had been steeped in superstition, barbarism and irreligious practices and whose intellects were ordinary and unable to comprehend high philosophical truths. Hence Christ's teachings consist of short suggestive sayings, full of depth, yet free from all affections or obscurity.

Jupiter and the Moon are quite powerful indicating keen mental perception and righteous conduct. One of the ten

Commandments of Christ worth noting is "Do not kill". This is indeed noble. But it looks pathetic when we remember that the European nations, mostly composed of Christian units, have vied with each other in resorting to war on the flimsiest grounds. Saturn's presence with the Moon indicates Christ's meekness, modesty and compassion.

It is the major planets, especially Jupiter and Saturn, disposed in kendras that make one an entity. His popularity with the masses, his public life and accessibility and the fullness and completeness of his life so rich in action and varying experience bespeak an exceptionally powerful disposition of Jupiter and the 9th house.

His celibacy and spotless virtue are denoted by the non-affliction of Venus. His death by treachery by mob-violence is too well shown by the disposition of Mars. The resurrection also took place in Ketu Dasa on 9-4-30 A.D., when Jupiter was transiting the radical Moon and the 7th from Lagna. The transit of Jupiter lends extraordinary colour to the biblical narrative of resurrection.

A careful study of the horoscope of Jesus reveals his real personality. He has no doubt altered the whole current of the stream of history and the horoscope presented above testifies not only to the unique character of his individuality, to his devotion and self-sacrifice and to his sinlessness but also to the fact that he furnished to the Western nations, an ideal and moral code which the otherwise most enlightened Christian nations have shamelessly set at naught to serve their selfish ends.

No. 7.—EMPEROR NERO

Birth Details.—Born on 15th December 37 A.D.(O.S.) at about 7.28 a.m. (Long. 12° 46′E., Lat. 41° 29′N.)

Planetary Positions.—The Sun 267° 30′; the Moon 139° 2′; Mars 271° 2′; Mercury 245° 2′; Jupiter 229° 32′; Venus298° 2′; Saturn 182° 2′; Rahu 278° 50′: Ketu 98° 50′; and Lagna 267° 32′. Ayanamsa +5° 2′.

			Rahu		Mercury
			Ketu		
	RASI			NAVAMSA	
Mars Venus Rahu			Moon Mars		
Lagna Sun Mercury	Jupiter	Saturn	Sun Lagna Jupit.	Saturn	Moon Venus Ketu

Balance of Venus' Dasa at birth: Years 11–5–12.

Special Features.— The Lagna is Dhanus or Sagittarius and the lord Jupiter is in the 12th (practically at the end of the 11th Bhava) while Lagna is occupied by the Sun lord of the 9th and Mercury lord of the 7th and 10th and aspected powerfully by Saturn lord of the 2nd and 3rd. The ascendant, therefore, while quite strong, has a predominance of malefic influences over it rendering the native wily, unscrupulous and headstrong. The Moon, karaka of the mind, is in Leo a fixed sign owned by the Sun a natural malefic and is powerfully aspected by Mars suggesting his childish vanity and ungovernable selfishness while his savage temper is indicated by the conjunction of Mars and Rahu in the 2nd in the house of Saturn.

Atmakaraka Sun is doubtless strongly disposed having obtained Vargottama, but Saturn's aspect over him both in the Rasi and Navamsa, and the complete absence of Jupiter's 'touch' is strikingly illustrative of Nero's personality. Sagittarius rising with the Sun and Mercury endowed Nero with a wonderful physique and robust health. He was said to be remarkably beautiful, his perfect limbs, bright red curly hair and dignified carriage compelling admiration.

Nero's mother was a powerful factor in his life and the presence in Lagna of the lord of the sign the Moon is placed in, accounts for this. Mark the fact that the Lagna, the Sun and the Moon are all in fixed signs while Mars and Saturn are in the Hora of the Sun, 8th being aspected by Saturn—all these suggesting that the instinct for cruelty was innate in the man and that mad and furious passions for blood, accompanied by extreme violence of temper would seize him. The enormity of his cruel actions, unparalleled in history, are also shown by exalted Saturn aspecting Lagna and the lord of the 5th Mars and the lord of the 2nd and 3rd Saturn aspecting the 5th (manas) and the Moon, karaka of the mind aspecting the 3rd house.

The Moon's presnce in Karakamsa made him a musician. Venus in the 2nd in Rasi and getting Neechabhanga in the 10th in Navamsa—besides being Atmakaraka, endowed Nero with a phenomenal artistic temperament and a love for music. He was no mean singer, he was famed throughout Italy and Greece for the possession of a superb voice. The 7th lord Mercury is in Lagna aspected by Saturn while Kalatrakaraka Venus is slightly afflicted in the sign of Saturn by association with Mars and Rahu while in the Navamsa Venus is debilitated and in conjunction with Ketu. The desposition of Mars in Vargottama in the house of family is significant.

These dispositions of Mars, Venus and the 7th lord suggest that Nero was highly excitable and a victim of unnatural vices and a sensualist of the worst type. It is alleged that his sexual life was of a most depraved character and that he was morally gross. He had Alpayu or short life as could be seen from the presence of lords of Lagna and the 8th in Panaparas or succeedent houses.

Important Events.—Nero's father's death occurred in Jupiter's Dasa Venus Bhukti. Jupiter is in the 12th from Pitrukaraka, while Venus is in the 2nd maraka. His marriage with Claudius's daughter, the ill-fated Octavia, took place in Mercury's sub-period in the Dasa of the Sun. Mercury the sub-lord owns the 7th and is in Lagna with the major lord who owns the 9th house. In the Navamsa also, Mercury owns the 7th. The 7th house is ill-disposed and hence the intrigues and scandals characterising the married life of this Emperor.

The most important event in Nero's life was his adoption by Claudius in 50 A.D. during the sub-period of Mars in the Sun's Dasa. Mars is extremely powerful being exalted and obtaining Vargottama. This adoption was responsible in a large measure for Nero to become the Emperor. He ascended the throne on 13-10-54 A.D. in the sub-period of Venus in the Dasa of the Sun. It will be seen that apart from his inherited evil nature, the Sun is highly powerful. As lord of the 9th he is in Lagna, while Venus is equally strong and capable of doing immense good by virtue of having obtained Neechabhanga in the 10th from Navamsa Lagna, by being in Karakamsa and by owning the 2nd and 9th from Chandra Lagna and posited in Chandra Lagna. No wonder that Vargottama position of the major lord, the Lagna and the dignified position of Venus, conferred an Empire on Nero.

Nero killed his mother, of course at the instance of his mistress, in Jupiter's Bhukti in the Moon's Dasa. Jupiter is in Scorpio an insect sign, owning the 8th from Matrukaraka and being placed in the 4th from the Moon. The burning of Rome took place in Venus' Bhukti in Moon's Dasa—both the sub and Major lords being aspected powerfully by Mars—the planet of incendiarism.

Finally the revolt of the people and his death took place in Saturn's sub-period in Mars' Dasa. Saturn owns the 2nd and 3rd from Lagna and the 7th from Chandra Lagna, while Mars rules the 5th and 12th. In Navamsa Mars rules the 3rd and 8th from Chandra Lagna and occupies the 2nd maraka.

Remarks.—Nero's horoscope is interesting as illustrative of certain fundamentals of astrology. His cruelty, his base sexual life and his imperial office are brought out in his chart. There are several Rajayogas in the horoscope which are worth noting. The determined struggle carried on by Agrippina to win for Nero the throne which it had been predicted by the Chaldean astrologers to be his are brought out by the fact of the Moon fortifying the 9th house and the 9th lord being placed in the 10 from the 4th.

There are of course several yogas, such as Gajakesari, Mahabhagya, Parivarthana, etc., but the most important Raja-yogas are the disposition of exalted Mars, Lagna, the Sun and exaltad Saturn in Vargottama, the presence of the lords of the

9th and 10th in Lagna, Neechabhanga for Venus in the 10th from Navamsa Lagna. Even a low-born, is supposed to become a king if the Moon be aspected by an exalted planet. This combination is present in Nero's horoscope, as the Moon is in the royal sign of Leo aspected by exalted Mars.

When Nero was hardly three years old, his father died and his mother had been banished on a charge of treason and conspiracy by Emperor Caligula and Nero thus early deprived of both parents found a bare shelter in the house of his aunt Domitia. With the death of Caligula the new Emperor Claudius recalled Agrippina from exile. Britanicus, the sun of Claudius, was by common consent regarded as the next in succession. To outweigh Britanicus' claims as the son of the reigning emperor, Agrippina relied on the double prestige which attached to her own son as being at once the grandson of the popular favourite Germanicus and the lineal descendant of Augustus himself.

In 49 A.D., she married her own uncle Claudius and in A.D. 50 Nero was adopted by the Emperor thus ensuring the throne. This adoption is clearly indicated by lord of 9 (the Sun) being aspected by Saturn and lord of 12 (Mars) being strongly disposed. The Matrukaraka being posited in a malefic sign and receiving the aspect of Mars rendered Nero's mother highly cruel, immoral and unscrupulous. Vargottama is a highly beneficial combination—in fact more beneficial than exaltation and when Vargottama occurs for exalted planets, the resultant would, of course, be powerful Rajayogas as in the case of Nero.

Lagna, the 9th lord, the 2nd lord and the 5th lord have all obtained Vargottama and this is indeed a unique disposition. The Sun and Mars are the planets for power and when they are so powerful, it is no wonder that Nero revelled with childish delight in the consciousness of absolute power. The afflictions of Venus especially by Mars, Rahu and Ketu favour those homo-sexual attachments reminiscent of classical Greece.

Two powerful combinations for making Nero a musician are present, viz., the Moon occupying Karakamsa and the Moon being placed in a Navamsa of Mercury and being associated with Venus. Nero was prouder of the reputation as an artist than of his glory as an Emperor. Clad in the humble garments of the professional actor (Saturn aspecting Lagna and hence setting at naught conventionalities) he would await his turn to appear before the musical adjudicators imploring judgment only on the merits of his performance. Born in a double-bodied sign, viz., Sagittarius, his was a complex personality. His horoscope does not reveal him to be as bad as he is depicted in history.

Adored by the people of Rome and worshipped as God by the Greeks, he was nevertheless dispelled by the senatorial and patrician families of Rome (Mars and the Sun in Dwirdwadasa). The fire of Rome is said by all authorities later than Tacitus to have been deliberately caused by Nero himself. But with Sagittarius rising and Jupiter being placed in Lagna in Navamsa, coupled with the Tacitus' description of Nero's energetic conduct at the time justifies us in acquitting the Emperor of so reckless a piece of incendiarism. Nero showed unusual public spirit during this time and opened his magnificent parks to the fugitives and the homeless.

The position of Saturn is intriguing. As 2nd lord he is exalted and is actually in the 10th house powerfully aspecting the Sun thus delegating much of his power to the Sun and it was during Sun's Dasa that Nero really ascended the throne. Saturn's aspect over the Sun is adverse. Consistent with the dictum that Saturn's position in the 10th drags one from power suddenly, we find that Nero had an ignominious flight and death.

No. 8.—PROPHET MAHAMUD

Birth Details.—*Born on 20th April 571 A.D. (O.S.) at 1-10 a.m. (Lat. 21° 20′ N., Long. 40° 14′ E.)

Planetary Positions.—The Sun 28° 45′ ; The Moon 136° ; Mars 90° 35′ ; Mercury 2° 24′ ; Jupiter 209° 50′ ; Venus 39° 29′ ; Saturn 211° 46′ ; Rahu 35° 31′ ; Ketu 215° 31 ; Lagna 304° 47′ ; 10th house 227° 1′. Ayanamsa 2° 26′.

	Sun Mercury	Venus Rahu		Venus	Mercury		Jupiter
Lagna			Mars	Rahu			Mars Saturn
	RASI				NAVAMSA		
			Moon				Moon Ketu
	Ketu Saturn	Jupiter		Sun	Lagna		

Balance of Venus' Dasa at birth :   Years 15–3–0.

Special Features.—Aquarius rising with Scorpio in Navamsa seems to fit in with the traditional description of

---

* The data given by Prof. B. S. Rao in *Royal Horoscopes* appears to be correct but not the chart. The rectified time of birth is 1-10 a.m. Prof. Md. Abdul Khaleque, in a letter addressed to me, observes thus

4

Mahamud, as "of middle height, greyish, with hair that was neither straight nor curly, with a large head, broad shouldered with thick hands one feet". The lord of Lagna Saturn is actually in the 10th Bhava and with Jupiter in Bhava associa- tion and with Ketu in Rasi association. Lagna is rendered strong by Lagna lord Saturn being in close association with Jupiter who also aspects Lagna. Kumbha or Aquarius is a mystic sign and consistent with the nature of Saturn, the Prophet "lived a life of severe simplicity". The 2nd lord being Jupiter and the 2nd house being unafflicted gave him a "deep and pleasant voice". The karaka of the mind Moon is in Leo aspected by Saturn Lagna lord. In the Navamsa again, the Moon is afflicted. Consequently, (it is said) that "he was in the habit of giving violent expression to the emotions of anger and mirth". The last days of the Prophet, however, (Jupiter Dasa) were remarkable by a calmness and serenity of mind. The 4th house is highly afflicted indicating that he was illiterate.

According to classical texts, when the Sun is in a Dusthana

---

regarding the Prophet's birth details : "As to the month of the birth of the Prophet, the opinions also differ. The majority of the opinions are that he was born in the month of Rabiul Awal. One or two narrators have said that he was born in the month of Ramadan. It has been proved that the latter are not at all reliable persons; so their words cannot stand against the words of the most trustworthy and vastly learned scholars of the age. So it is certain that he was born in the month of Rabiul Awal. As to the date of his birth almost all the historians are of the opinion that he was born on the 12th of Rabiul Awal corresponding to the month of April, 571 A.D." The views of the great historians and the traditions of the Prophet clearly indicate that he was born on the 12th of Rabiul Awal. The Halabi, taking all the different views together and judging the merits of the assertions in the critical light, has shown that it can undoubtedly be said that he was born on the 12th of Rabiul Awal.

and the Lagna is in the Dwadasamsa of Pisces or Leo, the native would be a posthumous child. It will be seen that in the Prophet's horoscope, the Sun is in the 3rd and the Lagna has fallen in Meena (Pisces) Dwadasamsa, suggesting clearly that he was a posthumous child. Mark the fortification as well as affliction of Venus, Kalatrakaraka. In his own house in the 4th Venus gets positional as well as directional strength while his association with Rahu and his being aspected by Saturn renders him afflicted. The lord of the 7th is exalted and is in the last Navamsa, aspected both in Rasi as well as in Navamsa by Jupiter. The Prophet married eleven wives, and the first wife Khadija was a widow and was his senior by 15 years. Mark Rahu-Venus association.

Two powerful Rajayogas are to be found—one in the 3rd house by the association of the Sun (lord of the 7th) and Mercury (lord of the 5th) aspected by Jupiter lord of the 2nd and 11th ; and the other having reference to the 10th by the mutual aspects of Lagna lord Saturn and the yogakaraka Venus. Jupiter the planet of wisdom is in the 9th or Dharmasthana aspected by Mars, lord of Karmasthana who in his turn has obtained Neechabhanga and is Vargottama and hence strong *par excellence*. The emphasis on the 9th and 10th—involving Jupiter and Saturn—Ketu gives us the clue as to the methods employed by the Prophet in spreading his doctrines, especially his encouragement of the shedding of kindred blood in the cause of Islam. He wanted to spread his Dharma (Jupiter in the 9th) but the means (Karma) was in consonance with the nature of Mars. In the Navamsa again, it will seen that Mars and Saturn are in the 9th.

Important Events.—His mother died in his 6th year when he was having Venus Dasa Rahu Bhukti. Mark the position of these two planets in the house of the mother. Marriage with Khadija, a widow and senior to him by 15 years, took place when the Prophet was 25, during the Moon's Dasa

Saturn's Bhukti. It will be seen that the major lord is in the 7th from Lagna and the sub-lord Saturn owns the 7th from the Moon and occupies the 7th from Kalatrakaraka. His flight to Yathrib intitiated the Mohammedan era (Hijira) and this happened in Rahu Dasa Venus Bhukti. Mark again the disposition of these two planets in the 4th. The turning point in his career began in the same year and under the same directional influences. The campaign of Mahamud for the spread of Islam involving violence took place in Rahu Dasa. Mutual aspects between Rahu and Saturn are not desirable. One of his sons died in Jupiter Dasa Mercury Bhukti. It is significant that the major lord Jupiter is aspected by the Sun a maraka and Mercury the sub-lord is associated with the maraka planet Sun. In the Navamsa, again, Jupiter as owning a maraka place is in the 8th while Mercury is lord of another marakasthana from the Moon.

Remarks.—In the world's religious history, Mahamud is certainly a most extraordinary character. He was a prophet, philosopher and politician. The peculiar disposition of Jupiter in the 9th, Lagna lord in the 10th and the Sun and Mercury in the 3rd and Venus in the 4th—each powerful in its own way, and each bringing into play its peculiar indications due to ownership, association. etc.,—render the horoscope a remarkable one. Mahamud influenced the world in no ordinary way. Deep thinkers who have studied his works carefully admit the grandeur of his religious system and the depth of his wisdom and all this is due to the blessings of Jupiter's position in the 9th. Mokshakaraka Ketu's situation in the 10th in the house of Mars is significant. This made Mahamud a real *gnani* but because the sign involved is that of Mars, he did not adopt an entirely peaceful method to propagate his religion. The Prophet has influenced the lives of millions of his followers during the last thirteen centuries and the clue to his unique personality is to be found in his horoscope,

No. 9.—SRI RAMANUJACHARYA

Birth Details.—*Born on the 4th April 1017 A.D. (O.S.) at about 12 Noon. (Lat. 11° 14′ N., Long. 78° 56′ E.)

Planetary Positions.—The Sun 11° 32′; the Moon 73° 50′; Mars 121° 24′; Mercury 24° 42′; Jupiter 63°; Venus 16° 36′; Saturn 260° 18′; Rahu 43° 42′; and Lagna 102° 2′. Ayanamsa 8° 40′.

	Venus Sun Mercury	Rahu	Moon Jupit.
	RASI		Lagna Moon
			Mars
Saturn	Ketu		

Mars	Rahu		
	NAVAMSA		Sun
			Venus
Ketu Mercury	Lagna Jupiter Saturn		

Balance of Rahu Dasa at birth : Years 8-3-27.

Special Features.—Jupiter-Saturn influences focussed on Lagna lord in Rasi and Lagna in Navamsa indicate attractive

* Sri Ramanuja is said to have been born on Thursday, 13th day of the Chaitra month, in the constellation of Aridra, in the year 939 of Salivahana. This corresponds to 4th April 1017 A.D. I am indebted to Mr. A. S. Sowmyanarayana Iyengar of Madras for this information. The time of birth is given as at about midday.

physical features and handsome appearance, a broad forehead, large eyes, long arms reaching up to his knees and a face endowed with the lustre of genius; lord of the 2nd Sun is in association with the intellectual and the poetical planets Mercury and Venus respectively, suggesting uncommon powers of intellect but great humility also as Saturn aspects Lagna lord.

Venus, lord of the house of education, with Mercury the planet of intelligence and the Sun, lord of the house of speech, all aspecting the house of education and otherwise unafflicted, gave Ramanuja erudition, intellectual vigour and intense yearning for knowledge. It must be noted that Ramanuja's early education was under the formidable Yadava Prakash, a staunch Advaitin. In the Navamsa, again, the 4th house is equally well disposed, as the 4th lord Saturn is exalted in Lagna with the divine planet Jupiter. Ramanuja's mastery of all the intricate argumentations of Vedanta was remarkable. At times Ramanuja began to feel that Yadava Prakash's interpretation of certain Vedic texts were not quite up to his satisfaction and this led to differences between master and pupil.

Jupiter who indicates Brahmagnana or divine knowledge is in the 12th or Mokshasthana with the emotional planet Moon who happens to be lord of Lagna and the combination receives the aspect of the philosophical planet Saturn. Hence, Ramanuja propounded a system of philosophy—Visishtadwaita—that stressed the need for a personal God and a more emotional and a less intellectual approach to the problem of religion. Venus occupying Karmasthana with Atmakaraka Sun is suggestive that making *bhakti* as the pivot of religion was one of the most important points in the life-work of Ramanuja. There is a certain harmonious blending of reason, intuition and revelation in the method of Ramanuja's approach to the problem of reality, consistent with the harmonious disposition of the lords of Lagna, the 12th and the 10th.

The 7th lord Saturn is in the 6th (12th from 7th) aspected by the lords of Lagna and the 6th. In the Navamsa, again, the 7th house is considerably afflicted by the combined influences of Saturn and Mars though Jupiter's aspect lends a slight relief. Consequently, Ramanuja's domestic life does not appear to have been very happy. It is said that he did not find in his wife that ready sympathy and compliance to his own wishes he expected of her. He took advantage of an invitation from his father-in-law to send away his wife and immediately assumed Sanyasa. Mark the fact that Mokshasthana is aspected by Saturn, lord of the 7th, and lord of Mokshasthana is with Kalatrakaraka suggesting that in a sense, she was indirectly instrumental for his taking Sanyasa. The 5th, house of children, is considerably afflicted by the presence of Ketu and the aspect of Mars.

Important Events.—Venus Bhukti in Jupiter Dasa was of great significance, for it was under these directional influences that Ramanuja married Kantimati, his father died and the family had to shift to Kancheepuram. The major lord Jupiter owns the 7th from Chandra Lagna, is aspected by the lord of the 7th (in Navamsa) while the sub-lord Venus is Kalatrakaraka; and hence marriage took place. Father's death was due to the fact that the major lord, as owning the 9th from Lagna, is aspected by Saturn (lord of the 12th from 9th) while the sub-lord owns maraka places from the sign occupied by Pitrukaraka. During the Sun's sub-period there was an attempt to kill Ramanuja by his own Guru. The Sun is a maraka from Lagna while Jupiter is a maraka from the Moon. In Jupiter Dasa Rahu Bhukti, the master sent away his wife and became a

Sanyasi. Mark the position of Rahu in the 12th from the 7th lord (from the Moon) and the unique disposition of Jupiter from Chandra Lagna. During Saturn Dasa, Ramanuja got himself initiated into every department of learning and philosophy which then constituted the Vaishnava lore. There was again another attempt on the life of the saint during Saturn Dasa. It will be seen that Saturn's disposition in the 7th from the Moon and his ownership of the 7th from Lagna has conferred maraka power on Saturn. But owing to the Purnayu nature of the horoscope, nothing untoward happened.

The discovery and consecration of the temple at Melkote took place in Venus Dasa Saturn Bhukti. From Chandra Lagna, the disposition of Venus, as lord of the 5th with the lord of Chandra Lagna, in the 11th, is ideal while Saturn and Venus are in mutual trine. Owing to the lordship of a kendra by Venus, Ramanuja, during Venus' Dasa, had to undergo considerable persecution under the Chola king Kulottunga. In the Sun's Dasa—mark his exalted position in the 10th—Ramanuja received considerable support from Vishnuvardhana which enabled him to actively spread his doctrines in Mysore State.

He died in Rahu Dasa Mercury Bhukti, when he was 120 years old. The major lord Rahu is in the house of Venus who in his turn, along with the sub-lord Mercury, has joined the Sun a powerful maraka planet. It will be seen that in the Navamsa, Rahu is in the 8th while Mercury is in the 2nd aspected by the major lord.

Remarks.—Ramanuja's horoscope is illustrative of an active, long, useful and eventful life. From a spiritual point of view, the horoscope has many virtues. Firstly, Jupiter the planet of wisdom is in the 12th (Mokshasthana) with the lord of Lagna Moon. Atmakaraka Sun is in the 10th (house of action) with the intellectual planet Mercury. Obviously, his wisdom did not merely culminate in verbose but there was a certain amount of spiritual attainment which enabled him to save himself from the clutches of desires and attachments.

Mark again Saturn's aspect on Jupiter–Moon association. Ramanuja played a notable part as a fearless and faithful worker in the field of religious and social reform. In making Hinduism a "religion of loving devotion to an all-powerful and all-merciful God what Ramanuja mainly did was that he combined the old religious views of the Bhagavatas with the Vedantic ideas of Sankara's higher pantheism, so as to make his *advaita* (absolute non-dualism) become *visishtadvaita* (qualified non-dualism)". Ramanuja emphasised the value of devotion, service, self-surrender to God, and the need for moral conduct, sinlessness and selflessness in life.

No. 10.—OMAR KHAYYAM

Birth Details. — *Born on 18th May 1048 A.D. (O.S.) at 4-48 a.m. (L.M.T.). (Lat. 36° 13' N., Long. 58° 45' E.)

Planetary Positions. — The Sun 53° 12'; the Moon 79° 54'; Mars 28° 36'; Mercury 57° 36'; Jupiter 297°; Venus 67°; Saturn 278° 48'; Rahu 161° 6'; and Lagna 49° 1'. Ayanamsa 9° 6'.

Ketu	Mars	Lagna Sun Mercury	Moon Venus	Moon Sat.	Rahu		Lagna
							Sun
Jupiter Saturn	RASI			NAVAMSA			
			Rahu	Mars Venus		Ketu	Mercury Jupiter

Balance of Rahu Dasa at birth :   Year 0–1–18.

Special Features. — Lagna occupied by the Sun, the planet of vitality and Mercury, the planet of intelligence and aspected by Jupiter endowed the native with a healthy physique and

* This is the data given by Swami Govinda Thirtha in his *Nectar of Grace*. The birth date of Omar Khayyam (as quoted by Prof P. S. Sastri in December, 1945 issue of THE ASTROLOGICAL MAGAZINE is given by Zahiruddin Abdul Hasan in his *Futimma Siwan Al Hikmat*, thus:

good memory and intelligence. There is interchange or Parivarthana between lords of Lagna and the 2nd, *viz.*, Venus and Mercury, indicating proficiency in different branches of knowledge. The association of Venus with the Moon gives a virile and energetic mind. Venus is a planet of materialism, poetry, and to a certain extent, reason. His disposition in a common sign in Rasi and his association with Mars in Navamsa, which is a common sign, made him a rationalist, a lover of all the good things of life and a man of versatile interests. It will be seen that Lagna, the Sun and Mercury are all aspected by Jupiter, the divine planet from the 9th house giving him high philosophical knowledge, powers of observation and profound scholarship.

The house of education is considerably fortified as lord of the 4th happens to be the Sun who is in Lagna with Mercury lord of the house of intelligence. Mercury is the planet of mathematics. Obviously, he was a great astronomer and mathematician. His standard work on algebra written in Arabic and other treatises of a similar character raised him to the foremost rank among mathematicians of age.

The 9th house being afflicted by the presence of debilitated Jupiter deprived him of his father early in life. Both the Matrukaraka and the 4th house are well disposed, assuring long life to the mother. Both in Raṣi and Navamsa, the 5th house has

---

"Omar's ascendant was Gemini. The Sun and Mercury were in the degree of the ascendant in the third degree of Gemini. Jupiter was aspecting the Sun and Mercury from triangulation." On the basis of this information Swami Govinda Thirtha has fixed the birth details of Khayyam after elaborate researches. Obviously, the positions of planets given by Zahiruddin, as per the then prevailing calendar, correspond to the Sayana zodiac. On the basis of the ascendant degree givan, the time of birth has been found to be 4-48 a.m.

the influences of the nodes focussed on it. It is said he was childless. The 7th or house of marriage is not well disposed indicating no marriage. Kalatrakaraka Venus is in Mercury's place in association with the Moon. In the Navamsa Venus is considerably afflicted. All these indicate sensuousness and a pleasure-seeking nature.

Important Events.—He lost his father in the beginning of Saturn Dasa. Note the presence of Saturn in the 9th. By the end of Jupiter Dasa he had already become a versatile scholar. Jupiter aspects the 4th lord in Lagna conferring proficiency in different branches of knowledge. At the age of 26 (Saturn Dasa Sun Bhukti) Omar was already the head of an observatory. Saturn is yogakaraka and occupies the 9th while the Sun, who has also caused Rajayoga (involving 4th and 5th houses) is in Lagna.

Before the end of Rahu's sub-period in Saturn Dasa he had become a metaphysician, philosopher, logician, doctor, and mathematician, and had also developed poetical talent. Rahu as sub-lord gave all the results due to Mercury whose house he has occupied.

Just at the fag end of Mercury's Dasa, he went on a pilgrimage to Mecca. And in 1103, when Ketu Dasa was in progress, he retired from public life. Mark the position of Ketu in the 10th from Chandra Lagna and the debilitation of Jupiter, whose results he should give. He died in 1123, when Venus' Dasa and Saturn's Bhukti was in operation. The major lord Venus occupies *marakasthanas* both in Rasi and Navamsa. The sub-lord Saturn is with Jupiter, a maraka from Chandra Lagna. In the Navamsa also he is aspected both by Jupiter and Mercury who are marakas respectively from Lagna and Chandra Lagna.

Remarks.— To attain proficiency in a variety of subjects such as metaphysics, medicine, astrology, philosophy and mathematics planetary groupings must be of a certain significant pattern. We find that the intellectual planet Mercury and the intuitional planet Jupiter are in mutual trines Mercury having the important ownership of Poorvapunyasthana, denoting great devotion to God and the ability to intellectually perceive the reality of the Absolute. The Parivarthana between the poetic Venus and the intellectual Mercury accounts for Omar's poetical renown which he owes to his *rubaits* or quatrains. And finally the disposition of the Sun, Atmakaraka in Lagna with Mercury aspected by Jupiter, reveals that although some of his quartains are purely mystic and pathetic, most of them "are the outpourings of a thinker who protests both against the narrowness, bigotry, and uncompromising austerity of the orthodox and the eccentricity and the ravings of extremist Sufis".

No. II.—CHENGIZ KHAN

Birth Details.—*Born on 16/15 September 1186 A.D. (O.S.) at about 1-30 a.m. (L.M.T.). (Lat. 37° N., Long. 65° E.)

Planetary Positions.—The Sun 169° 23′ ; the Moon 198° 12′ ; Mars 179° 38′ ; Mercury 155° 33′ ; Jupiter 170° ; Venus 155° 24′ ; Saturn 174° 18′ ; Rahu 3° 10′ ; What about Ketu and Lagna 100° 40′. Ayanamsa 11° 2′.

RASI			
Rahu		Moon	
			Lagna
	Moon Ketu	Sun Mars Merc. Jupiter Venus Saturn	

NAVAMSA			
Rahu			Sun Jupiter
Merc. Venus			
			Saturn
Ketu Lagna			Mars

Balance of Rahu Dasa at birth : Years 2-5-5.

Special Features.—Chengiz Khan's father Yasuki was absent at the time of the native's birth in a campaign against

* The data is from the *National Astrological Journal* for August 1933, wherein it is stated that Chengiz Khan was born on 29th Jumada 582 A.D in the night corresponding to 16-9-1186. The Lagna Cancer has been fixed by us taking into consideration salient life events. Latitude and longitude of birth are only approximate.

a Tartar. This is explained by the fact of Saturn's (the birth being at night) association with Mars and the Lagna being unaspected by the Moon. The Lagna is a watery sign. It will be noted that the Khan was born on the banks of the river Onon. At the time of birth, the child had in its clenched fist a clot of coagulated blood like a red stone. In Chengiz Khan's horoscope, all the planets are confined to two signs causing what is called Yuga Yoga. Astrological writers have condemned this yoga as causing irreligiousness and childlessness ; but here as the yoga has been peculiarly disposed inasmuch as the reference is to the 3rd and 4th houses, its indications have been fully neutralised by the presence of the other formidable Rajayogas.

Chengiz Khan was a wanderer and a conqueror. As *Saravali* says, when there is Shadgraha Yoga (six-planet combination) the person becomes a wanderer, a fighter and a man of good conduct. The Lagna lord Moon is in a kendra but in association with Ketu. The Moon rules the populace and hence men who enjoy great name and popularity are born under Cancer, the sign ruled by the Moon. Here as the Moon is with Ketu an incendiary planet, it signified a crafty, violent and dangerous person.

The yogakaraka Mars, owning the 5th and 10th, the Sun lord of the 2nd or house of wealth, Jupiter lord of the 9th and Venus lord of the 4th and 11th, Saturn lord of the 7th (and 8th) have all gathered in the 3rd the house of courage which house is the virgin sign of Virgo, with Mercury the lord in exaltation. This curious association of all trinal and quadrangular lords is a most powerful Rajayoga indicating power, wealth, conquests and certain victory over enemies.

Important Events.—He lost his father at the age of 13 in

Jupiter Dasa Venus Bhukti. Jupiter as owning the 9th is in the 3rd in association with Mars, a maraka for the 9th house. The sub-lord Venus is in a maraka from the Pitrusthana, owning a maraka from Pitrukaraka. Under the same directional influences, the Rajayoga part of Jupiter's indications manifested as the native succeeded to his father's interests.

Again from the Sun's Bhukti he was involved in almost unbroken warfare till the end of his 43rd year, when his power was firmly established. In Mercury Dasa Sun Bhukti, he adopted the name and title of Chengiz Khan. Mark the association of Saturn, lord of the 7th (war and foreign relations) with Mars, the martial planet who happens to be the yogakaraka indicating continuous military expeditions. Mercury lord of the 3rd is exalted in the 3rd on upachaya, while Ketu occupies the 4th in the constellation of Mars, thus becoming capable of producing results due to Mars the yogakaraka.

Throughout the remaining part of Mercury's Dasa and the whole of Ketu Dasa, wars spread his dominion west beyond the Jaxartes river in Turkestan and to Bokhara. His armies penetrated through Samarkhand into Khorasam to Merr and into Georgia, across the Indus into Peshawar and Lahore and campaign in China which made him ruler over almost the whole of the Chinese empire.

He died in his 65th year in Mongolia, on the banks of the river Sai when he was undergoing the major period of Venus and the sub-period of the Sun. The major lord Venus is in the 3rd in association with two powerful marakas the Sun and Saturn while the sub-lord Sun is himself a maraka indicating death.

Remarks.—Chengiz Khan was one of the greatest conquerors that has ever lived. And this is satisfied by the peculiar disposition of Mars, as yogakaraka, the 3rd house, in Vargottama. There is a certain blending of the influences of the 7th (conquest), 10th (career), 2nd (wealth), 9th (general fortune), and 5th (intelligence).

Son of a petty Mongol chieftain, he lived to see his armies victorious from the China sea to the banks of the Dneiper. *Laghu Jataka Sarwaswa*, verse 537, says that when all the planets are in the 12th from the Moon and aspect the 6th, a peculiar type of Rajayoga is caused and that the person would live for 68 years. This yoga applies *in toto* to the horoscope of Chengiz Khan. It will also be seen that all the six planets the 12th from the Moon have caused Anapha Yoga which usually denotes "well-formed organs, majestic appearance, good reputation, generous instincts, self-respect and famous for sense pleasures".

Birth Details.—*Born on the 11th April 1296 A.D. (O.S.) at 10-58 p.m. (L.M.T.). (Lat. 15° N, Long. 77° E.)

Planetary Positions.—The Sun 16° 30′ ; the Moon 100° 7′ ; Mercury 358° 48′ ; Jupiter 260° 6′ ; Venus 346° 24′ ; Saturn 64° ; Rahu 42° 30′ ; and Lagna 262° 29′. Ayanamsa 12° 34′.

RASI

Mercury Venus	Sun	Rahu	Sat.
Mars			Moon
Jupiter Lagna	Ketu		

NAVAMSA

Mars Merc.	Rahu		
			Sun
Saturn Venus	Moon Ketu Lagna Jupiter		

Balance of Saturn's Dasa at birth :   Years 9-4-0.

Special Features.—Jupiter rising almost in conjunction with Lagna, which is Sagittarius, conferred a manly and noble

---

* The age of Vidyaranya has been variously given, much of the uncertainty being due to the confusion of the name of the Sage in his Purvasrama (Madhavacharya) with Madhava Mantri, a Saraswat Brahmin minister, who was also known as Madarasa and who was the son of Chaunda of Angirasa Gotra. In some of his own works, written

appearance, with well-proportioned limbs, broad chest and a magnetic personality. The Moon karaka of the mind is in his own house free from affliction indicating a "pleasant disposition free from passion". Atmakaraka Sun lord of the 9th is exalted in Aries, aspected by Jupiter lord of Lagna. Such a position of the Sun always makes one a leader in ideals and a poineer of advanced thought.

The Sun and the Moon in mutual kendras from each other and the Sun and Jupiter in mutual trikonas, devoid of malefic aspects or associations, gave to the native great mental energy, remarkable foresight, extreme ideality, self-will, generosity and combativeness, the last quality being expressed in constructive channels, owing to the absence of malefic influences.

Mercury the planet of intellect governing the 10th house or karmasthana is in debility in the 4th or house of education but there is neechabhanga caused by the presence of Venus as

----

before he took Sanyasa, Vidyaranya speaks of himself as a Brahmin of Bharadwaja Gotra, his father being Mayana and his mother Srimathi. Prof. B. Suryanarain Rao has very ably discussed this matter in his monumental work *Never-to be Forgotten Empire* and has clearly shown that Sage Vidyaranya and Madhava Mantri are two different persons, the former being the founder of the Sangama dynasty and the spiritual head of Vijayanagar Emperors while the latter was merely a minister under the rulers of Vijayanagar. The findings of oriental scholars like Robert Sewell and Lewis Rice are not at all helpful in the matter. By a consideration of the relevant literature bearing on the history of S. India during the 13th and 14th centuries, I am inclined to conclude that Vidyaranya was born in the last decade of the 13th century. For the exact birth details of this Sage however I am indebted to Prof. P. S. Sastry, who says that according to *Renuka Tantra*, the Sage was born on the 7th day of the bright half of the lunar month Vaisakha of Kaliyuga year 4397. This information was provided to Prof. Sastry by Sri Kalyanananda Bharati. The longitude and latitude of the birthplace

well as Jupiter in kendras from Lagna. This gave the Sage,
intellectual versatility and vigour and masterful spirit. It will be
seen that Vidyaranya was an intellectual giant. "His brain was
ever active and looking to the quantity, quality and the vast
number of subjects he has handled with such ease and mastery,
one cannot but be struck at the gigantic nature of his intellect
and the erudition he has brought to bear in his immortal commentaries upon the Vedas."

Mark the position of Mars as lord of the 5th in the 3rd,
again unafflicted, but in association with Mercury in Navamsa.
This made him an independent character with clear and decided
ideas and a spirit that is fearless, dauntless and aspiring.

It will be seen that Vidyaranya lived at a time when
political and cultural anarchy prevailed in South India due to
the onslaught of Mohammedan invasions and the disorgani-
sation of Hindu kingdoms. Tenth lord Mercury, neechabhanga,
9th lord the Sun exalted in the 5th and aspected by Lagna lord
Jupiter, the 10th being aspected by two benefics, gave the
Sage not merely spiritual and intellectual attainments, but a
sense of patriotism, love for national Dharma, and a spirit of
determination to stem the rot that had set into the very vitals
of Hindu leadership.

---

are given only approximately. The followiug is the relevant verse from
Renuka Tantra :

    Chatvaryabda sahasreshu chatvaryabda sateshu cha ;
    Tribhiruneshu varsheshu gateshasmin kalouyuge.
    Durmukhyabde radhamase saptamyam soumyavasare ;
    Ravibhagevayo svochcha samsthayo vrishagettvagou.
    Punyarshe chandra samyukte nutuune samsthithe sanou ;
    Chape gurou kumbha samsthe bhoume jatastu madhavah.

    In the original horoscope, Mercury's position is given in Aries, while
calculations according to modern constants give the position as 358° 48′.

The two powerful Panchamahapurusha yogas enabled him to establish firmly the famous Sangama dynasty upon the throne of Vijayanagar which later on extended its influence and might practically throughout South India, and thus became the chief instrument for the preservation of the political and cultural independence from Mohammedan aggression.

It will be seen that Jupiter's presence in Lagna identical with *swakshetra* and the position of Venus in the 4th identical with his exaltation have caused two Panchamahapurusha yogas, *viz.*, Hamsa and Malavya, the former indicating "distinction, righteous disposition and pure mind" and the latter denoting "strength of mind, wealth, clean sense-organs, renown and learning", all of which he possessed to a remarkable degree.

Lord of the 2nd Saturn is in the 6th Bhava and in a *trikona* from the lord of the 5th, while the lord of the 11th Venus is exalted in a kendra, with lord of the 10th Mercury. From Chandra Lagna again, Dhanabhava is very well pronounced, especially that the 2nd lord the Sun is exalted in the 10th while the 9th is occupied by two benefics, both endowed with Rajayoga tendencies. As a consequence, he used his great spiritual influence in collecting huge funds which were used for endowing the empire with financial security.

Ketu, Mokshakaraka, is in the 12th, Mokshasthana, while the 12th from the Moon has Saturn aspected by Jupiter, lord of the 9th. These planetary influences made him a real Yogi and Sanyasi and enabled him to lead a life of complete detachment, austerity and simplicity. Other yogas of significance present in this horoscope are Vallaki, Sarala, Lakshmi and Vidyut. Each of these has contributed its share to make the man what he was: an intellectual and spiritual colossus, shaping the destinies of an empire and rebuilding the cultural

life of millions of people according to the great ancient traditions of India, yet keeping himself away from the political
atmosphere and power politics of the day.

Important Events.—Throughout Saturn Dasa which lasted
till about the age of 9 years 4 months, financially, the family
was in very bad circumstances. Mark the fact that though 2nd
lord Saturn is in the 6th Bhava, he is aspected by the 12th lord
Mars. It will be seen that Mars is Bhratrukaraka and aspects
Saturn from Bhratrubhava. Vidyaranya's two younger brothers
were born in the Dasa of Mars.

The house of education is pre-eminently strong by the
position of exalted Venus in association with neechabhanga
Mercury and aspected by Vaksthanadhipati Saturn. It was in
the Dasa of Mercury, that the native had his education under
three distinguished masters—Vidyatheertha, Bharathi Krishna-
theertha and Sankarananda. Due to the highly dignified situation of Mercury, in respect of the house of education,
Vidyaranya attained unparalleled distinction in all the Vedas
and Vedanta. Venus has caused Malavya Yoga in the 9th or
Dharmasthana from Chandra Lagna ruling the mind.

It was in Venus Dasa Venus Bhukti that Madhava was
ordained as Jagat Guru in Sringeri by Sri Vidyasankara Theertha.
The most important act of his life was the founding of the
grand empire of Vijayanagar and this happened in 1336, in
Venus Dasa Mars Bhukti. The position of Mars from Lagna is
ideal and he happens to be the yogakaraka from the Moon and
actually occupies the 9th Bhava from Chandra Lagna.

In Mars Bhukti Vidyaranya left Sringeri for Vijayanagar
and lived there, entrusting the pontifical office of Sringeri to
his brother Bhoganatha known after his initiation into Sanyasa
as Bharathi Theertha. This brother's (Bharathi Theertha) death

took place in Rahu Dasa Mercury Bhukti. Rahu, the major lord, is in the house of happiness from Bhratrusthana (3rd) and Bhratrukaraka Mars and occupies a marakasthana. Venus, whose results Rahu should give, is also in the 2nd maraka from Bhratrusthana. It is fitting therefore that the brother's death should have taken place under these directional influences.

The Guru's own death took place in Rahu Dasa Venus Bhukti. Rahu, the major lord, is in Bhava association with Saturn, lord of the 2nd, a maraka place, while Venus the sub-lord (whose results alone should be given by Rahu) is in association with Mercury, a maraka from Lagna, and aspected by another maraka Saturn. Lagna lord strong in Lagna and lord of the 8th in his own house conferred a long life of 91 years.

Remarks.—The gigantic nature of the task which Vidya-ranya had to accomplish to reorient the cultural, social and the political outlook of the Hindus, so well indicated in his horoscope, can be appreciated only against the background of the historical conditions that prevailed in South India in the 14th century.

Hoysala and Warrangal powers had collapsed under the irresistible pressure of Mohammedan invasions. A new Mohammedan power—the Bahmani kingdom—was rising. Hindu national outlook and culture were on the verge of extinction. In this anarchy Vidyaranya determined to establish a strong and centralised new state which would halt the forces of disruption and disintegration. Jupiter the divine planet is rising in Lagna, in his own house, aspecting the royal and political planet the Sun, lord of the 9th exalted. Therefore Vidyaranya's ambition to found an empire for safeguarding and reviving the national Dharma (signified by the 9th house) was fulfilled.

He became the rallying point for the scions of the disorganised Hindu royal families who had been waiting for the appearance of a selfless and brave leader, who could give them scope to defend their country, their honour and their religion and who would enable them to cope with the Mohammedan incursions, and in Vidyaranya they found an ideal personage.

Two planets in own house, two planets exalted and one planet neechabhanga and Vargottama, constitute three powerful Rajayogas favouring the "command of all the insignia of royalty". Hence Vidyaranya was able to found the empire of Vijayanagar and earn the gratitude of posterity.

The shattered political forces of ancient Hindu dynasties were formed into a strong bulwark against Mohammedan invasions and an empire established under whose benevolent administration the whole of South India, including the East Coast from Cape Comorin to Bengal, witnessed peace, prosperity and unfettered cultural revival.

To a student of astrology, Vidyaranya's horoscope would be interesting in three ways : First, as indicating intellectual versatility, because of the powerful and favourable disposition of Mercury in the 4th house ; second, as revealing the depth of his spiritual and yogic attainments—he is alleged to have shown a number of miracles due to his Yoga Vidya, his spirituality being brought out by the dignified position of Jupiter in Lagna and Mokshakaraka Ketu in the 12th ; and third, as revealing his great political wisdom and statesmanship in founding an empire and entrusting it to deserving hands and centralising its administration so as to establish its authority throughout South India and thus paving the way for the cultural and political revival of the people.

These achievements should be traced to the unique positions of the Sun in the 5th, of the 10th lord in the 4th and that of Mars in an upachaya, ensuring success. As the celebrated Prof. B. Suryanarain Rao observes : ''it may not be possible to find many names if we search in the pages of the world history—which can furnish a career parallel to that of this wonderful personage and if Vidyaranya stands today as one of the greatest men among the historical and literary characters, he richly deserves that proud distinction by his gigantic intellect, his versatile genius, his political prudence and foresight, his simple and devoted life.''

His horoscope is an illustration of what an extraordinary man he was and how, despite his close association with mundane affairs, he withdrew himself from the ebb and flow of life's passions. Rajayogas and Parivraja yogas untainted by Saturn-Rahu or Saturn-Mars or Rahu–Mars associations or combined aspects are the special feature of this horoscope.

No. 13.—GURU NANAK

Birth Details.—*Born on 8th November 1470 (O.S.) at midnight (L.M.T.). (Lat. 31° 39′ N., Long. 74° 47′ E.)

Planetary Positions.—The Sun 220° 30′; the Moon 38° 18′; Mars 211° 24′; Mercury 232° 24′; Jupiter 164° 30′; Venus 186°; Saturn 39° 6′; Rahu 263° 48′; and Lagna 136° 28′. Ayanamsa 15°.

	Moon Saturn	Ketu	Moon Sat.			Jupiter Ketu	
			Lagna		NAVAMSA		Mars
RASI							Lagna
Rahu	Sun Mars Mercury	Venus	Jupit.		Venus Rahu	Sun Mercury	

Balance of the Sun's Dasa at birth : Year 0-9-23.

Special Features.—Simha or Leo rises unaspected by or unassociated with any malefics or benefics. The Lagna is

---

* I am indebted to Mr. Nahar Singh Gyani of Gujjarwal, Ludhiana District, for the birth details of Guru Nanak. According to most reliable sources, the Guru was born on the Full Moon day of Karthika, Samvat 1526, Thursday at midnight, in the nakshatra of Krittika, Simha Lagna.

Vargottama and even in the Navamsa, the Lagna is unafflicted. This gives an exalted nature and a strong will, and renders the horoscope fortified. The Sun, lord of Lagna, is in the 4th in association with Mercury and Mars and aspected by the Moon and Saturn. The Sun's position in a kendra, in the sign of yoga-karaka Mars, is highly favourable as it confers a frank and noble spirit and diverse capabilities. The Moon–Saturn association gives mental conflicts and a spirit of inquiry.

Born in a Kshatriya family to Kalu and Tripta, Nanak appears to have been even in his childhood a mystic disposition and given much to contemplation—blessings mainly due to the Moon's disposition with Saturn and the Sun's occupation of the secret sign of Scorpio. Lord of the 2nd Mercury, the planet of intelligence, is involved in Mercury Aditya Yoga with the lord of Lagna in the 4th house, while the 2nd or house of speech is occupied by Jupiter, lord of the 5th. These explain Nanak's deep and versatile learning and persuasive eloquence.

It will be seen that the 4th and 10th houses—two important kendras—are largely influenced by five planets—all natural malefics, except the Full Moon. Out of these five, the Sun happening to be Lagna lord, Saturn happening to be a Kendradhipati and Mars, a yogakaraka—have become benefics

The English date corresponds to 20th October 1469, but the weekday is Friday and nakshatra Bharani. If 21st October 1469 is taken, the nakshatra will no doubt be Krittika but the weekday would be Saturday. According to the custom prevalent in certain parts of North India, the year mentioned always refers to the past year (*gata*) and not to the current year. It is therefore reasonable to infer that the Guru was born in Krittika Sukla Pournimasi after 1526 Samvat, which actually means he was born in 1527th Samvat corresponding to 8th November 1470, on which date Krittika nakshatra and Thursday coincide. I am therefore inclined to feel that the correct date of birth is 8–11–1470.

by ownership. The martial planet Mars, the intellectual and emotional planet Mercury, the royal planet the Sun (also Atmakaraka) and the mental and the philosophical planets the Moon and Saturn—all involved in influencing two of the most important houses of the horoscope, *viz.*, the 4th indicating happiness and achievement and the 10th (Karma) or the house of action, filled the Guru with those great spiritual ideas and intuitions which led him to found a great sect.

Rahu's position in the 5th does not favour happiness from children, but it does confer a certain spiritual outlook and the spirit of renunciation and detachment. The Moon happens to be Mokshasthanadhipati and he occupies the 10th with Saturn, the planet of renunciation. In the Navamsa, again, the divine planet Jupiter with Mokshakaraka Ketu is in the 10th (Karmasthana) aspected by Saturn. These are formidable combinations capable of conferring real spiritual attainments after intense mental struggle, a conviction that he was born for achieving something unique in the world by spreading the gospel of the Fatherhood of God and the Brotherhood of man and sweet resignation to the will of God. Mark the fact that Saturn is also lord of the 6th. His association with the Moon indicates that Nanak had to overcome considerable opposition from hostile relatives and co-religionists.

Important Events.—Nanak was put to school in his 7th or 8th year when he was undergoing the Moon's Dasa. The Moon has favourable aspects from planets situated in the 4th house. Consistent with the lordship of the Moon (he owns the 12th or Mokshasthana) Nanak often surprised his schoolmaster and parents by his queer acts and utterances, and occasional sallies of free thought.

His spiritual prepossessions and mystic brooding spirit became clearly visible in the course of the Moon's Dasa. It was in the Moon's Dasa, that he was put to various secular tasks by his parents, but he began to get more and more absorbed in religious practices. Guru Nanak's marriage took place in Mars Dasa. Mark the fact that Mars is aspected by Saturn, lord of the 7th and is in the 2nd from Kalatrakaraka Venus. Under the same directional influences Nanak was appointed in the service of Daulat Khan.

However, as Rahu Dasa advanced, he abandoned his service and became an ascetic for all practical purposes. Note the fact that Rahu is in the constellation of Venus lord of the 10th. Throughout Jupiter Dasa he wandered all over the country preaching his gospel of love and faith in God. It will be seen that Saturn, as lord of the 8th in the 10th, is aspected by Jupiter, as lord of the 8th (we shall here, for the moment, ignore that other benefic ownership of these two planets).

Consequently, during Saturn's Dasa, Nanak and his favourite disciple Mardana were imprisoned by Babar's men. Subsequently, under the same Dasa influences, Nanak came in personal contact with Babar and exercised considerable influence on the life and conduct of this emperor.

Towards the close of his life, the Jupiter laying aside the garb of Fakir settled down with his family at Kharatpur and continued to teach the new faith to the large number of his followers. In Saturn's Dasa Jupiter's Bhukti, he appointed one of his most sincere disciples as his spiritual heir ignoring his own son whom he thought unfit for the task and died at the fag end of Jupiter Bhukti. The major lord Saturn owns the 7th, a maraka place, while the sub-lord Jupiter as owning the 8th is in the 2nd another maraka place.

Remarks.—The horoscope is significant inasmuch as the powerful Rajayogas caused in the 4th house involving the 4th, 10th, 1st and 2nd houses found expression in spiritual channels, conferring on the native fame, influence and extraordinary greatness. Owing to the glorified position of Lagna and the sobering influence of Saturn on Lagna lord, in spite of all his greatness, he was simple and unassuming.

Five planets involved in mutual aspects and associations may be construed as some sort of a Parivraja Yoga. Nanak's faith was monotheistic. His life and doctrines did not expose him to persecution for he declared that all men had a right to search for knowledge of God. The Sun is free from the effects of Rahu and Ketu. Hence the Guru played a patriotic part by ably influencing Babar and turning him into a kind ruler.

No. 14.—SRI CHAITANYA

Birth Details.—Born on 18th February 1486 A.D. (O.S.) at 8-56 p.m. (Long. 88° 25′ E.. Lat, 23° 23′ N.)

Planetary Positions.—The Sun 323° 52′ ; the Moon 142° 52′ ; Mars 282° 56′ ; Mercury 342° ; Jupiter 261° 40′ ; Venus 6° 7′ ; Saturn 236° 2′ ; Rahu 328° 10′ ; and Lagna 184° 24′. Ayanamsa 15° 14′.

Mercury	Venus				Mars	Sun Venur	Rahu
Rahu Sun			Sat.				
	RASI				NAVAMSA		
Mars			Moon Ketu				
Jupiter	Saturn	Lagna		Ketu	Lagna	Moon Jupiter Mercury	

Balance of Venus Dasa at birth :   Years 5-8-12.

Special Features.—The Lagna or the ascendant is strong being aspected by Venus its lord, and Venus in turn being aspected by Jupiter from his own sign. The forces of Mars and Venus being primarily concentrated on the Lagna, Sri Chaitanya was very beautiful and was hence called *Gauranga* or fair-complexioned. This combination also gave him a fair face, sparkling eyes, eloquence and a musical voice. He was born at the time of a lunar ealipse and it is alleged that at the time of his birth, the parents could notice on the body of the child 32 marks of the person of Narayana.

Mercury the planet of intellect is neecha but he has obtained a distinct neechabhanga (cancellation of debility). Moreover in Navamsa the disposition of Mercury (planet of intellect), the Moon (planet ruling mind and emotion) and Jupiter (planet of knowledge) — all in one sign without any malefic aspects excepting that of Mars, lord of Navamsa Lagna, accounts for Chaitanya's keenness in mastering all branches of Sanskrit learning, especially grammar and logic.

Dhana Yoga is well marked by the presence of Saturn, the yogakaraka, in the 2nd and by the *Parivartana* (exchange of houses) between the 2nd and 5th lords and the exaltation of the 2nd lord in the 4th being aspected by the 4th and 5th lord Saturn. This is suggestive that Sri Chaitanya was a very rich and prosperous man. His prosperity and learning seem to have turned his head. But the *dwirdwadasa* positions of planets explain that he intensely struggled within for the rejuvenation of his soul.

After he renounced the world he became the embodiment of humanity, avoided all publicity and display. The Sun and Rahu in the 5th aspected by the Moon lord of the 10th is a powerful combination for Sanyasa, as also lord of Lagna and lord of Chandra Lagna being in the 7th. The lord of the house of speech is exalted while from the Chandra Lagna the 2nd lord gets neechabhanga. These gave him that musical voice and eloquence which held the hearts of his listeners spell bound as he poured forth his rapturous discourse rich with stirring verses from Bhagavata or the aphorisms of Sri Vyasa or the great utterances of Upanishads.

The Sun is *Atmakaraka* and the Moon *Manahkaraka*. His birth at the time of a lunar eclipse (hence the Moon's conjunction with Ketu) the Moon–Ketu combination receiving the combined aspects of Saturn (Yogakaraka), Jupiter (Gnanakaraka), Mars (Tarkakaraka) and the Sun and Rahu (Atmakarakas) gave the saint true *Atmavidya* or knowledge of the Self which he attained through *bhakti* or devotion.

Another equally important combination for renunciation is the Moon occupying the Drekkana of Mars and receiving Saturn's aspect. Chaitanya had two marriages. Kalatrakaraka Venus in the 7th is bad as also Mars aspecting the combination. In the Navamsa also Mars is aspected by Saturn. The house of children is completely afflicted by being occupied by the Sun and Rahu. Jupiter, Putrakaraka, is hemmed in between malefics. His father died early. Mercury, the 9th lord, is neecha and Pitrukaraka, the Sun, is afflicted. Sri Chaitanya was the last of the 10 children born to his parents, of whom 8 died.

The 3rd house is fertile as the lord of the 3rd is in the 3rd and Bhratrukaraka Mars is exalted. But as the 3rd house is hemmed in between malefics and Mars is aspected by Saturn, all the brothers and sisters died excepting one.

Important Events.—Sri Chaitanya married at 16 in the sub-period of Saturn in the Moon's Dasa. The major lord Moon is aspected by Mars lord of the 7th while Saturn the sub-lord not only owns the 7th from the Moon but also occupies the 2nd or house of family. He renounced the world at the age of 25 in the sub-period of Saturn within the Dasa of Mars. Note how both these planets have caused the ascetic combination—Mars as lord of Drekkana occupied by the Moon and Saturn as aspecting the Moon. The Swami died at the age of 47 in the beginning of Jupiter's Dasa. Jupiter owns the 3rd and occupies the 3rd. In the Navamsa Jupiter is the lord of the 2nd from Lagna and lord of the 3rd from the Moon and occupies the 12th in conjunction with lord of the 8th.

Remarks.—In Chaitanya we have a great teacher, reformer and master. Never, since the Buddha's death, had any saint more gentle and sweet, more humane, trodden the soil of India. Greater than his creed and reforms was his character, pure, gentle, ecstatic, full of sweetness and loving kindness. His heart flowed out in sympathy for all, for the poor and the lowly as well as for the scholar and the prince.

He had to meet with a lot of opposition from contemporary pandits. Mercury in the 6th enabled him to conquer all such opposition by the force of love. Lord of the 9th is Mercury and he was neechabhanga. Mercury is lord of the 9th and is in the house of *moksha*, in the Navamsa. Hence he preached a most impassioned type of Vaishnavism and left a great and historic sect behind him.

Nothing is more beautifully brought out in the life of Sri Chaitanya than his great spirit of self-sacrifice and humanity. When he was well on the road to worldly prosperity and fame, he suddenly renounced them all at the call of higher life. The sub-period of Saturn in Mars was the turning point. Throughout Mars Dasa Sri Chaitanya wandered about, dressed in the mendicant's quilt preaching of love and Divine service. Associating with all, the lowly, the outcaste and the poor—he ate, sang and prayed with them.

Among all medieval Acharyas of India, Chaitanya stands unrivalled for his clear and emphatic exposition of the principles of the new Vaishnavite creed. There is also a tradition that Chaitanya composed a commentary on Vyasa's Brahma-sutras. Full of his own deep personal mysticism, fired with poetry of Bhagavata, the discourses of Chaitanya are not mere expositions to be set side by side with the classic commentaries of other great Acharyas, but in themselves profound and stirring revelations of the Vaishnavite Dharma.

Sri Chaitanya was quite young at the time of his death. His physical frame broke down under prolonged mental convulsion and self-inflicted torments and he passed under circumstances over which the piety of his biographers has drawn the veil of mystery.

In all such horoscopes of Bhaktas and Acharyas, the disposition of the Moon and the Sun with special reference to Jupiter and Mercury is of supreme importanse.

No. 15.—AKBAR THE GREAT

Birth Details.—Born on 24th/23rd November 1542 A.D. (O.S.) at 4-9 a.m. (L.M.T.). (Lat. 25° 19′ N., Long. 69° 47′ E.)

Planetary Positions.—The Sun 235° 12′ ; the Moon 70° 0′ ; Mars 294° 42′ ; Mercury 251° 30′ ; Jupiter 187° 18′ ; Venus 200° 2′ ; Saturn 209° 12′ ; Rahu 309° 36′ ; and Lagna 203° 22′. Ayanamsa 16° 1′.

		Moon		Venus	Lagna	Ketu Saturn
Rahu			Sun			Mercury
	RASI			NAVAMSA		
Mars		Ketu				Mars
Mercury	Sun	Venus Jupiter Saturn Lagna	Moon Rahu Jupit.			

Balance of Rahu Dasa at birth : Years 13–3–1.

Special Features.—The Lagna is Thula or Libra occupied by Jupiter, a benefic, Venus the lord and Saturn a yogakaraka. Consistent with the propensities of the three planets Akbar was "tall in stature, of a ruddy or wheat complexion". Venus rising within four degrees of ascending point rendered his physical appearance "most captivating and handsome". His son Salim described him as "tall of stature, of a ruddy brown complexion, eyes full and dark while his great breadth of chest and long sinewy arms gave him strength of a lion". The karaka of the mind Moon is in Gemini aspected powerfully by two first-rate benefics, *viz.*, Mercury lord of Chandra Lagna. and Jupiter, lord of the 7th and 10th from Chandra Lagna. The Moon is free from affliction. This must give a clue to his mental make-up and character. As Meadows Taylor observes, "he had no deceits, no falsehood, no shifts, no intrigues". The Sun's position in Scorpio, otherwise unafflicted, made him "affable and majestical, merciful and severe, loved and feared of his own".

Libra is a movable and active sign, and marks the meeting point between the equator and the ecliptic. Hence it makes the native moderate in his quality and tastes. Rahu is in the 9th from Pitrusthana and Pitrusthana being aspected by Jupiter (a maraka from Pitrusthana) explains the birth of Akbar under strange circumstances, at a fortress when his father Humayun, driven from the throne of Delhi, was escaping to Persia.

Coming to Rajayogas with which we are mostly concerned in this horoscope, we find that, whilst Saturn alone is capable of conferring Rajayoga, his association with Venus, lord of the Lagna, has augmented the yoga to a considerable extent. Jupiter by virtue of owning the 3rd and 6th is a temporal malefic but is rendered harmless owing to his disposition in a Bhava sandhi. The Moon is lord of the 10th, is full and occupies the sign of Mercury in Rasi with the full aspect of lord of the 9th Mercury. This is another Rajayoga. Mars who is Bhoomikaraka (lord of lands) occupies 4th house in exaltation, with Rahu, and powerfully aspects both 10th and 11th, with the attributes of Kosa (2nd) and Kalatra (7th) lordships. Again, lord of the 11th the Sun occupies Kosabhava (2nd) with Sthanabala (positional strength) and lord of 2nd Mars occupies Vahanabhava (4th house) in exaltation. Mercury is not combust being removed seventeen degrees from the Sun and occupies a dusthana (3rd) hemmed in between two malefics the Sun and Mars.

The horoscope bristles with Rajayogas and is one of the most brilliant ones one can come across. When he was born at Umarkot in Sind, his exiled father, Humayun, celebrated the event by distributing fragrant musk amongst those present with him, and wished that his son might fill the world with his fame even as the musk filled with fragrance the desert-air ! Akbar's innate royalty is due to Venus–Saturn conjunction in the ascendant.

His military prowess and personal courage are accounted for by Mars. Mars' ownership of the 7th and occupation of 4th powerfully aspecting the 10th and 11th amply explain Akbar's well-known policy of imposing Imperial dominion over Rajput Princes by contracting marriage alliances with their daughters.

Akbar's fine artistic and cultural tastes are to be ascribed to Venus in the Lagna. The confusion of his enemies and his career of conquest are due to the disposition of Jupiter who, representing debt, disease and enemy, occupies the house of destruction. But the colossal wealth, which history tells us Akbar was possessed of, is most certainly the result of lord of the 11th the Sun occupying the 2nd and lord of the 2nd Mars exalted and occupying the 4th and aspecting the 11th.

Important Events.—The fag end of Rahu Dasa was remarkable for two most important events in the career of Akbar, viz., death of his father Humayun and his being elevated to the throne at Delhi. Rahu's situation in the 9th from the 9th caused the death of the father. Rahu is strong, being in his own constellation and Saturn, whose results Rahu should give, is a yogakaraka and occupies Lagna. Hence the conferment of the throne. As soon as Jupiter Dasa commenced, Akbar's most formidable enemy Hemu was routed in Panipat.

Mark the weak disposition of Jupiter as lord of the 3rd in an inimical sign. Jupiter Dasa was a period of military success when Akbar achieved a series of conquests over his enemies, mainly owing to the superior strength of Lagna lord over that of the 6th lord. By the end of Jupiter's Dasa Akbar was master of almost the whole of Northern India.

Salim and Murad, Akbar's first and second sons, were born in 1569 and 1570 in Jupiter's Dasa, Mars and Rahu Bhuktis. The 3rd son was also born at the fag end of Jupiter's Dasa. Then commenced his Saturn Dasa lasting till 1591. Saturn is a yogakaraka and is ideally placed in Lagna with Lagna lord in Lagna and it was during Saturn Dasa that Akbar's career as an Emperor reached its zenith. He consolidated his empire and laid the foundations of the administration which has wrought the admiration of historians.

In Mercury Dasa the Moon Bhukti, his son Murad died. Another son Danial died in Jupiter Bhukti of Mercury Dasa. Mark the Moon is in the constellation of Rahu and Mercury in that of Ketu. His own end came on 13-10-1605, Mercury Dasa, Saturn Bhukti. The major lord Mercury is in the 7th from Chandra Lagna and in the 3rd from Lagna while the sub-lord Saturn, though a yogakaraka, has been rendered capable of causing death by his being natural Ayushkaraka, by his owning the 8th from the Moon and by joining Jupiter lord of the 7th Chandra Lagna. He occupies a death-inflicting house (2nd) in the Navamsa.

Remarks.—If Lagna could also be considered as a kendra, as it should be, then three Panchamahapurusha yogas obtain in Akber's horoscope, *viz.*, Sasa, Malavya and Ruchaka—Sasa and Malavya by Lagna being identical with Saturn's exaltation sign and the own sign of Venus respectively and Ruchaka by Mars being exalted in a kendra from Lagna. The results, attributed to these yogas, seem to have fully manifested in this case.

There was no Moghal empire before Akbar, but only the attempt to create one. But at Akbar's death his empire stretched from Hindukush to Godavari and from Bengal to Gujarat. Mark the absence of mutual associations or aspects between Rahu and Mars, Rahu and Saturn and Mars and Saturn and note the dominance of the influences of Jupiter and Venus on Lagna and that of Mercury on the Moon. He deliberately accepted compromise as the basis of his policy and sought to conciliate the Hindus and secure their loyalty. There is no trace of much fanaticism in his religious policy, because of the absence of mutual aspects between first-rate malefics. Akbar's conscious reaction to Islam is to be ascribed to the Papargala (an obstruction) in which Mercury lord of the 9th is bound up. Akbar did not believe in Islam or Christianity, but had the good sense to be tolerant towards all faiths. The distinction attained by Lagna lord Venus made him humane and merciful in conquest, just and considerate and yet firm and decided in action, with the result he secured the high respect and often the affection of his opponents. Akbar's horoscope is an illustration of the harmonious blending of different Rajayogas, to be admired by all students of astrology.

No. 16.—JOHN MILTON

Birth Details.—Born on 9th December 1608 (O.S.) at about 6-30 a.m. (Lat. 51° 31′ N., Lang. 0° 5′ W.)

Planetary Positions—The Sun 251° 48′ ; the Moon 42° 18′ ; Mars 336° 48′ ; Mercury 267° 48′ ; Jupiter 19° 18′ ; Venus 271° 40′ ; Saturn 281° 48′ ; Rahu 111° 24′ ; Ketu 291° 24′ ; and Lagna 226° 18′. Ayanamsa 16° 56′.

Mars	Jupiter	Moon		Moon Ketu	
			Rahu		Ketu Sun
	RASI			NAVAMSA	
Ketu Saturn Venus			Rahu Venus		
Sun Mercury	Lagna		Merc.	Lagna	Mars Jupiter

Balance of the Moon's Dasa at birth : Years 8–3–9.

Special Features.—Scorpio is rising and the Lagna is Vargottama aspected powerfully by exalted Moon, lord of the 9th. The lord of Lagna is in Pisces, a benefic sign, but aspected by Saturn. In the Navamsa again, the lord of Lagna is disposed in the 11th with Jupiter. Hence the Lagna is fairly strong. The disposition of the Sun in a dual sign with

Mercury gave Milton a fertile imagination and rendered him direct-spoken, fearless, impressionable, active and generous. Martian and lunar influences, being primarily focussed on the Lagna describe him as a slender figure, of middle stature, looking younger than he was and fair complexioned. Lagna lord being aspected by Saturn gave him feeble health. His "unaffected cheerfulness and civility" and his extremely courteous and affable treatment of his visitors are the blessings of the exalted Moon's aspect on Lagna. His intellectual pre-eminence is marked out by the Vargottama position of the intellectual planet Mercury.

The house of finance is well disposed, because of the fact it is owned and aspected by Jupiter, besides being joined by the Sun lord of the 10th and Mercury, lord of the 11th. Throughout his life he was well off financially but for a temporary period when he was an impoverished man.

The 3rd lord Saturn is in the 2nd house, but in his own sign having gained four Navamsas. He is neecha in Navamsa but has attained neechabhanga. Mars the lord of brothers has gained three Navamsas, but is well associated in the Navamsa. Though Milton's father had six children, only three survived including Milton.

The 4th lord Saturn is not very well situated but Matrukaraka the Moon is not only exalted but in kendra from Lagna. Besides this, lord of Lagna is in the 4th house. These dispositions gave Milton happiness from his parents, especially father. In his writings Milton speaks with gratitude and affection of the "ungrudging pains bestowed on him by his father in his early education". There was only one little matter of difference between them, viz., after the collegiate education, the son was bent on a "private life of literature and poetry".

The 5th house is unfortunately situated. The 5th lord, who also happens to be Putrakaraka, is in the 6th, the house of Mars. The 5th house is also aspected by Saturn while Rahu is in the 9th. In the Navamsa again, the 5th house is equally strongly afflicted on account of Jupiter's conjunction with Mars and the association of the Sun (lord of the 5th from the Moon) with Ketu. Evidently he had hardly any happiness from his children. The Aputrayoga clearly marked on account of the combination suggested above, rendered him lose his first and only son, while his three daughters—"poor motherless girls"—the eldest in her 17th year in 1662, the second in her 15th; and the youngest in her 11th who had grown up in their father's blindness and too great self-absorption, ill-looked after and but poorly educated, 'made nothing of neglecting him', rebelled against the drudgery of reading to him or otherwise attending on him and "did combine together and counsel his maid-servant to cheat him in her marketings and they had actually made away with some of his books".

The 7th house is equally afflicted; not in the sense of his not deriving happiness from his wives but in regard to loss of wives. No doubt the 7th is occupied by the exalted Moon, lord of the 9th. It only renders the persons highly passionate, "with just a shade of stateliness". The 7th lord Venus, who happens to be Kalatrakaraka, is in the 2nd house (though in 3rd Rasi) and both Venus and the 2nd house are associated with a number of malefics, viz., the Sun, Saturn and Mercury. On account of this the poet had three marriages.

We are concerned in this horoscope mainly with the combinations that made him such a great poet. We shall advert to this subsequently. There is another important aspect of great interest to astrological students, viz., his becoming totally blind in his 44th year. The 12th lord Venus is highly afflicted while lord of the 2nd, *viz.*, Jupiter is in the 6th, in the house of Mars, not aspected or joined by any benefics. Hence there was danger to his eyes through neglect. The 9th lord the Moon is exalted while Putrakaraka is in a benefic house. Milton's father lived upto a good old age.

Important Events.—He took his M.A. degree in 1632 during Rahu Dasa Mercury Bhukti. Rahu is aspected by Saturn lord of the 4th, while Mercury is in the 2nd and 9th from Vidyakaraka. Until practically the end of Venus Bhukti (in Rahu Dasa) he led a life "dedicated wholly to scholarship and literature". The poet's mother died in the same sub-period. Mark the disposition of the major lord Rahu in the 3rd from Matrukaraka and the 7th from Matrusthanadhipati while Venus is disposed in the 12th from Matrusthana, both in the Rasi and Navamsa.

He was on a foreign tour during the last part of Venus sub-period when he met distinguished intellectuals including the great Galileo, then old and blind and still "nominally a prisoner to the inquisition for his astronomical heresy". Mark that both Rahu and Venus are in movable and watery signs. Venus is in the 2nd Bhava while Rahu is in the 9th Bhava. Hence, Milton's continental tour remained one of the chief pleasures of his memory through all his subsequent life.

The beginning of Jupiter Dasa saw a most unfortunate event in his life, consistent with the fact that Jupiter owns the 2nd from Lagna, the 8th from the Moon and occupies unfavourable places from both these points. He married in 1643 and hardly were the honey-moon festivities over when his wife, a "frivolous, unsuitable and stupid girl", abetted by her mother, left Milton, Saturn's Bhukti was however more fortunate. Saturn though a malefic is in his own house in conjunction with Kalatrakaraka Venus and in a kendra position from the major lord. It was during Saturn's sub-period that reconciliation was effected between him and his wife. Saturn occupies a Neechamsa, but gets neechabhanga besides being aspected by Mars, lord of Lagna in Navamsa. Moreover Saturn is in the constellation of the Moon, lord of the 9th.

He had his first child during this sub-period. Mercury's sub-period saw the birth of another daughter and the death of his own father. The astrological explanations for this are simple. Venus Bhukti in Jupiter Dasa was perhaps the most unfortunate period of his life, though generally it is anticipated that Venus in Jupiter would always prove fortunate. Here Venus owns the 7th and 12th houses (both bad) and occupies the 2nd Bhava (ruling family and eyes) and is associated with two first-rate malefics, *viz.*, Saturn and the Sun. Even Mercury is a malefic here. Each planet is capable of a two-fold function. The results due to the ownership and malefic association manifested themselves in the death of his only son (born earlier in this same sub-period), death of his wife just after she had given birth to his third daughter and his becoming totally blind.

The planet causing the blindness gave rise to the unfortunate event during his sub-period. Added to all these, the poet was passing through *sadesathi*. No wonder that "with the three children thus left him, Anne but 6 years old, Mary not 4, and the infant Debora, the blind widower lived on in his house in such desolation as can be imagined".

His second marriage took place as also the death of his second wife at the end of Jupiter Dasa. As soon as Saturn Dasa commenced which coincided with the triumphal entry of Charles II into London, Milton had to be in hiding as he was considered to be 'a republican culprit' and had been named for special punishment.

Note Mercury and Ketu the sub-lords are disposed in *dwirdwadasa* positions from the major lord Saturn (Ketu is in the 3rd Bhava and Saturn in the 2nd as also Mercury). These two sub-periods were the time of his "deepest degradation" and he was now nothing more than "an infamous outcaste, the detestable blind republican and regicide who had, by too great clemency, been left uncharged".

He also got married for the third time during Mercury's sub-period and she proved 'an excellent wife'. His death took place in 1674 in Rahu Bhukti in Saturn Dasa. The major lord Saturn owns the 3rd and occupies the 2nd maraka while the sub-lord Rahu is in the 3rd from the Moon, and the latter planet who is to give the results of Rahu is in a maraka house.

Remarks.—We can glean from Milton's horoscope his intellectual pre-eminence and extraordinary literary genius. The planet of intellect, *viz.*, Mercury is in the 2nd house, here Sagittarius, a fiery and war-like sign. The blessings of this combination, *viz.*, skill in poetry and acquisition of wealth by his own talents had been fully conferred on Milton, while Venus in the 2nd house contributed its useful share in making him an outstanding poetical genius. Another equally noteworthy combination for making Milton a great author is the disposition of the Moon with a malefic in the 5th from Kara-kamsa. There was a marked tendency to the satirical and sarcastic (*Kudukanvita*) in his criticisms of men and things and this was primarily due to the disposition of the lord of the 4th, *viz.*, Saturn in the 2nd Bhava. The definition for proficiency in poetry given in *Bhavartha Ratnakara* applies *in toto* to this horoscope.

It will be seen that the 2nd Bhava has also the association of Saturn and the Sun while both Venus and Mercury are Vargottama. From the Moon, the 2nd is aspected by no less than three planets, amongst which Mars figures equally prominent. This made him bold, fearless and speculative and gave him a fondness for labours of scholarship and compilation. The centre of gravity in Milton's horoscope is the 2nd Bhava and the focussing on it of the influences of the intellectual Mercury, the emotional Venus, the philosophical Jupiter, the political Sun and the democratic Saturn must be noted. He was one of the best Latinists of his generation.

The Sun, a royal and political planet and lord of the 10th is in the 2nd house, aspected by Jupiter and associated with Saturn, the planet of democracy. This gives us a clue to appreciate the fact that he was not only the greatest poet of his age, but that there is no life of that time, not even Cromwell's in which the history of the great Revolution, in its successive phases, so far as the deep underlying ideas and speculations were concerned may be more intimately studied than Milton's.

His *Aeropagitica* and his other pamphlets contain the "precious life and blood of a master spirit". The Moon is free from affliction while Venus has malefic association. Evidently it cannot be said that Milton's genius was destitute of humour. Though Saturn in the 2nd is suggestive that his prevailing mood was severely earnest, there are pages in his prose writings (Mercury–Venus in the 2nd) of the most laughable irony, reaching sometimes to outrageous farce and some of them as worthy of the name of honour as anything in Swift.

Jupiter as lord of the 5th aspects the 2nd. Rahu's situation in the 9th house throws light upon Milton's mind and the greatness of his greatest achievement *Paradize Lost*. The above combination also reveals Milton's metaphysics. While ontologically Milton starts from a pure spiritualistic theism or from the notion of one infinite and eternal spirit as the self-subsisting God and author of all being (mark the philosophical planet Jupiter aspecting the 10th house), cosmologically his system is that of a pantheistic materialism.

The Sun–Saturn association in the 2nd Bhava explains his political leanings. He was a republican. In 1648 Milton was appointed to the secretaryship for foreign tongues and he did a lot of work for the cause of the republicans and in defence of the Republic against a complication of royalist intrigues and dengers. Milton was so much of a modern radical of extreme school in his own political views and sympathies that he could not but be vexed by the growing conservatism of Cromwell's policy. Note also the combined influences of Jupiter and Saturn on the 2nd and 12th Bhavas. It was Milton's fixed idea that there should be no such thing as an established church or state paid clergy of any sort or demonination.

Summing up, there are no special yogas excepting Mercury —Aditya, Anapha and Lakshmi, but there is a peculiar blending of forces in the 2nd house that could clearly explain 'the Miltonic something'—something more than mere perfection of literary finish which distinguishes all his writings. This 'something', due to the peculiar blending of forces in the 2nd house, rests upon a peculiar substratum of personal character, moral manliness and high literary effort.

No. 17.—AURANGZEB

Birth Details.—*Born on 3rd November 1618 (N.S.) at 1-43 p.m. (L.M.T.) (Lat. 28° 39' N., Long. 77° 13' E.)

Planetary Positions.—The Sun 203° 50' ; the Moon 35° 14' ; Mars 144° ; Mercury 199° ; Jupiter 310° ; Venus 259° ; Saturn 48° ; Rahu 280° ; and Lagna 313° 45'. Ayanamsa 17° 4'.

		Moon Saturn	Merc. Rahu			Sun	Saturn
Lagna Jupiter		Ketu	Moon Lagna				
	RASI			NAVAMSA			
Rahu		Mars					
Venus	Sun Mercury		Jupit.	Mars			Ketu Venus

Balance of Sun's Dasa at birth : Years 2-1-20.

Special Features.—The Lagna is the mystic sign of Aquarius, and has Jupiter rising. But the combined aspects of

---

* Aurangzeb was born, according to the details given to me by Pandit Srikanta Sastry, when I met him at Varanasi in 1938, in Margasira Krishna 1 Saturday, Samvat 1675 at ghaties 18-30 after sunrise in the constellation of Rohini, the Sun occupying 23° 25' Libra with Mercury, Venus in Sagittarius, Rahu in Capricorn, Lagna and Jupiter in Aquarius,

Mars and Saturn conferred the worst characteristics of bigotry and fanaticism. Whilst the exaltation of the karaka of the mind, *viz.*, the Moon in the 4th indicates vast ability and patience, his association with Saturn and his occupation of the constellation of the Sun, who is in debility, made Aurangzeb habitually suspicious. Mark the fact that except Lagna all the kendras have malefics, while Lagna is subject to malefic aspects, producing Daitya Yoga, the result being a detestable hypocrisy.

Lord of the 10th Mars, the planet of war and aggression, is in the 7th while in the Navamsa he is very strongly placed in his own sign. This gave him a spirit of aggression, an insatiable ambition and an unscrupulous employment of means to attain his ends. Jupiter, who is almost in conjunction with Lagna, despite Mars-Saturn aspects, could have neutralised the affliction of Lagna, but he actually occupies the constellation of Rahu, an incendiary planet. It is no wonder therefore that he had hardly any loyal workers. Those employed by him, knowing themselves to be surrounded by dangerous spies and informers, could not serve him faithfully or freely. The political planet Sun, lord of the 7th, has obtained neechabhanga, by virtue of Saturn's disposition in a kendra from Lagna. In the Navamsa he is subject to affliction by being aspected powerfully by Mars.

Saturn and the Moon in Taurus and Mars in Leo. In a small pamphlet published by the Anup Sanskrit Library, containing the horoscopes of some ancient Indian monarchs, the same birth details as above were given for Aurangzeb but there was no mention of the constellation. Samvat 1675, Margasira Krishna 1 (Karthika Krishna 1 according to southern reckoning) corresponds to 3-11-1618 (N. S.) Saturday, but the nakshatra happens to be Krittika. Planetary positions calculated for this date exactly corresponds with the chart as given above. I am quite convinced about the correctness of the birth details.

The mistakes of his political conduct are sufficiently evident by this disposition of the Sun. Ketu in the 6th or house of enemies aspected by Lagna lord Saturn, and the lord of the 6th fairly strong and associated with Saturn, gave him a formidable number of enemies, and the delusion of universal authority and the alienation of the affections of the Hindus carried with them their own seeds of destruction.

Six planets in kendras causing Chatussagara Yoga, lords of 4 planets in kendra – the Lagna (Saturn), the 2nd and 11th (Jupiter) and the 10th (Mars) involved in mutual aspects and thus generating powerful Dhana Yogas and Jupiter-Moon in mutual kendra giving rise to Gajakesari Yoga, are all factors whose importance must be clearly marked by students of astrology.

From Chandra a Lagna, very powerful Rajayoga is centered on the 10th involving Jupiter, Mars and Saturn. With all his hideous defects of character, this combination enables us to admire Aurangzeb's courage, energy and ability, with which to the very last, he conducted the affairs of his Government in person. The dominance of Mars in the chart made him an out and out autocrat and it is doubtful whether he ever sought or accepted advice from anyone. Jupiter, as Putrakaraka in Lagna, indicates that is natural love for his children was great. Consistent with the nature of Aquarius and the absence of Jupiterian influences on the 10th Bhava, he was niggardly in his personal money matters. It is alleged, despite the onerous duties of the State, he used to quilt caps and sell them. In fact he desired in his will that his funeral expenses should be defrayed from the sale proceeds of the caps.

Imporant Events.—Aurangzeb's marriage with Dilras Banu Begum, a Persian princess, took place just at the end of

Mars Dasa.   Mars is in the 7th or Kalatrabhava and in the 9th
from Venus the Kalatrakaraka.   Under the same directional
influences, his appointment as Viceroy of the Moghal Provinces
in the Deccan came about.   Mars as lord of the 10th aspects
the 10th from Lagna.   From Chandra Lagna also he aspects the
10th.   It is significant that these two events took place about
the end of Mars Dasa.

Rahu's situation. in the 12th from Lagna and the 9th from
the Moon and Saturn's disposition in Chandra Lagna, with
reference to which he also happens to be yogakaraka, account
for his unfriendly relations with his father, on account
of which he was transferred to Gujarat, during Rahu Dasa
Saturn Bhukti. His military operations, which formed part of
Shahjehan's aggressive schemes in Central Asia, proved a drain
on the finances of the empire. This was in Rahu Dasa Mercury
Bhukti.   Mercury, though lord of the 5th, is afflicted so far as
military operations are concerned, as he is in association with
debilitated Sun, lord of the 7th.   Throughout Rahu Dasa, he
was engaged in military operations which did not prove altogether successful. As lord of the 2nd and 11th, Jupiter aspects
Pitrukaraka Sun and Pitrusthana (9th house). In Jupiter Dasa
own Bhukti, Aurangzeb's father fell seriously ill. Mark the
fact that Saturn at Lagna lord aspects the 10th house as
well as Lagna and Jupiter is in Lagna aspecting the 9th.   Mars
lord of the 10th also aspects Jupiter and the 10th from the 7th.

It was in Jupiter's sub-period, in his own major period that
Aurangzeb engaged himself in the war of succession and
experienced little difficulty in defeating his brothers and in
imprisoning his father Shahjehan and in usurping the Government. As soon as Saturn Bhukti commenced, he crowned
himself as emperor. Saturn is highly powerful and free from

affliction excepting that he is in the constellation of the lord of
the 6th the Moon, denoting innumerable enemies even amongst
his own kith and kin. In Mercury's sub-period, he was able to
liquidate all his brothers and he did not spare even their off-
spring and he believed himself secure. Mark the fact that
Mercury is in the constellation of Rahu. The Sun's sub-period
in the major period of Jupiter started on 7th July 1666 and
Aurangzeb's father, Shahjehan, died in Agra Fort in December
1666. The sub-lord the Sun, as Pitrukaraka occupying Pitrusthana, and aspected by Jupiter lord of the 2nd and 11th,
brought about the death of the father.

It was again in the Sun's sub-period (Jupiter Dasa) that
the "formidable infidel" Shivaji, who had been invited to
Delhi, slighted and imprisoned, escaped causing the Emperor
real uneasiness. His long reign of 44 years, covering the greater
part of Jupiter Dasa and the entire periods of Saturn and
Mercury, can be divided into two phases : the first of consolidation and the second of fruitless efforts to conquer the Deccan.
All these three planets have to do with either Lagna, the 9th
or 10th. His death took place in the beginning of 1707, when
he was having Mercury Dasa Saturn Bhukti. The major lord
Mercury is a powerful maraka, as he owns the 8th from Lagna,
and the 2nd from the Moon and has joined the Sun, lord of the
7th. Saturn the sub-lord is in association with the Moon lord
of the 6th and the disposition of the major and sub-lords is
shashtashtak (6th and 8th). Note also the fact that Saturn
was transiting Taurus and thus causing *sadesathi* for the third
time.

Remarks.—Lagna is the hinge on which the entire horoscope revolves. Jupiter rising in Lagna, Lagna itself and
Mercury lord of the 5th (Poorvapunya) or house of intelligence
and understanding in the constellations of the incendiary planet
Rahu, give a clue to the innate fanaticism, savagery, barbarity

and inhumanity exhibited by Aurangzeb in the treatment of his own brothers and father, his enemies and his Hindu subjects.

The 10th and 4th (action and thinking) are not clean, subjected as they are to the aspects of two first-rate malefics. This gave Aurangzeb, hypocrisy and unscrupulous ambition. He imprisond his father in Agra, confined his brother Murad in Gwalior, beheaded his brother Dara, proclaiming him as an apostate from the faith by a mock tribunal Dara's sons were imprisoned, a son of Murad was poisoned and Murad himself put to death in prison. Ths Sikh Guru Tej Bahadur was put to death because he refused to become a Muslim, and Sambajee, the son of Shivaji, was executed with barbarous torture because he spurned the indecent offer of the Emperor that Sambajee would be spared if he could become a Mohammedan.

According to *Sambhhu Samhita*, Rakshasa Yoga arises, when the malefics are dominant in kendras and when benefics though occupying kendras are in the Nakshatras or Navamsas of malefics. When the yoga is present in the horoscope of an ordinary man, he destroys his own family by his violent and unscrupulous behaviour, while in the horoscope of a ruler, the consequences of the yoga become fatal to the interests of the nation. Aurangzeb's horoscope is an appropriate illustration of Rakshasa Yoga. The 5th is subject to Papakarthari Yoga and the 5th lord is with debilitated the Sun.

He lacked the vision of Akbar and the tact of Jehangir. Rahu in Mokshasthana is no doubt good but he is in the constellation of the Moon (lord of 6th) and occupies a malefic sign. Hence he was an "extremely orthodox and bigotted Moslem". His treatment of the Hindus was severe and barbarous. (Guru Chandala Yoga due to Jupiter's presence in Rahu's nakshatra.) Medows Taylore, the celebrated historian, observes thus: "He reimposed the detested jezia upon the Hindus. On the promulgation of the imperial edict, his palace was besieged by masses of clamorous petitioners ; and on the occasion of a State visit to the great Mosque, many of the people who had blocked up the streets in crowds in order to levy remission of the tax were trampled to death by his elephants."

Guru Chandala Yoga *plus* Rahu's position as suggested above are the combinations for his iconoclastic fury. Hindu fairs and religious festivals were prohibited and their gods, goddesses, temples and sacred shrines were destroyed, with a firmness and severity, cold-bloodedness and violence, unparalleled in ancient Indian history. The horoscope has its bright shades also. The inherent benefic nature of the divine planet Jupiter in the mystic sign of Aquarius, which is Lagna, suggests despite the hideous defects of his character, the innate austerity of the Emperor in his personal life, and the vast ability, patience and courage with which he conducted the affairs of his Government in person.

From Lagna, yogakaraka Venus is in the 11th, unafflicted. The Sun and Mercury lords of a quadrant and a trine have joined in the 9th, the Sun debilitated but neechabhanga. The 10th is aspected by its own lords Mars. From Chandra Lagna, the powerful Rajayoga of Sun–Mercury has reference to the 6th while the 10th is aspected by the yogakaraka Saturn from Chandra Lagna. With these combinations, it is no wonder that under Aurangzeb the Moghul empire attained its greatest extent. He was the last of the great Moghals. Jupiter in Rahu's constellation aspected by Saturn, and the 10th being aspected by Saturn and Mars, produced Rajayoga effects with seeds of decay and destruction inherent in the combinations. He committed acts which excited the utmost unpopularity and discontent in all parts of the empire, laid the foundation for a civil war which resulted in the revival of a national spirit before unknown, to throw off the hated Moghul yoke.

No. 18.—SHIVAJI THE GREAT

Birth Details.—*Born on 19th February 1630 A.D. (O.S.) at 6-26 p.m. (L.M.T.). (Lat. 18° 32′ N., Long. 73° 53′ E.)

Planetary Positions.—The Sun 323° 56′ ; the Moon 178° 48′ ; Mars 76° 37′ ; Mercury 338° 10′ ; Jupiter 307° 19′ ; Venus 10° 1′ ; Saturn 197° 37′ ; Rahu 60° 49′ ; Ketu 240° 49′ ; and Lagna 149° 9′. Ayanamsa 17° 14′.

Mercury	Venus		Mars Rahu	Sat.	Ketu	Sun	
Sun Jupiter					Mars		Venus
	RASI		Lagna		NAVAMSA		
Ketu		Saturn	Moon	Lagna Jupit.		Rahu	Mercury Moon

Balance of Mars Dasa at birth : Years 4-1-17.

Special Features.—The Lagna is Simha or Leo, a fixed and fiery sign and the lord of Lagna Sun is in the 7th with

* There has been some controversy amongst historians in regard to the date of Shivaji's birth. But I am inclined to prefer the data given above, as the horoscope explains Shivaji's wonderful career, while

Jupiter aspecting the Lagna. This combined aspect of Lagna lord and Jupiter on Lagna *plus* Sagitturius rising in Navamsa with Jupiter Lagna lord in Lagna, has rendered the Lagna very strong. His "medium stature, quick and piercing eyes and white complexion" are brought out by the nature of the rising sign. His generosity of character is well denoted by the Jovian aspect on Lagna. The lord of the Moon Lagna Mercury is debilitated in the 7th but has obtained a distinct Neechabhanga. Moreover, he is subject to a powerful Subhakarthari Yoga and is free from any malefic aspects. This combination clearly demonstrates the greatness of Shivaji's genius. Aquarius is a mystic sign. The Sun, Atmakaraka and Lagna lord in this sign, in conjunction with Jupiter, lord of the 5th, thus constituting a powerful Rajayoga, is of great importance as it endowed Shivaji with constructive statesmanship, political acumen and the gift of judging character at sight and choosing the fittest persons for his work.

------

historically also, sufficient proof is forthcoming in favour of the particular date. There is further corroboration by *Judhe Chronology* which is in old MSS, in possession of an ancient family whose ancestors activity helped Shivaji and who are said to be still enjoying the grants received in those times. I am indebted to Mr. D. V. Apte, B.A., Anandashram, Budhwarpet, Poona, for keeping me in possession of valuable information pertaining to Shivaji's birth date. The above date is corroborated by *Shivbharat* an epic poem composed by a court poet of Shivaji. A copy of *Shivbharat* was found at Tanjore in the Saraswathi Mahal Library and another copy was found among the collections of old MSS, in the possession of Upadhyayas who are the descendants of Shivaji's family priests. Mr. Apte says that he has carefully studied *Joahe Chronology* and *Shivbharat* and has every reason to believe that the dates and accounts supplied by these two works are reliable and based on contemporary evidence. Sir Jadunath Sircar is inclined to put the birth date as "Monday 10-4-1627" on the authority of the two **bakhars** composed

The Moon is doubtless in a common sign and aspected by Mars lord of the 4th and the 9th but Mercury, another ruler of the mind, is ideally situated. This denotes remarkable mental poise and self-mastery which goes with it. The 2nd lord Mercury aspects the 2nd and has obtained neechabhanga. The 2nd is also aspected by the yogakaraka Mars from the 11th who is in a kendra from the 2nd lord and a trikona from the Dhanakaraka Jupiter. These are very powerful combinations endowing the native with immense wealth.

The very position of Mars, the yogakaraka in the 11th, is indicative of his bravery, good character, liberality and great riches.

The 4th lord Mars is in the 11th in nominal association with Rahu but aspected powerfully by Jupiter. This coupled with the unique disposition of Matrukaraka both in Rasi and Navamsa explains Shivaji's intense love for his mother. It must be noted that his elastic mind during his young age was profoundly influenced by the deeply religious life of his mother Jeejabai which imparted a stoical earnestness to the character

---

about the last quarter of the 18th century. The accounts given in these two bakhars are found to be totally unreliable. For further details reference may be made to 'Birth Date of Shivaji', by D. V. Apte, B A., and Paranjpe, M.A., B Sc. in short the authorities in support of 1627 A.D. "are modern, unreliable and self-contradictory while the authorities in favour of 1630 A D. are reliable and coherent". The most authentic evidence is the horoscope of Shivaji in possession of Pandit Mithalal Vyas of Jodhpur which was obtained by Pandit Raghunatha Sastri, an eminent astrologer of Poona and in which the details of birth are given as "Samvat 1686, Phalguna vadi (Bahula) 3, Sukra (Friday) Ghati 30-9 (after sunrise)—the Sun—Aquarius 23° ; Lagna—Leo 29°. The horoscope is said to be in the handwriting of Shivaram (belonging to the family of Jyothishi Chandu) who is said to have died in 1777, and thus, a contemporary of Shivaji.

of Shivaji. It will be seen that whilst the 4th lord is fairly well disposed, the 4th house is subjected to Papakarthari Yoga. Evidently Shivaji was unlettered. But since Gnanakaraka Jupiter is strongly placed aspecting as he does the lord of the 4th, want of book-learning was more than compensated by his mastery of the great Hindu epics, and the noble examples of Sri Rama and the Pandavas awoke in him a spirit of daring and inspired an yearning to emulate the deeds of the ancient heroes.

The Moon in Vargottama, Mercury in the sign of Jupiter and the 4th lord in the intellectual sign of Gemini receiving the aspect of Jupiter did not leave his mind dull and sterile. On the contrary, they gave him an amazing capacity for constructive thinking and action. Leo and Sagittarius as Lagna in Rasi and Navamsa respectively enabled him to acquire great skill in archery, wrestling, riding and other accomplishments and great adventures fascinated his youthful heart.

There are several outstanding Rajayogas, but by far the most important one is the presence of a powerful Adhi Yoga by the disposition of three first-rate benefics, viz., Jupiter, Mercury and Venus in the 6th, 7th and 8th houses from the Moon.

The 5th lord Jupiter is doubtless well placed but the 5th is considerably afflicted by the position of Ketu and the aspect of Mars and Saturn. He had five children but was not very happy especially because the character of his eldest son filled him with gloomy anticipation.

The 6th lord Saturn is exalted in the 3rd and the 6th is aspected by Mars. But from Chandra Lagna the 6th is occupied by the Sun and Jupiter. Evidently he had plenty of enemies but he overcame them by statesmanship daring and personal valour. The 7th lord Saturn is exalted in the 3rd while the 7th house is occupied by lord of Lagna as well as Jupiter. Kalatrakaraka Venus is aspected by lord of the 7th. From Chandra Lagna, Kalatrakaraka is equally strong. Mark the predominance of benefic influences in regard to the 7th and 8th houses and complete absence of any sort of connection between Kalatrabhava and Mars or Kalatrakaraka or Mars. This denotes that he was scrupulously clean in his relations with other women.

We are told that even the most beautiful women captive was addressed by him as his mother. As Venus is aspected by exalted Saturn and as lord of the 7th in Navamsa is exalted, he married four or five wives. Shivaji was practically a stranger to his father for several years after his birth and in fact it was Dadaji that really trained Shivaji in all martial accomplishments. Mark the disposition of Pitrukaraka in an inimical sign, and his being aspected by Saturn in Navamsa. But the hero had filial respect for his father. The 9th house has been strongly fortified by virtue of the lord being situated in the 10th Bhava aspected powerfully by the divine planet Jupiter and Venus a natural benefic and lord of the 10th being placed in the 9th. This combination explains the fact that Shivaji remained free from vice throughout life and passionately fond of *sastras.*

The 9th being devoid of malefic influence rendered him truly religious and there was no trace of bigotry or fanaticism in him. He had perfect toleration for all religions. His chivalry to women and enforcement of morality in his camp has won the admiration of even his hostile critics. A student of astrology cannot but be impressed by the strength *par excellence* of Lagna, the 9th and 10th houses.

Important Events.—His first marriage took place in Bangalore in Rahu Dasa Bhukti. The major lord Rahu is in the house of Mercury (the 2nd lord) who occupies the 8th from Lagna and the 7th from the Moon. In the Navamsa, Rahu is of course in the house of Kalatrakaraka. He is supposed to have married the other two wives in 1657 in Jupiter Dasa Mercury Bhukti. Mercury as we have already seen is in the 8th from Lagna while Jupiter is in the 7th. The whole of Rahu Dasa may be said to be a formative period in his life. His association with Mars gave him an adventurous career.

Even as early as 1646 he had taken Torana Fort from its commandant and indulged in acts of 'aggression' against the Sultan of Bijapur. It was Jupiter Dasa that enabled him to found his kingdom in the face of unparalleled difficulties which he overcame by dint of his innate ability, diplomacy states-manship and above all inspiration and genius. Jupiter has caused a powerful Rajayoga because of his association, as lord of the 5th, with the Sun lord of Lagna, in a powerful kendra and of his having caused Adhi Yoga. The Sun, Mercury and Mars appear to be very important planets for those born in Leo Lagna, and this is fully illustrated in Shivaji's case.

Adhi Yoga, so powerfully constituted in this horoscope, all the planets causing the yoga being highly benefic by ownership, made him stand on a lofty pedestal, unparalleled in modern times. Adhi Yoga makes one ''the lord of men, wealthy, a ruler, famous, prosperous, high souled, overthrow his enemies and widely renowned'', all of which Shivaji possessed to a wonderful degree. The fight with Nowshar Khan took place in Jupiter Dasa Mercury Bhukti. Under the same directional influence Shivaji was blessed with an heir to the throne. The defeat at the hands of Nowshar Khan may be explained by the elarata influences Shivaji was under. As Jupiter is Putrakaraka and Mercury is Chandra-Lagnadhipati, birth of an issue is justified.

The next and the most critical moment in Shivaji's life was his successful encounter with Afzal Khan, for on this depended his hopes of future greatness. This took place in Ketu Bhukti Jupiter Dasa. Ketu is in the house of Jupiter and aspected by Mars. Consequently Shivaji's success was assured and he made Afzal pay for his treachery. The Moon Bhukti in Jupiter Dasa was noted for two important events, *viz.*, an attempt by the cowardly Inayat Khan to murder Shivaji and the death of Shahji. Both the major and sub-lords are in maraka houses but because there are other benefic influences, the plot did not succeed. Jupiter the major lord owns the 2nd from Pitrukaraka while the Moon is in the 8th. Moreover, Saturn was transiting the 4th from Shivaji's Janma Rasi. The first 12 years of Jupiter period made Shivaji great enough to challenge the prestige of the Emperor at Delhi with the result Jaisingh was sent by Aurangzeb to vanquish this 'mountain rat'. Shivaji realised that he was no match for the great Imperial army and with his usual foresight he sued for peace. And this single defeat for Shivaji occurred in Jupiter Dasa Mars Bhukti. Mars is doubtless a yogakaraka and aspected by the major lord Jupiter, but by transit, Mars and Saturn were afflicting the 9th and 4th houses respectively. The 3rd and 8th lordship of Mars from Chandra Lagna must have given this great reverse.

The end of Jupiter Dasa more or less synchronised with the visit of Shivaji to Agra, the studied insult shown to him by Aurangzeb, Shivaji's bold defiance of the Emperor, incarceration and the thrilling escape from the clutches of the treacherous tyrant. Rahu's association with Mars in the 10th from Chandra Lagna explains all these soul-stirring developments. Rahu–Mars association is always bad but because of their good location, Shivaji escaped from these ordeals quite safely.

Shivaji's insult at the hands of Aurangzeb marks a decisive turning point in the history of India. Consistent with the nature of Leo Lagna, Shivaji was indeed a "lion-hearted man of action". Saturn in the 3rd house exalted and aspected by Jupiter is said to produce a king, and this has been literally fulfilled in the case of Shivaji, for as soon as Saturn Dasa commenced, Aurangzeb recognised him as Raja and he completely broke off with the Moghals.

We now come to the greatest event in his life, *viz.*, Coronation or Rajyabhisheka which took place in Saturn Dasa Ketu Bhukti. Ketu is a shadowy planet and he is in the sign of Jupiter who in his turn is equally well placed. Saturn and Jupiter are mutually well disposed besides being inherently strong. His mother Jeejabai died under the same directional influences, Ketu being in the 4th from Chandra Lagna and the major lord occupying a maraka from Chandra Lagna. The great Shivaji died in Saturn Dasa Mars Bhukti. Saturn is definitely a maraka both by ownership and position while Mars rules the 3rd and 8th from Chandra Lagna both in Rasi and Navamsa. Consistent with the nature of Mars Shivaji's death was due to fever and blood dysentery.

Remarks.—What interests us in this great horoscope is the elusive character of some of the outstanding combinations that made Shivaji win and create a wave of triumph for Indian nationalism. He was certainly a chosen instrument of God. As students of astrology, we have to note the following :— The presence of strong Adhi Yoga caused by Jupiter, Venus and Mercury, out of which the last planet has become exceedingly strong by virtue of neechabhanga ; Chandra-Lagnadhipati obtaining Neechabhanga ; and the Moon occupying a Vargottama position and being aspected by two planets. This particular Rajayoga indicates that the native though born in a low family will become a king (provided four planets aspect the Moon), but here two planets aspect by special *drishti*. The Moon is practically full and is Vargottama. Out of the lords of the 11th (*viz.*, Mercury), 9th (*viz.*, Mars) and the 2nd (*viz.*, Mercury) if at least one planet occupies a kendra from the Moon (here two planets are in kendra) and Jupiter is lord of the 2nd, 5th or 11th (here he is lord of 5th) a very powerful Rajayoga is caused and the person is said to become a ruler of an empire. This yoga obtains very strongly in the case of Shivaji.

Then we have Moon in Virgo aspected by Mercury. This also indicates kingship. Thus there are quite a number of outstanding combinations. The one great asset in his horoscope is the complete absence of mutual aspects between Mars, Saturn and Rahu. There is doubtless the association of Mars and Rahu, but they are nearly 16° apart, the one in the 10th Bhava and the other in the 11th. Moreover, even the slight stigma, if any, due to this association, is more than compensated by the powerful aspect of Jupiter. Hence fundamentally, the horoscope is a constructive one. Shivaji therefore aimed at giving his subjects peace, and a beneficent administration. He sought for national development through action and not by platform orations. He had great personal magnestism and displayed the highest genius as a king and as a statesman, qualities not a little due to the unique blending of the influences of Jupiter, Sun and Mars.

Absence of bigotry, which is again due to absence of mutual aspects between malefics, universal toleration and equal justice for all his subjects were his distinctive policy. In any horoscope, the Sun, the Moon and Lagna from the

tripod of life.   When they are free from affliction, the horoscope becomes a very fortunate one.   Here, but for the Moon
being aspected by Mars, which indicates mental sharpness and
activity, both the Lagna and the Sun have no affliction.   Hence
Shivaji had a peculiar personal magnetism and the knack to get
the most devoted service from his officers. Like Akbar and
Hyder, he had the peculiar gift of judging character.   He was
not merely a dreamer ; Mars, the yogakaraka in the position he
is, cannot make him an idle dreamer.   It gave him an unfailing
sense of reality.   He started on loose soil but erected a substantial edifice. In the words of Sri Jadunath Sircar, "Shivaji's
real greatness lay in his character and practical ability, efficiency
of arrangements and instinctive perception of what was
practicable and most profitable under the circumstances.........
his personal morality and loftiness of aim ...... universal toleration and insistence on equal justice for all.   His dominion
spread first of all through the conquests of hearts which the
honest and strong administrator alone can achieve".

Shivaji imparted a self-reliant enthusiasm to Indians.   The
Moghals had not for centuries met with any noteworthy opposition.   Shivaji planned their expulsion and before the end of
his restless life had made much progress in the execution of
that design.   Indeed Shivaji left a name which has fired and
"which would continue to fire the spirit of man and strive
forth as an ideal for him for ages yet unborn".

The demoralisation born on account of constant defeats
had eaten into the vitals of the Indian Nation till it grew into a
superstition that the Moghal Emperor possessed a divine right
to rule.   And Shivaji dealt a death-blow to this superstition.
A study of the horoscope of such a celebrity should therefore
be of much more than casual interest.

No. 19.—HYDER ALI

Birth Details.—*Born on Saturday, December 8, 1722 A.D. (N.S.) at 2-15 a.m. (L.M.T.) (Lat. 13° N., Long. 5h. 10m. 20s. E.)

Planetary Positions.—The Sun 237° 24' ; the Moon 227° 42' ; Mars 222° 5' ; Mercury 216° 42' ; Jupiter 238° 12' ; Venus 281° 41' ; Saturn 239° 58' ; Rahu 65° 12' ; and Lagna 182° 28' ; Ayanamsa 18° 32'.

		Rahu	Sun Sat. Jupit.	Venus	Ketu
	RASI			**NAVAMSA**	
Venus					
Ketu	Sun Moon Mars Mercury Jupiter Saturn	Lagna	Moon	Rahu	Mars Lagna	Mercury

		Rahu	Sun Sat. Jupit.	Venus	Ketu
Venus					
Ketu	Sun Moon Mars Mercury Jupiter Saturn	Lagna	Moon	Rahu	Mars Lagna

Balance of Mercury's Dasa at birth : Years 15–8–6.

Special Features.—The Lagna is Libra, unconjoined or unaspected and the lord Venus is in the 4th. Six planets in the

---

* Hyder's birth details are differently given by different writers. According to some, he was born on the New Moon day of the cyclic year Sarwari in the constellation of Jyeshta. This falls in 1720. Others affirm

2nd or house of wealth constitute a significant neechabhanga Rajayoga. The Moon is no doubt in debility but his association with five other planets forms a grand Rajayoga. The Moon's association with two malefics may justify to a certain extent the description of Hyder's character by his biographer as "cold-hearted, cruel and possessing no affection to anybody". The nearness of the Moon and Mars to each other made him a man of strong likes and dislikes while the disposition of Lagna lord in the 4th, aspected by yogakaraka Saturn, rendered him dignified and statesman like towards his political enemies. It is said that Hyder never forgave or forgot the treacherous and the cowardly and this characteristic can be traced to the Navamsa Lagna being occupied by Mars.

---

that he was born in 1701. For the authenticity of the data employed by me, I have relied upon three sources. The first and the most important is the Rasi Chart given on page 17 of *Royal Horoscopes* by Prof. B. Suryanarain Rao who used to tell me that he believed in the genuineness of this Chart as it was given to him by his very good friend the late Dewan Sir P. N. Krishnamurthy the grandson of Dewan Purnayya, who was Hyder's colleague. Astronomically calculated this Chart gives the date as 8-12-1722 A.D. Secondly, Mr. Lewis Rice says in his *Mysore Gazetteer*, Volume I, Page 372, that Hyder was born in 1722 A.D. Thirdly, Col. Wilks, who was the political Resident at the Court of Mysore after the fall of Srirangrpatna and who came into close contact with Hyder's contemporaries, mentions in his *History of Mysore* that "Hyder, although 27 years of age, was not in service", this obviously referring to Hyder's age before the siege of Devanahalli in 1749. According to this statement Hyder's birth falls in 1722 A.D. I feel therefore justified in assuming that Hyder was born in 1722 and this is confirmed by the Chart given by Sir P. N. Krishnamurthy to the late Prof. B. Suryanarain Rao. The other details such as the actual date can be easily found from the Chart. Lagna is given as Libra in the original. The exact longitude and the Navamsa Lagna have been fixed by me by taking into consideration the physical and mental characteristics of Hyder as recorded by his biographers.

Mark the (9th from the 9th) being aspected by Mars (lord of the 6th and 11th from the 9th) explaining his humble beginnings. In his earlier years Hyder grazed cattle and tended a garden under the Brahmin Shanbhogue Venkappayya. The association of Moon–Jupiter-Mercury gave him an extraordinary memory. The 5th lord is with Saturn while the 5th is aspected by Mars. Putrakaraka is also not well disposed. Hyder was not happy with regard to his children and the period of prosperity that attended his son Tippu, after Hyder's death, was brief. The 6th lord Jupiter is in the 2nd while the 6th lord from the Moon is in Chandra Lagna itself. He was surrounded by many enemies, internal and foreign, and he waded through all the difficulties which obstructed his progress, and stood as a victor amongst his foes, as Lagna lord is not afflicted and is well disposed. In the Navamsa, the dispositions of planets are more brilliant, especially the presence of the Sun (lord of the 11th), Jupiter (lord of the 3rd) and Saturn (Yogakaraka) in the 6th.

From Chandra Lagna the influences of four important planets have been focussed on the 10th or Karmasthana. Mark the disposition of six planets in the 2nd or house of wealth involving the Rajyakaraka (and lord of the 11th) Sun, yoga-karaka Saturn, and Dharma and Karmadhipatis (9th and 10th lords) Mercury and the Moon respectively. There is a curious mixture of powerful Dhana and Rajayogas, the focus being the 2nd house. The Lagna or ascendant is in Libra or the sign of balance and is completely unafflicted. This gave him the noble capacity of administering justice impartially. The position of Rahu in the 9th indicates early death to his father. The Lagna is Vargottama and this is a very important point to note.

Important Events.—It was in the Sun Bhukti Venus Dasa that Hyder received an independent command in Mysore at the

siege of Devanahalli.   Mark the position of the Sun with Mars.
Tippu was born in Venus Dasa Mars Bhukti. Mark Mars is with
Putrakaraka Jupiter and the lord of the 5th Saturn while the
major lord occupying the Moon's constellation (and the Moon
is with Putrakaraka and Putrasthanadhipati) is in the 5th from
Chandra Lagna in Navamsa, Throughout Venus Dasa he had
brilliant victories and had a quick rise until by about 1761, he
was almost the undisputed master of Mysore.

Venus, lord of Lagna, occupies the 4th which house is the
sign of Saturn a friend and yogakaraka. Venus has full *digbala*.
He is powerfully aspected by yogakaraka Saturn and it is no
wonder that during Venus Dasa, Hyder reached the zenith of
his political career, all by sheer ability and efford.   In the first
few years of Sun (Jupiter Bhukti) Hyder suffered defeat at the
hands of the English. In the II Mysore war, which took place
in Saturn Bhukti Sun Dasa, Hyder inflicted a crushing defeat on
the English. At the fag end of the Moon Dasa, Hyder again
attacked the English but the campaign could not be completed.

His Mars Dasa commenced by the middle of 1781 and he
became ill. His death took place on 7–12–1782 in Mars Dasa
Jupiter Bhukti. It will be seen that Mars is a definite maraka
as he owns the 2nd and 7th from Lagna and occupies the 2nd.
The sub-lord Jupiter owns the 2nd from the Moon and 3rd and
6th from Lagna and has joined the major lord and Ayushkaraka
in the 2nd.

Remarks.—Hyder's career was a mixture of curious and
romantic events. Historians hold that excepting Shivaji the
Great, there is not one of the great adventurers of India in
recent times, who can be compared with Hyder, whether as to
ability or success. All the important planets (the nodes
excepted) have been confined to just two signs causing the

unfortunate yoga going under the name of Yuga, which explains Hyder's obscure early life. But the extraordinarily strong disposition of Lagna and Lagna lord the latter obtaining digbala and receiving the aspect of the yogakaraka from the 2nd house, and all the planets including Ketu joining the 2nd Bhava, and Mercury getting into Lagna Bhava, have rendered the horoscope extraordinarily significant.

Hyder became the most formidable rival of the British in India and who, if he had lived a few years more, would have probably changed the course of Indian history for the next couple of decades. As Prof. Rao observes : ''Hyder's military talents were in no way inferior to those of Napoleon and his calmness and self-reliance in the midst of the greatest difficulties were far superior to Napoleon whose heart sank with him at times and who ignobly yielded to the English''.

A combination of the lords of the 2nd, 4th, 5th, 7th, 9th, 10th, 11th in the 2nd is a formidable Dhana Yoga explaining the fact that when Hyder died, a fortune of 30 crores in cash, and crores worth of jewellery and gems, etc., were bequeathed to his son Tippu. The peculiar disposition of almost all the planets in the 2nd owning different lordships justify Hyder's ''daring to seize, and the capacity to wield supreme power and the natural sagacity of his mind, affable manners, and discerning character'' which won the affections of his followers and enabled him to establish his authority over almost the whole of the southern part of India.

No. 20.—JOHANN WOLFGANG VON GOETHE

Birth Details.—*Born on 29th August 1749 (N.S.) at 12-17 p.m. (L.M.T.) (Long. 8° 41' E., Lat. 50° 7'' N.)

Planetary Positions.—The Sun 136° ; the Moon 323° ; Mars 254° 30' ; Mercury 130° ; Jupiter 337° ; Venus 157° 30' ; Saturn 206° ; Rahu 267° ; Ketu 87° ; and Lagna 208°. Ayanamsa 18° 54'.

			Ketu	Venus	Moon	Saturn	Lagna Ketu Mercury
Jupiter							
Moon	RASI		Sun Merc.		NAVAMSA		Sun Mars
Mars Rahu	Lagna Saturn		Venus	Rahu			Jupiter

Balance of Jupiter's Dasa at birth : Years 12-4-24.

Special Features.—The Lagna is strong as Saturn the yogakaraka is exalted, and lord of Lagna is powerfully aspected

---

* Goethe himself gives his birth time as 'at noon'. We have fixed the time of birth as 17-30 ghaties after surprise corresponding to 12-17 p.m. (L.M.T.). The birth time was rectified on the basis of the followieg : (a) Goethe was the eldest son of his father, (b) he married late in life,

by Jupiter who happens to be lord of 2nd and 5th (according to Bhava considerations). Lord of Lagna Venus who in turn is aspected by Jupiter suggests Goethe's striking appearance, his broad brow and flashing eye. His generosity of character is well denoted by the same jovian aspect. Goethe tells us that when he was born, he remained 'as dead' for some time and was only brought into activity by the efforts of the obstretic attendants. Being an astrologer himself he attributes this to the opposition of the Sun and the Moon though, perhaps, based on his own theory of light, he tries to prove that the Sun-Moon opposition is a favourable aspect. Saturn's presence in Lagna accounts for the difficult labour of the mother. From Chandra Lagna the horoscope is very powerful. Jupiter is in the house of wealth ; a Rajayoga is formed in the 7th by the conjunction of Mercury and the Sun lords of the 5th and 7th respectively. Lord of Chandra Lagna is exalted in the 9th and Mars and Rahu are posited in the 11th—highly favourable combinations. The Sun's situation in a Vargottamamsa and the Moon being completely free from malefic affliction are suggestive of Goethe's singular individuality of character while the maturity and ripeness of his genius may be guessed by the disposition of Jupiter and Venus in benefic signs, the former in swakshetra and the latter, neechabhanga. The 3rd house is afflicted considerably by the presence of Rahu and Saturn's aspect. The 7th lord Mars is in conjunction with Rahu and

---

and (c) he had only one son who also died in Goethe's own lifetime. The Lagna or the ascendant is the last part of Libra and the beginning of Scorpio so that qualities of both the signs are blended together. The Sun and Mercury are exactly in the 10th Bhava, Venus in the 11th, Mars in the 2nd and the Moon in the 4th Bhava. In higher latitudes two Bhavas often merge together into one sign and this has been the case in the horoscope of this great poet.

aspected by Saturn. The 7th from the Moon however is somewhat favourably disposed. In the Navasmsa also the 7th is considerably afflicted. These dispositions indicate not only the disappointments in his love affairs but also his late and somewhat unconventional type of marriage. For, it was only in 1806 in his 57th year – that he actually married though she was wife in conscience from 1788. Vasumathi Yoga is present because of the situation of Jupiter and Venus in the 6th and 11th Bhavas respectively. The disposition of Jupiter in the 2nd from the Moon generates Sunapha Yoga which is of a powerful nature as Jupiter happens to be placed in his own house. Lords of the 5th and 6th (according to Bhava reckoning) happen to be Jupiter and Mars respectively and they are in mutual kendras giving rise to Shankha Yoga. Lord of the 9th (according to Bhava) is the Moon. He is in Aries in Navamsa. The lord of this Navamsa, viz., Mars joins the 2nd house and hence gives rise to what is called Samrajya Yoga which rendered the native equal to a king. What wonder then that Napoleon and Goethe are considered the two greatest men in Europe during their time. The 5th house is completely spoiled when viewed from Chandra Lagna—Mars, Rahu and Ketu all converging their effects. Goethe had but one son who also died which calamity Goethe could not stand as it happened just a few years before his own death. Goethe was the greatest poet of Germany. Apart from this he took interest in physiognomy, philosophy, alchemy, philology, astrology, art and mystical writings. In other words, he was a versatile genius. The Sun, the Moon, Mercury, Jupiter and Venus ars the planets that have rendered him a versatile genius. In the Navamsa all the kendras are occupied. The situation of Jupiter in the 4th and exalted Venus aspecting the 4th are significant combinations suggestive of the emotions that moulded his poetical thoughts.

Important Events.—Goethe's first great illness in August 1768 when he suffered from the weakness of the lungs and digestive troubles occurred in Ketu's sub-period within the Dasa of Saturn. In Rasi the major lord is in Lagna while in the Navamsa the sub-lord is in Lagna. Ketu is powerfully aspected by Mars (lord of the 6th according to Bhava). Venus' sub-period is much more significant. Venus is in the 11th both from Lagna and also from major lord. It was during this sub-period that he became Doctor of Laws. It was during this sub-period that Goethe came into active contact with most of those impulses of which his after-life was a development. In the Moon's sub-period of Saturn's Dasa he was employed as an advocate. Mark the mutual disposition of the Moon and Saturn. This was also the period in which his literary activity was most prodigious when he was more fully occupied with literary plans which had reference to the deepest problems of human nature. We next come to Venus sub-period in Mercury Dasa. Mercury (intellect) is in the 10th (action) and Venus (emotion) is of course in the 11th (gains). This was the most momentous epoch in the development of his intellectual life. His capabilities manifested themselves in full measure in the sub-period of Venus within the Dasa of Venus. Venus as lord of Lagna is in an enviable position especially that he is in the 11th having obtained neechabhanga. It was during Venus' sub-period that Goethe met Schiller whose friendship in the closeness of its intimacy and its deep effect on the character of both friends, has scarcely a parallel in literary history. Goethe married Christiane Vulpius in 1806 during the sub-period of Venus— Kalatrakaraka—in his own Dasa. Venus is both lord of Lagna and lord of 12th or house of loss. It was in this same sub-period that Schiller's friendship with Goethe was severed by the former's death. The Sun's sub-period was also memorable in that it was during this sub-period that Napoleon and Goethe met and conversed. The Sun is a political planet and occupies the 10th house. It was also in the Sun's sub-period that the first of the famous *Faust* was published in complete form. Goethe's wife died in Jupiter's sub-period while his only son whom he loved deeply died in Venus' sub-period in the Sun's Dasa. The last twelve years of Goethe's life were occupied by his criticisms on the literature of foreign countries. He died in 1832 in Moon Dasa Mars sub-period. Mars is lord of the 7th and occupies the 2nd while in the Navamsa he is in the 3rd. The Moon owns the 2nd in the Navamsa. Thus Mars overpowered the major lord and inflicted death.

Remarks.—Jupiter gave Goethe the steadfastness of character which enabled him to pursue an independent career of self-culture. The Moon in the fixed and mystic sign of Aquarius and in direct aspect to Mercury suggests devotion to art in the midst of every kind of distracting influence. Venus bestowed on Goethe a joyous nature, lively sympathy, flow of language, and love of narration without which he could not have been a poet. Venus is neecha. This indicates sensual nature. Some of his writings are of an erotic character. Goethe describes them as moral—sensuous but they are more sensuous than moral. The same position of Venus accounts for his several disappointments in his love affairs. The Sun–Mercury combination always gives love for astrology and mystical studies. Goethe studied physiognomy under the auspices of Lavater. In his scientific research he succeeded in seeing as in a vision, the scheme of evolution applied to all phenomena of the physical and moral world, which the labours of the ancient Hindus had already revealed. Jupiter is the planet to make one an entity in any department of knowledge. He is the 2nd lord from the Moon and is in the 2nd while in the Navamsa he aspects exalted Venus in the 10th from Mercury's house. These are indeed subtle combinations whose importance is apt to be overlooked by students of astrology. Goethe's name is due to that famous *Faust*—the deepest and the most important work. With the completion of *Faust*, Goethe felt that the work of his life was accomplished. As we have observed above, the disposition of Venus, Mercury, Jupiter, the Sun and the Moon clearly reveal that his works have been woven according to his own life experience. Always striving after objective truth (Jupiter) and sometimes attaining to it, he exhibited to the world every phase of his plastic mind in turn and taught both by precept and example, the husbandry of the soul. His horoscope reveals that he learned by sad experience that the lesson of life is to renounce. It is also indicative that self-conflict and self-command moulded the exuberance of his impulsive nature (Mars in the 2nd) into monumental symmetry and proportion. Posterity must decide his exact precedence in that small and chosen company which contains the names of Homer, Dante and Shakespeare. As Homer concentrated in himself the spirit of antiquity, Dante of the middle ages and Shakespeare of the renaissance, so Goethe is the representative of the modern European spirit.

No. 21.—TIPPU SULTAN

Birth Details.— *Born on 1st December 1751 (N.S.) at 8 a.m. (Lat. 13° N., Long. 5h. 10m. 20s. E.)

Planetary Positions.—The Sun 229° 54' ; the Moon 24° 24' ; Mars 318° ; Mercury 227° 42' ; Jupiter 47° 30' ; Venus 194° 6' ;· Saturn 236° 24' ; Rahu 225°' ; Ketu 45° and Lagna 258°. Ayanamsa 18° 56'.

	Moon	Jupiter Ketu		Mars	Ketu	Jupiter
Mars				Venus Sat.		
	RASI			NAVAMSA		
Lagna	Sun Mercury Saturn Rahu	Venus		Sun Merc.	Moon Rahu	Lagna

Balance of Venus Dasa at birth : Years 3-4-24.

Special Features —Consistent with the Lagna being the war-like sign of Sagittarius and Lagna lord Jupiter being

* The date of birth has been ascertained on the basis of the Rasi Chart given in *Royal Horoscopes* by Prof. B. Suryanarain Rao to whom this Chart was given by Sir P. N. Krishnamurthy from his family records and can therefore be considered trustworthy.

aspected by the martial planet Mars, he was well built, brave, liberal and popular. Lagna As lord is also subjected to the combined influences of *all malefics*—particularly Saturn, Rahu and Mars, he lacked the prudence, diplomacy and foresight of his father and Tippu's "head and heart were both defective". The Moon is in Aries a movable sign aspected by the emotional Venus but otherwise unafflicted. Consequently he was subject to sudden fits of mental elevation and depression and lacked that calmness and equanimity which were the dominant characteristics of his father. The Lagna is no doubt a benefic sign. But the lord is subject to powerful malefic influences. Whilst this made him bold as an individual soldier, it is said, he was bigotted and fanatical and his treatment of his Hindu subjects was harsh and somewhat unbecoming. Until the commencement of Rahu Dasa, he possessed lovable qualities but as soon as Rahu Dasa commenced, he became a thoroughly changed person and as per the estimate given by Syed Hussain, one of Tippu's most confidential servants, "there was nothing of permanency in his views, no solidity in his councils, and no confidence on the part of the Government". Though English, French and some Indian accounts give details of murders, torture and mutilation which marked the reign of this monarch, the position of the 10th lord in his own nakshatra suggests that he could not have been as bad a tyrant as he is represented to be. A very powerful Rajayoga is caused by the association of the lords of the 9th, 10th, 2nd and 5th, indicating his high birth and great political power, but the yoga, having occurred in the 12th or house of loss, caused the disappearance of all the indications of the combined yoga.

Important Events.—Tippu attacked the English at Madras in the course of the Moon Dasa. But because of the Moon's

ownership of the 8th house, the campaign was not quite successful. It was in Rahu Dasa Rahu Bhukti that Tippu attacked
Baillie's detachment and Hyder's army met with glorious
triumph. His father's death took place in Rahu Dasa Jupiter
Bhukti when he was engaged in a war with the English. It will
be seen that Rahu the major lord is in the 12th in association
with Pitrukaraka (and also lord of the 9th) Sun and Jupiter the
sub-lord, who happens to be a maraka from Pitrukaraka
occupies another maraka place from the Sun. But because
Jupiter happens to be the lord of the 9th from Chandra Lagna
and has Samasaptaka disposition from the major lord, Tippu
succeeded to his father's great possessions without opposition
under the same directional influences. Rahu occupies the constellation of Saturn and is in the sign of Mars with Saturn and
the Sun, and Mercury lord of the 7th or foreign affairs. In the
Navamsa, he occupies the 3rd with the Moon. Therefore
throughout Rahu Dasa Tippu was very restless, bent on driving
away the English, who were his inveterate enemies. Mars
Bhukti in Rahu Dasa was highly significant. Mark the Upachaya
disposition of Mars from Lagna and the mutual kendra positions
of the major and sub-lords. It was during this sub-period that
Tippu sent a secret circular to the different powers in India
proposing to them all to unite in a common league for the
expulsion of the English from India. His heart was throbbing
for the indipendence of India. As soon as Jupiter Dasa started,
he sent ambassadors to negotiate with the French for the
expulsion of the English. In Saturn Bhukti of Jupiter Dasa,
the English stormed Srirangapatna and Tippu died bravely as
a soldier on the battle-field. Jupiter though Lagna lord
proved a maraka by virtue of his being aspected by two powerful marakas Saturn and Mercury and his being disposed in the

2nd from Chandra Lagna. He died on 4th May 1799, on a New Moon day. As Alison, author of the famous "French Revolution" says, "the Brahmins had predicted that the 4th of May would prove an inauspicious day to him. He made them large presents on that very day and asked them for their prayers".

Remarks.—Tippu's horoscope clearly domonstrates some of the basic principles of the astrological science. Lagna lord weak, Ayushkaraka afflicted and the 8th lord in a malefic sign conferred Madhyayu. The peculiar Rajayoga, formed by association of the lords of the 2nd, 9th and 10th having reference to the 12th or house of loss, deprived him of his head and empire. From Chandra Lagna, Jupiter and Saturn, lords of the 9th and 10th, though in mutual kendras causing another Rajayoga are considerably afflicted by Rahu, Mars and Ketu. This Rajayoga was lost during the Dasa of Jupiter and the Bhukti of Saturn. As Prof. Rao observes in his *Royal Horoscopes* "Hyder knew from the beginning that Tippu would lose the empire......he saw clear signs of bigotry and want of statesmanship and predicted what was to happen after nearly 20 years". It will be seen that the Sun lord of the 9th and Mercury lord of the 10th are in conjunction causing a powerful Rajayoga, but Mercury happens to be in combustion and these planets are in the grip of Rahu within hardly 5 degrees and thus eclipsed in a way, and the yoga has occurred in the 12th or house of loss. No wonder that Tippu lost his life and empire.

No. 22.—MARIE ANTOINETTE

Birth Details.—Born on 2nd November 1755 (N.S.) at about 8 p.m. (Lat. 46° 30′ N., Long. 30° E.)

Planetary Positions.—The Sun 201° ; the Moon 182° ; Mars 87° ; Mercury 224° ; Jupiter 169° ; Venus 202° ; Saturn 274° ; Rahu 156° ; Ketu 336° ; and Lagna 74° 1′. Ayanamsa 18° 57′.

		Mars Lagna	Sun Venus		Mars Jupiter
Ketu					
			Rahu Sat. Lagna		
	RASI	—		NAVAMSA	
Saturn					Ketu
	Mercury	Sun Moon Venus	Jupit. Rahu	Mercury	Moon

Balance of Mars Dasa at birth : Years 2-5-9.

Special Features.—The lord of Lagna Mercury in the 6th unaspected by or unassociated with any other planets, though Mars in Lagna Rasi, the Moon and the Lagna in odd signs (the Moon actually occupying the Trimsamsa of Mars) reveal her natural restlessness and give a clue to the character of the

9

native. Gemini rising shows how charitably she was inclined.
Venus in his own house in Chandra Lagna suggests that she
was an adept at mimicry, vivacious, somewhat proud. Her
thick eyebrows and the light russet hair may be accounted for
by the lord of Lagna occupying a Keetarasi. The concentration
of martian, mercurial and venusian influences on Lagna and the
Moon tells us that she was a delicately poised type, witty,
fascinating, charming, somewhat eccentric (Saturn aspecting
the 2nd). Mars is in the Lagna Rasi and consistent with his
nature, he gave Marie Antoinette enterprise, vitality and *Joie
De Vivre*. The 4th lord in this case is the *Sun and he is
debilitated occupying the 5th Bhava. It will be seen that the
Sun as well as Matrukaraka Moon are powerfully aspected by
Saturn. These will explain the queen's masculine minded
mother, Maria Theresa and the lack of intimate maternal super-
vision since the Empress was continually occupied with affairs
of State and for that matter was not very maternally inclined ;
she was interested in her children so far as they became pawns
in her ambitious political schemes. Bhratrukaraka Mars is in
the 9th Navamsa in association with Jupiter, lord of the 11th
ruling elder brothers and sisters. This may well account for
the fact that she was the fifteenth child of her mother. The
house of children is not well situated. The 5th lord Mercury is
in a Keetarasi and the 5th house being occupied by Putrakaraka
is further afflicted by Rahu. Her life was made more unhappy
by the constant harping on her barren condition which went on
all around her for years. The Moon in a sensitive place like
Libra and powerfully aspected by Saturn, invariably causes

* In higher latitudes it sometimes happens that two signs merge into
a Bhava or *vice versa*. Hence though Mercury should have been the lord
of the 4th, actually the Sun is the lord.

great apprehension and it is evidenced that Marie Antoinette had a nervous dread of childbirth. The 5th house is afflicted and Rahu's situation is not at all beneficial for the sacred function of motherhood. The 6th lord Mars is in the 2nd while the 6th from the Moon is occupied by Ketu. These planets are in the 6th Bhava. The court of France was hostile to her from the very beginning. She was always in the midst of confusion, intrigues, uncertainty, troubles through schemes and plots, deception and secret enemies. Three important planets including lord of Lagna in the 6th house—not the 6th Rasi—and the 6th lord Mars in Lagna thus causing a Parivarthana Yoga between the lords of Lagna and the 6th, a combination that is most undesirable can explain to an astrologer that a combination such as this engendered that marked unpopularity she laboured under throughout her queenly life. It was a contact that made for brusqueness, for tactlessness, for being too outspoken and hence exhibiting a serious lack of discretion that in its turn made her the target of unmerited attacks of a particularly bitter nature, the total accumulation of which swept her at last from the throne. Coming to the 7th house, we find the 7th lord Jupiter is in the 4th with Rahu. Jupiter is powerfully aspected by Mars. Kalatrakaraka Venus is with debilitated Sun aspected by Saturn. A contact such as this explains that "if ever there was a marital tragedy, long-drawn out and with its roots extending deep into the past, here was one : the fifteen-year-old girl brought up in the comparatively simple, homelike court of Vienna, unsophisticated and virginal, now suddenly thrust by maternal ambition coupled to the always heartless expendients of statecraft into the very midst of the most corrupt and licentious court in the Europe of that most dissolute age'.' In Navamsa, Saturn and Rahu aspect the 7th and

the 7th lord is aspected by Saturn, so that the husband was a
gawky youth of shuffling gait, taciturn, stubborn and stupid.
From Chandra Lagna there is a distinct Neechabhanga Rajayoga
for the Sun. Three planets are Vargottama. The significance
of all this is lost by the 10th lord Saturn being placed in the
8th powerfully aspected by Mars lord of the 6th.

Important Events.—The first shock in her life was
father's death in her 10th year, in the sub-period of Saturn in
Rahu Dasa. From Pitrukaraka Rahu is in the 12th while the
sub-lord Saturn owning the 9th is in the 12th from the 9th.
From Chandra Lagna, Rahu (who should give the results of
Mercury) is in the 12th. She was married in Venus Bhukti
Rahu Dasa, when she was in her 13th year. Rahu is with
Jupiter lord of the 7th, while Venus, the Kalatrakaraka as well,
is associated with the Moon lord of the 2nd or family. The
nearness of Kalatrakaraka Venus and lord of Kalatrabhava
Jupiter, and the nearness of the lords of Lagna and Kalatrakaraka to each other explain why marriage took place so early.
The next and the most momentous event in her life took place
in 1774 (Rahu Dasa Moon Bhukti) when the throne of the
Bourbons with its heritage of intrigue and political trouble
devolved on Louis XV's heir and the young Antoinette. Both
the major and sub-lords are in the 5th house while the 10th
lord Saturn aspects the sub-lord Moon. It is from the Moon's
Lagna that neechabhanga for the Sun is caused. Consequently,
the Moon conferred the throne on the native. The afflictions,
however, to which the Moon is subject, forebode the tragic
destiny awaiting the queen. She became a widow in Saturn
Dasa Saturn Bhukti. The 8th lord is in Aquarius Navamsa,
whose lord is also Saturn. Therefore Saturn is capable of
causing widowhood. The last and the most tragic event is her
own death. Saturn owns the 8th house and occupies the
8th. In the Navamsa, he powerfully aspects the 7th and is

associated with Rahu. The death actually occurred in the inter-period of Venus, sub-period of Saturn and the Dasa of Saturn.

Remarks.—Marie Antoinette is the tragic heroine of the vaunted revolution of 1791, martyr to what still currently passes for democracy, on innocent victim sacrificed by blood-thirsty mobs to stone for nine centuries of royal misrule. Whilst her horoscope, as a whole, is of interest as belonging to the last of Bourbons, we are concerned in this analysis with her tragic end, tragic marital life and tragic public career. Her horoscope reveals that her faults were caused by her education and position rather than her nature. The Lagna is in the sign of Mercury, the Trimsamsa being that of Jupiter. Consequently, she cannot be guilty of many of the libels against her. It may be asserted that she was personally a virtuous woman (Jupiter aspecting Lagna in Amsa and Mars, lord of Chandra Lagna in the 9th from the Moon with Jupiter) though always appearing to be the very reverse. The Jupiter–Moon Yoga should make one feel that innocence is not always its own protection and that circumspection is as necessary for a queen as for any other woman. Coming to her married life, it must be evident to any tyro in astrology that Mars and Saturn are prominent in regard to the 7th house, while Venus being afflicted has no relief. Supremely indifferent to all matters except his own particular pleasures, the husband (Louis XVI) treated her overtures with a complete lack of interest. The 7th lord Jupiter with Rahu evidences that neither domestically nor publicly was the husband able to give Marie any happiness. Leo rules France and Kalatrakaraka is with the ruler of Leo, suggesting that she became queen of France by matrimonial alliance. When the influence of Mars is powerful on the 7th or 8th house, a most inharmonious marriage is the indication. The affliction of Venus may also suggest some sort of impotance on the part of her husband. In fact, it is related of the inept Louis (her husband) that he left his princess at the door of the bridal chamber and spent that night and many to follow in *Solitudinam et Castam Quietalem*. If ever there was a marital tragedy, long drawn out and with its roots extending deep into the past, here was one. The nature of her death is clearly revealed by her horoscope. Death **takes place in captivity when the 22nd Drekkana happens to be either** *Nigala, Sarpa or Pasa*. In this case the 22nd Drekkana is the first of Capricorn and hence a *Nigala* one ; hence death in captivity. As Mars aspects the 8th and as Ayushkaraka is also in a *Nigala Drekkana*, the queen had to meet her end by being guillotined. Her death occurred in Venus Antara, Saturn Bhukti, Saturn Dasa. Venus it will be seen is in *Ayudha Drekkana* and by virtue of the influence both Saturn and Mars prevailing on the 8th house, in particular reference to evil Drekkanas, no wonder her graceful head fell to the insatiable maw of guillotine. She was born on the day of the great Lisbon earthquake during which, within the space of a few minutes, 40,000 people lost their lives. The wedding day was overshadowed by a terrible accident in Paris at the fete given in honour of the marriage. These were indeed the darkest portents. A careful analysis of this horoscope should reveal that the planetary positions tended decisively toward downfall and loss of status. In Bhava six planets are in *dwirdwadasa*. The luminaries and Saturn are inharmoniously disposed. As soon as the Venus inter-period commenced, she was imprisoned and on 16-10-1797, just a few days before the Antara ended, she was beheaded. It is said that she walked "with firm step and that peculiarly graceful carriage for which she was often admired, head up and looking straight ahead of her, up the steps of the platform to the instrument of death". Thus perished in her 38th year Marie Antoinette of Hapsburg-Bourbon consort of Louis XVI and martyr to what mankind still persists in calling "Liberty".

No. 23.—SRI THYAGARAJA

Birth Details.—*Born on 4th May 1767 A.D. (N.S.) at about 12 noon (L.M.T.) (Lat. 10° 47′ N., Long. 79° 10′ E.)

Planetary Positions.—The Sun 23° 9′ ; the Moon 96° 41′ ; Mars 64° 9′ ; Mercury 0° 21′ ; Jupiter 143° 14′ ; Venus 50° 57′ ; Saturn 59° 3′ ; Rahu 284° 17′ ; Ketu 104° 17′ ; and Lagna 115°. Ayanamsa 19° 9′.

	Sun Mercury	Venus Saturn	Mars		Mercury	Rahu	
			Lagna Moon Ketu	Lagna			Venus
	RASI				NAVAMSA		
Rahu			Jupit.				
					Mars Ketu	Sun Jupiter	Moon Saturn (Kara- kamsa)

Balance of Saturn Dasa at birth : Years 13–9–9.

Special Features.—The Lagna is a movable sign and the lord Moon, though in his own sign, is in the 12th Bhava. It is said that Sri Thyagaraja was very short-tempered in his younger days ; this is accounted for by the Moon's situation

---

* For birth data we are indebted to the Editor of *The Hindu*, Madras.

in the 12th house coupled with the presence of Saturn in the 2nd from Chandra Lagna in Navamsa. Though the native's physical build partakes of the characteristics of Cancer, the presence of Ketu in Lagna, the aspect of Saturn over Lagna and Aquarius rising in Navamsa, aspected by Jupiter—all go to influence the physical disposition—tall and lean, well-proportioned limbs, a broad chest and a dignified appearance—all due to the influences of Cancer blended to a considerable extent by Jupiter's aspecting Navamsa Lagna. The Sun and the Moon representing the eyes are in exaltation and own house respectively indicating that his eyes were full of brightness emanating a spiritual lustre. Note all the planets are in the 1st, 2nd, 7th, 10th, 11th and 12th Rasis. The 6th and 8th are not at all occupied. The 9th indicating Dharma is owned by Jupiter and the 10th ruling Karma has been the centre of the beneficial rays of Mercury and Jupiter. Hence his life of simple austerity, his insatiable zeal in the praise of Sri Rama and his indifference to worldly affluence and the glamour of royal patronage. The Sun and the Moon representing soul and the mind respectively are fairly powerful indicating the high degree of development of Atmavidya (self-knowledge) and strength of mind so very essential for achieving great deeds. The Sun is neecha in Navamsa and is hemmed inbetween Mars and Ketu on the one hand and Saturn on the other so that the native must have undergone intense mental and spiritual struggle within himself in the earlier days before perceiving truth and reality through the agency of music. Matrukaraka or indicator of mother is with Ketu while the indicator of father is neecha in Navamsa in the 9th. Lord of the 4th is in the 11th with Saturn, a malefic. These combinations explain the fact of his parents having died early. Between the 3rd lord and Mars the latter is more powerful. Mars is in the 2nd Navamsa suggesting that Sri Thyagaraja had only one brother. A noticeable characteristic of Cancer is the solemnity of its expression for it rules the soul, the inner life and religion ; and these are serious things. The Lagna is in Cancer, the Moon is in Cancer, Ketu is in Cancer and Saturn aspects Cancer. All these energies focussed on Cancer show the wonderful conception of this master-genius.

Important Events.—The first and the most important event is the serious illness (fever) when he was five years old. This occurred in the sub-period of the Sun in Saturn's Dasa. The Sun who is the planet of vitality owns the 2nd a maraka, while Saturn the major lord owning the 7th and 8th aspects Lagna. In the Navamsa, Saturn is in 2nd from Chandra Lagna while the Sun is in the 2nd from Saturn. This illness made his parents very sad. A holy man came to them at that time and assured the parents that Sri Thyagaraja would soon recover as he was destined to shed lustre on South Indian music. His marriage took place when he was 18 in Mercury Dasa Venus Bhukti. The major lord Mercury is with the 2nd lord Sun and occupies the nakshatra of Ketu who in his turn aspects the 7th. The sub-lord Venus being Kalatrakaraka is with Saturn, lord of the 7th. All these combinations suggest his marriage in the 18th year. Saturn is fairly well disposed owning the 7th and associated with Venus, lord of music. Saturn's Dasa was there-fore formative, enabling Thyagaraja to undergo the rigorous training necessary to master the technicalities of music and develop his talents in such a manner as to make him what he became. It is alleged that the great musician had known about the time and date of his death quite in advance. At the predic-ted moment the congregation of his friends and disciples, who had gathered there, heard a mysterious sound (*nadam*) ema-

nating from the saint's head. Soon they saw a bright halo of
light flying from his head and vanishing slowly into the atmosphere. The 8th lord is in a benefic sign with a benefic planet
while the 8th is aspected powerfully by the 8th lord and the
greatest benefic Jupiter. The exact year of his death is not
known. We are inclined to the view that Sri Thyagaraja died in
Rahu Dasa Jupiter Bhukti at the age of 85. Rahu is in the 7th
both from Lagna and the Moon. Saturn whose results Rahu is
to give is lord of the 7th and 8th. In the Navamsa he is in the
8th from Lagna. The sub-lord Jupiter is in the 2nd a maraka
place occupying a *shashtashtaka* position from the major lord.
In the Navamsa, Venus, whose results Rahu should give, owns
the 2nd from Chandra Lagna while Jupiter is a maraka both
from Lagna and Chandra Lagna.

Remarks.—Sri Thyagaraja is a household name in South
India and he occupies a pre-eminent place amongst the great
masters of South Indian music. Mark the positions of Jupiter,
Mercury and Venus. Jupiter is in the house of speech while
Mercury is in the 9th house (though in 10th Rasi) aspecting
the 4th house. Thyagaraja was not only a musician but a great
saint also. This is brought into light by the fact that devotion
and melody have been blended together in his compositions
in such a way that they cultivate the piety of the singer as well
as the listener.

His musical genius and philosophical eminence are clearly
explained by the presence of Jupiter and the Sun in the 2nd
from the Karakamsa. Mercury's presence in the 9th Bhava
indicates that the wonderful conceptions of this master-
genius entered his consciousness without any assistance of
the intellectual faculty—the several elements of composition
appearing to him before his inner vision. Jupiter's presence

in the second in the house of the natural Atmakaraka has invested Thyagaraja's compositions with a sense of exalted morality and sympathy for the forces that make for good and they furnish an ideal guide for human conduct.

Venus is the planet for emotion as well as devotion. His aspecting the 5th has made the songs highly devotional. His compositions re-echo in the human heart the infinite hormonies of pure untainted Being. The Sun and Mercury are in the 10th Rasi and Jupiter aspects the 10th. This means he had a mission to fulfil which he did fulfil. The unique feature of his music is the appeal it makes not only to the musical intellect and to the devout mind, but to the lay-man and the critic also. It is this peculiar feature in his songs that has immortalised Thyagaraja's name. No wonder the Sun, Mercury and Jupiter were not a little responsible to make him what he is even today. His life work was centered round musical creation. He brought music home to the hearts and minds of the people. He offered, not only to the musician but to all who have ears to hear and hearts to be touched, a spring of the purest and most elevated pleasure. He left the world happier and the better for his work in it.

No. 24.—ABRAHAM LINCOLN

Birth Details.—*Born on 12th February 1809 at 7-32 a.m. (L.M.T.). (Lat. 35° N., Long. 89° E.)

Planetary Positions.—The Sun 304° 6′; the Moon 275° 20′; Mars 185° 46′; Mercury 312° 44′; Jupiter 332° 16; Venus 347° 46′; Saturn 223° 16′; Rahu 197° 44′; Ketu 17° 44′; and Lagna 316° 39′. Ayanamsa 19° 40′.

Jupiter Venus	Ketu			Rahu			
Sun Lagna Mercury		RASI		Moon Lagna		NAVAMSA	Jupiter
Moon				Merc.			
	Saturn	Rahu Mars		Venus	Sun Mars	Saturn	Ketu

Balance of the Sun Dasa at birth : Years 2-1-6.

Special Features.—Consistent with the narure of Lagna lord and the sign occupied by him, which is one of long

* Abraham Lincoln is said to have been born "between 7 and 11 a.m.". The Lagna varies from 5° Aquarius to 4° Aries. Taking into cousideration the description of his physical features, the peculiarities of his birth, the vicissitudes of his life and the nature of his death, the Lagna has been fixed as Aquarius 16° 39′.

ascension, Abraham Lincoln had an "ungainly figure, with long arms and large hands and relatively small development of chest", but he possessed immense physical strength. The mystic sign Aquarius rising with Mercury placed very near the ascending degree made the native firm in principles, benevolent and humanitarian. Lagna lord Saturn is aspected by the divine planet Jupiter. He was therefore deeply religious and had an implicit faith in God. The sign Aquarius has the quality of usually making one somewhat queer and peculiar in his nature. True to this characteristic, "taste and minor sensibilities were a little deficient" in Lincoln. But rare occasions such as "can arouse a passionate sense of justice would kindle his kind nature with a sudden fire". Mark the position of the Moon in the 12th in the constellation of the Sun and aspected by two first-rate malefics, of which, Saturn as Chandra-Lagnadhipati becomes a benefic. Mercury is in Lagna with the Sun. Thus there was, in his mind, a blending of tolerance and humour with a singular purity of life. The Moon's situation in a saturnine sign and his affliction by Mars and Saturn, without any neutralising effects, denote that he was subject at times "to unrestrained emotional reaction, morbid depression and even temporary insanity". The 4th lord Venus exalted is in a trine from Lagna lord denoting a sensitive, good looking and pious mother, but as Matrukaraka Moon is afflicted the mother was short-lived. The 9th is occupied by two malefics. Lincoln's father was illiterate, shiftless and of no great help to the boy. The 4th lord Venus is exalted in the 2nd and is in association with Jupiter lord of the 2nd. This evidently reveals that Lincoln was struggling with self-education. Slavery came to be hateful to him because the planet of the downtrodden Saturn, happening to be lord of

Lagna, occupies the 10th aspected by the divine planet Jupiter from his own sign. Kalatrakaraka Venus is exalted in the 2nd, while the 7th lord Sun is in the nakshatra of Mars. The 7th itself is aspected by Saturn. Consequently, though Mrs. Lincoln "had a high temper" she was an admirable wife for her husband. But as Venus is in the constlellation of Rahu, Lincoln discovered that marriage "is a field of battle and not a bed of roses"—a battle in which it is said that he did not play his full part. Another interesting combination in his horoscope is the position of the emotional planet in the 12th subject to the aspect of Saturn. This indicates 'occult' tendencies. He believed in dreams as omens. According to classical works like *Jataka Tatwa*, when Saturn, Sun and Mars are in the 10th, 7th and 4th respectively, death takes place by assassination. Here we find Saturn is in the 10th ; Mars aspects the 4th and the Sun aspects the 7th. As a result of these combinations, Lincoln was assassinated.

Important Events.—The first and the most important event is the death of Lincoln's mother when he was 9 years old in Moon Dasa Saturn Bhukti. The Moon as Matrukaraka is considerably afflicted while from the 4th (house of mother) Saturn is in a maraka place. Throughout Mars Dasa, especially that Mars is afflicted by his association with Rahu, Lincoln had a chequered career and was poverty-stricken which continued almost right upto the end. As soon as Rahu Dasa commenced, Lincoln was appointed Captain of a company to serve in the Black Hawk war. Mark the excellent position of Jupiter who has caused Subhavesi Yoga. As soon as Jupiter Bhukti commenced, the native was elected to Illinois Legislature. As soon as Venus sub-period in Rahu Dasa dawned, Lincoln's marriage took place with Mary Todd. It was again under the directional influences of the yogakarakas Jupiter and Venus that Lincoln making speeches began to be talked of as a candidate for Presidentship. Jupiter has caused Vesi Yoga. The Moon is in the constellation of the Sun lord of the 7th. It was in Jupiter Dasa Moon Bhukti that Lincoln became the President of U.S.A. Mark the excellent position of Jupiter both in Rasi and in Navamsa. The fag end of Jupiter Dasa was equally remarkable because he was elected President for the second time and Lincoln succeeded in having passed the amendment to the Constitution which ended slavery in America. As soon as Saturn Dasa Mercury Bhukti started, Lincoln was assassinated. Saturn, as we have already seen above, by virtue of his position in the 10th, has caused Mrityu Yoga. From Chandra Lagna, he owns the 2nd, a maraka place. Saturn is further aspected by Jupiter, lord of the 2nd, a maraka place. These influences justify death in Saturn Dasa Mercury Bhukti. Mercury is in the 2nd from the Moon with the 8th lord. He is the 8th lord from Lagna and Navamsa Lagna. As regards the nature of death, the disposition of Saturn in the 10th points to death by weapon.

Remarks.—We can best understand the astrological causes which made Lincoln one of the world's greatest men by a close examination of his horoscope. "Born in a log cabin, in turn woodman, flat boatman surveyor, village postmaster, legislator, country-lawyer, member of Congress and finally President," Lincoln's fight in life was very hard consistent with the *dwirdwadasa* positions of planets. The most notable combinations are the presence of a very powerful Subhavesi Yoga caused by Jupiter lord of the 2nd, in the 2nd and Venus, the yogakaraka, exalted in the 2nd, the association in Lagna of the 5th lord Mercury and the 7th lord Sun, the political planet; the position of

Mars, as lord of the 10th in the 9th and the elevation of Lagna lord Saturn in the 10th, in the sign of the fighting Mars aspected by the beneficent Jupiter. It is Jupiter's aspect on the 10th that made him firm and absolutely independent where his conviction was concerned. It is again due to Jupiter's position that Lincoln had an intense belief in a vast and over-ruling Providence. It is birth in Aquarius Lagna that accounts for his benevolence, forgiveness and world-wide humanity. As the 2nd lord Jupiter and the 12th lord Saturn are in mutual trikonas he never developed even a reasonable desire to be rich, though he suffered from poverty in his early career. Lords of Lagna and the 9th are in excellent dispositions mutually, but lords of Lagna and the 10th are in *dwirdwadasa*. Conse-quently he faced the difficulties and terrors of his high office with detachment and strength with which he had earlier paved his way as a poor man. The harmonious disposition of the lords of Lagna and the yogakaraka Venus and the creative planet Jupiter made him "a signal benefactor of posterity, statesman, ruler and liberator".

No. 25.—LORD TENNYSON

Birth Details.—Born on 6th August 1809 at about 11.45 p.m. (Lat. 53° 32' N., Long. 0° 24' W.)

Planetary Positions.—The Sun 113° 45' ; the Moon 53° 45' ; Mars 196° 45' ; Mercury 95° 45' ; Jupiter 4° 45' ; Venus 67° 45' ; Saturn 217° 45' ; Rahu 187° 36' ; Ketu 7° 36' ; and Lagna 55°. Ayanamsa 19° 45'

	Jupiter Ketu	Moon Lagna	Venus	Mars		Jupiter	Ketu
			Sun Merc	Sun			
	RASI				NAVAMSA		
							Moon Lagna Mercury
	Saturn	Mars Rahu		Venus Rahu			Saturn

Balance of Rahu Dasa at birth : Years 6-1-26.

Special Features.—The ascendant is Taurus, a fixed sign and the lord Venus is in the 2nd. Lagna is occupied by the Moon. In Navamsa lord of Lagna is in the 7th aspected by Mercury and the Moon. These indicate a fine, large-featured, bronze-coloured, shaggy-headed man. The Moon ruler of the mind is exalted. This coupled with the presence of Anapha Yoga made the poet a 'brotherly' and solid-hearted man. His manners were rough and rude and this is partly accounted for by the combined aspect of Mars and Saturn on Lagna. Saturn also indicates a "naturally shrinking disposition preferring to live in seclusion, shyness and restraint". Of course the Sun is in Cancer in the 4th Bhava giving rise to emotion, love and warm-heartedness. His poetic greatness is due to the position of Venus in the 2nd and Gemini a sign of fertility and creation rising in the 2nd house. Mars lord of the 7th is in the 6th house. This disposition bears witness to Tennyson's version of the struggle between the higher and lower forms of sex impulse with its accompanying emotions. The Sun is in the 4th Bhava though in 3rd Rasi. In the Navamsa there is *Parivarthana* or exchange of houses between the 10th and 5th lords. The 9th being aspected by the 9th lord gave him spiritual understanding and his mind was focussed on events far in advance of his time, events that were to be the direct outcome of the process of growth, of which he was so keenly aware. The Kahala Yoga was also responsible for his becoming the poet-laureate.

Important Events.—Tennyson made his first real bid for public recognition in 1830. This was in the Sun's sub-period in Rahu Dasa. The Sun is in the 4th Bhava (though in 3rd Rasi) and the foundation for his future success was laid during this period. Jupiter's Dasa was one of expansion. Having caused Kahala Yoga, it was in his Dasa that Tennyson published the famous two-volume edition of his poems. 1850 was a very important year. His marriage took place in this year and he was also appointed as poet-laureate in succession to Wordsworth. These far-reaching events occurred in Saturn's

Dasa Saturn's Bhukti. Saturn is a yogakaraka and is in the 7th or house of marriage. In Navamsa he is in the second. As owning the 9th and 10th and occupying the 7th, Saturn conferred not only fame and fortune but also marriage. Saturn's sub-period in Mercury's Dasa was equally eventful because it was during this period that Tennyson was made a Baron. Saturn, as we have already seen, is a yogakaraka and Mercury as lord of the 2nd and 5th is in the 3rd with the Sun. Tennyson died in 1892 at the ripe old age of 83 years at the fag end of Ketu Dasa. Ketu is in the 12th and Mars whose influences Ketu is to partake owns the 7th. In the Navamsa again Mars is in the 8th both from Lagna and the Moon thus justifying maraka.

Remarks.—Tennyson was not only a great poet but an equally great philosopher too. Mark the exchange of the 5th and 10th lords, Jupiter and Venus respectively in Navamsa. Tennyson felt a deep and lively interest in the march of progress, as manifested in the social, economic and scientific achievements of his day. Venus made him the poet and Jupiter conferred the philosophical tinge. Jupiter ruling religion and philosophy is in the 12th or house of moksha and has caused Kahala Yoga with the Sun in a kendra from him. Therefore Tennyson, in the very depths of his nature, wrestled with faith and reason, with the scientific instinct and the desire to believe in the immortality of the soul. The fruits of his struggle are given to the world in the fine, clear, imaginative beauty of 'In Memoriam'. Tennyson says : "On stepping-stones of our dead selves we rise to higher things". This consciousness of growth by change is one of the most outstanding qualities of Tennyson's philosophy. It is everywhere evident in his poetry, and one receives the impression the word 'change' itself bears some magic connotation in the poet's mind. Venus is in the 2nd—unadulterated—in the house of imagination. Venus is the planet of emotion. There were times when he gave expression to such vehement emotion and such profound passion that he was scarcely intelligible to his readers. The poet was very regardful of public opinion, a quality that was the natural outcome of Saturn aspecting Lagna, as also the Sun and the 2nd lord Mercury being in the 3rd. The aesthetic Venus, placed in Gemini, the second house, made Tennyson one of the greatest masters of poetic workmanship, the world has ever known. The sources of Tennyson's greatness as revealed through his horoscope are many and they come out mainly through the disposition of Jupiter, Venus and Mercury in Rasi and Navamsa.

No. 26.—KARL MARX

Birth Details.—Born on 15th May 1818 at about 2 a.m. (L.M.T.) (Lat. 49° 44' N., Long. 6° 38' E.)

Planetary Positions.—The Sun 24° 18' ; the Moon 24° 8' ; Mars 90° 58' ; Mercury 40° 12' ; Jupiter 263° 5' (R) ; Venus 39° 12' ; Saturn 325° 59' ; Rahu 18° 39' ; Ketu 198° 39' ; and Lagna 302° 56'. Ayanamsa 19° 52'.

	Sun Moon Rahu	Mercury Venus		Ketu Venus	Mercury	Saturn
Lagna Saturn			Mars			Mars
	RASI			NAVAMSA		
Jupiter		Ketu		Sun Moon	Lagna Jupiter	Rahu

Balance of Venus Dasa at birth : Years 3–9–18.

Special Features.—The ascendant is Kumbha or Aquarius, a mystic sign, and the lord Saturn is situated in the Lagna. Both the ascendant and the ascendant lord are powerfully aspected by Mars (lord of the 3rd and 10th), who has just entered his sign of debilitation. These combinations no doubt gave him a robust constitution but the planet of vitality being

eclipsed by Rahu rendered him ruin his health through over-
work. The Navamsa Lagna being hemmed inbetween malefics
and aspected by Mars is further proof of the struggles he must
have undergone in early life. Lord of the house of speech is
situated in the 11th in his own sign. That Marx was an
independent thinker of great originality and force of character
is denoted by Mercury, the planet of intelligence—and in this
case the lord or house of intelligence, being placed in a benefic
and friendly sign and free from evil aspects or association.
Venus is yogakaraka and he is exalted in the 2nd or house of
speech while the lord of the 2nd joins his own Rasi in the 11th.
This combination illustrates the fact that Marx was never in the
habit of borrowing but of strongly asserting the results of his
own research and of impressing upon other men.

Saturns's presence in Lagna, in this case Aquarius, a mystic
sign, is of the almost significance and the great virtue of the
horoscope hinges to a large extent upon the fact that Lagna
(Aquarius) is occupied by the lord Saturn. We have said
several times that Aquarius is a mystic sign. Saturn in Lagna
loses digbala but in this case he gains sthanabala. If Rahu
were there instead of Saturn, Marx would probably have become
the greatest philosopher of his time. But, on the contrary,
Saturn is there aspected by the matter-of-fact planet Mars. No
wonder therefore that though Marx was at first a zealous
student and apparently an adherent of Hegelianism, his (Marx)
conception of the world is the Hegelian reversed. For Hegel
"the thought process", which he transforms into an independent subject under the same idea, "is the creator of the real,
which forms only its external manifestation"; with Marx, "on
the contrary, the ideal is nothing else than the material transformed and translated in the human brain". Saturn is glorified

as lord of Lagna in Lagna and that too in Moolatrikona.
Hence his deep concern for the labour and the acceptance in
all its logical consequences of the principle that labour is the
source of value. In fact it is the basis of a vast and elaborate
system of social philosophy devoid of spiritual moorings. Marx
attained no distinction as a statesman or as a ruler. The 10th
house is rendered null and void because the lord Mars is
neecha, he has not obtained neechabhanga, and he has caused
Parivarthana with the Moon lord of the 6th. Obviously the
Parivarthana here is in regard to the 3rd and 6th houses constituting a *Dainya Yoga*, and hence of absolutely no practical
importance. His proficiency in social and political matters may
be explained by the fact that Mercury is in Karakamsa. Another
combination of significance is the presence of *Dama Yoga*.

Important Events.—When Marx was six years old, his
parents embraced Christianity. This was in the Sun's Dasa.
The Sun is lord of the 7th and occupies the 3rd with the Moon
and Rahu, the combination receiving the aspect of Jupiter from
Sagittarius and that of Saturn from Aquarius. The Moon
represents the subconscious mind or the 'affect personality'
(of the psycho-analyst) and his conjunction with Rahu is of
great psychological significance in accounting for his revolutionary tendencies and his eagerness to lead human society
into new modes of thought and behaviour. Marx was born on
an eclipse day ; this fact, coupled with the effects created by
the concentration of five-planet energies in Aries, suggests that
there was in his unconscious a tendency to project a revolutionary behaviour in the form of a conscious and deliberate
attitude. Since the Sun who has contributed the 'sensitivity'
is the Pitrukaraka, it would symbolise his father's break from
his Jewish religious tradition. His marriage took place in Mars

Dasa, Venus Bhukti. From the Moon, Mars owns the 8th while in Navamsa he has the 2nd and 7th lordship. Venus the sub-lord however is Kalatrakaraka and he is in the 4th in his own house and the 11th from the major lord Mars, this indicating marriage in his Dasa. It was in the same Venus Bhukti that his interest in economics became particularly aroused and that he had his first meeting with Engels. Venus is in the constellation of the Sun and hence is capable of producing some of the results due to the Sun. As Rahu is placed in Aries, he must give, in a large measure, the results of Mars and of course to some extent those due to the Sun and the Moon. Rahu Dasa was one of expansion of his literary and revolutionary activities. Mars is in the 6th and this is indeed a good index of revolutionary activities. This accounts also for the enmity over his public activities. Rahu's sub-period in his own Dasa was particularly important because it was during this time that Marx wrote and travelled a good deal, becoming increasingly known among progressive thinkers. The advent of Jupiter's sub-period was noteworthy because of the famous *Communist Manifesto* which was the birth cry of Marxian communism. Jupiter aspects Rahu from Sagittarius and consistent with the nature of these 'directions', the work releases the dynamic power of the man who thundered against social evils with the prophetic passion of his ancient forbears. His death took place in 1883 when the sub-period of Mercury was operating in the Dasa of Saturn. Though lord of Lagna, Saturn, is the Ayushkaraka and presides over *Naidhana Tara* or the star of death counted from the birth constellation, he occupies Jupiter's constellation and Jupiter is lord of the 2nd from Lagna. In the Navamsa, Saturn owns the 3rd from the Moon and occupies the 7th with Mercury lord of the 8th. The sub-lord Mercury owns the 8th and occupies the 2nd from the Moon. Added to all these, Saturn was transiting Taurus, the 2nd from Marx's Janma Rasi, with the result he was having *sadesathi* for the third time in his life. All these factors justified his death during this period.

Remarks.—The horoscope is interesting in two ways, *viz.,*: (1) Saturn the planet of labour, and of course the masses, is in a highly favourable position and (2) the Sun-Moon-Rahu conjunction, occurring in a square to Mars and aspected by Saturn, rendered the man revolutionary. Mercury in the 4th endowed Marx with extraordinary dialectical skill and historical learning into the most complete system of socialism that has ever been formulated. The mystic sign of Aquarius rising would have certainly made Marx a great mystic and philosopher but the fact that a fallen Mars, who in this case is Karmasthanadhipati, aspects the Lagna and the lord made him turn his back against the idealism of Hegel and to transform his dialectical method into what was to become the logical basis of Marxism, *viz., Dialectical Materialism.* The 10th house has absolutely no benefic influence nor has the 9th anything to do with Jupiter, Mercury or unadulterated Rahu. *All the malefics* aspect the 9th while benefic Saturn aspects the 10th. These two sets of aspects suggest disillusionment, dissatisfaction with idealism and transition to *Realistic—Rather Materialistic—* ways of thinking. The devotion and enthusiasm which had previously been fixed on ideal and spiritual conceptions (Ketu in the 9th) became concentrated on humanity. Socialism (the pet child of Saturn) became a social, political and economic creed to Karl Marx. In analysing astrologically the theory of Marx we do not wish to take any position implying agreement or dissent with it. Marxism and of course the communist movement are historical facts and their rise, growth and world application must be studied and understood objectively and dispassionately whether or not one is in sympathy with their doctrines. In the Navamsa, Libra rises and Jupiter is in Lagna while Mars obtains a distinct neechabhanga in the 10th. Rahu is in the 12th. These dispositions lay the emphasis upon service and organising ability, mostly at the level of mental concepts. The emotional life (Moon in Aries) is entirely subservient to the intellectual (Lagna strong). The horoscope is of an indefatigable worker and a ruthless opponent. It must be evident to any student of astrology that harmonious aspects between malefics—particularly Saturn and Rahu—would direct the latent forces in constructive and useful channels. In this case Rahu and Saturn are in the 3rd and 11th from each other. This explains clearly that the fundamental principle of the Marx school and of the whole cognate socialism is the theory of 'surplus value'. It supplies the key to his explanation of the history and influences of capital. In Marx's chart, the house of wealth is doubtless well fortified but these influences have been denied manifestation by the predominantly evil—evil in respect of material gains—influences centered on the 9th and 10th apart from evidently weak disposition of the 10th lord. The whole position of the Marx school can be characterised as evolutionary and revolutionary socialism (Mars aspects Saturn, and Saturn aspects the Sun and Rahu based on a materialistic conception of the world and debilitated Mars aspects Lagna and lord of Lagna) and of human history.

The chart is a remarkable one. The combinations are elusive and they reveal that the great merit of Marx lies in the work he has done as scientific inquirer into the economic movement of modern times (Venus yogakaraka exalted in the 2nd) and as the philosophic historian of the capitalistic era. Students of astrology know that history, including economic history, is a succession of orderly phenomena, that each phase in the line of succession is marked by facts and tendencies more or less peculiar to itself (and consistent with dispositions of major planets), and that laws and principles, which we now condemn, had formerly an historical necessity, justification and validity.

No. 27.—QUEEN VICTORIA

Birth Details.—Born on 23rd/24th May 1819 at 4-4 a.m. (L.M.T.). (Lat. 51° 30′ N., Long. 0° 5′ W.)

Planetary Positions.—The Sun 42° 13′ ; the Moon 43° 40′ ; Mars 357° 42′ ; Mercury 19° 2′ ; Jupiter 297° 4′ ; Venus 6° 45′ ; Saturn 338° 53′ ; Rahu 358° 17′ ; Ketu 168° 17′ ; and Lagna 41° 19′. Ayanamsa 19° 53′.

Rahu Mars Saturn	Mercury Venus	Sun Moon Lagna		Mars Rahu	Sun Lagna	Moon	Venus
	RASI				NAVAMSA		
Jupiter							
		Ketu					Ketu Mercury Jupiter Saturn

Balance of the Moon's Dasa at birth : Years 7–3–0.

Special Features.—Two factors are significant as indices of the remarkable nature of the horoscope. The first is the conjunction of the three most vital centres of the horoscope, *viz.*, the Lagna, the Moon and the Sun in the sign of Taurus. And the second is the satelletium of four planets obtaining in the 12th Bhava. Taurus rising confers a mind that is practical and concrete but the lord of Lagna in the 12th, in Bhava association with Rahu, and the Lagna being aspected by Jupiter tends the mind to be obsessed by delusion of grandeur. The same position of Jupiter in the 10th Bhava, aspecting the royal planets the Sun and the Moon, gave the individual the sense of purpose that she was born for fulfilling a certain mission in life. It must be noted that the idea of an empire grew and developed round the symbolic personality of Queen Victoria. Lords of the 2nd (kutumba), and the 10th (occupation) are *dwirdwadasa*. Thus tensions are shown, a ''struggle in the adjusting of the personal life of the woman to the social and national destiny of the queen''. Lord of Lagna and the 7th (Venus and Mars respectively) are in Bhava association while Mars is in the constellation of Mercury, lord of the 2nd and 5th. This denotes that the subject was very much attached to her husband and dominated by his influence. He became the queen's partner in politics and being her superior in intellect and knowledge, became her master and guide. Mark the fact that, lord of the 5th, Mercury, is not only associated with Lagna lord Venus but occupies the constellation of Venus, while the 5th is aspected by Jupiter and three malefics. Jupiter the Putrakaraka has been rendered strong by sthanabala. The planet of vitality, *viz.*, the Sun, as owning the 5th (in Navamsa), occupies Lagna. All these factors account for the queen's prolific motherhood. It will be seen that she gave birth to nine children. Superficially studied, no outstanding Rajayogas are visible, but careful scrutiny reveals the presence of powerful yogas. The royal planet Moon is not only exalted but is Vargottama. Mars and Rahu in the 11th from the Moon are Vargottama. Saturn happening to be yogakaraka from Lagna and Chandra Lagna is in the 11th nearly 19° away from Mars, having obtained Parivarthana with Jupiter lord of the 11th. Jupiter is no doubt debilitated but since he gains sthanabala and is actually in the 10th house, in the constellation of Mars, lord of the 7th, "imperialism" became the queen's mood and the queen became the symbolic foundation of the new British Empire.

Important Events.—Victoria ascended the throne in 1837 when she was having Rahu Dasa Jupiter Bhukti. Jupiter is dominantly placed and Rahu the major lord is in Vargottama and in the constellation of Mercury. The years immediately following her accession "were the least sensible and satisfactory time in her whole life", probably due to the situation of Jupiter in the constellation of Mars who in his turn is afflicted. In 1840 she was married to her cousin Albert in Rahu Dasa Saturn Bhukti. Mark the fact that both major and sub-lords are in Rasi association and under the same directional influences the first issue, a daughter, was born. As the major lord Rahu is in the constellation of the 5th lord Mercury, seven issues were born in Rahu Dasa and two issues in Jupiter Dasa. Her husband's death which occurred in Jupiter Dasa Venus Bhukti produced an emotional condition which lasted for a couple of decades. Her emotional life became indrawn and weighed down under the fatality of her husband's death. The major lord Jupiter is considerably afflicted in Navamsa while Mars has joined Kalatrakaraka Venus in the 12th Bhava. The queen groaned under the labours of her self-imposed isolation and for many years she kept herself almost entirely secluded in her palace. Saturn, as lord of the 10th and 11th Bhavas (lord of the 9th and 10th Rasis) in the 11th and being involved in Parivarthana with Jupiter lord of the 9th Bhava, represents the expansion of the empire during his Dasa. It will be seen that

Disraeli's vigorous imperial policy was congenial to the queen, who warmly applauded the acquisition of the Suez canal shares and welcomed the measure which conferred upon her the title of empress of India in 1876, this important event having taken place in Saturn Dasa Venus Bhukti. With the commencement of Mercury's period, the Silver Jubilee of her reign was celebrated and for the country, a period of unprecedented material prosperity set in. Mercury as lord of the 2nd in the constellation of Lagna lord is capable of conferring very good results. The queen died in 1903 in Mercury Dasa Saturn Bhukti. Mercury is a maraka as 2nd lord while Saturn as Ayushkaraka occupying the constellation of the 7th lord Mars is empowered to kill the native.

Remarks.—True to the dominant position of the royal planets the Sun and the Moon in Lagna, that too within 3 degrees from each other, the queen was out and out an imperialist. Consistent with the peculiar position of Rahu, she received a crown that "had been tarnished by ineptitude and vice" and she wore it for 63 years. If you look at the Bhava chart, you will find that all the planets (excepting Ketu) have been grouped within an arc of 103°, involving the 10th, 11th, 12th and 1st houses. This is a unique feature making her reign extraordinarily eventful. Neither the Lagna nor Lagna lord has anything to do with Saturn. Lagna is occupied by the Sun and the Moon. These combinations explain why the queen did not accept the modern notion that politics should be left to politicians. The harmonious disposition between the lords of the 2nd (family) and the 9th (Jupiter) brings into relief the intensity of her devotion to duty as wife, mother and queen and the transparent honesty of her character.

No. 28—SRI RAMAKRISHNA PARAMAHAMSA

Birth Details.—Born on 18th February 1836 at about 6-23 a.m. (Lat. 22° 53° N., Long. 87° 44′ E.)

Planetary Positions.—The Sun 308° 19′; the Moon 323° 15′; Mars 293° 9′; Mercury 316° 33′; Jupiter 76° 0′; Venus 339° 29′; Saturn 195° 10′; Rahu 214° 20′; Ketu 34° 20′; and Lagna 304° 53′. Ayanamsa 20° 6′.

Venus	Ketu		Jupit.		Moon	
Mercury Lagna Sun Moon		RASI		Rahu Merc Jupit. Sat.	NAVAMSA	Mars
Mars						Ketu
	Rahu	Saturn		Sun	Lagna	Venus

Balance of Jupiter Dasa at birth : Years 12-1-6.

Special Features.—Lagna is Kumbha or Aquarius and the lord of Lagna Saturn is exalted in the 9th being aspected powerfully by Jupiter. Lagna is also aspected by Jupiter. The conjunction of the Sun, the Moon and Mercury in Lagna aspected by Jupiter indicates a great change in life which made him undergo peculiar yogic experiences. The Sun, the Moon and Lagna—

representing the soul, mind and body respectively—are all in the fixed sign of Aquarius. The Atmakaraka Sun being aspected by Jupiter is suggestive of the grand development of the soul. The Moon in a similar situation is indicative of the direction in which his mind was working from his very young age and the way he controlled his mind. Venus, a yogakaraka for Aquarius, is in the second exalted. Venus is not subject to any malefic combinations or aspects both in Rasi and Navamsa. He is of course debilitated in Navamsa. The 7th lord Sun is in Lagna—unaspected by any malefics—but powerfully aspected by Jupiter. The disposition of Venus—free as it is from any malefic association—accounts for the complete absence of *passions* and *sensual feelings* even towards his own wife whom he looked upon as the Mother—the mother who gave birth to him and the embodiment of motherhood. Three planets are in exaltation—a combination which has made him one of the greatest saints of India, who brought about a mighty awakening of the Hindu religion with all that it stands for. Strictly speaking no *Parivraja yoga* (combination for asceticism) is revealed in the horoscope but a careful scrutiny suggests that the combination, "if Saturn or lord of Lagna aspect the lord of the sign occupied by the Moon, an ascetic is born" is present because Saturn happens to be the lord of both Lagna and the Chandra Lagna. One takes to renunciation when the Moon occupies an Amsa of Saturn or Mars and is aspected by Saturn. In this horoscope the Moon is in the Amsa of Mars aspected by Saturn. The *Pragnakaraka* Mercury occupies a Vargottama position.

Important Events.—Sri Ramakrishna Paramahamsa was married in 1859 in his twenty-third year. The *marriage* took place in Saturn Dasa Moon Bhukti. The acquisition of a wife may happen in the Dasa or Bhukti period of a planet (*i*) occupying the 7th, (*ii*) aspecting the 7th, (*iii*) owning the 7th, (*iv*) or when the lord of Lagna transits the 7th. In this case Saturn was transiting Leo the 7th and as his Dasa was operating he brought about the marriage. The Moon aspects the 7th house and is in conjunction with the 7th lord. Hence the marriage took place in Saturn Dasa Moon Bhukti. The period between 1856 and 1864 was very important inasmuch as it was during this period that Sri Ramakrishna followed *Adwita Sadhana*. 1864 was very important because he met Totapuri an Advaitic monk at the close of this year, who influenced Ramakrishna's thoughts considerably. This occurred in the sub-period of Jupiter within the Dasa of Saturn. Mark the dispositions of Jupiter and Saturn especially the fact that Saturn is not subject to any malefic aspects or conjunction but on the other hand is aspected by Jupiter the divine planet. Saturn, though classified as an evil planet, will give real knowledge and he alone can give real renunciation.

Remarks.—Ramakrishna's life was a web of spirituality. The mysticism and devotion to God and peculiar psychic experiences which may be called the full realisation of God in this life may be explained from the concentration of the Sun, the Moon and Mercury in Aquarius—which also happens to be the Lagna and the whole combination deriving the aspect of Jupiter. To Sri Ramakrishna the Divine Mother-Kali represented the highest and the absolute. He saw through illusory nature of the universe with the search-light of his own discrimination under the direction of an illumined Guru (Master) and developed by constant renunciation and meditation, an unshakable faith in his essential identity with the impersonal God. Mars is exalted in the 12th house whereas the forces released from

Jupiter (*gnana* or knowledge), Mercury (*buddhi* or intellect), the Sun (*atma* or soul), the Moon (*manas* or *mind*) have all been focussed on *Aquarius*—a philosophical sign. Ramakrishna's life was therefore a beacon light meant to illumine the upward path of human civilisation and direct it towards a great world-wide spiritual awakening. The horoscope is full of significance for a student of astrology.

No. 29.—BANGALORE SURYANARAIN RAO

Birth Details. — Born on 12th February 1856 at about 12-21 p.m. (L.M.T.) (Lat. 18° N., Long. 84° E.)

Planetary Positions. — The Sun 301° 12′ ; the Moon 18° 29′ ; Mars 180° 53′ ; Mercury 308° 27′ ; Jupiter 321° 38′ ; Venus 260° 33′ ; Saturn 63° 20′ ; Rahu 6° 9′ ; Ketu 186° 9′ ; and Lagna 43° 9′.   Ayanamsa 20° 24′.

	Moon Rahu	Lagna	Sat.		Lagna Jupiter	Rahu	
Sun Mercury Jupiter							
	RASI				NAVAMSA		
Venus		Mars Ketu		Merc.	Ketu	Sun Saturn Venus Mars	Moon

Balance of Venus Dasa at birth : Years 12-3-9.

Special Features. — The student will at once be struck with the beautiful situation of planets free from *shashtashtaka* (6th and 8th from each other) and *dwirdwadasa* (2nd and 12th from each other) dispositions. Mark the concentration of three planets, the Sun, Mercury and Jupiter in Aquarius—a philosophical sign all in the 10th or Karmasthana from Lagna. This made him a real *Karmayogi* and a practical philosopher. Compare this combination with the Sun and Mercury in Aquarius being aspected by Jupiter in Sri Ramakrishna's horoscope given on page 160.

The Lagna is a fixed sign aspected by Mars, and the lord of Lagna derives strength only on account of his disposition in the Navamsa. Lagna is powerfully aspected by Mars. He had a magnetic personality, domineering and of very independent spirit. The Navamsa Lagna and the situation of Jupiter rendered his physical features very attractive. Both in Rasi and Navamsa, almost all the planets are in *chara rasis* or movable signs. He had a tendency to move about frequently delivering lectures and for expounding the cause so very dear to his heart. Saturn in the 2nd, Venus in the 8th and Mars and Ketu in the 7th from the Moon are indicative of not much happiness from wife. The Moon is with Rahu aspected by Mars ; though this combination gave him mental worry, it enabled him to cultivate that strength of mind and spirit of optimism which stood him in good stead at the most critical times of his life. A powerful Rajayoga is caused in the 10th house by the conjunction of Mercury and the Sun. Jupiter as a natural benefic has added dignity to the combination. This combination brought him good reputation and wide influence and made him an authority not only in astrology but in the Indian sciences and history as well. The Parivarthana (exchange of houses) between the 2nd and 9th lords (Mercury and Saturn respectively) and the disposition of Saturn who is the yogakaraka for Taurus Lagna in the 2nd enabled the native to earn considerable wealth but Saturn in the 2nd made him spend (of course on good purposes) all his earnings without saving anything.

Important Events.—Prof. B. Suryanarain Rao graduated in 1884 from the Central College, Bangalore. This took place in Sun Bhukti (Sun's sub-period) in Moon Dasa (Moon's period). The major lord owns the 4th from Lagna in Navamsa while the sub-lord owns and aspects the 4th from Lagna. THE ASTROLOGICAL MAGAZINE was founded in 1895, in Rahu Dasa Jupiter Bhukti and the magazine had a very checked career until it was taken over and restarted by the present Editor. The first wife's death took place in Venus Bhukti within Rahu Dasa. Rahu as a shadowy planet should give the results of Mars, and Mars owns the 7th and occupies the 7th from the Moon. The sub-lord Venus owning the 2nd and the 7th from Chandra Lagna occupies the 8th. Rahu, Jupiter and Saturn built up his career and gave him international reputation. Jupiter is a maraka for Taurus Lagna. Prof. Rao fell seriously ill and his life was in danger at the end of Jupiter Dasa. A great grandson was born in the Moon Bhukti in Saturn Dasa. His own death took place under the same directions. Saturn became a maraka as occupying the 2nd from Lagna and the 3rd from the Moon in Rasi and 7th from Lagna in Navamsa. The Moon became capable of killing him as owning the 3rd and placed in the 12th from Lagna.

Remarks.—Prof. B. Suryanarain Rao was a versatile genius. He was not only a scholar in astrology but equally well versed in Sanskrit, Law and History. Mercury, the Sun and Jupiter all posited in the 10th gave him a fertile intellect. His mastery of the English language was superb. His faith in God was firm and implicit. Three planets in *Karmasthana* particularly Jupiter and Mercury made him an authority on astrology and history, and they gave him that power of intuition which made his predictions wonderfully accurate. The Sun in the 10th brought him into contact on almost equal terms with Maharajas, Governors and Viceroys. His spirit of independence and capacity in conversation and arguments were admired by all those who came in contact with him. He has written about 70 books on a variety of subjects—history, astrology, biography, novels and fiction and several of them are still unpublished. Five planets in a kendra in the Navamsa and the absence of *dwirdwadasa* situation made him a man of immense strength of mind and tremendous magnetic power. It was he who was responsible to a very large extent in creating a taste for learning in subjects like astrology and foster a spirit of 'national existence' in the intellectual sphere at a time when, due to the influence of Western education, scepticism and derision were the predominant features which characterised the majority of the then educated Indians. He was eminently proud of his culture and nationality which he was wont to carry a little aggressively. His chart reveals that he possessed a character and personality which profoundly influenced all those who came into contact with him.

No. 30.—BALA GANGADHARA TILAK

Birth Details.—*Born on 23rd July 1856 at 6–24 a.m. (L.M.T.) (Lat. 18° 32′ N., Long. 73° 53′ E.)

Planetary Positions.—The Sun 99° 55′ ; the Moon 349° 15′ ; Mars 185° 10′ ; Mercury 82° 32′ ; Jupiter 348° 44′ ; Venus 100° 24′ ; Saturn 76° 53′ ; Rahu 358° 57′ ; Ketu 178° 57′ ; and Lagna 110° 23′. Ayanamsa 20° 24′.

Moon Jupiter Rahu		Merc. Sat.	Sat. Rahu	Mercury		
		Lagna Sun Venus				
RASI			Lagna	NAVAMSA		
Mars	Ketu	Moon Jupit.	Mars	Venus		Sun Ketu

Balance of Mercury Dasa at birth : Years 13–8–14.

Special Features.—The lord of Lagna Moon in the 9th in exact conjunction with the 9th lord Jupiter denotes generosity, sincerity and courtesy of manner and confers a sound, healthy

* The data (given on page 357 of September 1908 issue of *The Astrological Magazine*) were supplied by Mr. Tilak himself to late Prof. B. Suryanarain Rao when the latter was the Lokamanya's guest in 1907 or 1908 at Poona. The time of birth is mentioned as Gh. 2.5 after sunrise.

constitution of great vitality. The Lagna is occupied by the Sun and Venus, aspected by Jupiter making the native sober and manly in address, amiable, generous, faithful, just, honest, religious and hating all mean and sordid actions. That Tilak was a man of various and no mean gifts—a great Sanskrit scholar, a powerful writer, and a strong, subtle and lucid thinker—becomes evident by the kendra positions of the intellectual Mercury and the poetic Venus in the Navamsa. The Moon-Jupiter conjunction going under the name of the Gajakesari has also produced another Rajayoga by virtue of the Moon being lord of Lagna and Jupiter being lord of the 9th. Whilst the powerful nature of the Rajayoga indicates his pride in indigenous culture, his unperturbed sense of duty, and his invincible patriotism, Rahu's association and the aspect of Saturn hardens the political life obstructing the expression of the yoga in concrete terms, *i.e.*, the actual enjoyment of the yoga results is denied. But for this affliction he might have wielded power as a great statesman. Yogakaraka Mars is in the 4th aspecting the 7th and 10th houses. This signifies a world-conquering will and determination to overcome obstacles. There are quite a number of Bandhana yogas, prominent ones being : the association of the Sun with Venus lord of the 11th in Lagna ; Saturn as lord of the 8th aspecting Lagna lord the Moon in the 9th ; Ketu posited in the constellation of the lord of the 3rd and afflicting Lagna lord ; and (in Navamsa) Lagna lord Saturn and the lord of the 8th Sun in mutual aspects and subject to Rahu-Ketu influences. Jupiter is the planet of tradition, religion and wisdom. His position in Navamsa *vis-a-vis* Lagna lord Saturn was responsible for making Tilak revive the memory of Shivaji and organising the Ganapati festivals. It was the same combination that "enabled him to effect the union of the new political spirit with the tradition and sentiment of the historic past and of both with the ineradicable religious temperament of the people''.

Important Events.—In September 1897, Tilak was sentenced to eighteen months' rigorous imprisonment. This occurred in Sun Dasa Moon Bhukti. As we have already suggested above both the Sun and the Moon have caused Bandhana Yoga, by virtue of the former joining lord of the 11th in Lagna and the latter joining Rahu in the 9th aspected by Saturn. In Rahu Bhukti he was released as Rahu could give the results of the benefic Jupiter. The split in the Congress in 1907 resulting in Tilak breaking his connections with the organisation occurred in the Moon Dasa Jupiter Bhukti while as soon as Saturn Bhukti started, he was convicted to transportation for life. How a planet, who is Lagna lord and who has caused a Rajayoga in an important house like the 9th is also capable of conferring extremely evil results in his Dasa, when subject to Rahu–Saturn effects, becomes clearly evident in regard to Tilak's horoscope. During the remaining period of Moon Dasa Tilak confined in the Fort of Mandalay, suffered from diabetes, alone and unfriended but full of fortitude. It was again under the same directional influences that some of his great monumental works, such as *Geeta Rahasya, Arctic Home of the Vedas*, etc. were produced. Mark the fact that the Moon, lord of the Dasa, is with Jupiter and in the constellation of Mercury. He was released with the dawn of Mars Dasa. It will be seen that Mars is a yogakaraka and is not subject to afflictions either by Saturn or Rahu. He aspects the 10th or house of action. In the Navamsa Mars is subject to Subhakarthari Yoga, caused by Venus and Jupiter a yogakaraka and malefic by ownership respectively. In Mercury Bhukti Mars Dasa, Tilak embarked upon a big litigation against Valentine Chirol, who called him a seditionist for defamation, went to England in this connection and the suit went against Tilak because Mercury as lord of the 3rd and 12th is in the 12th in association with lord of the 8th Saturn. He died in August 1920 as soon as Rahu Dasa commenced. Rahu is in the constellation of Mercury, who as lord of the 3rd is in the 12th in conjunction with Ayushkaraka Saturn who is also a maraka. From Chandra Lagna, Rahu aspects the 7th and Mercury is a maraka by ownership.

Remarks.—The most outstanding combinations in this horoscope are : the glorified position of lord of Lagna in the 9th with the 9th lord and affliction of this combination by Saturn and Rahu, resulting in obstruction of the free flow of fortunate influences and the presence of Bandhana yogas or combinations for incarceration causing great suffering. Tilak suffered a lot for the country. He was a born fighter as revealed by the dominating position of Mars and he will be remembered for ever for the inspiring legacy that he has left to India in the thought "Swaraj is my birthright". He was essentially a man of religion as revealed by the position of Jupiter. It may be asked whether Jupiter–Rahu association has not caused *Guru-Chandala Yoga*. The answer would be that the yoga stands neutralised by the fact that Rahu is in the constellation of Mercury and is removed from Jupiter by nearly 10°. Rahu's situation in the nakshatra of Mercury who is Mokshasthanadhipati and the entire combination receiving the aspect of Saturn from Mokshasthana gave him a living faith in God. Otherwise, he would not have said at the time of his conviction that 'there are higher powers that rule the destinies of things and it may be the will of Providence that the cause which I represent should prosper more by my suffering than by my remaining free". Arishta yogas for suffering evenly balanced with Rajayogas and Lagna and Lagna lord fully fortified reveal Tilak's stainless purity of life, immense sacrifice in the cause of the country, deep devotion to the people and principles, and the moral stuff and quality of the man which left him uncrowned king of India.

No. 31.—GEORGE BERNARD SHAW

Birth Details.—Born on 26th July 1856 A.D. at about midnight (Lat. 53° 2' N., Long. 6° 16' W.)

Planetary Positions.—The Sun 103° 36' ; the Moon 44° 36' ; Mars 186° 36' ; Mercury 88° 36' ; Jupiter 348° 36' ; Venus 105° 36'; Saturn 77° 36' ; Rahu 358° 14' ; Ketu 178° 14' ; and Lagna 44° 36'. Ayanamsa 20° 24'.

Rahu Jupiter		Moon Lagna	Merc. Sat.	Rahu Sat.		Lagna Moon	Mercury
			Sun Venus				
RASI				NAVAMSA			
						Sun Venus Mars	
	Mars	Ketu	Jupit.				Ketu

Balance of the Moon Dasa at birth : Years 6-6-18.

Special Features.—The Lagna, the Moon, Mercury and Rahu have all occupied Vargottama positions, and this is a unique feature. Mercury, the planet of intelligence and intellect, and Jupiter, the planet of wisdom, have been posited in their own houses while the Moon, the planet for mind, is exalted. Lord of Lagna is with the Sun aspected by Jupiter while in the

Navamsa, lord of Lagna aspects Lagna. The position of Mercury in his own sign in the 2nd or house of intelligence indicates Shaw's rapidly working mind and Saturn's association suggests his tantalising yet charming perversity. The same disposition of Mercury made him a witty conversationalist giving him his paradoxical and extremely complex nature. Mercury is in the house of wealth elevated by Vargottama and his association with the 9th and 10th lord Saturn—a yogakaraka for this horoscope—is suggestive of his financial gains and public favour through writing ; Mercury also gave him the power of searching analysis. Venus in conjunction with the 4th lord made him a successful music and art critic. The Moon (mind) aspected by Mars, Mercury (intelligence) associated with Saturn and Jupiter (wisdom) associated with Rahu and aspected by Saturn (both in Rasi and Navamsa) made him a "crank and visionary". Shaw's mother was a powerful factor in his life and the Moon's presence in Lagna accounts for this. The benefic disposition of Matrukaraka gave good longevity to his mother. The typical *Rajayoga* indicated by Lagna and the Moon being in Vargottama and aspected by three planets in Navamsa suggests Shaw's early difficulties, how he tried very hard to make a living with his pen and how a slow ascent in his fortunes began. The Sun, ruling vitality, is so completely free from malefic associations or aspects that Shaw possessed very good health and spirits. The Sun, the Moon and the ascendant forming as they do, the tripod of life, are very well disposed as to give him that gorgeous optimism for life. The presence of *Kahala Yoga* made him noble, benevolent, kind and respected. The *Dama Yoga* made him liberal and a bene-factor. Jupiter in the 11th with Rahu (forming more or less *Guru Chandala Yoga*) made him a religionist or philosopher, his philosophy sometimes taking perverse shape. He had no issues and this is corroborated by the presence of Ketu in the 5th house, the fifth lord's conjunction with Saturn and Putrakaraka being associated with Rahu. Mark the affliction in the 5th house in the Navamsa also.

Important Events.—In Rahu Dasa, he had smallpox which left him unscared. From then on, he became an opponent of vaccination. His real financial prosperity began only from Jupiter Dasa and Venus Bhukti. Jupiter is Dhanakaraka and occupies the 11th and Venus as lord of Lagna is in an upachaya. Rahu Dasa extended till 1888 and Rahu enabled him to expand his intellectual outlook. Between 1876–1885 he wrote five novels. He married in 1898 in Jupiter Dasa Venus Bhukti. Venus is Lagna lord and Kalatrakaraka while Jupiter is in the 9th from Venus. In the Navamsa Venus is in the 7th while Jupiter lord of Dasa, is in the 8th (house of marriage thread). He won the Nobel Prize for literature in Ketu Bhukti Mercury Dasa. The sub-lord Ketu as well as the major lord Mercury are in Vargottama besides being situated in very favourable positions both from Lagna and from each other. The major lord ruling the house of intelligence and situated in the house of wealth was responsible for the financial benefits the native enjoyed. Mercury Dasa commenced in 1923 and Shaw's reputation reached a climax. The combinations for longevity are also unique—the 2nd lord is in the 2nd, the 3rd lord is in Lagna and the luminaries are free from affliction. He died in 1950 in Venus Dasa Venus Bhukti.

Remarks.—The horoscope is typical for longevity, temperate habits and intellectual attainments. Shaw was a champion of anti-vaccination and vegetarianism and had many times tilted his lance at the medical profession. He delighted in exposing the weakness of mortals but he was sincere in the goodness of man. Through his entire literary structure runs a noble and high purpose. He may have been impractical in many ways but he endeavoured to destroy false ideals and illusions which obsess mankind. For a student of astrology, the horoscope is of great significance on account of (i) Swakshetra and Vargottama disposition of planets and (ii) the benefic dispositions of the Lagna and the luminaries. Note how Mercury, Saturn and Jupiter have contributed to his literary greatness.

No. 32.—SRI NARASIMHA BHARATHI

Birth Details.—Born on 11th March 1858 at 9 p.m. (L.M.T.) (Lat. 13° N., Long. 5h. 10m. 20s.)

Planetary Positions.—The Sun 330° 23′; the Moon 283° 45′; Mars 216° 55′; Mercury 317° 53′; Jupiter 22° 58′; Venus 333° 7′; Saturn 91° 6′ (R); Rahu 327° 21′; Ketu 147° 21′; and Lagna 92° 50′. Ayanamsa 20° 26′.

Venus Sun	Jupiter		Merc.	Moon	Rahu
Mercury Rahu		Sat.			Venus Sun Saturn
	RASI			NAVAMSA	
Moon		Ketu	Lagna		
	Mars	Lagna	Ketu	Jupiter	Mars

Balance of the Moon Dasa at birth : Years 7-2-7.

Special Features.—Libra rising conferred a sweet and gentle nature. The lord of Lagna Venus is exalted and free from any affliction thereby rendering the horoscope very strong. Mercury's disposition in the 5th or house of intelligence endowed His Holiness with a cool, clear intellect while Jupiter's powerful aspect on Lagna gave him a great sense of justice.

Mars occupies the 2nd or house of speech, the house being his own, while from Chandra Lagna, the 2nd is occupied by both Mercury and Rahu. These dispositions rendered the native eloquent and persuasive making him at the same time a bit short-tempered. The Moon is doubtless in an evil Rasi and aspected by an evil planet. But yet, as the Moon is in his own constellation and in a favourable Navamsa, the subject had a mind capable of mastering recondite philosophical doctrines, and inclined to subtle and abstruse studies. As the horoscope relates to a sage. we shall confine our attention only to certain relevant Bhavas. The house of intelligence falls in the mystic sign of Aquarius associated with the spiritual planet Rahu. Whilst this is indicative of an intense mental struggle for breaking the cords of attachment from this world, it nevertheless made the subject a very learned man greatly advanced in tapas and yoga and commanding the real admiration of all classes of people. Saturn the yogakaraka occupies the 10th house aspected by the Moon, lord of the 10th. This is one of the most important yogas—Raja, as well as Parivraja, especially that there is Parivarthana between these two planets. Saturn as lord of Lagna in Navamsa aspects Lagna and has obtained a Vargottama position. This is a unique combination indicative of great influence, wealth and power, all of which he wielded not for personal gain or pomp but because of the fact he symbolised the spiritual aspirations of millions of Hindus.

Important Events.—The first and the most important event we have to consider is his ascending the pontifical throne of Sringeri in 1868 in Mars Dasa Mercury Bhukti. Mars is lord of the 2nd (and 7th) and occupies the 2nd unafflicted, while from Chandra Lagna, as lord of the 4th he occupies the 11th.

Mercury, the sub-lord, owns the 9th from the Moon and Lagna and occupies the 5th and 2nd respectively, besides occupying a favourable place from the major lord. These dispositions justify his "inheriting" the spiritual throne with all the attendant paraphernalia. The next important event is the installation of Sri Sankara and Sri Sarada at Kaladi in Saturn Dasa and Mercury Bhukti (1910). Saturn is the most important planet in this horoscope. He is a yogakaraka and his having caused Parivarthana with the 10th lord is suggestive of the activities. His Holiness engaged himself in. Beginning from 1910 he made a long tour of South India. This brought him great name and fame and earned for the mutt great respect. Saturn occupies a movable Rasi and is Vargottama and therefore the results he gave during his Dasa were consistent with the nature of his ownership and location. His Holiness died in 1912 when Ketu Bhukti in Saturn Dasa was operating. It will be seen that Saturn is in marakasthana from Chandra Lagna in Rasi while Ketu is in the 8th from the Moon, the major and sub-lords being disposed in *Dwirdwadasa* from each other. In the Navamsa again, Saturn occupies a maraka house while Ketu is in the 8th from Chandra Lagna.

Remarks.—His Holiness was noted not only for maintaining unsullied the noble, religious and moral traditions of the most important seat af Adi Sankaracharya but also for his own great intellectual and yogic achievements. He was a profound thinker and a man of broad intellectual gifts and this is clearly brought out by the situation of Mercury in the 5th house. The 9th from Karakamsa is aspected by Jupiter. This acquires a vital meaning, as it brings to light the fact that His Holiness had truth as his ideal and motto. The Moon is in the 12th from Karakamsa ; while the 4th from Karakamsa is aspected by Mercury. These two combinations symbolise spiritual creativeness and transcendental activity making him a Paramahamsa.

As Jupiter has joined the 5th from Karakamsa, he became highly proficient in Vedic literature and Vedanta. It will be seen that lord of the 4th (intellect) in Navamsa is in the 9th (religious faith and dharma). No wonder he became a great exponent of dharma through intellectual appeal. Summing up, a student of astrology must note (a) the disposition of Mercury, Jupiter and the Moon from Karakamsa, (b) Mercury's situation in the 5th from Lagna and the exaltation of lord of the 5th from the Moon, (c) Gajakesari Yoga, and (d) the powerful Parivarthana caused by the disposition of the 10th lord in the 4th and the 4th lord in the 10th in Vargottama. The Moon ruling the mind is in a malefic sign aspected by a malefic planet. This suggests a conflict between the forces of evil and those of good in the initial stages of life and the triumph of the spirit, especially that the natural Atmakaraka Sun is in a benefic sign. The Mercury-Rahu association must have contributed its share to distract the subject in his spiritual and yogic adventures but because the combination has occurred in a mystic sign and in the 12th from the Atmakaraka Sun, it made this man a seeker after illumination through original ways— through paths of individual mysticism. Mark the position of Ketu in the 12th in Navamsa, denoting moksha or final liberation.

Here is a horoscope in which a typical Rajayoga has expressed itself in terms of Parivraja, especially because of the fact, that the Yogakaraka Saturn is in the 10th while the lord of Dharmasthana is so placed, that the native could only enjoy the spiritual aspect of the Rajayoga. The horoscope suggests that while the Swamiji was by nature a recluse and an ascetic eager to lead a life of contemplation and meditation, rich in intellectual study and creative activity, he had been forced by his Karma, perhaps against his personal propensities, to assume a position of public authority and leadership in matters of religion.

Birth Details.—Born on 30th November 1858 A.D. at 4–25 p.m. (L.M.T.) (Long. 90° 2′ E., Lat. 23° 33′ N.)

Planetary Positions.—The Sun 227° 1′; the Moon 170°; Mars 291° 52; Mercury 243° 48′; Jupiter 56° 39′; Venus 247° 38; Saturn 111° 17′; Rahu 312° 49; Ketu 132° 49′; and Lagna 32°. Ayanamsa 20° 26′.

RASI

	Lagna Jupiter		
Rahu			Sat.
Mars			Ketu
Mercury Venus	Sun		Moon

NAVAMSA

		Mercury	Moon Venus
			Mars Ketu
Rahu Lagna Sat.			Jupiter
Sun			

Balance of the Moon Dasa at birth : Years 2–3–0.

Special Features.—The Lagna is strong as Venus, its lord, is in association with Mercury lord of the 2nd and 5th and Lagna is occupied by the benefic Jupiter. From Chandra Lagna, the horoscope gains considerable strength. The association of Mercury (Lord of the 1st and 10th from Chandra Lagna) and Venus (lord of the 2nd and 9th from the Moon) in the 4th aspecting the 10th from Chandra Lagna is a powerful combination indicating that Jagadish Bose showed a marked bent towards inventions from a very early age. Bose attained acknowledged distinction in physics but his sphere of activities extended to the domain of physiology also. He brought to light many of the activities pertaining to plant life. Look at the Parivarthana or exchange of houses between Venus (lord of the house of speech, fortune and intellect) and Jupiter (lord of the house of education and the karaka of wisdom) with reference to Chandra Lagna. The 2nd, 4th, 5th and 9th houses are important in assessing the intellectual greatness and worth of an individual. The exaltation of Mars (ignoring for the time being the evil due to his 3rd and 8th lordship) in the 5th from the Moon and in direct aspect to lord of the 5th from the Moon is another important combination. From Lagna, Mars is in the 10th Bhava while Saturn is in the 4th Bhava. Bose's eminence in his own field is due not a little to the position of Mars in the 10th in exaltation along with Rahu. The Moon is aspected by Saturn as well as Jupiter. He was the victim of prejudice and race discrimination. Saturn's aspect over the Moon must have given him lot of worry but Jupiter's aspect enabled him to cultivate that strength of mind which is so very essential for achieving great objects. He had to encounter a lot of opposition from other scientists who did not relish his intrusion into the domain of physiology. Rahu in the 6th from the Moon is mainly responsible for this. Bose's paper 'The Electric Response' was under consideration for publication. But on the ground that Bose refused to change the name of the paper from 'Electric Response' to 'Certain Physical Reactions' the paper was rejected by the Royal Society. This had its own reactions (of course temporarily) on his scientific reputation, because the public could not know that prejudice

and personal antipathy were behind this rejection. Rahu in the
5th enabled him to overcome all opposition. Truth prevailed in
the end and his theories were accepted. Even the Royal Society
is not without its shade of vanity of learning. The house of
profession is very well fortified from Chandra Lagna and the
Subhavesi Yoga from the Sun has contributed not a little to his
inventive genius. Jupiter in the 2nd house made Bose a clear,
forceful and convincing speaker. Jupiter in the Lagna Rasi
rendered him intensely human who could see deeply that the
essential brotherhood of man was a growing reality and not a
mere abstraction.

Important Events.—He passed his B.A. in the sub-period
of the Moon in Rahu Dasa. Rahu is strongly entrenched in
his own star aspecting the 4th; while the Moon, sub-lord, is in
the 5th. The latter part of Jupiter Dasa witnessed the expansion
of his intellectual activities. The Dasa of Jupiter was a period
of expansion while that of Saturn was one of consolidation. It
was in the year 1896 (Jupiter Dasa Venus Bhukti) that he
sent the result of his research to the Royal Society. Mark the
dispositions of Jupiter and Venus from Chandra Lagna. In Venus
sub-period the University of London conferred on Bose the
degree of Doctor of Science. The Sun Bhukti was equally
important as it was during the Sun's sub-period that he was
first asked to deliver before the Royal Society, the Friday even-
ing discourse. The Sun is lord of the 4th and is in the 7th both
from Lagna and the major lord, and in the 3rd from the Moon.
His reputation reached its zenith in the course of Mercury Dasa.
His death took place in Ketu Dasa. Ketu being a spadowy planet
must give the results of the Sun who in turn is in the 7th from
Lagna and in the 3rd from the Moon.

Remarks.—Bose's horoscope is interesting for the simple reason that we seek to find in it combinations which made him a genius and an inventor. His discovery proves that there is no sharp dividing line between the nervous life of plants and animals. All the three benefics Mercury, Jupiter and Venus are completely free from malefic association or affliction and they are placed in beneficial signs. These three benefics indicating knowledge, intelligence and wisdom have brought about a link between Lagna, the 2nd, 4th, 9th and 10th houses from Chandra while Mars and Saturn have been disposed equally favourably. Saturn is the real philosopher and his aspecting the 10th Bhava makes Bose a great philosopher—rather a scientific mystic. Aquarius is in the cusp of the 10th house, and Rahu's presence there made him highly philosophical. Both Rahu and Aquarius are idealistic and have great affinity for invention, research and invisible things. Hence J. C. Bose astonished the world with the results of his discoveries, first on the property of invisible electric rays, then in revealing the inner and invisible activities of plant-life and finally in establishing the unique generalisations of the unity of all life—a truth already perceived by the great Maharshis of Aryavartha.

No. 34.—HAVELOCK ELLIS

Birth Details.—Born on 2nd February 1859 at 8-30 a.m. (L.M.T.) (Lat. 51° 22′ N., Long. 0° 6′ W)

Planetary Positions.—The Sun 292° 34′ ; the Moon 285° 4′ ; Mars 340° 34′ ; Mercury 270 34′ ; Jupiter 51° 4′ ; Venus 247° 34′ ; Saturn 108° 4′ ; Rahu 310° 4′ ; Ketu 130° 4′ ; and Lagna 307° 4′.   Ayanamsa 20° 26′.

Mars	Jupiter			Moon	Venus
Lagna Rahu		Sat.			Sun Jupiter Ketu
	RASI			NAVAMSA	
Sun Moon Mercury		Ketu	Merc. Rahu		
Venus			Sat. Lagna	Mars	

Balance of the Moon Dasa at birth :   Years 6–2–12.

Special Features.—The Lagna is Kumbha or Aquarius, a mystic sign and Rahu the planet of mystery is in conjunction with the rising sign. This is significant. Classical books on astrology suggest that when Rahu is in Lagna, it inclines one to "appear rather odd and eccentric". It is no wonder therefore that Havelock Ellis was, in the late Victorian era, "the rebel, the lone distrusted path-finder, probing into the things the Victorians preferred to consign to secrecy". Consistent with the nature of Aquarius, he was "reserved and shy" and in his avoidance of the public he had a record of never having made a public speech. Lord of the 2nd, Jupiter, is in a kendra in the constellation of the 6th lord Moon, aspecting the 10th or Karmasthana showing that his bent was that of a philosopher in his own way. Yogakaraka Venus, the planet of sex, is actually in the 10th Bhava in the constellation of Ketu. This disposition gives a clue to the subject-matter of his studies and specialisation. Mercury, the planet of intellect, and lord of the 5th or house of intelligence in the 11th Bhava suggests that Ellis brought to bear upon his writings literary brilliance, sharp intelligence and daring wit. The disposition of the political planets—the Sun and the Moon—lords of the 7th and 6th respectively in the 12th aspected by Saturn is an unfortunate combination which involved him in trying lawsuits, brought against him by the authorities for his 'obscene writings'. It will be seen that *Anapha Yoga* caused by Venus is a signature of fame through the sources ruled by Venus, *viz.*, sex. Mark the fact that Mars as lord of the 10th is in the 2nd aspecting the 5th. He qualified for the medical profession and for a short time he engaged in general practice, but abandoned it for literary work. Mars is also the planet of sex and his kendra position from the karaka of sex, *viz.*, Venus gave him courage to attack the problem of sex with a realism which was as acute as his idealism. The Moon, karaka of mind, is with the Sun in the 12th, a house of spirituality aspected by the philosophical Saturn and in association with Mercury. This combination made his mind synthetic and detached. It will be noted that he searched the extremes of the thoughts of others but maintained his own equilibrium.

Important Events.--When he was having Rahu Dasa Jupiter Bhukti, Ellis made a journey to Australia with his father which made a tremendous impression upon his young mind. Rahu and Jupiter are in mutual kendras, Jupiter's position, as lord of the 2nd having reference to the 4th or house of education. As soon as Saturn Bhukti commenced, his head became full of sexual thoughts and he determined to devote his life to the study of sex problems. It was in Jupiter Dasa Ketu Bhukti that proceedings were instituted against Ellis for his *Studies in the Psychology of Sex*, "a wicked, bawdy, scandalous and obscene book". Ellis himself was not molested. Jupiter is in the constellation of the 6th lord Moon while Ketu is strongly disposed in the 7th justifying the litigation. With the advent of Mercury Dasa, the native began emerging from the "shadowy regions of sex heresy into light of world recognition". Mercury as lord of the 5th is ideally placed in the 11th Bhava. From Chandra Lagna, he owns the 9th house and occupies the Chandra Lagna, being aspected by Jupiter. In the Navamsa again, Mercury is strongly disposed. Havelock Ellis died in Mercury Dasa, Saturn Bhukti. It will be seen that the major lord Mercury owns the 8th and has joined the Moon, lord of the 6th and the Sun, lord of the 7th a powerful maraka and is aspected by Jupiter, another maraka. The sub-lord Saturn is, of course, in the 7th or house of death.

Remarks.—Unless the Moon and Saturn are involved in some sort of mutual aspect, real achievement in life—political, social or intellectual—cannot be attained. Saturn is the planet of discipline and the Moon is the planet of emotions. When they are in association or mutual aspect, it means severe discipline of the mind to the point of making impressions. In this horoscope, such a configuration is present involving not only the

Moon and Saturn, but also the Sun, Mercury and Saturn. Rahu is the planet of repugnance. As Rahu is in Lagna, the native's writings at first roused repugnance of the ordinary reader. But as he came under the directional influences of Mercury, his works began to be adjudged without prejudicial heat. Whether or not books like Ellis' *Studies* can benefit married people by their frank discussion of intimate aspects of married life or they are likely to occasion lascivious thoughts and create in the minds of the readers, especially the youth, lustful desires the native was considered the foremost authority in the psychology of sex and his *Studies in the Psychology of Sex* are a classic of their kind. It is the disposition of Rahu in the mystic sign of Aquarius, which is the Lagna and the presence of Saturn Lagna lord in Rahu's constellation that made Havelock Ellis what he was in the field of sex-psychology.

No. 35.—RABINDRANATH TAGORE

Birth Details.—Born on 7th May 1861 at 2-51 a.m. (L.M.T.) (Lat 22° 40′ N., Long. 88° 30′ E.)

Planetary Positions.—The Sun 25° 48′ ; the Moon 351° 59′ ; Mars 61° 36′ ; Mercury 9° 18′ ; Jupiter 117° 24′ ; Venus 24° 32′ ; Saturn 132° 37′ ; Rahu 266° 17′ ; Ketu 86° 17′ ; and Lagna 336° 9′.   Ayanamsa 20° 28′.

Moon Lagna	Venus Sun Mercury		Ketu Mars	Jupit.		Ketu	Mercury
			Jupit.				Saturn
	RASI		---	NAVAMSA			---
			Sat.	Moon			Lagna
Rahu				Rahu Sun Venus	Mars		

Balance of Mercury Dasa at birth :   Years 16–2–20.

Special Features.—Tagore's intellectual aristocracy is brought out by the Parivarthana Yoga (interchange of houses) between lords of Lagna and the 5th, *viz.*, Jupiter and the Moon respectively and the exaltation of lord of Lagna in the 5th. The karaka of the mind who is also lord of the 5th is not only unafflicted but is highly fortified, conferring an intuitive and

Mark again the position of Rahu in the 10th. This is a good combination. As soon as Rahu Dasa commenced, there was a windfall in the shape of the poet getting an annual endowment of Rs. 5,000 for rural reconstruction work. Rahu is capable of giving the excellent results of Jupiter. It was again during Rahu Dasa that the poet toured Europe, America and Japan. He met the great intellectuals of these countries—authors, statesmen and thinkers. In conformity with his philosophy which advocates a synthesis between the East and West he founded the intellectual university of Viswabharathi. The Bhukti of Jupiter in his own Dasa, consistent with the ideal position of Jupiter in the horoscope, was one of the most richly creative periods of his life. It is said that he was able, even in his sick-bed, to write not only several books of poems and addresses but also a short autobiography. And finally his death took place in Jupiter Dasa Jupiter Bhukti. Ordinarily Jupiter as lord of Lagna could not confer maraka results, but here Jupiter occupies the constellation of Mercury, a powerful maraka, both by ownership and occupation and hence Jupiter gets the power to kill.

Remarks.—In Tagore's horoscope, there is a unique blending of the influences of the emotional and intellectual Mercury, the philosophical Jupiter, the poetic Venus and the political Sun. The Moon's position in the 11th from Jupiter in Navamsa indicates fame and renown. Because of the exaltation of Lagna lord Jupiter in a trikona which constitutes *Parvatha Yoga*. Tagore was known and respected throughout the world. His writings embody the compressed wisdom of a lifetime, a lifetime, of intense religious introspection and experience. Mark the presence of the lords of Lagna and the 4th in movable signs. The poet travelled practically throughout the world. It is the prominent position of Jupiter and the presence of the outstanding yogas of *Parijatha* and *Saraswati* that were responsible for his greatness as a seer, as an upholder of moral values and as a teacher.

No. 36.—SRI SWAMI VIVEKANANDA

Birth Details.—*Born on 12th January 1863 at 6-33 p.m. (L.M.T.) (Lat. 22° 40′ N., Long. 88° 30′ E.)

Planetary Positions.—The Sun 270° 52′ ; the Moon 168° 54′ ; Mars 7° 46′ ; Mercury 283° 13′ ; Jupiter 185° 28′ ; Venus 278° 32′ ; Saturn 165° 2′ ; Rahu 233° 41′ ; Ketu 53° 41′ ; and Lagna 267° 31′. Ayanamsa 20° 30′.

	Mars	Ketu			Venus Mercury	Saturn	Moon Mars
				Rahu			
Mercury Sun Venus	RASI			Sun	NAVAMSA		Ketu
Lagna	Rahu	Jupiter	Moon Sat.	Lagna	Jupiter		

Balance of the Moon Dasa at birth : Years 3-3-27.

Special Features.—The ascendant or Lagna is Sagittarius or Dhanus, a war-like and common sign. The lord Jupiter is in the 10th house (though in the 11th Rasi) and is powerfully aspected by Mars lord of the 5th and hemmed inbetween Rahu on one side and the Moon and Saturn on the other. The Lagna is Vargottama as also the Sun. The predominance of

---

* For data we are indebted to late Mr. F. C. Dutt of Calcutta and Sri Ramakrishnashrama of Madras.

Jupiterian factors *pius* the powerful aspect of Mars over lord of Lagna indicate his athletic form, his inclination towards corpulence, and his tall stature. The 3rd lord Saturn is in a common sign, and the 4th is occupied by Mars. He was therefore square shouldered, broad chested and rather heavily built. The fine disposition of Lagna lord, and Jupiter's Navamsa rising, gave the Swami an olive complexion, a full face, a vast forehead and a sparkling personality. The fortunes are dualistic in keeping with the dual nature of both Janma and Chandra Lagnas. One of the netrakarakas (indicators of eyes) in Lagna and the Rasi dispositions of Venus in the 2nd gave him a pair of magnificent eyes, large, dark and rather prominent with heavy lids whose shape recalled the classic comparison to a lotus petal. Though a sanyasi, his prominent characteristic was kingliness, so well denoted by the position of the Sun in Lagna Bhava, itself being a war-like sign. Whatever may be the views of his biographers, associates and admirers, the strong currents of Mars, the Sun and ascendant accentuate the impulsive and head-strong tendencies of the sign as a whole, while at the same time, Jupiter's excellent disposition combined with the static influence of the third Drekkana of Sagittarius quickens the intuitional and inspirational nature giving an ability to prophecy and foresee the future. He was a born orator and his rich, deep and beautiful voice is brought out by the disposition of Jupiter in the 2nd from Chandra Lagna. Mercury, who was responsible, not a little in making the Swami a great speaker, is abutting on the 2nd house. The concentration of the Sun, Mercury, Venus, Mars and Jupiter influences in regard to Lagna is deeply significant and explains the fact that his glance, whilst capable of sparkling with

wit, irony or kindness, could easily lose itself in ecstasy. His
majesty comes into bold relief by the disposition of the Lagna.
The second lord Saturn is in the 9th house with the Moon in an
inimical sign. Though Jupiter is in the 2nd from Chandra Lagna,
it is aspected by Mars lord of the 3rd and 8th and Jupiter is
rendered weak as a kendra lord. The 4th Bhava is occupied by
Mars lord of the 5th or house of intelligence which in its turn
is powerfully aspected by Jupiter lord of Lagna. These combinations reveal the rare potentialities with which he was
endowed. If there were no Jupiter's rays blending the powerful aggressive influences of Mars, in regard to the fourth and
fifth houses, his tremendous energy would not have been
directed in a spiritual channel and would certainly have been
misused. The 6th house representing debts, diseases and
enemies is occupied by Ketu while the 6th lord is in Lagna.
There is no other benefic aspect on this. This gave him a lot of
opposition : Vivekananda's success, in his first address to the
Parliament of Religions, roused bitter rancour amongst the
Christian missionaries and sharpened the jealousy of certain
Hindu representatives. Saturn's situation in the 6th in Navamsa
is equally significant ; as a result of the 6th house disposition,
Vivekananda was the buttend of considerable malevolent
interpretations. Venus, lord of the 6th and 11th, in the ascendant, with Mercury lord of a kendra, must have made him
misunderstood by his adversaries whose bitterness did not stop
short of the use of the most dishonourable weapons. The
Moon–Saturn conjunction denotes lot of mental conflict and
agitation. For instance, this combination, occurring in a
sensitive sign like Virgo, gave him the capacity to realise the
relativity of virtue and broadened his moral conceptions. The
7th house ruling sensual passions is free from affliction ; nor

has Venus been rendered evil. In the Navamsa, whilst Venus is exalted and pure, being aspected by Jupiter, the 7th is occupied by Mars. This fine disposition should have really made him control his senses and he must doubtless have been a true Brahmachari. The scornful lesson, taught to Christian missionaries in America that they were not Christians in the true sense, made some of them spread infamous calumnies of the Swami's life in America. When Venus is well situated, the indication is clear that the Swami did actually sublimate his sensual desires and he could never have been guilty of the charge made by a vulgar-minded clergyman that the Swami had wronged a servant dismissed by the Governor of Michigan. We are referring to this little yet important incident, in order to impress upon the readers that the disposition of Venus testifies to the moral dignity of Vivekananda. The 8th house being aspected by Mars and lord of Lagna subjected to *Papakarthari Yoga*, coupled with the association of the Moon lord of the 8th with Ayushkaraka, did not give him good longevity.

Important Events.—From an astrological point of view, the first and the foremost important event is the death of Vivekananda's father in 1884. This occurred in Ketu Bhukti Rahu Dasa. Mars whose results Rahu should give is in the 8th from the 9th (house of father) and 12th from Pitrukaraka. In the Navamsa, Rahu is in the 7th from the 9th and in the 2nd from Pitrukaraka. Ketu the sub-lord is in the 6th from Pitrukaraka and in the 9th from Lagna Navamsa. These positions are enough to deprive the native of his father. The next event that profoundly influenced the subject is the passing away of his Guru Sri Ramakrishna Paramahamsa. This occurred in 1886 in the sub-period of Venus, Rahu Dasa. It will be seen that Venus by virtue of being a member of the satellitium formed in Lagna, which has given rise to a powerful Parivraja Yoga, was instrumental in a large measure, in making Vivekananda the successor to the spiritual gadi of Ramakrishna. Rahu is in Mokshasthana (12th) and is capable of bestowing spiritual leadership. The end of Rahu Dasa and the beginning of Jupiter Dasa saw him in a frenzy. He was seized by a sacred madness to escape. As soon as Mars sub-period commenced, he left alone without a companion for a tour all over India. Rahu in the 12th was solely responsible in kindling the innermost springs of spirituality. Mars and Rahu are in *shashtashtaka* (6th and 8th from each other). From Chandra Lagna, Mars is in the 8th and Rahu in the 3rd. These are unfavourable positions. Even Jupiter is ill disposed in an inimical place from Chandra Lagna. No wonder therefore that for two years (end of Rahu and the first year of Jupiter), he lived in a seething cauldron ; he suffered from hunger, from thirst, from murderous nature and insulting man. Probably these experiences were necessary to make him fit for the fulfilment of the mission. The end of Rahu Dasa was therefore a period of intense preparation in the direction of spiritual realisation. He left India for America in May 1893 just before the end of Jupiter Bhukti in Jupiter Dasa. He addressed the Parliament of Religions in Chicago in September 1893 in the sub-period of Saturn. In Vivekanand's horoscope, Saturn, Rahu and Jupiter are the tripod of spiritual life. Jupiter, the major lord, is in the constellation of Mars, ruling the 12th while Saturn is in Hasta ruled by the Moon. Saturn as lord of the 2nd is in the 9th house (though in the 10th Rasi). He was now in danger of being overwhelmed by riches. American snobbery threw itself upon him. But, as Saturn has also caused Parivraja Yoga, Vivekananda was able to put up stout resistance aganist these distractions. In fact, he stigmatised the vices and crimes of the Wastern civilsation with its characteristics of violence, pillage and destruction. Mercury is an intellectual planet. The disposition between Mercury, the sub-lord, and Jupiter the major lord is harmonious. While Mercury represents intellect, Jupiter rules wisdom. From karakamsa, Mercury is in the 11th. It was therefore during this sub-period that he was able to meet and contact such celebrated thinkers and intellectuals as Maxmuller, Deussen and Tesla. Ketu Bhukti was remarkable because it was during this sub-period that the Swami went to Amarnath. Ketu's presence in the 9th from Chandra Lagna is full of astrological significance. His second trip to Europe and America was the period between June 1899 to December 1900, in the Bhukti of Venus. Venus is in Capricorn a movable sign and in the 10th from Karakamsa in Pisces, a watery sign. The last and the most tragic event was of course his untimely death in the prime of life on 4-7-1902 in the sub-period of the Sun in Jupiter Dasa. Jupiter is undoubtedly a maraka because he owns the 7th from Chandra Lagna, occupies the 2nd, being subjected to *Papakarthari Yoga*. In the Navamsa he owns the 7th from Chandra Lagna and is in the 12th from Lagna. The Sun is in the 2nd from Lagna with 7th lord Mercury. Therefore, even though according to medical opinion, death was due to heart failure or apoplexy, the end was certainly peaceful, as the 8th house is completely free from affliction.

Remarks.—To an astrological student, Vivekananda's horoscope is interesting so far as the *Parivraja Yoga* is concerned. The end of Sagittarius rising, the same being owned by a benefic, and Jupiter occupying a kendra Bhava are strongly indicative of final emancipation. Another

powerful ascetic combination is that the Moon, occupying
the Drekkana of Saturn, is with Saturn in the 9th house.
Again, the presence of Rahu in the 12th is a powerful factor
while the dispositions of Jupiter and Lagna in good houses
have contributed not a little in making him a successful
ascetic. As Jupiter is in Karmasthana, Vivekananda became a
great exponent of *Advaita Vedanta* consistent with the dictum
Vedanta Gnaninamva Yativara Mamavekshya meaning that
Jupiter would make one well versed in Vedanta philosophy
or an eminent ascetic.

Viewed purely from an astrological point, we find that
whilst in Ramakrishna Paramahamsa's horoscope, the ascetic
combination has occurred in a mystic sign Aquarius which is
also his Lagna, in that of Vivekananda, the stress is on
Sagittarius, a war-like sign. This distinction gives a clue as
regards the spiritual aspirations of both. Ramakrishna's life was
a web of spirituality. The mysticism and devotion to God and
his peculiar psychic experiences, which may be called that full
realisation of God in this life, may be explained from the
concentration of the Sun, the Moon and Mercury in Aquarius.
He was God-intoxicated. On the other hand, the emphasis
laid on Sagittarius, the Moon–Saturn conjunction and the
association of Mercury and Venus in Lagna, in Vivekananda's
horoscope, suggest a more intellectual and rational approach
to problems of philosophy. There is in this approach a
blending of the intellect (Mercury) and knowledge (Jupiter).
The harmonious disposition of Mercury and Jupiter rendered
him reconcile the metaphysics of Upanishads and the profound
views of Hindu philosophers with the coneptions of Western
metaphysics and principles admitted by modern science.
The Moon-Saturn conjuuction suggests the periodic crises

traversed by this stormy genius and the mental torments he was subjected to which apparently are contradictory but really logical, and which can never be understood by ordinary men.

Any tyro in astrology would be able to recognise at once the import of the situation of three planets in Lagna. Jupiter in the 10th, Rahu in the 12th and the Moon–Saturn conjunction in the 9th and the exaltation of Venus in the 10th from Karakamsa. The Parivrajaka combination is latent. These certainly indicate his moral intransigence, his virile idealism, and his dauntless loyalty towards his self-imposed mission. The Saturn–Moon conjunction in the 9th is alone accountable for his burning love for the Absolute and the irresistible appeal of suffering humanity. Mark the *dwirdwadasa* positions in the Navamsa. Indeed he was a true patriot, a friend of the poor. Summing up, his horoscope indicates that as a thinker he evinced great speculative boldness (Sun–Mercury conjunction), that as a man he had a deep desire to make the whole world enjoy the *bliss* of the spirit, and as a patriot he showed growing eagerness to restore India to her former glory.

No. 37.—SAYAJI RAO III, GAEKWAR OF BARODA

Birth Details.—Born on 12/11th March 1863 at 2-3 a.m. (L.M.T.) (Lat. 22° 20′ N., Long. 4h 53m. E.)

Planetary Positions.—The Sun 329° 30′; the Moon 220° 31′; Mars 40° 56′; Mercury 302° 40′; Jupiter 186° 42′; Venus 351° 17′; Saturn 162° 31′; Rahu 230° 38′; Ketu 50° 38′; and Lagna 258° 40′. Ayanamsa 20° 30′.

Venus		Ketu Mars		Mars Saturn		Sun
Sun Mercury	RASI			NAVAMSA		Ketu
			Venus Rahu			
Lagna	Moon Rahu	Jupiter	Sat.	Jupit. Moon	Mercury	Lagna

Balance of Mercury Dasa at birth : Years 14–7–6.

Special Features.—Sagittarius, as Lagna, aspected powerfully by Mars, gives a healthy constitution and a temperament principally of heat and dryness. The lord of Lagna is in the 10th house (though in the 11th Rasi) subject to *Papakarthari Yoga* by being hemmed inbetween Rahu and Saturn. In Navamsa, the Lagna is free from affliction and the lord is in

the 2nd aspected by Mars and Saturn. These indicate the
prominence of martian, jupiterian and mercurian qualities making the native quiet, self-possessed and persevering. The
Moon is debilitated and is in conjunction with Rahu aspected
by Mars, Ketu and Saturn. The Moon is thus subjected
to a series of afflictions which are considerably relieved by his
Navamsa position in Sagittarius, a benefic sign with the powerful benefic Jupiter and causing a powerful Gajakesari. The
Sun, lord of the 9th, is in the 3rd with Mercury aspected by
Jupiter. These dispositions of the Sun, the Moon and Lagna,
taken collectively, ensure a strong foundation. Mars and
Jupiter give a magnetic personality, and a keen sense of his
position as an independent ruler, value of method and economy
of time. Rahu in the 12th indicates broad toleration to all
religions. The Sun–Mercury combination in Aquarius explains
the extreme activity of the brain. The Moon is practically
eclipsed. His affliction and his debilitation are noteworthy
features suggesting that the Gaekwar belonged to an ordinary
family before he was adopted. The first legend connected
with the birth of this peasant boy with a king cobra spreading
its powerful hood, offering homage and protection to the babe
is astrologically explainable by the presence of Rahu with the
Moon. The *neechabhanga* here is of more than ordinary interest
because it merges into the realm of *Maharaja Yoga* announcing
that though born as a peasant boy he was destined to become
a powerful king. The Moon is neecha (in debilitation) and the
lord of the house where the Moon would get oocha (exalted)
is in kendra from Lagna. And again, the lord of the house in
which the Moon is neecha aspects the Moon. These two
combinations constitute a distinct Rajayoga of a high order.
Mark the conjunction of the lord of the 9th (Sun) and 10th

(Mercury) in the house of courage. Lord of Lagna is in the 10th house. The 2nd lord Saturn is in the 10th and the 10th lord Mercury is in the 2nd Bhava. The 10th is aspected by exalted Venus. Thus, the influences of the 1st, 2nd, 4th, 9th, 10th and 11th are so interrelated in this horoscope that they account for the immense wealth and power the Maharaja commanded. Mark the *parivarthana* or exchange of houses between Jupiter and Venus and Mercury and Saturn. In the Navamsa again, Saturn, the Sun, Jupiter and the Moon have focussed their influences on the 10th house. The royal planets, the Sun and the Moon, have been afflicted and the circumstance made him the most hated object of the Political Department of the Government of India, not failing at the same time to make him the darling of nationalist India. The 5th lord is afflicted while Jupiter the Putrakaraka is subject to *Papakarthari Yoga*. Even in the Navamsa, the 5th house is spoiled with the result the Gaekwar was very unfortunate in regard to his children as most of them died during his life-time. Venus, Kalatrakaraka, though exalted, is in a common sign aspected by Saturn while the 7th from the Moon is occupied by Ketu and Mars. In the Navamsa again, Venus is with Rahu while the 7th from the Moon has the influences of the Sun. The relief of the evil is to be found in the 7th from Lagna (in Navamsa) being free from evil aspect, Jupiter aspecting the 7th from the Moon and Venus being exalted in Rasi. As a result, he lost his first wife and had to marry a second one. Resoluteness and wealth are shown not only by the combinations already pointed out above but also by the presence of *Malavya Yoga*. The powerful *Sunapha* and *Subhavesi* have also contributed their quota of strength to make the horoscope a decidedly powerful one.

Important Events.—Seldom did fate play a stranger trick than when she selected this little boy and placed him on the throne of Baroda. The year 1875 was the most important in the life of the subject of this horoscope because he was adopted as Raja of Baroda. This occurred at the fag end of Mercury Dasa. Mercury is lord of the 10th and he is in the 3rd house with the 9th lord. In the Navamsa again, as lord of the 10th from Chandra Lagna he is in the 11th. As soon as Saturn Bhukti started, the adoption took place. Saturn rules over the 9th or Atimitra (very friendly) star and as lord of the 2nd he is in the 10th aspected by exalted Venus. In Ketu Dasa Venus Bhukti the Gaekwar had his first marriage. The sub-lord is Kalatrakaraka while the major lord Ketu being placed in Taurus must necessarily give the results of Venus. Ketu as lord of the Sampat or favourable star was full of significance. It was in Jupiter's sub-period in Ketu Dasa that the Maharaja was invested with full ruling powers. Note Jupiter is in the 10th Bhava and Ketu is with Mars. Note also their respective positions in Navamsa. 1881 to 1885 were years of consolidation, expansion and change. With the advent of Venus Dasa, the first wife died. Venus is lord of Vipat or "dangerous" constellation and as Kalatrakaraka is considerably afflicted he caused the death of the wife and also the second marriage. Venus is in a watery and common sign in Rasi and in a movable one in Navamsa. This situation of Venus gave the Maharaja his first trip to Europe. The beginning of Venus Dasa, as could be appreciated, did produce extremely adverse results—death of wife, climax of strain, loss of health and deep mental worry. The last part of the Sun Dasa caused the death of the Maharaja's eldest son. Venus is in the 5th from the Moon and in the 5th from Lagna in Navamsa afflicted by Rahu.

It will be seen that the afflictions to the Sun and the Moon pointed out above found their expression in the last part of the Sun Dasa and in the beginning of the Moon Dasa—especially in 1911. The Moon, besides being afflicted heavily, rules over Pratyak or 'obstruction' star. The Maharaja was accused of deliberate insult to the British King by turining his back upon him during the 1911 Durbar. The charge was preposterous because through a mistake the Maharaja turned his back and no insult was ever meant to the late king. The Political Department made much of this 'sedition' and the imperious Viceroy bruised the Maharaja's sense of dignity. On account of the favourable position of the Moon in Navamsa, he was able to pass through the crisis. During Mars Dasa, the State of Baroda began to progress upon well-ordered and systematic lines, reforms were introduced and the State got a name and reputation throughout India. His Highness died in the beginning of Venus Bhukti in Rahu Dasa. Rahu is in the 12th from Lagna in Rasi and in the 2nd from the Moon in Navamsa. Rahu who should give the results of Mars owns the 5th and 12th and is in the 7th from the Moon. In Navamsa, Mars owns the 3rd and 8th and is in the 8th with Ayushkaraka Saturn. Venus the sub-lord owns the 2nd in Navamsa and occupies the 2nd from the Moon.

Remarks.—His Highness the Gaekwar's horoscope interests us because it is an illustration of an ordinary peasant boy becoming a ruler, consistent with the obtaining of certain Neechabhanga Rajayogas. The combinations for wealth present in this horoscope enable us to appreciate that the same principles can be extended to suit the horoscopes of even mediocre persons with a view to judging their financial dispositions. Superficially looked at, the Maharaja's horoscope does not present a vivid perspective of its immense potentiality. However, a careful scrutiny reveals important combinations. The position of Saturn in the 10th is of much significance to a student of astrology. Such a combination makes one a democrat, a nationalist, a patriot, a man to whom the weal of the down-trodden would be of much concern. The Gaekwar was a patriot in the truest sense of the word. The Sun and the Moon afflicted with Saturn placed in the 10th rendered his position rather delicate because his sturdy independence made him cross swords with the Government of India. The Moon's debilitation and association with Rahu rendered him worried and unhappy in spite of the great wealth and power. He had himself said once that he had never known the true felicity of domestic life such as less exalted folk enjoy. His ardent nationalism was liable to misconstruction. The Sun in Aquarius made him taciturn, the Moon in Scorpio made him sensitive and Jupiter as lord of Lagna rendered him a man of honourable intention. Mercury gave him intellectual curiosity. Immense wealth is always shown where the influences exercised by the 2nd, 1st, 9th, 10th and 11th lords are sympathetically blended. The 2nd lord in the 10th, the 10th lord in the 2nd Bhava with the 9th lord, exalted Venus in the 4th and lord of Lagna in the 11th and the Parivarthana between Venus and Jupiter and Mercury and Saturn coupled with the yogas already described show a remarkable blending of forces showing money, influence, power and opposition.

Brought as he was, an unlettered boy living in obscurity in an obscure village, to a throne where he was the master of absolute power and unlimited wealth, living only six years in an atmosphere of law and order, of high ideals and of intensive study and exposed soon after to the temptations of traditions

and customs he could easily have stepped back into bad ways.
A weakening of purpose or a slackening of moral fibre during
those critical years would have been a signal for whisper, an
insinuation, a suggestion which adroitly followed up might
have led to incalculable disaster.

Against this background, study the Gaekwar's horoscope.
Of course he shares with us the imperfections of humanity.
But you will find in him a great statesman, a kind ruler, a true
patriot and one who recognised his limits as a ruler by the
simple rule that every earthly ruler is also subject to a mightier
one.   The Indian Princes were made to feel that they were
nothing but subservient creatures of the British in India.   In
spite of this, the Gaekwar of Baroda was hailed as the ablest
(excepting of course the late Maharaja of Mysore) and the
most patriotic amongst the princely order.

No. 38.—HENRY FORD

Birth Details.—Born on 30th July 1863 at *2 p.m. (L.M T.) (Lat. 42° 5′ N., Long. 83° 5′ W.)

Planetary Positions.—The Sun 106° 34′ ; the Moon 290° 12′ ; Mars 127° 35′ ; Mercury 102° 32′ ; Jupiter 179° 56′ ; Venus 151° 44′ ; Saturn 160° 32′ ; Rahu 223° 5′ ; Ketu 43° 5′ ; and Lagna 211° 52′. Ayanamsa 20° 30′.

	Rahu		Ketu Saturn		Mars
RASI		Sun Merc.	NAVAMSA		Moon Lagna
Moon		Mars	Venus		
	Rahu Lagna	Venus Jupit. Sat.	Sun	Mercury Rahu	Jupiter (Kara-kamsa)

Balance of the Moon Dasa at birth : Years 2-4-6.

Special Features.—The Lagna being Scorpio, an insect sign, is occupied by Rahu and aspected powerfully by Mars and Saturn. Though three important malefics focus their influences on the ascendant, yet Mars and Saturn have become temporary benefics by virtue of owning the Lagna and a kendra

---

* Rectified by us as 2 hrs. 9 min. p.m.

respectively. Rahu being aspected by Saturn is in a way harmonious in the sense that their attributes, according to the dictum *Sanivudrahu*, are similar. The presence of Rahu in Lagna makes the native a deep thinker and even, when excited, of strong character. The lord of Lagna is placed in a benefic Navamsa though aspected by debilitated Saturn. The Chandra Lagna is powerful enough as the lord is in the 9th with two benefics, Venus and Jupiter—the former being a yogakaraka. The malefic influences on Lagna indicate that the early days were hard. Scorpio rising makes the native bold. The will is strong. Ford was endowed with an 'eagle eye'. The presence of Rahu pulls down and destroys existing theories and this is effected by the acute penetration of the mind. Scorpio being a secret sign and in this particular case being occupied by Rahu a reptile planet, the native possesses an insatiable thirst for finding out the secret nature of things. Mars, the planet of engineering, and Saturn, the planet of labour, aspecting Lagna, should suggest the groove in which Ford's aptitude was directed in the early days of his life and how those instincts were responsible for making him a great engineer and industrialist. Again, the fact of Scorpio rising with the influences of Rahu, Mars and Saturn converging on it suggests that Ford's imagination was fertile and his nature, very resourceful. The same combination coupled with the fact that the Moon is in Capricorn made his manners somewhat brusque but outspoken and fearless. The 6th, 8th and 12th houses are completely free from benefic and malefic occupation and this is indeed a unique combination. The presence of *Sankha Yoga* indicates philanthropy, charitable disposition and long life. *Marutha Yoga* has considerably contributed to his social, financial and professional eminence. The 4th house indicates land, real estate and all solid foundations. Saturn owning the 4th is in the 11th with yogakaraka Venus in neechabanga. This is highly significant inasmuch as it indicates the degree of position, wealth and influence which Ford attained especially during the Dasa of Saturn. The presence of the Sun lord of the 10th in the 9th and the 9th being aspected by the Moon are factors indicating how the house of fortune is powerfully fortified. This combination also hints how Ford could influence politics in his country. The situation of all the important planets excepting of course the Moon and the shadowy ones Rahu and Ketu in the 9th, 10th and 11th houses is full of astrological significance ; lord of Lagna in the 10th, the 10th lord in the 9th and the 2nd and 7th lords in the 11th suggest how the centre of gravity has been disposed. Mark the interrelations between finance (Jupiter), estate, factory and labour (Saturn) and engineering and industry (Mars) reinforced by political influence (Sun and Moon) all being further fortified by the neechabhanga of Venus. Pitrukaraka Sun in the 9th is not quite conducive to happy relations with father. Ford's father was not in sympathy with his bent towards mechanics. Mark the favourable dispositions of the 3rd and 8th lords indicating good longevity.

Important Events.—Ford says in his autobiography that he left school at the age of 17 and became an apprentice. This happened in Rahu Dasa. Rahu is placed in the house of Mars, a planet indicating fire, chemicals and factories. His marriage took place in the Moon's sub-period in Rahu Dasa when Jupiter was transiting Scorpio. Rahu is in Lagna aspecting the 7th while Jupiter, being placed in the 9th from the Moon with Kalatrakaraka Venus, gave the gain of a wife while transiting the 11th. In the Navamsa the sub-lord Moon aspects the 7th house. He completed his first motor car in 1892 as soon as Jupiter Dasa began. This was the starting point for his future prosperity. Jupiter has a unique position forming a powerful Dhana Yoga besides being the Atmakaraka. The year from 1902, which embraces the Moon Bhukti, was one of investigation because Ford worked on the development of a four-cylinder motor. It was at the fag end of Mars Bhukti that Ford Motor Company was founded and to this achievement, the *Marutha Yoga* to which we have already referred has contributed not a little. Saturn's period is indicative of steady increase in business. Mercury Dasa is again very significant because it was during Venus sub-period that Ford started to build enormous works at Dagenham,

Remarks.—As students of astrology we are concerned with the financial and professional aspects of this horoscope. Henry Ford as every one knows was a great industrialist, engineer and manufacturer of automobiles besides being one of the richest, if not the richest man in the world. The horoscope is somewhat elusive inasmuch as combinations which made him what he was financially and industrially, cannot be deciphered easily by the ordinary students of astrology. Three astrological factors making for immense wealth may be noted, *viz.*, (*a*) the presence of *Marutha Yoga*, *viz.*, Jupiter being disposed in a trine from Venus, the Moon in the 5th from Jupiter and the Sun in a Kendra from the Moon, (*b*) Mercury in Cancer and Saturn in the 11th, and (*c*) the 2nd lord in the 11th. Ford was a man of original thinking and an inventor and this is justified by the presence of the Moon in Capricorn, a movable sign, and aspected by Jupiter and in Cancer (in Navamsa) aspected by Venus. From Chandra Lagna the house of fortune is immensely fortified by Venus—the yogakaraka being neecha-bhanga and in association with Saturn, lord of Chandra Lagna. From the special Dhana Lagna (vide *How to Judge a Horoscope*) which in this case happens to be Sagittarius, three planets are situated in the 10th. The 11th is the house of gains while the 10th is the house of profession indicating the means. The 9th is the house of fortune and Mercury is the planet of trade and business. The presence of the Sun (lord of the 10th) and Mercury in the 9th gives furtune through trade and Government favour ; Mars lord of Lagna in the 10th suggests factories, burning gases, engineering, steel, iron and laboratories. While Saturn in the 11th is significant because he shows gain through mines, iron, labour, and so on, Jupiter, lord of wealth, in the 11th in this particular circumstance, suggests the afflux of wealth. The motor car is a luxury for the ordinary man. It is a *vahana* and Venus is the *Vahanakaraka*. Consistent with this, Venus being placed in the 11th with Jupiter Dhanakaraka advanced the fortune of the native through the manufacture and sale of automobiles.

Being born with the Sun and the Moon in movable signs, Ford's life had ever been one of activity. He hated red-tapism. He was highly sympathetic and was more or less a pacifist. His philosophy was practical. He believed in service. As Venus happens also to be the 12th lord, he did not believe in the theory that business is a mere money-making game, yet strangely enough he made millions. Rahu in Lagna suggests that Ford by nature must have been a man of vision—a man who saw life with a broad vision and whose approach to special problems was that of the reformer. Saturn's position in the chart gave him a spiritual and truly human perspective, a sense of the common man which transcends what is usually meant by such a phrase. Jupiter (ignoring his being lord of the 2nd) in association with Venus and Saturn in the 11th indicates that Ford was not greedy. The harmonious blending of jupiterian, solar and saturnine influences made him a capitalist yet striving for the welfare of labour, a man of active habits detesting a life of ease, actuated by fine motives and human sympathy, opposed to war, full of self-confidence and a realization of the limitations of humanity. In his *Life and Work* he says that 'service comes before profit and that the sort of business which makes the world better for its presence is a noble profession'. This is fully justified by the disposition of Jupiter in Vargottama.

No. 39.—SIR ASHUTOSH MUKERJEE

Birth Details.—Born on 29th June 1864 at about 3-55 a.m. (L.M.T.) (Lat. 22° 35′ N., Long. 88° E.)

Planetary Positions.—The Sun 76° 50′ ; the Moon 16° 19′ ; Mars 2° 39′ ; Mercury 57° 50′ ; Jupiter 207′ 36′ (R) ; Venus 71° 26′ ; Saturn 170° 59′ ; Rahu 205° 24′ ; Ketu 25° 24′ ; Mandi 266° 48′ ; and Lagna 56° 43′. Ayanamsa 20° 30′.

Mars Moon Ketu	Lagna Mercury	Sun Venus	Sun	Mars	Rahu	Jupiter
						Saturn
	RASI		Venus	NAVAMSA		Moon
Mandi	Rahu Jupiter	Sat.	Mandi	Ketu		Mercury Lagna

Balance of Venus Dasa at birth : Years 15-6-9.

Special Features—Taurus, a fixed sign, as Lagna and the lord Venus in the 2nd in conjunction with the Sun, lord of the 4th receiving the aspect of Saturn and Jupiter, Mercury fortified in Navamsa Lagna aspected by Saturn and the Sun denote that his whole look was aggressive and dominating. The impression of a powerful personality was completed by the predominance of the solar and saturnine influences on the Lagna lord tempered by those of Jupiter to some extent. His "strong broad forehead and thick shaky eyebrows" are typically suggestive of the influence of the ascending sign, viz., Taurus. The Moon is almost in conjunction with Ketu but the fact that the sign happens to be Aries, and the 12th from Lagna, removes much of the stigma due to this combination. On the other hand, the Moon gets fortified by his association with Mars and being aspected by Jupiter—thus giving rise to *Chandramangala* and *Gajakesari yogas*. This accounts for the bull-dog expression that predominated his look. The Moon's position gives a pure and fertile mind. Mercury the planet of *buddhi* is rising exactly on the ascendant and is devoid of any malefic aspect. This fine disposition of Mercury endowed him with talents of a very high order. It will be seen that while yet a boy of 12, he had developed a thirst for useful knowledge which was later on a feature of his busy, strenuous life. Lord of Lagna has the aspect of Saturn and is with the Sun while the planets of health and vitality, viz., the Sun and Venus are in their turn subjected to the powerful aspect of Saturn. Hence he was not robust in his young age. That Sir Ashutosh owed a good deal of his mental peculiarities and gifts to the educative influence of his father during the formative days of his youth becomes evident in the conjunction of Venus, lord of Lagna with Pitrukaraka Sun. Consistent with the dictum that Mercury strong would make one well-versed in mathematics, we find here Mercury is strong in three ways, viz., as rising in Lagna, as lord of the 2nd, and as lord of the Navamsa Lagna. This accounts for the native's distinct bent for mathematics. It is said that in the course of his studies as a boy in the suburban school, he discovered certain errors and inaccuracies in Barnard Smith's

Arithmetic. The capacity for keen debate and effective speaking, which he had shown so much in life, are due to the fact that Venus is in the 5th from Karakamsa and that Venus and the Sun are associated in the 2nd or house of speech aspected by Jupiter. Academic brilliance is not always the test of true greatness. In the case of Ashutosh, it was the result of Jupiter as Vidyakaraka aspecting powerfully the Sun, lord of the house of education who in his turn associates with Venus, that gave rise to the high gifts of intellect, diligence and the method of conscious endeavour. The eminence and personality of Sir Ashutosh revolved on the harmonious disposition of the benefics and the ideal *parivarthana* or interchange of houses between Mercury and Venus. The chart gains further strength by the presence of *Gajakesari*, *Lakshmi*, *Sunapha*, *Vasi* and *Chandra-mangala yogas* each of which has contributed its quota of strength to make the native what he was. The house of children is unfortunately afflicted as Saturn occupies the 5th and as Putrakaraka is in conjunction with Rahu. The general strength of Jupiter has however resulted in at least one issue becoming prominent. The Sun, the Moon and Lagna representing the tripod of life are in common, movable and fixed signs respectively indicating middle life or Madhyayu.

Important Events.—The first significant event in the life of Sir Ashutosh was his securing the B.A. Degree with honours at the fag end of the Sun Dasa. The Sun is lord of the 4th and is in the 2nd with lord of Lagna and hence highly propitious to confer this distinction. The second event that profoundly influenced the native was his father's death in 1889 at the fag end of Rahu Bhukti in the Moon Dasa. The Moon owns the 2nd from Pitrukaraka and the 7th from Pitrusthana and is otherwise afflicted while Rahu, who should give the results of Venus, afflicts the 5th from Pitrukaraka and joins the lord of the 3rd from Pitrusthana. The first honour which fell on the subject was in the beginning of Jupiter's sub-period in the Dasa of the Moon, when as a young man of 24, he became the examiner of M.A. students along with Professor Booth. This created quite a sensation in Calcutta. Jupiter and the Moon are eminently situated mutually, justifying such a distinction. It was again in Jupiter Bhukti that he took his B.L. Degree and became an articled clerk under Sir Rash Behari Ghose. Mars is lord of the 7th and 12th and is in the 12th. Because he is in his own house, much of the evil, which he would have otherwise given, did not happen during his Dasa. It enabled the subject to gain a lot of legal experience. During this Dasa, Ashutosh did not find the profession of law, a bed of roses. It exacted the most assiduous toil which Ashutosh ungrudgingly offered at its altar. After Rahu Dasa commenced, he rose quickly to a position of prominence. In fact the beginning of Rahu Bhukti almost synchronised with his elevation to the Bench. Rahu's position in the 6th from Lagna is favoured as it indicates success over enemies. He is associated with Jupiter, lord of the 9th from Chandra Lagna. He occupies the house of Venus who in his turn is well placed. In Navamsa also, he is situated in the 9th. Thus indirectly Rahu has gained sufficient strength to promote the fortune of the native to such an extent that he was a Judge of the High Court from 1904 till the end of 1923. Finally, Sir Ashustosh died in 1925 as soon as the sub-period of Saturn commenced in Jupiter Dasa. Jupiter owns the 8th from Lagna and occupies the 7th from the Moon. In the Navamsa also, he owns the 7th and hence gets maraka power.

Remarks.—Mark the ideal situation of Lagna : His legal erudition is not a little due to the strong position of Mercury.

It may be argued that Jupiter being the planet of justice, his conjunction with Rahu could not be quite propitious for the even-handed administration of justice. But it should occur to any student of astrology that such a conjunction under certain conditions has its own importance. The very fact that Jupiter is in Libra in the 6th is a strength to reckon with.

Rahu is equally propitious in the 6th, and the conjunction can therefore find expression only in constructive channels. The same combination explains his zeal for the ancient learning which he reverenced no less, perhaps more than the light of the West. He persistently adhered to Indian dress and to the orthodox Hindu methods of living and performed pujas in the old orthodox style and this fits in with the presence of the lord of the 6th in the 2nd aspected by Jupiter.

Sir Ashutosh is held to be by far the most powerful educationist India has yet produced. This may be attributed to "a planet (Mars) occupying his own house and Amsa (Mars) aspected by another friendly planet (Jupiter)". The Moon–Mars conjunction, Jupiter–Mars opposition and Jupiter–Moon opposition have resulted in a series of constructive yogas, thereby rendering Jupiter highly powerful. Jupiter in his turn aspects the Sun (lord of the 4th) and hence the greatness of the individual in the educational sphere.

Sir Ashutosh's prominence as judge and jurist was universally recognised and there was a consensus of legal and judicial opinion that he raised the prestige of that office by his own singularly luminous judgments. Clarity of thought, ability, marked independence, unerring patience and uniform courtesy are all the gifts of a harmonious blending of benefic influences. Nowhere in the chart could we see mutual aspects between natural malefics. Mars and

and Ketu are nearly 23° apart that it is a case of association and not conjunction. Even this association according to the dictum *Kujavad Ketu* is a favourable one. The lord of Chandra Lagna strong, and the 4th and 9th lords in mutual kendras show the mettle the man was made of. The planet of memory, the planet of knowledge and the political planets, all strongly and harmoniously disposed, indicate an outstanding personality.

The presence of *Mridanga Yoga* by virtue of the lord of the Navamsa occupied by the lord of the 5th joining a kendra exemplifies the catholicity of Sir Ashutosh's interest and the wide range of his learning. Mark the position of the political planet Sun in Gemini receiving the aspect of Saturn and mark also the fact that Mercury and Jupiter are free from evil aspects. The native seldom threw himself heart and soul into the politics of the country. Education claimed most of his time. As Saturn is a yogakaraka and occupies the 5th, there was none to excel him in the steadiness of independence and consciousness and pride of power, the special characteristics of Taurus Lagna.

No. 40.—HERBERT GEORGE WELLS

Birth Details.— *Born on 21st September 1866 at 3-33 p.m. (G.M.T.). (Lat. 51° 24′ N., Long. 0° 1′ E.)

Planetary Positions.—The Sun 157° 52′ ; the Moon 300° 3′ ; Mars 76° ; Mercury 148° 25′ ; Jupiter 271° 54′ ; Venus 204° 9′ ; Saturn 199° 11′ ; Rahu 162° 15′ ; Ketu 342° 20′ ; and Lagna 273° 16′. Ayanamsa 20° 32′.

RASI

Ketu			Mars
Moon	RASI		
Lagna Jupiter			Merc.
		Venus Saturn	Sun Rahu

NAVAMSA

Sun Sat.	Rahu	Venus	
Mars	NAVAMSA		
Jupit. Lagna			
Merc.		Moon Ketu	

Balance of Mars Dasa at birth : Years 3–5–21.

Special Features.—The ascendant is Capricorn, a movable and saturnine sign and the lord is exalted in the 10th. Jupiter

---

* Mr. Well's birth time is not correctly known. His biographer Geoffry West states that Wells was born in "mid-afternoon", this of course being an approximate time. By a careful consideration of his life incidents and intellectual achievements, and by the application of rectification rules, we have been able to fix up the time as 3-33 p.m. (G.M.T.).

is in debility in Lagna, but has obtained neechabhanga. These two suggest that his early home-life was amidst very meagre circumstances Capricorn rising, and the aspect of Mars powerfully cast on it, made the native endowed with a quiet yet ambitious, persevering and persistent spirit capable of enormous effort towards attainment of a desired object. The ascendant configuration in Navamsa, especially the Vargottama dispositions of Lagna and Jupiter, coupled with Lagna lord Saturn occupying Pisces Navamsa, denote the physical constitution inclining to a decidedly square body build. The bony structure of his head is revealed by the predominance of the saturnine influence. Jupiter's impress, and the situation of the Moon in Aquarius, made the lips cancerian in their flaccidity and condensed the stature. Martian aspect on Lagna tended to accidents and this was fulfilled by a broken leg in his 7th or 8th year and a crushed kidney when he was twenty or so. The Moon's situation in Aquarius, a mystic sign, denotes the calibre of the mentality of Wells. Breadth and vision are characteristics of this position. The temper is strong, forceful and enduring and the mind should have been suspicious and melancholic. (The Sun in Virgo is highly significant giving as it does the capacity to blend the ideal with the practical in a marvellous manner. The same position makes the native very discriminative giving him large reasoning powers. Rahu's association with the Sun adds a certain amount of spirituality and the idealism becomes more manifest.) In several places in his autobiography he remarks about his inability to recall facts and this is seen in the Moon's association with Ketu in Navamsa. Wells was the youngest of four children. Ketu is in the 3rd while the lord Jupiter is neecha aspected by Mars. On the other hand, the 11th, ruling elders, is well disposed indicating elder brothers and sisters, but because the 11th lord is in the 8th from the 11th, none of them survived the native. (Ketu's presence in the 3rd is also suggestive of an illegitimate half-sister.) The 4th lord is actually *Venus. He occupies the 10th from Lagna and the 9th from the Moon in conjunction with Saturn. In the Navamsa, Jupiter aspects Venus, while Rahu is in the 4th. The natural Matrukaraka whilst not afflicted is not strong. The part-lordship of Mars suggests that the mother was ever busy, assuming all the responsibilities of the house, acting as house-keeper, and attending the shop when his father was out. The house of children is not favourable. Mercury, the 5th lord from the Moon, is in a barren sign while Putrakaraka Jupiter is neecha and aspected by Mars, who also occupies the 5th from the Moon. Even in Navamsa, the 5th is aspected by Mars while the 5th from Chandra Lagna and Karakamsa respectively have Mars and Rahu. Wells had two sons by his second wife, the eldest son 'having a fine precise brain'. The 7th house is extremely interesting. Mars in the 6th makes him 'exceedingly smitten with love' while Mars, aspecting the 9th from Karakamsa, denotes illegal gratification. Capricorn gives sex potency. The fact that Lagna is aspected by Mars and that Venus is in association with Saturn and Mandi is a signature of a strong, emotional and passionate nature. Venus, though in his own sign, loses his natural refinement and tends to grossness because of this affliction. Wells' sex experiences are rather flagrantly flaunted in his autobiography, though, Mercury's situation in the 7th from the Moon, makes him conceal the details of his personal experiences although he readily admits their existence. The 7th lord Moon

---

* In higher latitudes, it sometimes happens that two houses merge into a sign or *vice versa* with the result lordships are also merged.

is in the 2nd in Aquarius while in the Navamsa he is with Ketu. No wonder the coolness of his married partners and their lack of ardour is readily revealed. The affliction of Kalatra-karaka accounts for the break-up of marriage and his early 'romantic' career. The 8th from the Moon is occupied by the 7th lord Sun and Rahu, and aspected by Mars. This not only indicates complete absence of marital happiness but his extra marital sex excursions. Mercury lord of the 9th in the 8th (which happens to be the 7th from the Moon) probably explains the fact that his second wife 'was the business head of the family, taking care of his income, investments and the like', so that he 'was a paying boarder' in his own house. If rumour is to be believed in, still another woman figured in his life but the nature of the afflictions to Venus expressed itself in the way of that woman's marriage to another.

His father was a middle class man in accordance with the association of Pitrukaraka with Rahu and the 8th lord occupy-ing the house of father. Mars is the planet of sports and if this is admitted, then martian aspect on the 9th and the Sun gives us a clue that the father was a professional bowler and a cricket teacher. Planets ruling the father have no vitality. No wonder that the father was running a second-hand goods shop.

Important Events.—The Sun, planet of vitality, is asso-ciated with Rahu and aspected by Mars. Throughout Rahu Dasa several haemorrhages occurred and necessitated periods of confinement. The kidney trouble which occurred just about the time of Rahu Dasa termination is seen in the affliction Virgo and Rahu receive. His first marriage and divorce took place in the sub-period of Saturn in Jupiter Dasa. Jupiter owns the 2nd from Chandra Lagna and Saturn is with Kalatrakaraka. As Mandi has also joined the combination, there was early divorce. His second marriage occurred in Ketu's sub-period. It will be seen that Ketu can give the results of Jupiter and Ketu is in the 2nd or house of family from the Moon. The beginning of Saturn's Dasa was marked by the death of the mother. Saturn afflicting the 9th from Matrukaraka and aspecting the 4th was strong enough to deprive the native of his mother. His father died in 1910 in Ketu's sub-period. Ketu, it will be seen, is in the 7th from Pitrukaraka and Pitrusthana. Now we come to Venus sub-period in Mercury Dasa marked by the death of the 2nd wife. Venus, as we have already seen, is afflicted while Mercury, occupying the 8th from Lagna, is completely overpowered by the affliction of the major lord. A law suit began in 1928 (Venus in Mercury) and terminated in 1933 (Rahu in Mercury). Mercury is lord of the 6th and his situation in the 8th explains the above litigation. His own death occurred in Ketu Dasa, Mercury's sub-period. Ketu is in the 3rd from the ascendant and the 2nd from the Moon. In the Navamsa he is with Mandi in the 10th. The sub-lord Mercury is in the 8th from Lagna and the 7th from the Moon. All these dispositions were certainly such as to cause death at the fag end of the Dasa.

Remarks.—The vocation, earning capacity and the intellectual eminence of Wells should interest a student of astrology. While his writings give us an insight into the man, the planetary positions reveal a singular freedom from any subconscious complexes. The 10th lord Mars is in the intellectual sign of Gemini while the 10th house has exalted Saturn associated with Venus. Mercury lord of the 5th from Chandra Lagna is equally well placed in the 7th. This, coupled with the harmonious disposition of Venus and Mercury and the debilitation of Jupiter, indicates his prolific output since he was unhampered by any inhibitions. His earning capacity was indeed very good because Saturn lord of the 2nd is exalted in the 10th and joins Venus thus forming a Rajayoga. The presence of *Pushkala Yoga*, *Lakshmi Yoga* and *Harsha Yoga* gave him happiness, fame, enjoyment and good fortune. The Lagna is marked by a neechabhanga. His renown is explainable by the presence of Mercury in the 8th. Equally auspicious is the disposition of Ketu in the 3rd. The literary work of Wells may be divided into three periods : scientific romances, social novels and utopian books. His early writings generally deal with sex. These are attributable to Saturn, the Dasa lord, who has joined Venus and Mandi in a sex area, *viz.*, Libra. "Ann Veronica" is ultra frank in its presentation of sex. It was banned by libraries and denounced by the clergy. Throughout Saturn Dasa, he seems to have written books almost all of them dealing with the problem of sex,* love, passion, jealousy and the like.

It cannot be merely an astrological coincidence that only after the advent of Jupiter's sub-period in Saturn Dasa and of course in Mercury Dasa that Wells confined himself exclusively to subjects of political and sociological interest. The presence of the Moon in Aquarius, the *only truly mystic sign of the zodiac*, is reflected in his historical writings particularly his *Outline of History* and *Shape of Things to Come*, and *The Dream*, in which later work the chief character projected into a future age, dreams through a life-span of the present, presumably through the revelations of his subconscious mind of a former incarnation. The group of books which deal with world citizenship, the perfection

---

* *The Passionate Friends, The Wife of Sir Issac Harman* and *Marriage.*

of world Government, and an economic system in keeping with it are distinctly attributable to Aquarius and the nearness of the Sun and Saturn to each other. Rahu in the 9th from Lagna and Jupiter Vargottama in Lagna give him prophetic power, by means of which he anticipated many of the events and most of the problems which beset our times. In fact he is supposed to have anticipated the atom bomb (which he lived to see) 1914 in his book *The World Set Free*. It is a characteristic of Aquarius that the natives will not be aware of their own talents. Because Mars powerfully aspects the Lagna (which is a movable sign) Wells led an active life socially as well as mentally unlike many other imaginative writers. The 2nd lord Saturn is with Mandi, while Ketu is in the 2nd from the Moon. Hence he was always a tentatve writer putting forward his inchoate views, inviting criticism and stirring controversy, till he finalised his views. The Moon's situation in Aquarius is significant. Aquarius is the sign of a perfected world citizenship and a World State. It is utopian by nature and universal by scope. Whatever history may think of him, his horoscope reveals that Wells was more a stimulating thinker confronting mankind with the reality of certain problems than a literary artist.

No. 41.—MOHANDAS KARAMCHAND GANDHI

Birth Details.—Born on 2nd October 1869 at 7-45 a.m. (L.M.T.) (Lat 21° 37° N., Long. 69° 49 E.)

Planetary Positions.—The Sun 168° 22′ ; the Moon 120° 10′ ; Mars 207° 39′ ; Mercury 193° 9′ ; Jupiter 30° 25′ ; Venus 205° 53′ ; Saturn 229° 57′ ; Rahu 103° 36′ ; Ketu 283° 36′ ; and Lagna 193° 14′. Ayanamsa 20° 35′.

		Jupiter		Moon Ketu	Venus	Sun Mars
			Rahu			
	RASI			NAVAMSA		
Ketu			Moon	Jupit. Lagna Merc.		
	Saturn	Mars Mercury Venus Lagna	Sun	Sat.		Rahu

Balance of Ketu Dasa at birth : Years 6-10-28.

Special Features.—The Sun is in the 12th house powerfully aspected by Jupiter, who though a natural benefic, is lord of the 3rd and 6th. Jupiter is in the 10th from the Moon aspected by Saturn. This gives considerable spirituality. Jupiter the planet of wisdom and religion is neecha in Navamsa and has not obtained neechabhanga. This accounts for his tirade against the orthodox Hindus and the forcing of his views on conservative elements in Indian social and religious life. Libra is rising with Mars, Mercury and Venus, the latter two forming a Rajayoga. Here as Lagna is subjected to Papakarthari Yoga and as lord of Lagna is with Mars, a bloody planet, physically the native was not upto the mark. The influence of Mars is considerable. It gives a hot constitution rendering the subject to suffer from blood pressure and the like. The Moon, the natural index of the mind, is again hemmed inbetween Rahu on the one side and the Sun on the other powerfully aspected by Saturn. These combinations do not give mental peace. The soul of every man, with all its egoism, self-love and deep-seated desires is vested in the Sun. As he is in the 12th, it gives him spirituality. Mercury in the ascendant produces keen-ness of mind. The 10th is Karmasthana. Rahu's location there is always indicative of good work. Gandhi always advocated non-violence or *ahimsa*. Mars is in Libra—a sign of balance—and in conjunction with benefics. The 3rd lord Jupiter is aspected by Saturn and Mars and in the 3rd from the Moon there are Mars, Mercury and Venus. To say that Gandhi's non-violence breeds of cowardice is to betray our ignorance. The presence of Mars in the 3rd from the Moon made Gandhi delight in his independent spirit of sacrificing everything rather than bear restraint. The presence of Saturn or his aspecting the 10th house (either from Lagna or from the Moon) has great bearing on the influence one wields amongst the masses. If one has to have a following, be it in any sphere of activity—political, religious, social or literary—one should have the 10th fortified by an aspect or conjunction of a major planet. Of course this is a general statement and may have exceptions. Jupiter is in the 10th from the Moon and Saturn aspects the 10th.

Important Events.—The commencement of Rahu Dasa (11-6-1919) synchronised with Gandhi's active political programme involving the fight for swarajya. Rahu is in the 10th from Lagna and the 12th from the Moon. The 12th indicates losses, prisons, jails, underground cells, etc., and the 10th governs Karma, political authority and livelihood. In Rahu Dasa Rahu Bhukti, Gandhi was arrested for the civil disobedience campaign but was released in Jupiter Bhukti. In Ketu's subperiod (Rahu Dasa) he revived his campaign of mass civil disobedience. He was again arrested in 1942 in the sub-period of Mercury in the Dasa of Jupiter.

It was in Venus Bhukti of Jupiter Dasa that Gandhi saw his greatest dream, *viz.*, the Independence of India realised. But this did not make him happy, because of the partition of the country resulting in the massacre, physical as well as psychological, of millions of his countrymen. Note both Venus and Jupiter, the sub and major lords, have the contact of bloody Mars and Jupiter has the aspect of both Mars and Saturn. He was shot dead by a fanatic in Sun Bhukti in Jupiter Dasa. Jupiter is in the 8th aspected powerfully by Mars—a maraka and the Sun is in the 12th from Lagna and in the 2nd—another maraka from the Chandra Lagna. Because of the strong martian and saturnine influences on the 8th – 22nd Drekkana, Gandhi, an apostle of non-violence, had a *violent end.

Remarks.—Libra is rising with Mars, Mercury and Venus, the latter two forming a Rajayoga. Mars is in Libra a sign of balance and is in conjunction with benefics. The Moon, the natural index of the mind, is hemmed inbetween two malefics while the Sun ruling the soul is in the 12th or Mokshasthana

---

* In the March 1955 issue of *American Astrology* Mr. Cyril Fagan observes thus regarding Gandhi's death: "In April 1947 issue of *The*

powerfully aspected by Jupiter. These combinations explain the three cardinal virtues, *viz.*, *Satya* (truth), *Ahimsa* (non-violence) and *Brahmacharya* (continence), whereon the Mahatma laid most stress. Truth with him is a divine quality and he had realised the profundity of *Satya*. His conception of Satyagraha is based on the inward strength of the soul (*atma sakti*) and is not merely the negative virtue of abstaining from violence. There is a fundamental distinction between the animal and human worlds and the advocates of the use of force, who generally adopt a crude version of the Darwinian struggle for existence, simply exalt a biological generalisation into a doctrine of human destiny.

The second virtue is *ahimsa*, which is crudely translated as non-violence. According to the Mahatma's definition, just "as the hardest metal yields to sufficient heat, even so, must the hardest heart melt before the sufficiency of the heat of *ahimsa*".

Astrological Magazine, the Editor Dr. B. V. Raman made one of the most successful predictions of modern times, when he penned these words: 'Mars and Saturn will be in conjunction in the last degree of Cancer on November 12, 1947. These combinations also point to the loss (by assassination as violent Mars is with Saturn in the 12th) of a respected mass leader of this country.' (p. 247). There cannot be the slightest doubt that Dr. B. V. Raman had Gandhi's Rasi chakra before him when he wrote these ominous words, for the conjunction of Mars and Saturn, to which he refers, occurred at 11h. 21m. 45s. (U.T.) on November 12, 1947, when the sidereal longitude of the malefics was Cancer 28° 06′ 28″ and therefore close to Gandhi's Moon in Cancer 26° 55′. Gandhi was assassinated at New Delhi on January 30, 1948 (see horary chart) so that Dr. B. V. Raman's prediction which was published at least 10 months before the event, found an astonishingly accurate, if tragic, fulfilment. **The confirmation of this forecast puts Dr. Raman in the foremost rank of the world's successful astrologers, and renders the study of Jyotisha really worthwhile."**

As far as humanly possible, Gandhi put into stern practice the dictum of the sacred texts, viz., *Ahimsa Paramo Dharma* (*ahimsa* is the supreme virtue). *Ahimsa* does not imply passive resistance in the face of untruth but rather its active condemnation. Mars and Venus are at the fag end of Lagna, while Mercury the intellectual planet is almost in exact conjunction with the Lagna Madhya. This coupled with the presence of Jupiter in the 10th from the Moon explains Gandhi's incessant struggle to free men from shackles of *avidya* or ignorance.

The third cardinal virtue on which the Mahatma has laid stress is *Brahmacharya*. By sublimation of the sex function spiritual energy is generated which becomes a divine power and wonderful in its potency. The Mahatma had disciplined himself in all these cardinal virtues which go to make one a real saint and therefore he knew no distinction between the relatives and strangers, countrymen and foreigners. Essentially as a man of action, he had a constructive faculty—a characteristic of the balancing nature of the rising sign in his horoscope. His philosophy and the way of life had their roots deep in Indian culture and no wonder he was able to influence the unthinking masses, the bourgeois and even leaders of thought in the West. His ideals of simplicity, plain living and high thinking, calm and cool approach to problems in the face of the greatest provocation, and a life of service and dedication made him a great moral, spiritual and political leader.

No. 42.—CHITTARANJAN DAS

Birth Details.—Born on 5th November 1870 at 6-49 a.m. (L.M.T.) (Lat, 22° 40' N., Long, 88° 30'E.)

Planetary Positions.—The Sun 201° 48'; the Moon 345° 47'; Mars 133° 14'; Mercury 191° 8'; Jupiter 65° 36'; Venus 193° 36'; Saturn 245° 1'; Rahu 82° 35'; Ketu 262° 35'; and Lagna 210° 13'. Ayanamsa 30° 26'.

Moon			Rahu Jupit.	Sun Rahu	Saturn
	RASI		Venus	NAVAMSA	Lagna Mars
			Mars Merc.		
Saturn Ketu	Lagna	Sun Mercury Venus		Moon Jupiter	Ketu

Balance of Saturn Dasa at birth: years 1-3-4.

Special Features.—Though Lagna is devoid of the aspect or association of benefics, Lagna lord Mars occupies a dignified place in the 10th from Lagna and is otherwise unafflicted. The Lagna is more or less a *sandhi* or junction, partaking to a certain extent the characteristics of Libra and as a consequence of Venus too. The blending of martian and venusian influences gave him a sound body and a sound mind. Das was a poet and had a poet's emotional outlook, consistent with the presence of Venus in Lagna Bhava. The Sun is neecha but has obtained neechabhanga, due to Saturn's position in a kendra from the Moon. The subject's remarkable organising capacity and powers of leadership are due to the disposition of the Sun in Lagna Bhava. The 4th lord Saturn is in the 2nd, a sign of Jupiter and aspected by Jupiter; while from Chandra Lagna, the 4th lord is Mercury and he occupies a benefic position in the 8th giving rise to some sort of an *Adhi Yoga*. Jupiter occupies the 4th as lord of Chandra Lagna and aspects the 10th from Chandra Lagna. These combinations conferred on him legal brilliance. Because of the influences of Rahu and Ketu on the 4th lord from Lagna and the 4th house from the Moon, he had to give up legal practice. Lord of the 2nd Jupiter aspecting the 2nd and Mars the 2nd lord from the Moon, posited in an Upachaya therefrom, are excellent *Dhana Yogas* favouring amassing of wealth, but as lord of the 11th (Mercury) is in the 12th, again aspected by the benefic Jupiter, he divested himself of almost all his property which he left as a legacy to the nation for some charitable purposes. His patriotism, sense of humanism and love of the country are explainable on the basist of the presence of *Parijata Yoga*, and that of *Parvata* from the Moon. Lord of the 8th Mercury in the 12th from Lagna and lord of the 3rd Saturn, who is *Ayushkaraka*, in association with Ketu, conferred *Madhyayu*.

Important Events.—He was sent to London for studies at the age of 8 when he was having the Dasa of Mercury and the sub-period of the Sun. In Ketu Dasa, he failed in the I.C.S. Examination but he learned a great deal about

British politics and how elections should be fought. Mark the association of Saturn, lord of the 4th, with the Dasa lord Ketu. Consistent with the position of Jupiter in the 9th and in a kendra from the Moon and that of Venus in Lagna and the 8th from the Moon, it was during Venus Dasa Jupiter Bhukti that the Swaraj Party was founded. When he returned to India in 1893 to practise law, he was a briefless lawyer. He was then having Ketu Dasa. Just about the commencement of Venus Dasa, this struggling lawyer had a windfall. His younger brother who had been adopted by a rich man died, and bequeathed all his property to his mother, who in her turn bequeathed it to her sons. Venus, by virtue of the *Adhi Yoga*, enabled the native to get this unexpected fortune. It will also be seen that Venus is associated with the 10th lord Sun (neechabhanga) and aspected by Jupiter lord of the 2nd. It was again in the Dasa of Venus and Bhukti of Jupiter that C. R. Das woke up to find himself famous, when he pleaded for Aurobindo who was acquitted. The Sun, lord of the 10th, is neecha. It was in the Sun Dasa, latter part, that Das was incarcerated. The Moon is lord of the 9th and occupies the 5th, aspected by Lagna lord Mars from the 10th. This has given rise to some sort of a Rajayoga. Consequently, it was only after the advent of the Moon Dasa (in Mars Bhukti) that he became President of the Congress. It will be seen that unlike the Sun who is neecha in Lagna Bhava, the Moon is not afflicted. He is in a benefic sign and is free from the association or aspect of Saturn or Rahu. It was only after the coming in of the Moon Dasa that the Swaraj Party under the leadership of Das contested the elections and captured the majority of seats. His death took place in the Dasa of the Moon and the Bhukti of Jupiter. The Moon is in the

nakshatra of Saturn who in his turn occupies a maraka place
in association with another powerful maraka Ketu. The sub-
lord Jupiter not only owns a maraka house but also aspects it.

Remarks.—The horoscope is somewhat elusive as it does
not reveal, by a superficial examination, the worth or achievements of the native. In the Navamsa, the dispositions are
more arresting. In Rasi the Lagna is very strong, as the lord
Mars is in the 10th aspecting the Lagna. Mars is endowed
with considerable digbala. The political planet Sun is neecha
in Lagna Bhava but has obtained neechabhanga and is otherwise unblemished. The intellectual and emotional planets
Mercury and Venus respectively have caused *Adhi Yoga*, and
are subject to the aspect of Jupiter, lord of Chandra Lagna.
These combinations conferred on Das intellectuality, honesty
and political realism. His interest in politics was lofty for he
wanted a new order, In the Navasma again, yogakaraka Mars
is neecha in Lagna, but has obtained neechabhanga, as Jupiter
is in a kendra from the Moon. Jupiter happens to be the lord
of the 9th and has joined Lagna lord who was entered
parivarthana with Mars, the yogakaraka. Consequently, Das
had an unerring instinct for the weak points in an adversary's
position and a tenacious resolution in the execution of his own
plans which raised him far above the level of the ablest of his
associates. Unlike the philosophical Jupiter and the idealistic
Saturn, Venus is a realist *par excellence*. The house of speech
is occupied by Ketu and Saturn and aspected by Jupiter.
Ketu is in the constellation of Venus while Jupiter is in the
constellation of Mars. No wonder, Deshbandhu Das's speeches
were considered as marvels of logic, erudition and practical
idealism. Again, the dominant position of Mars made him a
skilful strategist and tactician. A careful study of his horoscope
is necessary if we have to understand the real worth and
achievements of this great patriot and leader.

No. 43.—AUROBINDO GHOSE

Birth Details.—*Born on 15th August 1872 at 5-17 a.m. (L.M.T.) (Lat. 22° 30′ N., Long. 88° 20′ E.)

Planetary Positions.—The Sun 121° 47′ ; the Moon 247° 11′ ; Mars 96° 50′ ; Mercury 144° 57′ ; Jupiter 113° 2′ ; Venus 129° 59′ ; Saturn 265° 2′ ; Rahu 48° 4′ ; Ketu 228° 4′ ; and Lagna 116° 42′. Ayanamsa 20° 37′.

RASI

	Rahu	Lagna	
RASI		Lagna Mars Jupit.	
		Sun Venus Merc.	
Moon Saturn	Ketu		

NAVAMSA

Lagna Jupit.	Sun		Rahu Moon Venus
		NAVAMSA	
	Ketu	Mercury Saturn	Mars

Balance of Ketu Dasa at birth : Years 3-2-22.

Special Features.—The Lagna is conspicuously strong, inasmuch as it is occupied by Jupiter, gnanakaraka, and lord of the 9th or Dharmasthana, and Lagna lord Moon is in a

---

* The Secretary, Aurobindo Ashram, Pondicherry, in a letter to the author has given the time of birth as one ghati before sunrise on 15-8-1872.

benefic sign. Cancer rising gives intuition, benevolence, sympathy, useful imagination and fondness for subtle things in life. Venus, the planet of poetry, is posited in the 2nd house. It will be noted that Aurobindo revealed unusual powers of intellect and a poetical genius of no mean order. Mark again the fact that the 4th lord Venus is in Lagna Bhava while the planet of intelligence Mercury has joined the Sun causing *Budha-Aditya Yoga*. The 4th is aspected by the yogakaraka Mars. From Chandra Lagna the 4th lord Jupiter has a prominent disposition, exalted in the 5th from the 4th. Aurobindo was a brilliant scholar having passed the tripos in Cambridge in the first division. Mars, Jupiter and Venus influencing the house of education and culture enabled him to know several languages—Greek, Latin, German, Italian, French and Sanskrit. Lagna lord is a political planet and Mars lord of the 10th (Karmasthana) is in Lagna, while the Sun, another political planet, is also in Lagna Bhava. He plunged into political activity for about 10 years, at first working behind the scenes and later on initiating more forward and direct political action. Lagna lord Moon is in Sagittarius, a war-like sign, in association with Saturn, lord of the 8th (and the 7th). The Moon is, in a sense, subject to Papakarthari Yoga, hemmed inbetween Ketu (228°) and Saturn (265°). There is no relief to this affliction. The circumstance coupled with the presence of *Pasa Yoga* landed him in jail for a period of one year. Between the Sun and the Moon (political forces) on one side and Jupiter (wisdom and spirituality) on the other, the strength of the latter is decidedly more pronounced as lord of the 9th Jupiter is exalted and is within 3° from the rising degree. As a result of this unique combination, Aurobindo's leanings were more towards development of the inner vision and *Yogic Sadhana* than political activity. Sri Aurobindo withdrew from politics in 1910 and devoted himself entirely to a life of spiritual contemplation and illumination. Saturn and the Moon are nearly 18° apart while Mercury without being combust has given rise to *Budha-Aditya Yoga*. This gave the sage clarity of thinking and inner knowledge. His works embody much of the inner knowledge that had come to him in his practice of yoga. In the Navamsa, the Moon is afflicted in Gemini by association with the incendiary Rahu and the sensual Venus. Obviously he must have passed through stages of intense mental and spiritual conflict before he realised that the ancient yoga systems of India sought to cut the guardian knot of mundane existence by treating it as a field of self-preparation which is to be transcended in taking possession of the highest state of abiding peace.

Important Events.—At the age of 7 (Venus Dasa Sun Bhukti) he went to England for education and lived there for 14 years. Lord of 4th house Venus is with the Sun lord of the 2nd. His education was completed in Venus Dasa. In Saturn's sub-period his father died. Note Saturn happens to own a maraka house from Pitrukaraka Sun. As soon as Mercury's sub-period commenced, he joined the Baroda service. Note Mercury is lord of the 10th from the Moon and occupies the 9th with Venus the major lord. He gave up Baroda service to join the agitation against the partition of Bengal in 1905. Aurobindo was prosecuted for sedition in 1907 in Saturn Bhukti of Moon Dasa. It will be seen that the association of the Moon as Lagna lord with Saturn as lord of the 8th has caused *Bandhana Yoga* and it was under the directional influences of these two planets that the native was prosecuted. In the Navamsa, Mercury as lord of Chandra Lagna is in the 6th with

Saturn lord of the 8th. It was during Mercury's sub-period in Moon Dasa that he had to spend one year in jail. The last part of Moon Dasa saw him completely cut off from politics and he took up residence in Pondicherry. Mars as yogakaraka is almost in the 12th Bhava (Mokshasthana) but in the constellation of Saturn, a planet of philosophy. In the Navamsa again, Mars is lord of the 2nd and 9th and occupies the 7th. It was in Mars Dasa that he began silent yoga. Rahu Dasa saw the publication of most of his important works such as *Isha Upanishad*, *Essays on Gita*, etc., and some of these works embodied much of his inner yogic experiences while others dealt with the spirit and significance of Indian civilisation and culture. In Jupiter Dasa, his name spread far and wide and he became an institution attracting admirers and disciples from all over the world. His death took place in Jupiter Dasa Rahu Bhukti. Jupiter the major lord is in the constellation of Mercury who is a maraka from Chandra Lagna and who occupies a maraka house in association with a maraka (Sun) from Lagna. Venus who should give the results of Rahu is in a maraka house with the Sun.

Remarks.—Aurobindo's horoscope is important from two aspects : First, the vitality of Lagna, derived mainly from the presence of exalted Jupiter, lord of the 9th or Dharma, rendered the man visionary and yet practical for he felt that there was a secret purpose controlling the whole process of evolution and that purpose was the complete self-manifestation of God in matter. The India he presented to the world was not the India of the politician but an eternal India with a message for the world evolving the supreme oneness of man and in resolving thereby the inherent contradictions of human living in a superior creative synthesis. And second : From

Chandra Lagna a powerful Rajayoga operates in the 9th or Dharmasthana, generated by the association of the Atmakaraka Sun (lord of the 9th) with the intuitional and intellectual Mercury (lord of the 10th or Karmasthana) and the literary and poetical Venus lord of the 11th. This yoga reveals his unusual powers of poetical genius and the stupendous activity of the intellect, all being directed in the channel of drawing human beings into association with each other and interpreting the soul of the nation that had put its impress on the history of humanity since times immemorial.

Venus Rahu	Mars	Moon	Sun		
					Mars Saturn
Mercury	RASI		NAVAMSA		Moon
					Mercury
Lagna Jupiter	Sun Ket			Lagna	Rahu

Balance of the Sun Dasa at birth: Years 3-6-26.

Special Features.—Pisces XII was a most auspicious and progressive astrological configuration. The presence of Jupiter in Lagna ... and Mars is in an upachaya, which happens ...

The presence of Jupiter in Lagna ... a configuration of the same ... the lord of Lagna (Saturn) ... and comes to ... planetary combination ... was associated about the greatest British statesman and orator, was carrying about himself the feelings of a born "radical."

No. 44.—POPE PIUS XII

Birth Details—Born on 2nd March 1876 at 0-39 a.m. (L.M.T.) (Lat. 41° 53′ N., Long. 12° 28′ E.)

Planetary Positions.—The Sun 321° 6′; the Moon 32° 42′; Mars 11° 29′; Mercury 295° 36′; Jupiter 221° 5′; Venus 358° 33′; Saturn 309° 29′; Rahu 339° 33′; Ketu 159° 33′; and Lagna 221° 6′. Ayanamsa 20° 33′.

Venus Rahu	Mars	Moon	Venus Ketu	Sun		
Sun Saturn						Mars
	RASI			NAVAMSA		
Mercury			Moon			Mercury
	Lagna Jupiter	Ketu	Sat.		Jupiter Lagna	Rahu

Balance of the Sun Dasa at birth : Years 3-6-25.

Special Features.—Pius XII was a man of broad and progressive intellectual gifts because of the presence of Jupiter in Lagna. *Lagna lord Mars is in an Upachaya, which happens

---

* The time of birth is speculative. By a consideration of his life events, the time of birth has been fixed at 0-39 a.m. Consistent with the nature of Lagna (Scorpio) and Lagna lord (Mars), in appearance cardinal Pacelli, "was somewhat above the average height, thin both in ascetic and athletic way, carrying himself with the bearing of a true aristrocat".

to be his own sign. This is a strong point. But Saturn's aspect
on Lagna is not desirable. In the Navamsa, the Lagna is
occupied by Jupiter and the lord of Lagna is exalted. Indeed
these combinations suggest that the life of the native, before he
became the Pope, had been a long process of spiritual testing.
The Moon is exalted and the lord of Chandra Lagna is not only
exalted but is Vargottama. These dispositions denote his
culture, his affability and graciousness, his tact and his sincerity. Jupiter's presence in Lagna as lord of the 2nd and 5th is
highly auspicious. Because of the aspect of Saturn on Lagna
lord Mars, a certain amount of fanaticism is apparent in his
approach to religion. He had been fearlessly outspoken against
every Governmental regime and every ideology that invaded
the spiritual supremacy of the Church. The Sun–Saturn association, involving the lordships of the 4th and 10th, two
important kendras, signifies spiritual (Sun is Atmakaraka)
activity and a contemplative temperament. In Rasi Venus-Rahu
in the 5th aspected by Jupiter, and in Navamsa the Sun
aspected by Jupiter, and Mercury well disposed, made him a
cultured gentleman, a polished diplomat and a statesman of
sincerity. Leadership in matters of religion and public authority
are the blessings of the powerful *Gajakesari Yoga* present both
in Rasi and Navamsa. Presence of Venus in the 5th house, a
double-bodied sign with Rahu, suggests a conflict between
the pulls of grosser human instincts and spirituality, between
a strong intellect and the spiritual mind. But Jupiter's aspect
on this combination from his dominant position in Lagna made
the man a seeker after illumination rather than yield to the
temptations of the flesh. Saturn, the planet of philosophy,
aspects Lagna. Jupiter in Lagna and Karmasthana or 10th

house, conferring vast knowledge of ecclesiastical procedure and diplomacy. In the Navamsa all the kendras are occupied, Mars having obtained neechabhanga.

Important Events.—After completion of education at the Capranica seminary and the pontifical institute, he was ordained priest in 1899 when he was having Rahu Dasa Jupiter Bhukti. Both Rahu and Jupiter are in a sense "planets of religion". Rahu is in Jupiter's sign. Consequently, throughout his Dasa, Pacelli devoted his energies to the "care of the souls", conducting spiritual retreats and acting as Chaplain to religious communities. As soon as Jupiter Dasa commenced, the native was appointed Secretary of the Department of Extraordinary Affairs. It will be seen that Mars aspects Jupiter. Under Jupiter Dasa Jupiter Bhukti, he actively engaged in spiritual ministrations to the German, Austrian and Italian soldiers. In Saturn Bhukti—note Saturn aspects the 10th and is with the 10th lord—Pacelli became the titular archbishop of Sardes and carried on his peace representations though his efforts did not succeed. In Mercury sub-period Pacelli was appointed the first Papal Nuncio to Berlin. From Chandra Lagna Saturn is a yogakaraka as lord of the 9th and 10th. Here, as lord of the 9th, he has joined the lord of the 4th causing another Rajayoga. As soon as Saturn Dasa commenced, he was appointed as Secretary of State for the Vatican City State. Under the sub-period of Mercury—note Mercury is well placed from Chandra Lagna—he was appointed Papal chamberlain. As soon as the sub-period of Venus commenced the native was crowned as Pope. From Lagna, Venus is in the 5th exalted and Vargottama and in the 2nd from the major lord Saturn. As Chandra Lagnadhipati he is uniquely disposed in the 11th. In the Navamsa Saturn is yogakaraka and occupies the 3rd while

Venus as lord of Lagna is in the 6th, an upachaya place. The major and sub-lords are disposed in mutual kandras, thus enabling the native to be raised to the lofty responsibility and position of Pope—the religious head of millions of catholics throughout the world.

Remarks.—The Pope's horoscope has three salient features, *viz.*, the presence of Jupiter, the planet of wisdom, owning the 2nd (speech) and 5th (Poorvapunya) in Lagna, the Lagna being aspected by lord of Lagna and Saturn and the fortification of the 10th and 11th houses from Chandra Lagna. The hormonious disposition of the Sun and the Moon in mutual kendres *plus* the presence of *Asatyavadi Yoga* has made him a polished diplomat while yogas like *Mridanga and Parijata* indicate an aristocratic bearing, an essentially sincere statesman and a saintly Churchman. The lord of the 9th Moon is exalted in the 7th and aspected by the lord of 5th Jupiter. A more ideal combination for a Pontiff cannot be conceived.

No. 45—ALBERT EINSTEIN

Birth Details.—Born on 14th March 1879 at 11-30 a.m. (L.M.T.) (Lat. 48° 24' N., Long. 10° E.)

Planetary Positions.—The Sun 332° 46'; the Moon 233° 48'; Mars 276° 12'; Mercury 342° 25'; Jupiter 306° 44'; Venus 356° 16'; Saturn 333° 28'; Rahu 280° 46'; Ketu 100° 46'; and Lagna 81° 47'. Ayanamsa 20° 43'.

Sun Mercury Venus Saturn			Lagna		Rahu Lagna	
Jupiter			Ketu	Moon Mars Venus		Sun
	RASI				NAVAMSA	
Mars Rahu						
	Moon			Jupit.	Saturn	Mercury Ketu

Balance of Mercury Dasa at birth : Years 7-10-26.

Special Features.—The intellectual sign Gemini rising gives a sympathetic and sensitive nature, mental restlessness and inherent intuitional ability. The Lagna is aspected by the Gnanakaraka Jupiter from the mystic sign Aquarius suggesting that Einstein gave the world gnana—not merely an abstract conception like Euclid's space—but knowledge of a real medium—space-time—in which physical processes act and are observed. Lord of Lagna ideally placed and not involved in any sort of affliction with either Rahu or Mars (in Navamsa, there is a slight affliction) conferred humility, gentleness and forbearance and charming manners. He was of a slender frame and possessed phosphorescent eyes being the blessings of Gemini Lagna. Lord of Lagna Mercury is in conjunction with Saturn, lord of the 9th and in association with the Sun, lord of the 3rd, and Venus, lord of the 5th (and 12th). This is an interesting combination having reference to the 10th Rasi from Lagna and the 5th from the Moon, signifying an active, able and penetrating mind. Mercury lord of Lagna as well as of the 4th or house of education is debilitated but gets cancellation of debility (neechabanga). Mercury's excellent position clearly explains the fact that at 14, Einstein taught himself integral and differential calculus and analytical geometry from books. The presence of *Buddhi Chaturya Yoga* enabled Einstein to revolutionise physics with deep and challenging ideas. The karaka for music, *viz.*, Venus is with Lagna lord. Consequently, Einstein was better than an average violinist, his favourite composers being Bach and Mozart. Lagna in Navamsa being occupied by Rahu, a planet of backward motion, made the scientist "a man of eccentricities", such as most great men are, but most of his eccentricities were merely efforts to simplify his life. Mark the situation of Jupiter, the planet of wisdom, in the 9th or Dharmasthana, between two malefics and thus subject to Papakarthari Yoga. Einstein was a sane man in a mad world, as scientist as well as saint. Mark the ideal disposition of the Sun in the 10th from Lagna and as lord of the 10th from the Moon in the 5th conferring great independence of thought. When in 1914, the German Government anxious to find intellectual support for its imperial ambitions put great pressure on its leading men, 93 of them signed a manifesto in support of Germany's entry into I World War, but Einstein did not sign. The Moon is debilitated in the 6th and the 6th lord is in the 8th with Rahu. These combinations exposed him on two flanks. On one flank was the rising Nazis to whom he was "un-German". To men across the Rhine, Einstein was a German scientist of whom too much fuss was being made. Dhanakaraka is well placed but Dhanadhipati (2nd lord) is *neecha* but otherwise unafflicted. He was without concern for money. All the money he received with the Nobel Prize, he gave away by way of charity.

Important Events.—In 1901, Einstein married the gifted mathematician Mileva Mavel, when Rahu Bhukti in Venus Dasa had commenced. Venus is Kalatrakaraka and Rahu is in the 8th (marriage thread) from Lagna and the 11th (gains) from Kalatrakaraka, while in Navamsa he aspects the 7th. Under the same directional influences (major lord Venus in the 10th or house of profession and Saturn, whose results Rahu should give, in a similar situation) Einstein started working as a Patent Office examiner. Saturn, lord of the 9th and Venus lord of the 5th, are together with Mercury lord of the 4th and Lagna. It was during Venus Dasa Saturn Bhukti that he first appeared before a large gathering of physicists, whom he impressed with his ability to unite his new ideas of relativity with those of quantum physics. Immediately after the commencement of Mercury's sub-period, Einstein got a job as Professor of Physics in Prague. The Sun's Dasa commenced in 1914 and this synchronised with his becoming the Director of Kaiser Wilhelm Research Institute for Physics in Berlin. It was in Moon Dasa Mars Bhukti that Einstein received international recognition

when he was made a Nobel Laureate. It will be seen that the
Moon is *neecha*, but as he is in the constellation of Mercury,
he is capable of giving the results of Mercury—intellectual
distinction as well as financial gains. Mark the position of
Mars, lord of the 6th and 11th exalted in the 8th with Rahu.
Even since his Dasa commenced in 1930, life had been made
intolerable for Einstein in Germany. His citizenship was
revoked ; he was expelled from the Academy of Sciences and
he was an exile with a price of 20,000 marks on his head.
That a malefic like Mars owning two dusthanas and occupying
the 8th, strong, and in association with Rahu, is capable of
giving hell to the native is clearly brought out in this horoscope.
In 1932 (Jupiter in Mars) he went to America and joined the
Institute at Princeton. Rahu, despite his incendiary nature, is
aspected (in the Navamsa) by Mercury (karaka for intellect)
and Jupiter (karaka for wisdom). Rahu Dasa commenced in
1937 and lasted till January 1955. It was during Rahu—due
to his peculiar disposition—that Einstein went on thinking,
speculating and "braiding together not only some strands of
experience, time with space, mass with energy, gravitation
with space-time but to braid together the whole of our physical
experience in a single theory" and looked for unity in all
nature. Rahu gave him success. But because Rahu is in the
8th with the planet of destruction, Mars, Einstein who "at 26
had for the first time equated mass with energy now saw the
equation threaten the world". Einstein's death took place as
soon as Jupiter Dasa commenced. It will be seen that Jupiter
is a maraka as he is lord of the 7th and is in the constellation
of Rahu.

Remarks.—Four planets having reference to the 10th and
the lordships involving Lagna, the 4th, 5th and the 9th have

caused some sort of Parivraja Yoga which made Einstein a Gnana yogi. He worked in abstruse mathematics most of which is incomprehensible to the average man. Relativity, over and above its scientific import comprises a major philosophical system. One cannot but be impressed by Einstein's equation—energy is equivalent to mass multiplied by the square of the velocity of light, that is $E = MC^2$ because it gives a unity to nature. When Jupiter is pre-eminently placed in a horoscope, either in the 9th or 10th or in Lagna, it makes the man philosophical. In this case, the emphasis is on Dharmasthana (9th) by virtue of the presence of Jupiter, and Karmasthana (10th) by virtue of the situation of four planets which made Einstein "incorruptible in the search for truth". He was not merely a scientist, but a humanitarian as is revealed by the presence of the Sun in the 10th. He spent his last years, warning against the misuse of power with all the force at his command. Lagna lord, subject to *neechabhanga* in the 10th by Venus, who in his turn has caused *Malavya Yoga*, clearly reveals that Einstein was undoubtedly one of the greatest mankind has ever produced.

No. 46. – SRI RAMANA MAHARSHI

Birth Details.—Born on 29th/30 December 1879 at 1 a.m. (L.M.T.) (Lat. 9° 50′ N., Long. 78° 15′ E.)

Planetary Positions.—The Sun 257° 4′ ; the Moon 89° 58′ ; Mars 23° 26′ ; Mercury 234° 36′ ; Jupiter 317° 57′ ; Venus 211° 57′ ; Saturn 348° 32′ ; Rahu 265° 23′ ; Ketu 85° 23′ ; and Lagna 182° 18′. Ayanamsa 20° 43′.

Saturn	Mars	Ketu Moon	Jupit.		Ketu	Moon
Jupiter			Merc.			Venus
	RASI			NAVAMSA		
Rahu Sun	Mercury Venus	Lagna	Sat.	Rahu Mars	Lagna	Sun

Balance of Jupiter Dasa at birth : Years 4–1–20.

Special Features.—The Lagna is Libra, the sign of the balance is Vargottama, and gains considerable vitality bacause of the aspect of Jupiter and the association of the lord of the Lagna with Mercury. The Maharshi was of medium height, fair-complexioned and had a dignified appearance, not a little due to the combined influences of the three important planets.

Mark the disposition of the Sun and the Moon in benefic signs and association with spiritual planets. His eyes were full of brightness emanating a spiritual lustre. He had a normal childhood. That he was inconspicuous in the school and had meagre education is revealed by the 4th lord being Saturn and the 4th house from the Moon being aspected by Saturn. Though the 3rd house is somewhat afflicted, the 3rd lord is fairly well placed while the 3rd from the Moon receives the aspect of Jupiter. The 3rd lord has gained six Navamsas, and allowing margin for the intervening malefics, it can be said that the number of brothers and sisters including the subject was 4. The Vargottama disposition of the Moon in a benefic sign and Jupiter's powerful aspect denotes a fairly good longevity to the mother. The situation of the yogakaraka, Saturn, in the 6th is highly significant. It demonstrates the pitfalls and the struggles the sage had to face before attaining the plane of bliss. He was a Brahmachari and sublimated his sex instincts into spiritual channels. This is revealed not only by the presence of Mars in the 7th but also by the disposition of Venus, Kamakaraka, in the 2nd with Mercury, lord of the 9th or Dharma. What little mischief Mars, as lord of the 7th in the 7th, could do has been offset by his occupying the constellation of Ketu, the mokshakaraka. There is no doubt that Jupiter aspecting Chandra Lagna in the 9th weaned the mind of the subject away from any thought of sex. Lagna lord aspecting the 8th and Saturn Ayushkaraka in a benefic sign denote good longevity. Pitrukaraka, Sun, afflicted by Rahu's association and the 9th lord being aspected by Mars, rendered the native fatherless at an early age. The Sun and the Moon representing the soul and the mind respectively are in benefic signs and are fairly powerful indicating the high degree of development of Atmavidya and the strength of mind. Rahu is with the Sun and Mars, the planet of passions, is in the house of passions. The native must have undergone an intense mental and spiritual struggle within himself before perceiving reality.

Important Events.—The first and the most important event is the father's death. This occurred in 1892 in Venus Bhukti Saturn Dasa. The major lord Saturn owns the 9th and is in a maraka house from the Pitrusthana (9th). And the sub-lord Venus in the 2nd in association with the 9th lord and aspected by Mars the combination occurring in the 12th from Pitrukaraka. Moreover, Saturn acquires the power to kill the father because of his 4th lordship. And Venus becomes equally empowered to kill because Venus, the lord of Lagna, should produce the results pertaining to the 9th Bhava, with whose lord he is associated. As Venus is in the house of Mars being aspected by the same malefic, evil results pertaining to the father happened. August 29, 1896 was perhaps a red letter day in the life of the Maharshi, for on this date he left his house in response to the call from Arunachala. At so early an age, his mind was already ripe for renunciation. These deve-lopments have reference to Saturn Dasa Mars Bhukti. It will be seen that both Saturn and Mars are yogakarakas—the former as lord of a kendra and kona and the latter as having caused *Ruchaka Yoga*. Mark the *parivarthana* between Saturn and Jupiter, lords of the 9th and 10th respectively from Chandra Lagna. This *Dharma-Karmadhipa Yoga* caused by the two philosophical planets is a unique combination which enabled him at such a tender age to transcend all limitations of body, mind and intellect. Rahu Bhukti in Saturn Dasa saw the death of the Maharshi's elder brother. Rahu is in the 3rd aspected by

Saturn and associated with the Sun. The next important event
is the death of his mother. This occurred in Ketu Dasa Moon
Bhukti. The sub-lord is of course Matrukaraka while the major
lord Ketu is in conjunction with the Matrukaraka. The Moon is
subject to the powerful aspect of Mars and Saturn in Navamsa.
The Maharshi's own death took place in Saturn Bhukti in Sun
Dasa. The Sun is in the 3rd from Lagna and as lord of the 3rd
from the Moon occupies the 7th, a maraka house. Saturn, the
sub-lord, besides being Ayushkaraka, occupies the 3rd from
Lagna and the 7th from Chandra Lagna in the Navamsa. These
various ownerships and dispositions have conferred on the Sun
and Saturn maraka power.

Remarks.—This is the horoscope of an extraordinary man
hailed as Bhagawan by his innumerable disciples and admirers.
The Moon is the Atmakaraka and is very strongly placed in
Vargottama aspected powerfully by Jupiter the divine planet.
Jaimini's dictum that Ketu in the 12th from Karakamsa gives
one *Kaivalya* or final emancipation is literally applicable in
this case. His appreciation of the oneness of the individual and
the universal spirit was not intellectual. On the contrary, he
was a witness to the truth that is beyond intellectual comprehension. What are the combinations that made this simple,
silent and frail human frame, a superman? There are no outstanding *Parivraja Yogas*. But the powerful *Dharma-Karmadhipa Yoga* involving Saturn and Jupiter, the latter planet
occupying the mystic sign of Aquarius, which happens to be
the 5th from Janma Lagna *plus* the disposition of Ketu in the
12th from the Karakamsa, should give the clue to understand
the personality of the sage. Mark the strength of the Moon. He
is in a benefic sign, Vargottama and in the 9th form Lagna,
unaspected by or unassociated with malefics like Saturn and

Mars. But nevertheless, as the Sun aspects the Moon, the Maharshi must have subjected himself to long and preliminary discipline, with the aim of attaining mental introversion, the first step towards self-realisation. Saturn in the 6th no doubt indicates troubles and opposition during his own Dasa but the *parivarthana* with Jupiter enabled the sage to overcome all obstacles. Mercury Dasa which lasted from 1903 to 1920 must have been very important in his life. Mercury is dharma-dhipa (9th lord) from Lagna and is in the 2nd, Scorpio, a secret sign, in association with Lagna lord Venus and aspected by Mars from the 7th house. This must have been a period of intense conflict between the inner "I" (the real) and the superimposed outer "I" or ego. Mercury in the 6th from the Moon has given rise to a trace of *Adhi Yoga*. The conflict between the forces of Mars—*Avidya* or egoism, ignorance, fear and lust and those of Mercury or *Jnana*—true knowledge so well indicated by the *shashtashtaka* disposition of these planets, ultimately resulted, through a process of self-discipline, self-analysis, and questioning and searching within (Scorpio) – in self-realisation or Brahma or Atmagnana. Another formidable aspect, no less important, in making the sage what he was, is the disposition of Jupiter and the Sun in the 6th and 4th Bhavas respectively. His horoscope, when carefully studied, doubtless reveals that the Maharshi belongs to the galaxy of those great sages and saints who have kept the light of India eternally burning.

No. 47.—FRANKLIN DELANO ROOSEVELT

Birth Details.—Born on 30th January 1882 at 8 p.m. (L.M.T.)   (Lat. 40° 43' N., Long. 73°.59' W.)

Planetary Positions.—The Sun 290° 20' ; the Moon 75° 5' ; Mars 66° 15 ; Mercury 306° 23' ; Jupiter 26° 10' ; Venus 285° 16' ; Saturn 15° 20' ; Rahu 224° 55' ; Ketu 44° 55' ; and Lagna 143° 32'. Ayanamsa 20° 46'.

	Saturn Jupiter	Ketu	Moon Mars		Venus Ketu
Mercury				Moon	Sun
	RASI			NAVAMSA	Saturn
Sun Venus		Lagna			
	Rahu			Mercury Lagna Mars Jupiter Rahu	

Balance of Rahu Dasa at birth :   Years 6-7-20.

Special Features.—The horoscope becomes significant by the *Chandramangala Yoga* in the 11th caused by the association of the Moon and Mars, the latter being a yogakaraka. From Chandra Lagna another Rajayoga is formed in the 11th by the conjunction of Saturn and Jupiter owning the 9th and 10th houses respectively, Saturn obtaining *neechabhanga*.

Mercury (lord of Chandra Lagna), being placed in the 9th, is highly significant. *Chandramangala Yoga* has occurred in the house of Mercury and Lagna is powerfully aspected by Jupiter. As President he did his best to alleviate suffering and to increase happiness in his own country. One cannot imagine what Britain's plight would have been but for the repeal of the neutrality legislation in 1939 and the ingenious innovation of Lend–Lease assistance. Mars is pretty strong in the horoscope and this was responsible for the unparalleled production of war material in America which changed the whole aspect of the war. The Sun, lord of Lagna, who is also the planet of vitality, is in the 6th or house of disease, in association with Venus and aspected by Saturn, lord of the 6th, and Mars. As a result of this affliction, Roosevelt was stricken with infantile paralysis at the end of Saturn Dasa. Some sort of *Vipareetha Rajayoga* has arisen by the very same combination of the Sun, as Lagna lord, in the 6th (an upachaya), in association with lord of the 10th Venus the aspect of yogakaraka Mars. This combination enabled Roosevelt to reach the highest position in life that is possible in a democratic country and to live the hard and exacting life of a great statesman.

Important Events.—In Jupiter Dasa, Roosevelt's father died when he was eighteen. Mark the position of Jupiter in the 9th from Lagna with Saturn. Roosevelt lived the life of a young man of independent means, slowly proceeding on his path, though interested all round and concerned at once with his own education and the conditions of American life. Saturn Dasa commenced in 1904. Saturn, lord of the 7th, in conjunction with Jupiter, lord of the 5th, has caused a distinct Rajayoga. Though Saturn is in debility, there is neechabhanga or cancellation of debilitation. Saturn aspects Venus, karaka of wife.

On St. Patric's day 1905, Roosevelt married Elaenor, a niece of Theodore Roosevelt. The first task of his public career started, when Rooseve't, 29 years old, went to Albany as senator for New York State. Lagna lord as well as lord of the sign occupied by the Moon are in watery signs in Navamsa. The sea had always allured Franklin Roosevelt. He was an excellent navigator. At the time of the Great War, Roosevelt was Assistant Secretary of the Navy. In 1918 he was sent under secret orders to Europe on a destroyer visiting some 50 naval bases in the Mediterranean and on the Scottish coast. Saturn had been very good to Roosevelt but as lord of the 6th and 8th from Lagna and the Moon respectively, during the last days of his Dasa, he was responsible for completely paralysing him from the hips down by an attack of infantile paralysis. Overnight a man of sparkling vitality had been reduced to a wreck.

Mercury is lord of the 2nd and occupies the 7th. In the Navamsa Mercury occupies a fairly good position. His Dasa commenced in 1923 and lasted till the beginning of 1940. In the house of Mercury (Gemini) there is *Chandramangala Yoga*, a unique combination. Jupiter casts a beneficial aspect on Lagna. Saturn in the 9th house is an excellent situation. Ketu Dasa commenced on 19-2-1940 and was a momentous one in his life. He won two presidential elections : the famous Atlantic Charter was born, and the major share was taken in winning the war. Ketu is in the 10th from Lagna and Venus, whose result Ketu should give, is lord of the 10th and is placed in the 6th with the Sun, lord of Lagna. From Chandra Lagna, Ketu is in the 12th—the house of losses. In Navamsa, Ketu occupies the 7th aspected by Mars and Jupiter and is in the 4th from Chandra Lagna. Thus Ketu is well placed to give Roosevelt name, power, influence, prestige and victory over enemies. But for Ketu's strong disposition Roosevelt would not have been able to retain his hold on the imagination of the people, nor could he have successfully battled against the cash and carry legislation which prevented utmost and being given to the Western allies. He died as soon as Saturn's sub-period commenced in Ketu Dasa. It will be seen that Ketu presides over the 3rd star, from that held by Saturn, going under the name of vipat (danger). The sub-lord Saturn owns a maraka house and is associated with Jupiter, lord of the 8th from Lagna. In the Navamsa, Saturn owns the 3rd from Lagna and occupies the 7th from the Moon. Ketu is in the 12th from the Moon and 2nd from the sub-lord. Added to all this, Roosevelt was having the Elarata for the third time in his life and Saturn–Rahu conjunction was taking place in his Janma Rasi, all these hastening his end.

Remarks.—In Roosevelt's horoscope, the Rajayogas are peculiarly balanced in the 6th (opposition and overcoming opposition), 9th (general fortune) and the 11th (gains and consolidation). The presence of *Chandramangala Yoga* in a sign of Mercury is a unique combination. Jupiter casts a beneficial aspect on Lagna. Hence in championing human liberties, he endeavoured to vindicate the moral rights of man. Saturn, the planet of democracy in the 9th house, is an excellent situation which made Roosevelt, the leader of World Democracy during the worst crisis in modern history. Lagna lord in an upachaya rendered him capable of handling the most difficult problems which he faced with tact, courage and imagination. In the Navamsa again, the Sun, as lord of the 10th, is in the 9th while Mars, lord of Lagna, is in Lagna with Jupiter, lord of the 2nd and 5th. Hence, he lived the moral and exacting life of a great statesman and genuine leader of a great people at a time when World Democracy was on trial.

17

No. 48.—AN EXAMPLE FOR RELIGIOUSNESS AND LOSS OF SIGHT

Birth Details.—Born on 24th March 1883 at 6 a.m. (L.M.T.) (Lat 13° N., Long. 77° 35' E.)

Planetary Positions.—The Sun 342° 17' ; the Moon 165° 20' ; Mars 317° 33' ; Mercury 321° 50' ; Jupiter 62° 43' ; Venus 298° 38' ; Saturn 31° 51' ; Rahu 202° 49' ; Ketu 22 49' ; and Lagna 340° 37'. Ayanamsa 20° 47'.

Lagna Sun	Ketu	Saturn	Jupit.	Mars	Mercury Rahu	Moon
Mercury Mars	RASI				NAVAMSA	
Venus				Sat.		
	Rahu	Moon			Ketu Lagna Sun Jupiter	Venus Kara-kamsa

Balance of Moon Dasa at birth : Years 6.

Special Features.—The ascendant is Pisces, a common and watery sign and the Sun and the Moon are also in common signs. The ascendant lord is in the 4th unaspected by benefics or malefics. The nearness of Mars to ascendant and the conjunction of Mercury reveals the subject's character. The Sun and the Moon, opposing each other and in dual signs, suggest a critical nature and inspiration. The Moon's position reveals that the mental side of the native is well developed and the disposition is receptive, showing reserve, diffidence and coldness. The absence of any malefic aspects over Lagna lord is an important factor denoting an affectionate nature. The Lagna and the Sun are both subject to Papakarthari Yoga, while the Moon receives the powerful aspect of Mars. This suggests a nature tormenting itself with curious fancies and readily moved by the proximity or association of others. The Karakamsa is free from affliction excepting that it is aspected by Mars. The mind is upright, kind, and the spirit, contemplative. The mutual aspect of Mars and Saturn suggests stubbornness ; the will, though changeful, is strong and he could be often content with a noble vengeance. The lord of the 2nd is in the 12th aspected by Saturn and the second itself is considerably afflicted though the 2nd lord derives some relief by Jupiter's aspect. Whilst the position of Venus in the 11th is always a good feature, in this case, the significance is lost partly by Venus being lord of 3 and 8 and partly by the *parivarthana*, the 11th lord has with Venus, the 3rd lord. In a sense, this combination has taken away much of the value or worth of the horoscope from the point of view of material gain and prosperity. The native never enjoyed the opportunity of asserting his individuality as the environmental factors were such that no effort on his part was needed even for meeting his own family responsibilities. Though the 3rd house is not well situated, the 3rd lord and karaka have harmonious dispositions. Mars, the indicator of brothers, has gained six Navamsas, Saturn intervening in the middle. The native had 6 brothers and sisters one of whom died early, he being the eldest. The presence of Jupiter in the 4th is significant while he was not much educated in the literal sense, he had the capacity of intuitional perception and experience. The house of children is fairly well disposed, the 5th lord being in the 7th and forming a yoga with Putrakaraka, suggesting happiness through children and coming to prominence of the eldest issue. The 9th and 10th lords, Mars and Jupiter respectively, are in the 12th and 4th and the real significance of this combination should be carefully noted by students of astrology. The subject had no definite occupation, as support was forthcoming voluntarily from his father and son.

Important Events.—The first marriage took place in Jupiter's sub-period in the Dasa of Rahu, who, it will be seen, is in the 8th, indicating marriage thread, while the sub-lord is in the 9th from the major lord. Mother's death occurred in 1902 when the sub-period of Saturn was operating. Saturn is in the house of fortune from the Moon and aspects powerfully the lord of the 4th from Navamsa Chandra Lagna. The first issue, a son, was born in the sub-period of the Moon in Rahu Dasa. The Moon is lord of the 5th and is in the 7th in a favourable position from Jupiter, the Putrakaraka. Mars' sub-period in Rahu Dasa was significant inasmuch as the wife died of smallpox. Mars is lord of the 2nd (family) from Lagna and is in the 12th; while from the Moon, Mars is lord of the 8th. In the Navamsa again, Mars occupies the 7th from Karakamsa. Rahu is in the 2nd from Chandra Lagna so that just before Rahu Dosa ended, the native had to lose his wife. Jupiter, being lord of Lagna and of the 7th from the Moon, the second marriage took place as soon as his Dasa began. The sub-period of Rahu, marking the end of Jupiter Dasa, was the most tragic because it was during this time that the subject lost his power of sight completely. This occurred just before the birth of a son. Rahu, it may be noted, aspects powerfully the 2nd from Lagna and Rahu is in the 2nd from the Moon. Jupiter is considerably afflicted in Navamsa. The next significant period was 1937 when the father, the guardian angel, died. Saturn the major lord is in the 7th from the 9th while Ketu the sub-lord is in the 2nd from Pitrukaraka, justifying the death of the father. The native's own death occurred in Mars sub-period, Saturn Dasa. Saturn is in the 3rd and aspects the 3rd from the Moon. Mars lord of the 2nd is in the 12th. In the Navamsa again, Saturn aspects the 2nd while Mars is in the 7th being lord of the 3rd and 8th from Karakamsa. As soon as the sub-period of Mars commenced the native's health gave way.

Remarks.—The horoscope interests us in two ways : firstly, the native had defective sight till 1928, *i.e.*, he could not see clearly during nights and he lost his vision completely in 1928 ; secondly, he was a great religious disciplinarian.

The Sun and the Moon indicate the eyes while the 2nd and 12th are associated with the right and left eye respectively. Even Mars is supposed to have governance over the eye. The Sun is subject to a *Papakarthari Yoga* in Lagna ; the Moon is powerfully aspected by Mars. The 2nd and 12th have the evil influences of all the planets centered on them. Mars and Mercury placed in the 12th aspected by Saturn, and Rahu and Ketu focus their combined influences on the 2nd. Thus, all the sensitive points pertaining to sight have been severely afflicted. Even in Navamsa, the 2nd receives considerable evil aspect. These influences suggest that the head was the seat of disease and the native lost his sight due to excessive partial headache. The affliction of Mars indicates extreme heat. Saturn–Mars square suggests pressure upon the pneumo gastric nerve, where it leaves the head.

He was a *Tapasvi* in its real sense. Unmindful of the tragedy that had befallen him in the shape of loss of sight and indifferent to the distractions which an unhappy domestic life had forced on him, he pursued with unabated zeal the task of performing more than 21 lakhs of Gayatri japams and thereby created around him a spiritual halo. Jupiter, aspecting the 2nd from the Moon and the Moon free from affliction, rendered him pure at heart. The 10th house is free from any trace of affliction. If he had no love for many, he had hatred for none. Words of abuse were perhaps foreign to him. His were the qualities of a cultured mind and an evolved ego. Frank and out-spoken and often blunt, diplomacy and sycophancy were completely absent. These are indeed great virtues.

The fact that a trace of *Virinchi Yoga* exists, by virtue of Jupiter and the lord of the 5th being placed in friendly kendras, should account for his deep religiousness. The 9th house from Karakamsa is occupied by a benefic and hence he was intent on doing virtuous actions ; always spoke the truth and respected parents and elders. He would not swerve in any way from the conduct prescribed in the Vedas and shone with real Brahminical lustre, qualities typically illustrative of *Virinchi Yoga*. It is the 9th that rules the religious tendencies, while the 10th has governance over karma. Mars, lord of the 9th, in Mokshasthana being aspected by lord of the 12th and Jupiter, Mokshakaraka and lord of Lagna and the 10th is unique inasmuch as it made him train his faculties in such a way that in spite of all physical and mental odds he faced, he made determined efforts in his spiritual aspirations with the result we could see in his face that calm and serene disposition which could only belong to a real yogi. If greatness consists also in asserting one's individuality in the direction of spiritual evolution and not in merely getting newspaper publicity, the subject was a truly great man.

The *dwirdwadasa* positions, *parivarthana* between the 3rd and 11th lords and the *Papakarihari Yogas* subjecting Lagna and the Sun to their influences, intermingled with *Virinchi*, *Gajakesari* and *Parivraja* combinations are of deep significance to students of astrology.

No. 49.—VINAYAK DAMODAR SAVARKAR

Birth Details.—Born on 28th May 1883 at 9-25 p.m. (L.M.T.) (Lat. 18° 23' N., Long. 73° 53' E.)

Planetary Positions.—The Sun 46° 10'; the Moon 304° 28'; Mars 8° 5'; Mercury 60° 26'; Jupiter 74°; Venus 15° 51; Saturn 39° 45'; Rahu 199° 20'; Ketu 19° 20'; and Lagna 266° 45'. Ayanamsa 20° 43'.

	Mars Ketu Venus	Sun Saturn	Jupit. Merc.	Rahu Sat.		Sun	Mars
Moon				Jupit.			
	RASI				NAVAMSA		Venus
Lagna		Rahu		Lagna	Moon	Mercury	Ketu

Balance of Mars Dasa at birth : 1–1–26.

Special Features.—The ascendant is Sagittarius, a war-like sign and Jupiter, the lord, aspects the Lagna. Sagittarius, being a fiery sign, denotes fire, an open mind and an honest and generous disposition. Mars is in Aries, an aggressive sign with Ketu, while there is a conjunction of the Sun and Saturn in the 6th. This combination makes him highly courageous. Savarkar's jumping into the sea near Marseilles while on his way to India under police custody is an example of his daring and courage. The same combination suggests also that there is a certain watchfulness and distrust of others which leads to deception while trying to avoid it. Lagna, being a sign of Jupiter and Lagna and Chandra Lagna being aspected by Jupiter, gave him the ability even as a lad, of divine communion. Lord of the 2nd (vak or speech) Saturn is in a benefic sign free from combination. The 2nd lord from the Moon is with the intellectual planet Mercury, in the sign of Gemini indicating great eloquence, fertile imagination, polished direction and a sense of perspective. It must be noted that by the time Jupiter Dasa commenced, he had already blossomed into an accomplished orator famed for his charming fluency and soundness of argument. From Chandra Lagna, the 10th lord is Mars and he is in the 3rd with Ketu and Venus, a yogakaraka. The combination has reference to the 5th house which, in a horoscope, denotes latent forces. Mars being a revolutionary planet, instilled into his mind revolutionary ideas which later in life he practised with considerable zeal and risk. Mark the fact that the 10th house is completely free from affliction. The 10th lord Mercury is in his own sign in the 7th in association with Lagna lord, Jupiter. But the 10th from Chandra Lagna has the aspects of three first-rate malefics, one of which is the Sun, the political planet. It is the focussing of the combined influences of these three malefics—Mars indicating revolutionary trend, the Sun indicating authority and Saturn indicating the spirit of patriotism and democracy that made Savarkar a patriot and a nationalist to the core and brought him into violent clash with the rulers. The horoscope has a number of *Bandhana yogas*, the most important ones being the association of the lords of Lagna and the 7th in a kendra from Chandra Lagna ; Ketu's disposition in Navamsa in the 10th from Lagna aspected by all the three worst malefics, and the 8th lord the Moon occupying the constellation of Mars indicating a checkered career, suffering and confinement in chains all of which Savarkar had in plenty.

Important Events.—Savarkar lost his mother when he was about 13 years old and his father died when he was 12 or 13, both events happening in Rahu Dasa. Mark the position of Rahu in the 8th and 3rd respectively from Matrusthana and Pithrusthana. His revolutionary activities also started under the same directional influences and they found full expression during Jupiter Dasa. Superficially Jupiter's position in the horoscope as Lagna lord does not warrant all the sufferings, risks and dangers which the native faced during Jupiter Dasa. But if you scrutinise the disposition of Jupiter, you will find that he is not harmless. He is in the Drekkana of *Ayudha* placed in a marakasthana. Occupying as he does the constellation of Rahu who, in his turn, is afflicted both in the Rasi and Navamsa, Jupiter conferred on him all the results due to Rahu's disposition. The native graduated in Jupiter Dasa Jupiter Bhukti. The position of Jupiter as lord of the house of education in the 7th is quite good. Under Saturn Bhukti in Saturn Dasa he sailed for England for further studies. In Saturn, Mercury and Ketu Bhuktis—note Saturn is in the nakshatra of Rahu and Mercury is in the nakshatra of Rahu—he kept contact with Sein Fein and other Irish Revolutionary parties and carried on the campaign of the nationalist struggle so vigorously through Abhinava Bharat Society in Europe, that at last in the I World War, India became an international issue. His arrest, his attempt to escape from the ship by jumping into the sea under the most hostile circumstances, with hundreds of foreigners keeping vigilant watch on his movements—took place in Ketu Bhukti of Jupiter Dasa. At the time Savarkar was escorted to the cellular jail of Andamans with fetters on hands and legs the sub-period of Venus was running in the major period of Jupiter. Mark the affliction of Venus as lord of the 6th and 11th in the 4th Bhava with Mars and Ketu. When he was running *sadesathi* for the first time, the native was persecuted, arrested, tried and finally convicted. He was brought back to India in Saturn Dasa Mercury Bhukti and interned in Ratnagiri. The beginning of Mercury Dasa was synchronised with his final release from internment. He had again to face trial in connection with the assassination of Gandhi and this happened in Mercury Dasa Moon Bhukti. Both the Moon and Mercury are in the constellation of Mars.

Remarks.—This is the horoscope of a selfless patroit who sacrificed his all for the freedom of his country. What would interest an astrological student is the occurrence of yogas which rendered the native display a heroic fortitude, a reckless spirit of sacrifice in the interests of the motherland, and the dignity with which the anguish of separation from the dear and near ones, was borne. The Sun, lord of the 9th with Saturn, lord of the 2nd, has conferred undying fame on the native, but as the political planet is afflicted both in Rasi and Navamsa, and as it occupies the constellation of the Moon, lord of the 8th, his sufferings and sacrifics did not receive that gratitude and aknowledgment which were bestowed on lesser men whose sacrifices were nil or nominal. *Bandhana yogas* are well pronounced especially that lord of the 6th and 11th Venus is in a kendra with Mars, lord of the 12th, and Ketu. Chandra Lagnadhipati Saturn and the 8th lord therefrom are also in conjunction in a kendra from the Moon. How an apparently benefic planet is capable of producing the most unfortunate results by virtue of occupying a destructive constellation, is clearly brought out in this case. Lagna is aspected by Jupiter lord of Lagna, who is unafflicted. This gave the native an indomitable spirit. In the Navamsa again, the Lagna is aspected by two first-rate malefics—Saturn (with Rahu) from 4th and Mars from 7th, a sign of aggression indicating that Savarkar combined in himself a dangerous rebel and a dauntless revolutionary. The horoscope of Savarkar, one of India's greatest revolutionists, deserves more than a casual study in the hands of astrological students.

No. 50.–BENITO MUSSOLINI

Birth Details.—Born on 29th July 1883 at 2 p.m. (L.M.T.) (Lat. 41° N., Long. 16° E.)

Planetary Positions.—The Sun 105° 13′; the Moon 48° 21′; Mars 52° 13′; Mercury 104° 43′; Jupiter 87° 43′; Venus 90° 43′; Saturn 46° 43′; Rahu 196° 4′; Ketu 16° 4′; and Lagna 211° 43′. Ayanamsa 20° 47′.

	Ketu	Moon Saturn Mars	Jupit.		Moon Saturn Jupiter
		Sun Merc Venus	Rahu		Mars Lagna Venus
RASI				NAVAMSA	Ketu
	Lagna	Rahu		Mercury Sun	

Balance of Moon Dasa at birth: Years 3–8–26.

Special Features.—A horoscope may be considered and searched from different points of view. In order to obtain a first impression we must consider first of all the ruler of the nativity. Lagna is Scorpio or Vrischika. Lord of Lagna Mars is in the 7th with a malefic Saturn aspecting Lagna. In the Navamsa, Lagna is Cancer and Mars is neecha but has obtained neechabhanga or cancellation of debility. This disposition of Lagna suggests Mussolini's instinctive sense of of dominion and an insistent, determind, positive energy. His personality expression is belligerent and aggressive because Scorpio is rising. Mars gives him dynamic energy and makes him bold, penetrative and gives him fiery enthusiasm But the conjunction of Mars with Saturn, lord of the 3rd, directs his capacities in quite destructive channels. If Mars were alone, he would probably have been one of the greatest conquerors, but Saturn has sapped up all the vitality so that he brouhgt ruin not only to himself but to his mother country also. A man influenced by Mars—and Mussolini is one of them—is an active and energetic worker but again there is the affliction of Saturn's combination with Mars. The position of Mars alone would have given him intellectual courage and optimism, positive thought, and critical abilities but Saturn again takes away much of the good with the result that at the last moment in a crisis, the person could lose his balance of mind, especially because the Moon representing the mind is with Saturn and Mars which denotes loss of temper on the slightest provocation. The lord of the 10th (the Sun) being in the 9th endowed Mussolini with a regal consciousness. He instinctively felt the right of rulership by Divine endowment. This was a wrong feeling for Saturn aspecting the Sun made him too selfish. Mars receives both favourable and unfavourable aspects—the bad ones producing many enemies and many dangers. All the planets are concentrated in three signs. This explains the sudden about face in his policies at times when it became easier to lead his flock by telling them that which they wished so hear even if it was exactly opposite to his expressed opinion of the day before. Mussolini did not create and mould his environment but took full advantge of conditions presented to him. Western astrologers thought that the most fortunate position in Mussolini's chart was the conjunction of Jupiter and Venus in the 8th house. These two benefics, they said, afforded a powerful protective influence over the physical body. We differ entirely from this deduction. According to Hindu astrology if the 8th is occupied by benefics—especially Jupiter and Venus—the combination goes under the name of Asura Yoga. This makes the native a tyrant taking pleasure in the sufferings of others. According to Mantreswara, "One born in Asura Yoga will become mean, a tale-bearer, will spoil others' work and will always be intent on securing his own interests. He will be head-strong. He will do vile acts and become miserable as a result of his own evil and mischievous doing". The situation of Jupiter and Venus should be viewed from the Moon as it causes a powerful *Dhana Yoga*. Moreover from the Moon, Sarurn is a yogakaraka and hence, during his Dasa which commenced somewhere in 1928, he reached the highest position as dictator. Saturn aspects the 10th from the Moon and he powerfully aspects the 10th lord, the Sun, from Lagna. It is this aspect that supplies the answer to the question why Mussolini fell. The heavy aspects involving the 7th, 8th and 9th houses increase his desire for position and status in life and show somewhat the methods he used to attain his ambition. When Mars is in the 7th in a leader's horoscope he will not generally hesitate to use the destructiveness of open warfare to gain his desires. The Moon's exaltation suggests that often he knew just how much he could bluff. But the conjunction of Saturn often misled him.

Important Events.—A close examination of the horoscope reveals the presence of *Subhavasi* and *Lakshmi Yogas*. These led him to power and that power he lost. In Mussolini's horoscope all the planets are located above the horizon and all of them are in the west. This has a very special meaning. If the planets are in the west it indicates rise during the second half of one's life. In this case they are found from the 9th to the descendant. We therefore could see that the ascent of Mussolini started at the beginning of the second half of his life. It was in Jupiter Dasa that he marched on Rome. Saturn Dasa enabled him to build an Empire but Saturn aspecting the lord of Karmasthana rendered its destruction inevitable. Atmakaraka is Jupiter and he is in the Navamsa of Gemini. Venus is in Karakamsa. It was this that gave him political power. Saturn Dasa began in 1928 and it lasted till 1947. From Lagna, Saturn is not a benefic whereas from Chandra Lagna he is a benefic. Hence he produced good results in the first half of his Dasa while in the second half he necessarily gave rise to very unfavourable results. In 1929 when Saturn Dasa had just then commenced, Mussolini succeeded in ending the quarrel between the Government and the Vatican. From 1935 onwards Mussolini became very aggressive under the auspices of the Dasa of Saturn who, in conjunction with Mars, is in the 7th house. He was ever ready to bluff and fight rather than to relinquish safety, territory and prestige. And with that affliction to the 7th house it was not surprising that his relations with other powers were inharmonious. Mussolini entered the II World War in Saturn Dasa and Moon Bhukti. Mark the situation of both these planets in the 7th along with Mars. In the Navamsa, Saturn owns the 7th and 8th houses and is situated in the 12th while the sub-lord owning Lagna is also placed in the 12th house thus indicating loss. Saturn tempted him to sacrifice himself for greedy ambition and self-aggrandisement. It is the same position of Mars and

Saturn that made the Duce use the modern technique of mass suggestion combined with the relentless use of force which enabled him to ensure that no currency was given to anything but his own accounts of events. In the Navamsa there is a conglomeration of four planets—the Moon (lord of Lagna), Saturn (lord of 8), Venus (lord of 11), and Jupiter (lord of 6)—all occurring in the 12th or house of loss. This satellitium is full of significance. This made the native overforceful, restless and disruptive. His death took place in Saturn Dasa Jupiter Bhukti. Saturn owns the 3rd and 4th from Lagna and occupies the 7th, a maraka place. In the Navamsa again, Saturn owns the 7th and 8th houses. The sub-lord Jupiter is a maraka, as he owns the 2nd and occupies the 8th with Venus, lord of the 7th. The major and sub-lords are in *dwirdwadasa* and the former in association with Mars. Hence Mussolini had a *violent end.

---

* In November 1943 issue of THE ASTROLOGICAL MAGAZINE, we made the following prediction about Mussolini :—

"In the birth chart of Mussolini, Saturn is in the 17th degree of Taurus while Mars is in the 23rd. Jupiter is in the 27th of Gemini. Saturn by transit passes through the orb of this degree by about October 1944 and the exact degree is transited by about July 1945. Thus about this time something tragic may happen to the Duce. There will be a conjunction of Mars and Saturn about the last part of Taurus in March 1944. This will be an exciting time for him. Things will happen quickly and unexpectedly. Rahu is incendiary in nature and Saturn does a thing with certainty. Mussolini's chart is no doubt powerful but the conjunction of Saturn and Mars and the conglomeration of evil forces occurring in the Navamsa are weak points suggesting that even though Mussolini has been rescued by Hitler, the Duce is most likely to have a tragic end. He will no more have any political power or authority. The star is about to set and the time will be the present sub-period of Rahu in the major period of Saturn."

Remarks.—It will be seen that the political planet Sun (lord of the 10th) in the 9th is aspected by Saturn, while Mars is in association with Saturn. Lagna lord Mars, 10th lord Sun and the 9th or house of fortune are all afflicted considerably clearly indicating fall from power and proving the dictum that mutual afflictions between Saturn and Mars involving the 9th or 10th are always of sinister significance.

No. 51.—HARRY S. TRUMAN

Birth Details.—Born on 8th May 1884 at 4-26 p.m. (L.M.T.) (Lat. 39° 7′ N., Long. 94° 30 W.)

Planetary Positions.—The Sun 27° 54′ ; the Meon 194° 27′ ; Mars 116° 27′ ; Mercury 40° 29′ (R) ; Jupiter 97° 19′ ; Venus 73° 13′ ; Saturn 49° 30′ ; Rahu 181° 1′ ; Ketu 1° 1′ ; and Lagna 178° 15′. Ayanamsa 20° 47′.

	Sun Ketu	Mercury Saturn	Venus		Mercury Ketu		Saturn
			Mars Jupit.	Moon Mars			
	RASI				NAVAMSA		
				Venus			
		Rahu Moon	Lagna	Sun		Rahu	Lagna Jupiter

Balance of Rahu Dasa at birth : Years 7–5–27.

Special Features.—The Lagna is Virgo or Kanya, a sign of quick perception. This makes the native modest, thoughtful, contemplative, prudent, economical and cautious, sometimes rather undecided but usually precise though nervous and lacking self-confidence, perceptive and somewhat intuitive. Mars, lord of the 3rd and 8th houses, is in the 11th from Lagna and the Sun ruling political power is in the 8th or a house of death. This may explain the fact that Truman reached power through a death. Jupiter exalted is actually in the 10th house though in the 11th Rasi. Mars has obtained cancellation of debility in the 10th which is further fortified by the occurrence of *Chandramangala Yoga*. These are dominant vibrations in his character and circumstances. The *Gajakesari Yoga* has reference to the 2nd, 4th, 7th and 11th and its effects are further augmented by the disposition of Venus, lord of the 2nd and 9th—wealth and fortune respectively, in the 10th. The aspect of Saturn upon Mars is not desirable. Saturn crystallises ; what we may call, collective destiny. As lord of the 5th and associating with the 10th lord in the 9th, thereby having caused a powerful Rajayoga, Saturn is capable of endowing the man with continual reinforcement of vitality as well as a progressive view-point of life. Mark the disposition of the majority of the planets in the second half of the zodiac. Stress is therefore laid on the 9th, 10th and 11th houses indicating respectively, fortune, action and realisation, the last being restricted by the intermingling of jupiterian, martian and saturnine forces. The Sun is very strong in Aries and Mars in the 10th has obtained neechabhanga and digbala. These stress the political sense and an eagerness for reform and a social enthusiasm for new theories.

The Moon is in association with Rahu in Libra. The Moon rules over the mind and Rahu rules over intuitional faculties. Their association in the 2nd house suggests that Truman had a mind which depended more upon unseen intuitional guidance than upon actual material fact. Mars has nothing to do with the 7th nor is there mutual aspect between Mars and Saturn. Obviously, Truman was not one for aggressive activity or forceful oral manoeuvres. President Truman's steadfastness, his resoluteness and his sense of balance are qualities of the Moon's situation in Libra. The most important Rajayogas in our opinion are the exchange of houses between the 9th and 10th lords, the association of Mercury and Saturn in the 9th, the exaltation of Jupiter in the 10th, neechabhanga of Mars In the 10th and Vargottama of Jupiter. Of course, due allowance must be made to the evil lordships of some of these planets causing the various yogas, but their inherent capacity to confer the blessings of the yoga are in no way affected or lessened, though the evil due to lordsip could manifest in terms of accidents, etc. Jupiter exalted and aspecting the 12th from Pada Lagna and the lord of the 4th from Karakamsa being aspected by Venus are factors indicating wealth and riches.

Important Events.—He became President during the sub-period of Venus in the Dasa of Ketu. Venus, as would be seen, is lord of the 2nd and 9th and is posited in the 10th having had Parivaathana with Mercury, lord of Lagna and the 10th. This is a unique combination. The major lord Ketu is in the 7th house and in a Vargottama. He occupies the 9th from Lagna in the Navamsa. Ketu is in his own constellation. Ketu is in the house of Mars. As such, he is capable of producing martian results. Mars, though had by ownership from Lagna, is enviably placed from Chandra Lagna. In the latter circumstances, he owns the 2nd and 7th and occupies the 10th in conjunction with exalted Jupiter. Mars is also placed in the constellation of Mercury. All these, combined. rendered the circumstances very favourable for Truman to become Head of the State. Owing to the dominance of martian trends during Ketu Dasa, Truman's foreign policy did not really ease the international tension. Truman laid down his office in Venus Dasa Venus Bhukti. Venus, though owning the 2nd and the 9th and occupying the 10th, is rendered weak because of his disposition in Rahu's constellation and his affliction in Navamsa by being subject to Papakarthari. Rahu is a maraka and the power is delegated to Venus. The Rajayoga part of the results iddicated by Venus were conferred by him as sub-lord in Ketu Dasa.

Remarks.—Here in Truman's horoscope, there are no indications to suggest his election. In fact, he is said to have not wanted executive responsibility, even as Vice-President. He was said to be "one of those average, everyday Americans —a veteran of the last World War, a small town-lawyer, an honest honourable, sincere individual who has never shown any particular tendency towards greatness". It was therefore a break of fortune for him to have been elected by the people because he never stood for any election but still the exalted office of President fell on him unexpectedly. This is indicated by the exaltation of the Sun in the 7th from the Moon and the association of the Sun with Ketu. The distance between Ketu and the Sun is more than 27° so that there is no fear of affliction. The Lagna or ascendant being vargottama is strongly disposed. Lagna lord Mercury in the 9th with Saturn lord of the 7th constituting a Rajayoga ; the Sun being exalted in the 7th from Chandra Lagna ; *parivarthana* between lords of the 9th and 10th ; and Mars, the planet of action *neechabhanga*, are the special features of this horoscope.

No. 52.—SRI KRISHNARAJA WADIYAR IV

Birth Details.—Born on 4th June 1884 at 10-18 a.m. (L.M.T.). (Lat. 12° N., Long. 76° 38′ E.)

Planetary Positions.—The Sun 53° 9′; the Moon 182° 56′; Mars 128° 54′; Mercury 32° 44′; Jupiter 101° 28′; Venus 92° 54′; Saturn 52° 52′; Rahu 179° 37′; Ketu 359° 37′; and Lagna 117° 40′. Ayanamsa 20° 47′.

Ketu	Sun Mercury Saturn	Lagna Ketu	Mars
RASI	Lagna Jupit. Venus	NAVAMSA	Sun Venus Saturn
RASI	Mars Mandi · Merc.	NAVAMSA	Mandi
	Moon	Rahu	Moon Jupiter · Rahu

Balance of Mars Dasa at birth: Years 1–11–16.

Special Features.—The ascendant or Lagna is Cancer, a movable and watery sign and the lord of Lagna the Moon is in the 4th, thus strengthening the Lagna. The Lagna is occupied by two first-rate benefics, Jupiter and Venus, and aspected by Saturn from another benefic sign. This disposition has doubt-less given vitality to the horoscope. Consistent with the inherent nature of Cancer and the predominating influence of Jupiter, His Highness had a magnetic personality of erect bearing and handsome features. Framed in a turban, His Highness carried himself with the innate reserve of royalty but without any suggestion of its pomp. The Sun's disposition in Taurus, which happens to be the 11th from Lagna, denotes conservatism, a strong will, persistence and a firm and authoritative attitude. It will be seen that Jupiter is exalted in Lagna. This is an ideal position denoting an optimistic spirit, a jovial disposition and pleasant manners. The Moon ruling the mind and the 'affect' personality of an individual is in Libra, in a kendra from Lagna and from Venus and in a sign of the latter. This combination gives fondness for music, poetry and fine arts generally with some ability in this direction. In fact, His Highness was well versed in Carnatic music and was a great patron of arts and letters. A fertile imagination, a quiet reserved nature, an adventurous disposition and the faculy of absorbing other people's ideas are the key-notes of Cancer being the Lagna. There are several Rajayogas revealing the true personality of the Maharaja. But the most outstanding combination is the exaltation of Jupiter in the 10th from Chandra Lagna with Venus, lord of Chandra Lagna. Lord of the 2nd Sun, in the 11th, Mars the yogakaraka in the 2nd and Jupiter the Dhanakaraka and lord of the 9th exalted in the Lagna constitute powerful Dhana yogas. The 5th lord Mars is associated with Mandi while the 5th itself is afflicted by the aspect of three malefics. The 5th from Chandra Lagna is aspected by Mars and Mandi. These afflictions rendered the native issueless. In spite of the wealth and the great qualities of head and heart he possessed, the Maharaja was not happy so far as marriage life was concerned. The 7th lord Saturn is disposed in a kendra from Mars lord of the 2nd and 7th from Chandra Lagna and Mars and Mercury afflict the 2nd or house of family. Venus, Kalatrakaraka, is aspected powerfully by Saturn while his association with Jupiter enabled the subject to sublimate his passions. The house of fortune is considerably fortified by its lord being exalted in Lagna and Mars, the yogakaraka aspecting the 9th powerfully. From Chandra Lagna, the 10th house gets immensely strengthened because of the exaltation of Jupiter and the presence of Venus. Jupiter is doubtless somewhat evil because of his ownership of the 3rd and 6th. But this inherent benefic nature asserts itself especially that he is in the 10th house. This combination also made His Highness's life one of religious sanctity. He was an orthodox Hindu in the true sense. He held in equal esteem the learned Pandit or the pious missionary. The most outstanding combination in the horoscope, is the occurrence of powerful *Gajakesari* and *Hamsa Yogas*. The results ascribed to *Hamsa Yoga*, *viz*., the person becomes a king, extolled by the good, will eat pure food and will be a man of righteous disposition holds good *in toto* in this horoscope, especially because, like the ancient Raja Rishis, he had consecrated all his endeavours to the welfare of his subjects. Venus, Rahu and the Moon in Vargottama, coupled with the attainment of digbala by Jupiter, the Sun and the Moon, gives rise to yet another powerful Rajayoga while Rahu in the 12th from the Moon indicates great piety, devotion and firm faith in God. The conjunction of Saturn and the Sun in the 11th made His Highness a constitutional monarch and he exercised an influence more pervasive and lasting than any power that a despotic monarch could have, because that influence proceeded from personal example and devotion to duty.

Important Events.—He was installed on the ancestral throne of Mysore on 8th August 1902. This took place in Rahu Dasa, Moon Bhukti. Rahu, the major lord, is in the house of Mercury who is in the 11th house from Lagna, associated with Saturn, a yogakaraka for Chandra Lagna. The sub-lord Moon having caused powerful Rajayogas such as *Hamsa, Gajakesari* and several others is eminently justified in bestowing a kingdom. His father Chamaraja Wadiyar died at the end of 1894, when the Maharaja was having Rahu Dasa Mercury Bhukti. Mercury is with Pitrukaraka and in the 9th from Rahu while Rahu occupies a maraka from the 9th house. In the Navamsa, Rahu is in the 3rd from Pitrukaraka and Mercury in the 7th empowering them to cause the father's death. The Sun's sub-period in Saturn's major period saw the death of the mother. The Sun is in the 8th from Matrukaraka in association with major lord Saturn, who owns the 4th from Chandra Lagna. His only brother, the Yuvaraja, died in Mercury Dasa, Mercury Bhukti, and he himself died under the same directions. Mercury is lord of the 3rd and is in conjunction with the Sun and Saturn, both powerful marakas. From Chandra Lagna, Mercury occupies the 8th. In the Navamsa again, Mercury owns the 7th from Lagna and is aspected by Mars, lord of the 2nd (and 9th) and Venus (lord of the 3rd and 8th). All these dispositions rendered Mercury capable of causing death.

Remarks.—The horoscope in question is typically illustrative of certain well-known principles of predictive astrology especially in regard to Rajayogas. Throughout his long and memorable reign of 40 years, His Highness showed a rare conscientiousness and disinterested zeal for the promotion of the welfare of his subjects which deservedly secured for him a moral authority and popular confidence which many heads of democratic States might well envy. This is due not a little to the strong *Hamsa Yoga*, especially having reference to the 10th house from Chandra Lagna. The lord of Lagna in a kendra and in Vargottama, and the lord of the 9th in exaltation is another powerful Rajayoga. The Full Moon's disposition in a kendra other than Lagna is itself a Rajayoga denoting the birth of the scion of a Royal family. Added to these combinations, the Full Moon's disposition in a Vargottama constitutes yet another asset illustrating the soundness of the astrological principles handed down to us by the sages.

The Sun-Saturn conjunction in the 11th is doubtless a good combination, but the fact that the Sun and Saturn are bitter enemies, the Sun ruling the 2nd or house of family and Saturn ruling the 7th or house of wife, made his domestic life quite miserable. Saturn's aspect on Lagna and on Venus may also be interpreted as denoting timidity on his part to check irregularities in religion and morals among his own close relations. The same aspect has also marred to a great extent what should otherwise have been very cheerful prosperity and jolliness of temper.

Leaving due margin for some of these evil combinations, it may be safely said that the horoscope has several virtues revealing that His Highness was the nearest approach in modern times to the ancient Indian ideal of true kingship ; for he firmly believed that the ultimate source and sanction of all true civil rule and obedience is the will and purpose of God and that behind the kings that are seen and temporal are things that are unseen and eternal. The horoscope, as a whole, is illustrative of very high qualities—personal as well as administrative and cannot fail to make a profound impression on the minds of the astrological readers.

No. 53.—RAJENDRA PRASAD

Birth Details.—*Born on 3rd December 1884 at 8-45 a.m. (L.M.T.) (Lat. 25° 36′ N., Long. 85° 10′ E.)

Planetary Positions.—The Sun 230° 47′ ; the Moon 55° 28′ ; Mars 247° 30′ ; Mercury 246° 7′ ; Jupiter 134° 33′ ; Venus 194° 35′ ; Saturn 60° 42′ (R) ; Rahu 169° 59′ ; Ketu 349° 59′ ; and Lagna 260° 10′. Ayanamsa 20° 47′.

Ketu		Moon	Sat.		Mercury	Rahu Mars
	RASI		Venus	NAVAMSA	
		Jupit.	Sun		Jupiter Moon
Mars Mercury Lagna	Sun	Venus	Rahu	Ketu	Lagna Saturn

Balance of Mars Dasa at birth : Years 5–10–17.

Special Features.—The Lagna is Sagittarius, a common and benefic sign and the lord Jupiter is in Leo, a friendly place. The Lagna is free from any malefic aspect. It has gained

---

* Mr. H. V. Kamath sent us Dr. Prasad's birth details, which he obtained from Mr. Chakradhar Saran, tne President's Secretary. I am indebted to Mr. H. V. Kamath for his kind help.

considerable strength by being conjoined with Mercury and aspected by Jupiter. The disposition of Lagna makes the native calm, subtle and collected. Jupiter, lord of Lagna, occupying the sign of the Sun endows the native with a quiet yet persevering and persistent spirit capable of immense effort. That he is self-possessed; of firm will, prudent and cautious, are indicated by the Lagna lord Jupiter being aspected by Saturn. The same saturnine aspect makes the temper strong, forceful and enduring. The Moon, karaka of the mind, is exalted in the 6th house. He is free from all evil aspects, save that of the Sun in Rasi and Mars in Navamsa. The Sun explains the moral stature and stamina of the man. His spirit of self-abnegation and self-sacrifice, his integrity of character and his idealised outlook are not a little due to the excellent position of the Moon and the powerful *Adhi Yoga* caused by him. The soli-lunar situations in this chart are of great importance as they emphasize mental purity making the native impartial, just, persistent, somewhat stern, and self-conscious of what he is. The influences of the Sun, the Moon and Lagna, summed up, reveal that the subject is broad-minded to a degree, not fond of show, sincere, catholic, modest and contented. The checkered financial career is due to the obviously unimportant position Dhanadhipati Saturn has been consigned to, though his presence in the 7th getting digbala can by no means be underrated. The 2nd lord Saturn is actually in the 6th house aepected by Mercury lord of the (7th and) 10th while in Navamsa the 2nd is occupied by exalted Saturn, Such dispositions generally denote financial stability giving way to difficulties, in consonance with appropriate directional influences. The 4th lord Jupiter is actually in the 9th house in a trikona from Mercury. This explains his high educational attainments.

Usually Mars-Mercury conjunction in Lagna inclines one to rashness and violence but as here Jupiter powerfully aspects the combination, the evil is considerably tempered giving rise to discrimination, acuteness of perception, and capacity to blend the ideal with the practical. The 6th lord Venus is in the 11th house, while the 6th is aspected by the Sun. Evidently he may entertain no enmity towards anybody but the same cannot be said of others towards him. Kalatrabhava is well fortified as Kalatrakaraka Venus is in his own sign while lord of the 7th Mercury is in Lagna. This denotes a fairly happy private life. The horoscope belongs to the category of *purnayu* or long life owing to lord of Lagna Jupiter aspecting the Lagna and the 8th lord Moon being exalted. It is the 10th or Karmasthana that is of the greatest significance. There are outstanding combinations such as *Sunapha*, *Amala*, *Obhayachari*, each of which has contributed its share of benefic influence to fortify the horoscope considerably.

Important Events.—Rahu Dasa, which ruled till 1909, saw the completion of his education. Mercury, whose results Rahu is to give, is in Lagna in conjunction with Mars lord of the 5th and aspected powerfully by Jupiter the Vidyakaraka. His legal career was built up in Jupiter Dasa. He is said to have had a lucrative practice. Dhana karaka Jupiter has given rise to *Gajakesari*. He aspects the 10th from the Moon. Being Vargottama, he is very strongly disposed. Jupiter gave him money, name, esteem and respect, all these being the blessings of the *Gajakesari Yoga*. He suspended his extensive practice in 1920, and plunged himself into the struggle for freedom in Jupiter Dasa, Moon Bhukti. Mark the disposition of Mars in Sagittarius a war-like sign. Mars owns the 12th or house of loss. Jupiter's ownership of the 8th and 11th from Chandra Lagna expressed itself in the shape of his undergoing much loss and suffering. Mark the mutual favourable dispositions between Saturn and Ketu. It was during this sub-period that Dr. Prasad visited England and the Continent. Both the Dasa and Bhukti lords are aspected by Mars from a common sign. Ketu is in Pisces a common and watery sign, while Saturn is in Gemini, a common and airy sign. It cannot be an anomaly that the Sun's sub-period in Saturn Dasa should have conferred the presidentship of the Congress on the native. Just because the major and sub-lords are both malefic and mutual enemies, it does not mean that only evil results should happen under their directional influences. From Chandra Lagna, the Sun owns the 4th and occupies the 7th while the situation of Saturn, the yogakaraka from Chandra Lagna, in the 2nd is equally propitious. Above all, the Sun's situation in Jyeshta, a constellation of Mercury, is of great significance. The same distinction of Presidency was again conferred on him in 1939, during Rahu's sub-period. Rahu being in the sign of Mercury has to give the results due to the strength of Mercury, who, it will be seen, has caused *Adhi Yoga* besides being placed in the 7th from the major lord and in Lagna aspected by Jupiter. The end of Saturn Dasa saw him in prison, being the result of the affliction due to his being aspected by Mars. Ketu as sub-lord seems always to have been beneficial to the native. It was only during Ketu Bhukti in Mercury Dasa that he was released from prison. The disposition of Ketu in the 4th from Lagna and the 11th from the Moon are clearly benefic dispositions. The President had Mercury Dasa practically till the end of 1960. He joined the Interim Ministry during Venus Bhukti. Venus is ideally placed as lord of 11th in the 11th both from Lagna and the major lord. Mercury Dasa Moon Bhukti was a landmark in his life, for the highest honour and the greatest position that an Indian could aspire for was conferred on him in his being elected as the First President of the Indian Republic. Mark the ideal disposition of the Moon and Mercury the sub and major lords —and the full manifestation of a powerful *Adhi Yoga* and *Kesari Yoga*. His end came in Ketu's major period. It will be seen that Ketu is in Revati ruled by Mercury who is a powerful maraka.

Remarks.—The horoscope of Rajendra Prasad, though seemingly unimportant, reveals combinations illustrative of a distinguished career and markedly rare patriotism. The 6th and 8th (*shashtashtaka*) disposition between the Sun and Saturn is always indicative of struggles, conflicts, opposition and incarceration unless relief is given by a powerful benefic. Here the mutual aspects between Saturn and Mars are a key to unlock the nature of the conflict that raged in the breast of the native between the responsibilities of a realist and the aspirations of an idealist. The *Adhi Yoga* is very powerfully marked by the disposition of Venus and Mercury in the 6th and 8th respectiyely from the Moon while the association of Mars in the 8th merely denotes liability to accidents and violence in the course of his own sub-period under Mercury Dasa. According to classical works, one born in *Adhi Yoga* will be resolute, wealthy, blessed with family and happiness, and he will become famous and learned. But here the scope for this yoga to manifest is restricted as the native was enjoying Mercury Dasa, Venus being able to function only as a sub-lord. The subject became a Minister with the advent of Venus Bhukti in Mercury Dasa. The horoscope has also *Anapha Yoga*.

Amala Yoga, *Obhayachari Yoga*, and *Parijatha Yoga*,—the lost being again caused by Venus. Evidently there is a merging of three first-rate yogas—with the result *Adhi Yoga* has been considerably strengthened. The mere presence of an *Adhi Yoga* is no open-sesame for the free flow of fortune. There are dagrees of variation. An *Adhi Yoga* caused by a benefic occupying an inimical or debilitated place, cannot be equated with an *Adhi Yoga*. where the Moon is exalted and other benefics are fortified by dispositions in auspicious places or by deriving strength due to their having caused simultaneously other equally fortunate yogas. Here, Mercury, one of the members of the *Adhi Yoga*, is in Lagna, in a sign of the benefic, Jupiter, who being Vargottama aspects Mercury while Venus, another planet causing the yoga, is in his own sign. Thus the three benefics are involved in causing this particular yoga. The Moon, the real generator of the yoga, may be said to be *par excellence* as he is exalted in the 6th and otherwise unafflicted. On account of these various sources of strength, Mercury is empowered to confer the most significant favourable results during his Dasa. Mercury Dasa indicates fame, reputation and service to the country. Mark also the concentration of the combined influences of Mars representing political and military power and Mercury representing Rajayoga on Lagna. The horoscope is of more than casual interest on account of combinations that elude easy analysis but are nervertheless full of potentiality. A horoscope such as the one under discussion rendered strong by the predominance of Rajayogas and the absence of a soothing influence of the benefics on Lagna or Lagna lord makes the subject stand out as a pathetic figure of great force and moral grandeur, a selfless worker, who has dedicated himself to the cause of the country and the people. The Moon, ruler of one's emotional set-up and mental leanings, is free from any sort of afflictions. Evidently he never allowed his vision to be clouded or his judgment to get warped. The horoscope clearly reveals that Rajandra Prasad was of stern stuff and that he represented an idealistic type of humanity displaying all those great qualities which make a man really great, lovable and saintly. The crux of the horoscope lies in the powerful Rajayoga caused in Lagna by involving Mars (lord of the 5th), Jupiter (lord of Lagna), and Mercury (lord of the 10th).

No. 54.—M. N. TANTRI

Birth Details.—*Born on 6th October 1885 at 1–36 a.m. (L.M.T.) (Lat. 20° 30′ N., Long. 72° 58′ E)

Planetary Positions.—The Sun 171° 58′ ; the Moon 140° 9′ ; Mars 110° 24′ ; Mercury 164° 2′ ; Jupiter 151° 19′ ; Venus 211° 11′ ; Saturn 77° 24′ ; Rahu 153° 43′ ; Ketu 333° 43′ ; and Lagna 112° 4′.   Ayanamsa 20° 48′.

Ketu		Sat.	Sat.		Mercury
		Lagna Mars	Rahu		Sun Venus
RASI				NAVAMSA	
		Moon	Mars Lagna Jupit.		Ketu
		Rahu Sun Jupit. Merc.		Moon	
Venus					

Balance of Venus Dasa at birth :   Years 9-9-9.

The ascendant or Lagna is weak as it occupied by debilitated Mars and the lord is in the 2nd aspected by Saturn lord of the 7th and 8th, making the native extremely sensitive, restless and nervous.   The 2nd lord Sun is associated with

* I am indebted to Mr. H. R. Desai of Bulsar for the birth particulars of this horoscope.

exalted Mercury, the planet of intellect and intelligence and the 9th lord Jupiter, the planet of thinking and reason. Unfortunately, Jupiter is in exact conjunction with the incendiary planet Rahu, both occupying the constellation of the Sun. These combinations indicate disappointments, frustration and a distorted outlook on life, due to wrong thinking and perverted reasoning. Mercury's exaltation made the native a brilliant writer in politics (Sun's association) and literature (Jupiter's association). Rahu's association with these two planets *plus* the affliction of the Moon rendered the native highly sarcastic. Due to the neecha position of Mars, lord of the 5th house, in Lagna, the native was liable to be obsessed with curious fancies. Lord of the 4th Venus in the 4th Bhava made him highly educated. It will be seen that he was a First Class M.A. Houses of finance (2nd), fortune (9th) and profession (10th) have all been afflicted in some way or other. The Sun as lord of the 2nd and Jupiter Dhanakaraka and lord of the 9th are considerably blemished by association with Rahu. Lord of the 10th Mars is neecha in Lagna, uchcha in Navamsa, but afflicted by association with Jupiter (lord of the 3rd and 12th) and aspected by the Sun, lord of the 8th. Both Lagna and Lagna lord are of course weak. Ill-health and financial troubles were too much for him. If at all there was any financial prosperity, it must have been only during Mars Dasa. As yogakaraka and feebly strong, Mars will have contributed his humble mite. But beginning from the latter part of Rahu Dasa, misfortune dogged him. The 7th house is equally afflicted, as lord of the 7th Saturn is in the 12th and from Chandra Lagna the 7th is occupied by Ketu in Bhava and aspected by Mars. Married happiness was almost nil. He married three times. The native committed suicide by throwing himself under a train on 5-11-1943. This happened in Jupiter Dasa, Ketu Bhukti. This major lord Jupiter is in the 3rd with the Sun a maraka planet, Rahu (occupying the constellation of a maraka) and Mercury (lord of the 3rd) occupying the constellation of a maraka. The sub-lord Ketu is in the 8th from the Moon in the constellation of Saturn, a powerful maraka. From Chandra Lagna he occupies the 7th a maraka, aspected by Mars, the planet of violence. The nature of death in this case is signified by Lagna lord Moon occupying an *Ayudha* Drekkana; Ketu in the 8th occupying a *Sarpa* Drekkana; and Saturn lord of the 7th occupying an *Ayudha* Drekkana. The native was an intellectual, a brilliant writer, thinker, somewhat of a cynic. He wrote a nasty book against Gandhi. The planets are so disposed as to cause great frustration and disappointment in life that unable to face these misfortunes, he finally decided to end his life by the extreme step of throwing himself in front of a train. The karakas for the mind, body and the soul (Moon and Sun) are all considerably afflicted.

No. 55.—THE NIZAM OF HYDERABAD

Birth Details.—Born on 6th April 1886 at 6-36 p.m. (L.M.T.) (Lat. 17° 30′ N., Long. 70° 30′ E.)

Planetary Positions.—The Sun 355° 50′ ; the Moon 19° 10′ ; Mars 135° 45′ ; Mercury 0° 20′ ; Jupiter 158° 18′ ; Venus 312° 8′ ; Saturn 71° 42′ ; Rahu 144° 2′ ; Ketu 324° 2′ ; and Lagna 181° 50′. Ayanamsa 20° 49′.

Sun	Moon Mercury		Sat.
Ketu Venus	**RASI**		
			Rahu Mars
		Lagna	Jupit.

	Jupit.	Mercury	Ketu
	Sun	**NAVAMSA**	
	Sat. Venus		Mars
	Rahu	Lagna	Moon

Balance of Venus Dasa at birth : Years 11–3-0.

Special Features.—The Lagna is Libra or Thula an airy sign aspected powerfully by Mercury and the Moon, lords of the 9th and 10th respectively, thus constituting a powerful Raja-yoga. The lord of Lagna Venus is in the 5th in association with Ketu and aspected by Mars and Rahu. These mutual aspects introduce an element of evil in an otherwise powerful

configuration. Mars aspecting lord of Lagna is suggestive of
an aggressive design and Saturn aspecting the Sun is a weak
point which could be made use of to break the strength of the
horoscope. The presence of Mars in Leo, a royal sign, aspected
by Saturn has great significance. Mars in the 11th gives good
character, while the Moon–Mercury combination gives him a
sense of justice and pride. It will be seen that almost all the
evil planets have mutual aspects and association. Thus Mars
and Rahu are aspected by Saturn ; Mars aspects the Sun and
the latter is again aspected by Saturn and of course Jupiter
also but the combined aspect of Saturn and Mars is so powerful
that it could set a naught the feeble benefic aspect of Jupiter.
These mutual evil aspects give the Nizam a driving desire for
power while Libra rising gives him the ability to recognise the
prevailing weakness in others. Libra ascending confers upon
the subject a gentle nature, flexible and sensitive and easily
influenced by prevailing conditions. It gives him courtesy,
honesty and a sense of justice. In the affairs of life, there will
be a certain lack of decision observed in him as he prefers
"to see what will be done" by others before moving himself.
The Lagna is occupied by Mandi and the lord of Lagna is with
Ketu. This gives rise to *Vanchnabheethi Yoga* so that the
native will always entertain feelings of suspicion towards
people around him and is afraid of being swindled or deceived
by others. The lord of the 4th, *viz.,* Saturn in the 9th and the
lord of the 9th, *viz.,* Mercury in a kendra constitutes a powerful Rajayoga. The lord of the 5th Saturn is strong and lords
of the 9th and 10th, *viz.,* Mercury and Moon are again in a
kendra. This is an equally strong Rajayoga justifying his
being the ruler of a premier Indian State. The Nizam is noted
for his fabulous wealth and this is shown by a number of

Dhana yogas out of which we propose to mention a few for the gratification of students of astrology. The lord of the 2nd is in the 11th, while Saturn the yogakaraka is in the 9th. Again, there is a combination of the lords of the 9th and 10th in the 7th. The very presence of Venus in the 5th accounts for his owning immense wealth.

Important Events.—He married Dulhan Pasha in 1906 in Moon Dasa Rahu Bhukti. The Moon is in the 7th or house of marriage while Rahu is in a similar position from Kalatra-karaka Venus. He ascended the Gadi in 1911 in Moon Dasa Venus Bhukti. Mark the fact that the Moon being a royal planet has caused a powerful Rajayoga in the 7th. As lord of the 10th he has joined Mercury lord of the 9th and is otherwise unafflicted. The sub-lord Venus happens to be Lagna lord and occupies a trinal house, which happens to be the 11th from the major lord Moon. In the Navamsa again, Venus is extremely powerful, as lord of Lagna, and occupies the 4th with yoga-karaka Saturn. It will be seen that the same Venus, who conferred power in his Bhukti in the Moon Dasa, deprived the Nizam of power and prestige, as sub-lord in Jupiter Dasa, when the police action took place. This is due to the fact that Venus is associated with Ketu and aspected by two malefics Rahu and Mars.

The major lord owns the 3rd and 6th houses and occupies the 12th in association with Rahu. The 6th indicates enemies, debts and diseases. The 6th here is Meena or Pisces and it is aspected by Jupiter, Mars and Rahu. Consequently, the Nizam used drastic means to intimidate his opposition, to prevent the gathering of individuals who were in opposition and to frighten the most courageous of them. The major lord owning the 3rd and the 6th, aspecting the 6th and occupying the 12th *plus* the

6th being again aspected by the incendiary Mars highlight the complacency of the Nizam in regard to the then fast deteriorating relations with the Central Government. According to some of the classical works on astrology, the major lord, aspecting the 8th, would prove highly injurious to the position and prestige of the subject. The results during the sub-period of Venus were highly adverse to the Nizam as both the lord and sub-lord of the Dasa either own or occupy the 8th or 12th. The sub-lord Venus is no doubt in the 5th but here he is aspected by both Mars and Rahu. This combination indicates that the person concerned "would lead the life of an incognito, suffer from fear, anxieties, loss of position and misfortune". Again the major lord Jupiter (owning 3rd) is posited in the 12th. This implies that evil counsel would prevail, there would be trouble through secret machinations, humiliation, discomfiture and loss of pride, all of which the Nizam had in large measure. He passed away during Rahu in Saturn. The major lord is Ayushkaraka and lord of the *Naidhana* or death star while the sub-lord is with Mars, a maraka.

Remarks.— The Nizam's horoscope is peculiarly disposed, as side by side with powerful Dhana yogas, there are combinations approximating to Rajabhanga Neecha yogas. Whilst Jupiter in the 12th and Lagna lord in a saturnine sign indicate simplicity, profound religious faith, calm resignation and serenity, the affliction of Lagna lord by three malefics and the political planet the Sun being aspected by Mars and Saturn deprive him of balanced judgment and sane thinking at times of crisis and give the native a wavering and weak mentality. Generally Lagna lord in conjunction with an incendiary planet, or subject to *Papakarthari Yoga*, denotes that the native would be misled by sycophants and toadies and the Nizam's case is no exception. The horoscope becomes significant from the point of view of Kalatrabhava. Mark the fact that the 7th lord Mars is subject to the combined aspects of Rahu, Ketu and Saturn while Kalatrakaraka Venus is equally strongly afflicted denoting *Bahukalatra Yoga*. It is rumoured that the Nizam had innumerable wives attached to his harem. Lagna lord weak and subjected to the aspects of Rahu, Ketu and Mars, and the political and royal planet Sun aspected by Mars and Saturn, without corresponding neutralising influences, are the draw-backs in this horoscope.

No. 56.— KASTURI SRINIVASAN

Birth Details.—Born on 7th August 1887 at 1–21 p.m. (L.M.T.) (Lat. 11° N., Long. 77° 1′ E.)

Planetary Positions.—The Sun 113° 38′ ; the Moon 332° 46′ ; Mars 86° 21′ ; Mercury 100° 16′ (R) ; Jupiter 188° ; Venus 156° ; Saturn 97° 44′ ; Rahu 118° 12′ ; Ketu 298° 12′ ; Mandi 269° 57′ ; and Lagna 222° 42′. Ayanamsa 20° 50′.

			Mars	Rahu		Mars	
Moon							
			Sun Merc. Rahu Sat.	Sun Venus			Moon
	RASI				NAVAMSA		
Ketu							
Mandi	Lagna	Jupiter	Venus	Mandi Jupit.		Lagna Mercury	Saturn Ketu

Balance of Jupiter Dasa at birth : Year 0-8-5.

Special Features.—The ascendant is Scorpio, an insect and fixed sign and the lord Mars is in the 8th in a friendly sign. The ascendant has no other beneficial or malefic association or aspects. The ascendant lord is powerfully aspected by Jupiter, lord of the 2nd and 5th. The ascendant is therefore strong and makes the native forceful and magnetic besides

No. 56.—KASTURI SRINIVASAN

Birth Details.—Born on 7th August 1887 at 1-21 p.m. (L.M.T.) (Lat. 11° N., Long. 77° 1′ E.)

Planetary Positions.—The Sun 113° 38′ ; the Moon 332° 46′ ; Mars 86° 21′ ; Mercury 100° 16′ (R) ; Jupiter 188° ; Venus 156° ; Saturn 97° 44′ ; Rahu 118° 12′ ; Ketu 298° 12′ ; Mandi 269° 57′ ; and Lagna 222° 42′. Ayanamsa 20° 50′.

Moon			Mars	Rahu		Mars	
			Sun Merc. Rahu Sat.	Sun Venus			Moon
Ketu	RASI				NAVAMSA		
Mandi	Lagna	Jupiter	Venus	Mandi Jupit.		Lagna Mercury	Saturn Ketu

Balance of Jupiter Dasa at birth : Year 0-8-5.

Special Features.—The ascendant is Scorpio, an insect and fixed sign and the lord Mars is in the 8th in a friendly sign. The ascendant has no other beneficial or malefic association or aspects. The ascendant lord is powerfully aspected by Jupiter, lord of the 2nd and 5th. The ascendant is therefore strong and makes the native forceful and magnetic besides

and in a detached manner. The 4th lord Saturn is in the 9th with Mercury and the Sun, as Rahu has gone to the 10th Bhava while the 4th is powerfully aspected by Jupiter, lord of the 2nd and 5th. The 4th is a fixed sign in this case. All these combined together denote immense immovable possessions. Long life to the mother is shown by the Moon's favourable disposition. The 6th lord is in the 8th and the 6th is powerfully aspected by Saturn and Jupiter, showing that for the most part, the native's health would be very good, that he would have the staunch loyalty from those who work for him. Nobility and magnanimity which are a part and parcel of his nature are also the blessings of Jupiter's aspect. There is a powerful *Adhi Yoga* present by virtue of the disposition of Venus and Jupitar in the 7th and 8th from the Moon. The peculiarity is that planets causing the yoga are themselves in benefic signs while the Moon from which the yoga generates is also in a benefic sign. This yoga has reference to *wealth and occupation*, giving at the same time influence, prestige and reputation. Good longevity is shown as Jupiter aspects the 8th powerfully and the 8th from the Moon is equally well situated by the presence of Jupiter. Some may raise the objection that such a situation causes *Sakata Yoga* and hence saps up the vitality of the chart. The objection can be ignored because the *Sakata Yoga* has been rendered feeble by the presence of more powerful combinations. Note the strength of the 9th house and the Sun indicating great fortune and inheritance. Another very significant combination is the presence of Venus, lord of the 12th, in the 11th debilitated. This weakens the 12th house considerably while the presence of Jupiter (the 2nd lord) in the 12th has contributed not a little to the reputation, philosophic outlook and self-confidence of the native.

Important Events.—Marriage took place in 1905 during the sub-period of Jupiter in the major period of Saturn. Saturn is in the 11th from Kalatrakaraka and in association with Mercury lord of the 7th and 8th respectively from the Moon and Lagna while the sub-lord Jupiter is in the 8th from Chandra Lagna. The most important event that happened in 1923 was the death of his father. This occurred at the fag end of Mercury Dasa. Both Mercury and Saturn are in the 9th house with the Sun Pitrukaraka and hence the end of Mercury Dasa coincided with this tragic event. Yet as Saturn, lord of the 4th, is in conjunction with the Sun (lord of the 10th) in the 9th, the native inherited substantial properties. As Saturn is the planet of responsibility, this was not without its risky aspect for equally immense responsibilities devolved upon his shoulders which for a man of lesser grit would probably have proved too unwieldy. The eldest boy was born in June 1927 in Ketu Dasa, Rahu Bhukti. The Moon whose results Rahu should give is in the 5th from Lagna while Rahu in his turn is in the 5th from the Moon. In the Navamsa also, Rahu is in the 9th from the Moon. Another son was born in 1936 in Venus Dasa Moon Bhukti. Venus is in the constellation of the Sun who in his turn is situated in the 5th from the Moon and 9th from Lagna while the Moon occupies the 5th Bhava. In the Navamsa again Venus is in the 5th in association with the Sun, and unafflicted. A daughter died as soon as Saturn Bhukti commenced in Venus Dasa. Saturn is in the 5th from the Moon while Venus rules the 5th constellation. In the Navamsa again Venus is in the 5th house from Lagna while Saturn rules the 5th. The native's mother died in Sun Dasa Mars Bhukti. The major lord Sun is in association with both Saturn and Mercury, lords of the 4th from the Lagna and the

Moon respectively while the sub-lord Mars is in the 4th from Matrukaraka. The Sun occupying a Chara Rasi, which happens to be a watery sign, gave the native trips to overseas countries, honour, fame and reputation, especially that he occupies an ideal position in the 9th. He died in 1959 in the major period of the Moon and the sub-period of Rahu.

Remarks.—Of all the Bhavas in this horoscope, those that would interest an astrological student are the 10th and the 2nd. The subject of the horoscope was the head of an institution which has still been playing a unique part in the creation and reflection of public opinion. The strength of the Lagna is of supreme importance whatever the Bhava under consideration. We have already seen how the Lagna and the lord are very powerful. What are the strong combinations for wealth and affluence in this chart? While the 2nd indicates wealth in general and the 9th, the extent of wealth, the source of earning it comes from the 10th. Thus in judging the degree of wealth, one must note the connection between the 2nd, 9th, 10th and 11th houses. The first and the foremost combination is the presence of a powerful *Adhi Yoga*. The 2nd lord aspects powerfully the lord of Lagna while the latter aspects powerfully the 2nd house. These two sets of combinations have fortified 'wealth' considerably. The 11th is occupied by Venus, who though in debilitation is strengthened by the fact that he is in the Sun's constellation. The situation of Saturn and the Sun (as lords of the 4th and 10th and hence causing a a Rajayoga), whilst having its own evil significance, is not without considerable strength in inducing flow of wealth and prestige. Mars is almost abutting on the 9th house and hence is highly fortified. Viewing from the Moon, we find that the 2nd lord Mars is in the 4th aspecting the 10th while the lord of Chandra Lagna and the 10th (Jupiter) aspects Mars. These mutual aspects between the 2nd lord and Lagna or the 2nd house and the Lagna lord always express themselves in terms of influx of considerable wealth. This is a combination the importance of which is hardly recognised by the average astrologer. The native was a newspaper magnate having to do with labour, machinery and trade. Mark the interrelations between Saturn, the Sun and Mercury. Since Saturn has caused a powerful Rajayoga gain by labour, responsibility and investments is indicated. The Sun indicates political influence and Mercury rules trade and journalism. No wonder he should have commanded immense influence with the ruling classes and in the newspaper world. The 10th house is Leo, a fiery sign. Rahu is the planet of machinery. When a fiery sign happens to be in the 10th house, a profession involving dealings with factories, printing machines, etc., is shown. The appropriate blending of the influences of Leo, Saturn, the Sun, Rahu and Mercury—a great journalist wielding much influence amongst classes indicated by the Sun, bearing the qualities of Mercury and coming into contact everyday with persons and properties indicated by Saturn —is noticeable. Mercury gave the subject tact and a clear mind, with fertility of resource, fluent speech and retentive memory.

The Sun is a creative planet. He rules aristocrats, kings and monarchs, persons highly placed in life, high political dignitaries, etc. Mercury rules authors, printers, booksellers and Saturn governs hawkers, factory and machinery workers. The blending of all these forces in a harmonious manner— the loci in this case being the 9th and 10th houses—has given an impetus to the financial aspect of the horoscope.

When a point of contact is established between the lords of
the 1st and 9th, fortune in general seems to receive an
impetus. This goes under the name of *Lakshmi Yoga*. Jupiter,
lord of Chandra Lagna, powerfully aspects Mars, lord of
the 2nd, and *Lakshmi Yoga* is given rise to. The horoscope
brings into relief an important astrological maxim that a
successful blending of saturnine and mercurian influences
coupled with the Lagna also being strong, with an equally
strong disposition of the Sun, would render the native highly
influential in high political circles.

Summing up, the horoscope belongs to an eminent man
well known in the public life of the country. He had mental
ambitions applied to universal services, a philosophic outlook
in tune with a steady mind, tactful yet independent, studious
and responsive to new thought, sympathetic towards others
and marked human tendencies. Mars in the 3rd from
Karakamsa made him brave and unyielding but not unsym-
pathetic. Venus in the 11th gave him an aesthetic sense of
appreciation, an ear for music and a taste for fine arts.
The horoscope in question is indeed a remarkable one, as the
subject was in charge of an institution which has been
instrumental not a little in regulating the political, cultural and
economic thought in this part of the country for over half a
century.

No. 57.—SWAMI SIVANANDA

Birth Details.—Born on 8/7th September 1887 at 4-16 a.m. (L.M.T.) (Lat. 8° 48′ N., Long. 77° 40′ E.)

Planetary Positions.—The Sun 144° 8′; the Moon 24° 13′; Mars 106° 41′; Mercury 141° 32′; Jupiter 192° 46′; Venus 164° 18′; Saturn 101° 28′; Rahu 116° 30′; Ketu 296° 30′; and Lagna 119°. Ayanamsa 20° 50′.

	Moon		Lagna		Venus
Ketu	RASI	Sat. Lagna Mars Rahu	Rahu	NAVAMSA	Ketu
		Sun Merc.	Jupit.		
	Jupiter	Venus	Mars	Sun Moon	Mercury Saturn

Balance of Venus Dasa at birth : Years 3–8–0.

Special Features.—Lagna lord the Moon occupying the tenth a martian sign, and otherwise unafflicted, confers a sturdy physical frame, an active and dynamic personality and an endearing nature. Mercury, the planet of intellect, is in the 2nd house with Atmakaraka Sun, who happens to be *Vaksthanadhipathi*. The native was an eloquent and witty speaker and even in his spiritual dissertations there is an element of humour. Both the Sun and Mercury in the constellation of Venus, the planet of poetry and music, makes Sivananda not only a realist in action and an idealist in vision, but confers a melodious voice capable of influencing the emotions of his listeners and creating in them an exalted mood when he sings kirtanas and devotional songs. Generally a man of studious habits, Sivananda had the capacity for hard work and this is largely due to the situation of Lagna lord in a martian sign. Mark again the *parivarthana* between the Moon and Mars, lords of Lagna and the tenth respectively. From Chandra Lagna Mars is in the 4th or house of education having obtained neechabhanga. These yogas have conferred on the native an all-round knowledge of the different branches of medicine and the spirit of service. But because Mars is with Rahu in the 12th from Atmakaraka Sun, from the healer of physical diseases, he had to change to a healer of spiritual ailments. The lord of the 4th or house of education, *viz.*, Venus is in the 3rd Bhava in association with the divine planet Jupiter, while the intellectual planet Mercury is in the constellation of Venus. While these combinations confer intellectual versatility, they also make one cosmic-conscious, enabling him to put forth his spiritual experiences in a style that is simple, yet captivating and dignified. It is suggested in astrological books that the mutual association of Saturn, Rahu and Mars is undesirable. In the case of Sivananda, all these three malefics are situated within an orb of 16 degrees. Naturally, the doubt may arise in the minds of some, as to whether, the existence of such an unfavourable combination could be reconciled with the career of a saint like Sivananda. The answer is yes. Saturn goes to the 12th Bhava which signifies philosophical insight. Both

Mars and Rahu are in the constellation of Mercury and therefore free from the otherwise incendiary results they would have
produced. Mars happens to be the yogakaraka and his presence
in Lagna with Rahu—and because the Moon, karaka of the
mind, is free from affliction—gives a catholic and tolerant
outlook but dogged persistence to achieve the aim of life. The
7th house is considerably afflicted as lord of the 7th Saturn is
with two malefics while the house itself is subjected to the
combined influences of Mars and Rahu. Evidently these
combinations have deprived the native of the "happiness" due
from Kalatrabhava. The 5th house is equally afflicted as the
lord Mars is with Rahu and Saturn. The disposition of Kalatrakaraka Venus, who is neecha and who is in Bhava association
with Jupiter, indicates high moral character and sublimation of
sex energy.

Important Events.—The Moon and Mars aspecting the
4th enabled him to have his education during their Dasas.
Just at the fag end of Mars Dasa—note Mars is lord of the
10th—the native, a full-fledged doctor, took up employment and
went away to Malaya. Rahu in Cancer, and hence capable of
producing the results of the Moon, gave him a successful
medical career practically throughout his Dasa in a foreign land.

The seeds of renunciation are inherent in Rahu. Side by
side with professional prosperity, cogitation of the final aim of
existence must have assailed the native. Even as a doctor, it is
said he was a humanitarian and a friend of the poor. With the
end of Rahu Dasa and the beginning of Jupiter Dasa, he
wound up his practice and got back to India. The important
position of Jupiter is to be noted. He is lord of the 9th
(Dharma) and is actually in the 3rd Bhava (an Upachaya) in the
constellation of Rahu—a planet of transcendentalism. In the

Navamsa Jupiter is no doubt neecha but has obtained neecha-bhanga.

Jupiter's qualities have been impressed on Rahu. Ketu is the natural Mokshakaraka. Both Rahu and Ketu have influenced the 10th from Chandra Lagna. Therefore, as soon as Ketu Bhukti in Rahu Dasa commenced, Sivananda was initiated into Sanyasa and he finally renounced the world. During Jupiter Dasa the Swami's activities expanded on an international scale and his name became widely known. The Rajayoga part of Jupiter's power became completely manifest. Jupiter's association with Venus enabled the native to bring out innumerable publications on his mission and philosophy. The very fact that Jupiter is in a kendra from the Moon is enough to indicate that during Jupiter Dasa, the native's fame was assured as an expounder of *gnana*—wisdom and knowledge —the exact nature of the *gnana* expounded depending upon the other aspectal and association influences. Saturn Dasa which commenced in the latter part of 1947 was equally significant. Saturn as lord of the 7th is well disposed. From Chandra Lagna, as lord of the 10th (and 11th) he is in the 4th in association with lord of Lagna. While Saturn made the native a focal point for the revival of spiritual aspirations, he also made him more introspective and inhibited. He was bound to meet with bitter opposition during this period. Saturn as maraka planet brought his earthly life to an end.

Remarks.—Generally birth in Cancer is a qualification for spirituality provided other yogas which can act as a catalyst are also present. In this horoscope seven planets have been disposed in four signs involving the 12th, 1st, 2nd, 3rd and 4th Bhavas while Lagna lord occupies the 10th. The situation of the Sun and Mercury in the 2nd, though in a state of combustion, confers intellectual equipment of a high order, as the two planets occupy different amsas. Though learned, there is no touch of pride as Lagna lord Moon is in mutual aspect with Jupiter, lord of the 9th. But because Mars, the yogakaraka, aspects the 4th from Lagna, there is a certain reluctant leaning for exhuberance of spirit which may express itself in the shape of pomp and pageantry. Quite a number of yogas are present. Cancer rising with the Moon in the 10th aspected by Saturn is a *Parivraja Yoga*. The 10th lord neechabhanga in Lagna is another Rajayoga. *Amala Yoga*, *Virinchi Yoga*, *Pushkala Yoga*, *Dhana Yoga* and *Parvata Yoga* are all present. There is a certain jumbling of Raja and Sanyasa yogas, the line of demarcation being slender. Jupiter and the Moon in mutual kendras have no doubt caused *Gajakesari* but the *Gajakesari* indications have become merged with the *Adhi Yoga*, as both Jupiter and Venus are in the 7th and 8th from the Moon. All these yogas render the horoscope significant making the native god fearing, philosophical, religious and humanitarian. Due to the position of Rahu and Saturn in Lagna, the Rajayogas have become transformed into *Parivraja Yogas*, indicating strength of character spirit of service and lofty idealism and making him one of the most outstanding saints inasmuch as his Vedanta is not abstract metaphysics but offers one a pattern for one's own life. Due to the disposition of Mercury and Jupiter in the 3rd and 11th from each other, there is a harmonious blending of the spiritual, mental and intellectual qualities, the result being an integrating personality capable of awakening the spiritual consciousness of renascent India. His contribution to the world of religious and philosophical literature in the English language is considerable. Despite all these, owing to the dominance of Mars and Rahu in Lagna, his quest for the overself was eternal because of the intensity of prarabdha karma.

No. 58.—ADOLF HITLER

Birth Details.—Born on 20th April 1889 at 6-30 p.m. (L.M.T.). (Lat. 48° N., Long. 13° E.)

Planetary Positions.—The Sun 9° 56′ ; the Moon 255° 46′ ; Mars 25° 31; Mercury 4° 48′ ; Jupiter 257° 23′ ; Venus 25° 50′ ; Saturn 112° 35′ ; Rahu 85° 6′ ; Ketu 265° 6′ ; and Lagna 180° 54′. Ayanamsa 20° 52′.

	Sun Mars Mercury Venus	Rahu		Mercury Rahu	Sun
		Sat.			
RASI			NAVAMSA		Moon
			Sat.		
Moon Jupiter Ketu		Lagna		Mars Venus Lagna Ketu	Jupiter

Balance of Venus Dasa at birth : Years 16-4-6.

Special Features.—Lagna is Libra, the sign of balance and it is aspected by a satellitium of four planets including Lagna lord Venus, who in his turn is aspected by Jupiter lord of the 3rd and 6th. Saturn in the 10th and Mars powerfully aspecting the 10th indicate a driving desire for power. The same combination gave the native the ability to recognise the prevailing weaknesses in others. The Sun's exaltation in the 7th gave determination. The Moon–Ketu association and the *Guru-Chandala Yoga* in Sagittarius give a clue to Hitler's mentality. The evil influences on the 7th house subjected the native's personal life to many disruptions. Mars–Venus association having reference to the 7th can also indicate sexual perversions. Whether from Lagna or from Chandra Lagna, the 7th house is considerably afflicted, creating for him innumerable enemies. Any tyro in astrology can recognise that Hitler's horoscope bristles with aggressive tendencies.

Astrologically the following yogas are present, *viz.*, (1) *Ruchaka*, (2) *Mahabhagya*, (3) *Kesari*, (4) *Lakshmi*, (5) *Sreekanta*, (6) *Sankha*, (7) *Papadhi*, and (8) *Neechakarma*. It must be noted that the mere occurrence of Rajayogas does not make one a good man.

Ruchaka is obtained by Mars occupying a kendra identical with his own sign. This gives him bravery, the native becomes powerful and will be arrogant (cf. *Phaladeepika*). *Mahabhagya Yoga* is caused by the occupation of odd signs by the Sun, the Moon and Lagna, when the birth is during day. This gives longevity, fame, and the yoga may be responsible for the native to cause immense pain (or pleasure) according as the Sun and the Moon are afflicted or not. He will be a *Kshithipati* or ruler. One who has a pure *Mahabhagya Yoga* will have spotless character, but here we have shown that the yoga is afflicted. *Kesari* is formed by the Moon and Jupiter conjunction in the 3rd house. Here the yoga is afflicted, because of Ketu's contact. *Kesari* has manifested in its lower plane. It made Hitler a ruler but instead of making him respected by all, he was rendered an object of hatred by the entire world. Lords of Lagna and the 9th (Venus and Mercury) have combined in the 7th. This is *Lakshmi Yoga* and the effects are well known to readers. But here again it is aspected by Saturn, a natural malefic. Saturn himself is a yogakaraka for Libra Lagna and his aspecting *Lakshmi Yoga*, no doubt, gave Hitler immense material possessions and power. The evil side of Saturn's influence manifested in the final collapse of the dictator—especially because Saturn is in the 10th house—further aspected by Mars. If the lord of the Lagna, the Sun and the Moon being in a kendra (quadrant) or trikona (trine) occupy the exaltation, own or friendly house, *Sreekanta Yoga* is caused. Here lord of Lagna and the Sun are in kendras but both being enemies remaining together in the same sign are bound to exercise baneful effects. The only effect is that Hitler felt that he was an agent of Providence sent for some special mission. The conjunction of the lord of Lagna and Mercury causes a Rajayoga and a similar one is formed from the Moon.

Important Events.—Hitler's father died when he was 13 years of age and he lost his mother two years later—both the deaths happening in Venus Dasa. Venus is with the lord of the 9th aspected by Saturn lord of the 4th. His sorrow and loneliness and his subsequent dependence upon the charity of relatives constituted the first of the great frustrations which are the key to his character.'' The following eight years—the last part of Venus Dasa and the first part of Sun Dasa—he earned his living by the building trade learning to be an architect's draftsman. In 1914 Rahu Bhukti Moon Dasa, Hitler enlisted himself in the Bavarian Army. The Moon is in Sagittarius, a war-like sign and this happens to be the 3rd or house of courage. It was in Mars Dasa beginning that he joined a progressive party and its name changed to National Socialists.

It was again in Mars Dasa, that the *Putsch* he organised to overthrow the Government was a failure and that he found himself in prison for treason. Mars is in conjunction with Venus (lord of Lagna and of 8th) and aspected by Jupiter, lord of the 6th. That a contact between lords of 1st and 6th, or 1st and 8th lands one in prison is an astrological maxim, proved in many a case. In 1933, Rahu Dasa Jupiter Bhukti. Hitler was appointed Chancellor of Germany. The major lord Rahu is in the 9th and Mercury who should give the results of Rahu is in the 7th in association with Mars, lord of the 7th, Venus, Lagna lord and the Sun, lord of the 11th—aspected by sub-lord Jupiter who has caused *Gajakesari yoga* in the war-like sign Sagittarius. Rahu's position is equally well fortified in Navamsa. Under the stimulus of Mercury's sub-period, Rahu Dasa—in view of Mercury's association with aggressive Mars, Hitler moved the German storm troops into the Rhine territory and thus began his series of aggressive acts or, in the words of his biographer Konrad Heiden, " the epoch of irresponsibility" culminating in the outbreak of the II World War in Ketu Bhukti Rahu Dasa. It was at the fag end of Moon Bhukti in Rahu Dasa that Hitler died with the fall of Berlin to the Allies. Rahu the major lord happens to be a maraka by virtue of his occupying the 7th from Chandra Lagna and the Moon becomes a *maraka, as he occupies the 3rd from Lagna and the 7th from the major lord.

---

* Writing editorially in the September 1944 issue of THE ASTROLOGICAL MAGAZINE we made the following observations about Hitler's end :

"Hitler is at present having the sub-period of the Moon in the major period of Rahu, lasting upto about 18-7-1945. The major lord owns the constellation from the birth star going under the technical name of *pratyak* or obstruction. Rahu, the major lord, is in the 9th from Lagna

Remarks.—Hitler's great hatred for the Jews was probably due to the conjunction of the Sun and Mars and the conglomeration of evil combinations. The most significant combination in Hitler's horoscope is the absence of *dwirdwadasa* positions which makes the nativity a remarkable one from an astrological point of view. The most powerful malefics—the Sun, Saturn

and in the 7th from the Moon. Rahu occupies Gemini and as a shadowy planet he must give the results of Mercury and in a secondary capacity those of Saturn also as he is similar in nature to Rahu (Sanivad Rahu).

"In the Navamsa again Rahu is in the house of death from Lagna and Karakamsa. Thus Rahu is decidedly malefic and is fully invested with the power of maraka. The Moon's sub-period continues till about 18th July 1945. The Moon, it will be seen, presides over Vipat tara or a constellation indicating danger. He is in the 3rd from Lagna. He is still powerful in Navamsa so that the evil effects in his sub-period can be accelerated only by Gochara or transit influences. The Moon is in the second hora of Sagittarius. Therefore it is only the latter part of his Bhukti that can prove harmful. The second part of the Moon's sub-period commences from about 18th October 1944 and continues for nine months. It is only during this period that Hitler's career must come to an end. Coming to Gochara effects Saturn is transiting the 8th from Hitler's radical Moon while Rahu is receding into the 8th. Before the end of 1944 Rahu will have entered Gemini and the distance between Rahu and Saturn will be about 10 degrees, implying for all practical purposes 'conjunction' according to Hindu astrology. The exact conjunction takes place in the second week of May 1945. Remember this conjunction occurs in the 8th from Hitler's Janma Rasi. Add to this the influence of the recent solar eclipse and the fact that his Dasa or directional influences are extremely adverse. You can yourself come to definite conclusion on the basis of the astrological evidence given above. The combinations of planets in Hitler's horoscope force us to lay further emphasis on the prediction we have already made that developments in Germany in the near future will be sudden, unexpected and dramatic, and that Hitler would have a violent end especially because of the powerful disposition of Mars."

and Mars—have centred their evil influences on the 7th or house of war. The Sun is exalted and Mars is in his own house and Saturn casts his powerful aspect. This made Hitler excessively aggressive and delight in human suffering and harvest of death. Medieval passion was stirred up. No conqueror since ancient times had dared systematically to enslave whole nations, and exterminate them when they dared to resist. Mars and Saturn gave Hitler a driving desire for power. The 6th house in a horoscope indicates enemies, debts and diseases. In Hitler's case the 6th is Meena or Pisces, a feminine and double-bodied sign. The 6th lord Jupiter, is in the 3rd with Ketu. From the Moon the 6th house is hemmed inbetween malefics. Saturn is in the 3rd from Karakamsa suggesting that he was really a brave and courageous man. A malefic planet is capable of doing good by virtue of owning certain houses or by being aspected by certain benefic planets. The affliction present in the 7th house in the Fuehrer's horoscope no doubt receives the aspect of Jupiter but here he is a *Chandala-Guru* having become incendiary by association with Ketu. Karakamsa has again the combined influence of Mars, Ketu and Venus. Thus these destructive influences made Hitler a man of peculiar psychological complexes. Hitler, therefore, paved the way for the return of archaeic ideas and feelings strengthening a new kind of chauvinism which made his victims receptive to his propaganda theories and undermined their resistance.

Saturn in the 10th or house of action and Mars in the 7th or house of war, in mutual aspect without any relieving features, was mainly responsible for Hitler's collapse. Hitler's horoscope is fully illustrative of the dictum that final fall is inevitable when Saturn occupies the 10th afflicted by Mars or Rahu.

No. 59.—JAWAHARLAL NEHRU

Birth Details.—*Born on 14th November 1889 at 11–3 p.m. (L.M.T.) (Lat. 25° 25′ N., Long. 82° E.)

Planetary Positions.—The Sun 211° 43′; the Moon 109° 20′; Mars 161° 25′; Mercury 198° 35′; Jupiter 256° 38′; Venus 188° 48′; Saturn 132° 15′; Rahu 74° 10′; Ketu 254° 10′; and Lagna 114° 25′. Ayanamsa 20° 52′.

			Rahu	Merc.	Mars		
			Moon Lagna	Rahu Lagna			Sun Saturn
	RASI				NAVAMSA		
			Sat.				Ketu Jupiter
Jupiter Ketu	Sun	Mercury Venus	Mars	Venus Moon			

Balance of Mercury Dasa at birth: Years 13–7–6.

Special Features.—The Lagna is Cancer hemmed inbetween two malefics and the lord of Lagna, *viz.*, the Moon is in Lagna, unaspected by any malefic or benefic. This has

---

The time of Mr. Nehru's birth had not been known, but we were able to fix it as 11-33 p.m. in the October 1942 issue of THE ASTROLOGICAL MAGAZINE on the basis of his life incidents particularly the 3rd and 5th

rendered the foundation of the horoscope quite strong.
Gravity and shyness are both denoted by Cancer rising.
His strikingly handsome figure, and the noble and cultivated
expression are due to the Moon's situation in Lagna.
The Sun is in Scorpio, an insect sign, suggestive sometimes
of strange contradictions. The Moon, the planet of
imagination and emotion, is quite free from affliction
except that he is hemmed inbetween malefics. This
denotes sympathy towards the suffering, and a highly
emotional nature. Jupiter aspecting the 2nd makes him
human and indicates responsiveness to feeling or opinion.
Cancer rules the subconscious memory of the past and
therefore he had often to carry upon his shoulders the
burden of the whole race. Saturn is actually in the 2nd
house making him extremely sensitive, fastidious and
detesting of indiscipline and disorder, sometimes very
autocratic and severe. His great intellectual attainments
are brought about by Mercury's disposition in the 2nd
from Navamsa Lagna. The Moon with Venus in the Navamsa
has gifted Nehru with a fertile imagination, delighting in
strange scenes of adventure, and the faculty of absorbing
other people's ideas. Pandit Nehru is a native of Cancer
and natives of Cancer in general are discreet and independent
in many things, the faculty of adaptation being enormous
though there is a high degree of nervous irritaibility, the

Bhavas. Subsequently we received a Rasi chart (as found in Pandit
Nehru's family records) from an esteemed friend in Delhi who says that
he contacted the Prime Minister and got the information. This gives the
ascendant as Cancer and the time of birth as 11-30 p.m. The Prime
Minister's Secretary has informed us in his letter dated 19th June 1962
that Mr. Nehru's time of birth was 11-30 p.m., thus almost confirming
our own findings.

result of extreme sensitiveness, this being a concomitant of lunar and fluidic nature. Lord of the third Mercury is in the fourth, hemmed inbetween two powerful malefics besides being aspected by Saturn. The third is occupied by Mars the indicator of brothers. In the Navamsa also Mars is in the 3rd from Lagna while Rahu is in the 3rd from the Moon. These combinations explain why Pandit Nehru had no brothers. The 4th lord Venus is in the 4th. Matrukaraka Moon is in Lagna. In the Navamsa also, the 4th house is well disposed. Lord of the 9th Jupiter is in his own house. These combinations explain the deep attachment Nehru had for his mother and father. The house of education is well fortified because of the presence of Mercury and Venus (besides the Sun also). The *Guruchandala Yoga* made Nehru an agnostic. He made no pretensions to an insight into the mysteries of the infinite. But yet, Rahu's presence in the 12th and Jupiter aspecting the 10th in Rasi and the Moon and Lagna in Navamsa, must have made him deeply religious in the sense that faith in progress, in a cause, in ideals, in human goodness and human destiny is closely allied to faith in a Providence. This faith sustained him under all circumstances. Putrakaraka Jupiter is afflicted. The 5th is a malefic sign and is occupied by a malefic planet. In the Navamsa again, the 5th from the Moon is highly afflicted. This explains his having only one daughter.

Important Events.—In 1905 Nehru sailed for England when he was having Rahu Bhukti in Ketu Dasa. Mark the positions of these two planets in Rasi and Navamsa. Venus Dasa Venus Bhukti (1912) saw him back in India—a politically quiet and dull India that offered no scope for the aggressive nationalism that the youth had already imbibed.

He settled down to the practice of law (Mercury, Sun, Venus
and Mars aspecting the 12th, indeed a powerful combination)
which offered possibility of a brilliant future but fate–rather,
luck ordained otherwise. Nehru married in 1916. Kalatrakaraka
Venus was responsible for this. Ketu Bhukti in Venus Dasa
saw him as President of the Indian National Congress—a
great honour and also a great responsibility. Venus is in the
4th having caused a powerful Rajayoga while Ketu is in the
6th—the sub and major lord being disposed in the 3rd and 11th
from each other—an ideal combination. With the commencement
of the Sun Dasa Nehru's popularity began to wax further. The
Sun is in a Keeta Rasi. He is a political planet. He aspects the
10th house. In the Navamsa he is with Saturn. The commencement of the Sun Dasa therefore saw him in prison.
Jawharlal's father died during Rahu Bhukti in Sun Dasa. Rahu
aspects Jupiter, lord of the 9th and the major lord Sun is
Pitrukaraka. The sub-lord is in the 8th from Pitrukaraka. Again
the end of Rahu Bhukti in Sun Dasa saw Nehru in jail. His
release took place in Sun Dasa Venus Bhukti (1935). In the
same period, his wife died. The major lord Sun owns the 2nd
(family) in Rasi and the 7th in Navamsa. The sub-lord is of
course Kalatrakaraka. Between themselves they are in the
2nd and 12th from each other. His last detention took place in
Moon Dasa Mercury Bhukti. Both the major and sub-lords are
hemmed inbetween malefics, the sub-lord owns the 3rd and 12th
and is in conjunction with the lord of the 11th. Rahu was then
transiting radical Saturn being the 2nd from the Moon. Mars
is a yogakaraka and he aspects the 10 house powerfully. As
soon as his Dasa began, Nehru became the Vice-President of
the Indian Interim Government. Though Rahu is in the 12th,
his disposition from Mars is very significant with the result the

influence of the major lord prevailed and Nehru became India's first Prime Minister. The end came in Ketu's sub-period in the major period of Rahu.

Remarks.—Nehru's horoscope is interesting in two ways: first as illustrative of certain typical Rajayogas and second as bringing to light the part played by planets causing and subjected to *Papakarthari Yoga* and how in spite of the general strength of the Lagna and the 10th house, they have their say. It will be seen that the disposition of benefics on either side of the Sun has given rise to a powerful *Obhayachari Yoga*. As the Sun Dasa commenced Nehru's popularity began to wax. Several factors must have contributed to his popularity, for popularity is a complex phenomenon. Astrologically, however, five planets—Jupiter, the Sun, Mercury, Venus and Mars—aspecsing the 10th were mainly responsible for making him the idol of India. Venus, Mercury and the Moon in kendras have conferred *Rajalakshana Yoga* making him too much of an aristocrat, Lords of the 5th and 6th are in mutual kendras constituting *Sankha Yoga*. His human sympathies, his wide culture, his internationalism seem to be the blessings of this yoga. Venus is in a kendra identical with his Swakshetra thus giving rise to a powerful *Malavya Yoga*, one of the five great combinations eulogised by the great Varahamihira. Three planets, *viz*, Jupiter, Venus and the Moon are all in their own houses. These and the concentration of the aspectal influences of five planets on the 10th have rendered the horoscope strong and reveal his sincerity frankness, single-mindedness, capacity for hard work and knowledge of the world. The planet strong in Lagna and the two benefics aspecting the 10th, *viz.*, Mercury and Venus are subjected to powerful

Papakarthari Yoga. The Sun is in a Keeta Rasi and in a kendra from Saturn. All these made Nehru, a celebrated 'jail bird'. His intellectual output in prison is prodigious. Mark the situation of the intellectual planet Mercury inbetween the Sun and Mars. His political doctrines are also revealed by his horoscope. Mars does neither aspect the 7th nor is he situated there. This makes him a democrat *cum* dictator. Summing up, the combinations of great significance to students of astrology are : (i) the presence of outstanding yogas like *Malavya, Raja-lakshana, Parijatha* and *Damini* ; (ii) the strength *par excellence* of Lagna and its lord denoting tremendous potentialities of his horoscope but preventing their early expression due to *Papakarthari Yoga* operating in regard to Lagna and the Lagna lord ; (iii) the situation of three important planets in their own houses; and (iv) the concentration of powerful aspectual influences on the 10th or house of action. The *Papakarthari Yoga*, to which the Moon is subjected, indicates often a feeling of loneliness and depression. Jupiter aspecting the 10th from his own sign gives him a pure heart and therefore in his case it is the means that justifies the end and not the end that justifies the means.

No. 60.—DWIGHT EISENHOWER

Birth Details.—*Born on 14th October 1890 at 5-15 p.m. (L.M.T.) (Lat 37° 45′ N., Long. 96° 32′ W.)

Planetary Positions.—The Sun 180° 2′; the Moon 192° 44′: Mars 263° 13′; Mercury 162° 40′; Jupiter 281° 54′; Venus 225° 14′; Saturn 141° 51′; Rahu 56° 27′; Ketu 236° 27′; and Lagna 357° 2′. Ayanamsa 20° 52′.

Lagna		Rahu		Lagna		Jupiter Mercury	
		RASI					Ketu
Jupiter	RASI		Sat.		NAVAMSA		Moon
							Rahu
Mars	Venus Ketu	Sun Moon	Merc.		Venus	Sun Mars Saturn	

Balance of Rahu Dasa at birth: Years 9-9-21.

Special Features.—The first thing that meets the eye in Eisenhower's chart is the proper alignment of benefic and malefic influences. With three elements in Vargottama and

---

* Eisenhower is said to have been born "late in the afternoon after a thunder-storm". By a careful consideration of his life events, we have been able to fix his Lagna as Pisces and the time of birth as 5-13 p.m.

Mars dominant in the 10th, we have indeed the General of the Army. Pisces rising makes the native rich, free and prudent. Natives of Pisces are capable of lifting themselves by their own merits to a position of celebrity and honour. The Moon in Libra aspected by Saturn makes the mind upright, benevolent, powerful, contemplative, studious but yet melancholic. Libra is the sign of balance. Hence the disposition of the Moon here confers ability to hold the balance of conflicting interests and duties. According to classical texts, Mars in the 10th makes one ''a king, liberal and admired by important men''. Mercury in the 7th ''makes one learned, he will dress himself well, will have greatness and a rich wife''. When Jupiter is in the 11th house, ''the person will be fearless, wealthy and long-lived''. Venus in the 9th blesses ''the person with wife, children and friends and makes him prosperous through royal favours''. When Saturn occupies the 6th house, the person will be ''wealthy, subdue his enemies, will be courageous and possessed of self-respect''. Mercury's exaltation gives him the knack of unusual discrimination. Saturn in the fiery sign of Leo, otherwise unafflicted by associations or aspects of Rahu or Mars, is here a planet of authority, exacting progress in a deliberate inexorable way. Mars in the 10th, unafflicted, makes one fearless yet soundly cautious. The position of Mars in Sagittarius makes

---

(L.M.T.). It is remarkable, as if to corroborate our finding, Cyril Fagan, by independent methods, based on the "primaries" and the "quotidians" has arrived at more or less a similar conclusion giving the time as 5-11 p.m. Our finding was published in February 1953 issue of THE ASTROLOGICAL MAGAZINE, and when the issue was in print, Cyril Fagan's article bearing on Eisenhower's time of birth arrived and it was published in the March 1953 issue of THE ASTROLOGICAL MAGAZINE.

soldiering a delightful career. Venus, the planet which imparts graciousness and charm to mortals, is associated with Ketu in Scorpio in the 2nd from the Moon. This combination can impart the gift of wit and repartee and lend dynamic ability for public speaking and conversation. Lagna lord Jupiter having neechabhanga in the 11th, otherwise unafflicted, enables the individual to perceive and cope with great issues. Despite the dominance of Mars on the meridian, Jupiter being Lagna lord and otherwise strong makes the General a man of peace. The most outstanding combination in the General's horoscope is the presence of *Bhadra Yoga* by the exaltation of Mercury in the 7th from Lagna. According to classical writers, one born in *Bhadra Yoga* will be "strong, will have a lion-like face, well-developed chest, well-proportioned limbs ; he will be taciturn and will live upto a good old age". Since this is one of the *Pancha Mahapurusha Yogas*, it makes the man, during the Dasa of Mercury honoured, admired and rise up to the pinnacle of fame and glory.

Important Events.—Dwight Eisenhower devoted most of his adult life to soldiering. He graduated from the U.S. Military Academy at West Point, New York, in 1915, just at the fag end of Jupiter Dasa. Mark the fact that Mars, the military planet, owning the 2nd and the 9th, is in the 10th. Sagittarius, a war-like sign. Mars aspects Lagna powerfully. He chose an army career although there had been no military tradition in his family. Saturn Dasa, Saturn Bhukti found Eisenhower serving as a Tank Instructor in World War I. From Chandra Lagna, Saturn happens to be a yogakaraka and he occupies the 11th from the Moon and the 6th from Lagna. Saturn is in the constellation of Venus who in his turn is in the 9th from Lagna and the 2nd from the Moon in the house of Mars. The

war ended a short time before he was scheduled to go overseas. Promotions came slowly as peace-time assignments gave him more executive than military experience. By far the most prominent combination is Mars in Sagittarius in conjunction with mid-heaven or *dasama* Bhava being precisely that which is expected of a famous general. He saw duty in the Panama Canal zone and in continental United States until 1935 (when Saturn Dasa ended) when he went to the philippines with Mac Arthur. From 1935 to 1939 "Ike" was a member of the American Mission to the Philippines headed by Mac Arthur, where, among other accomplishments, he organised the Philippine Air Force. Mercury Dasa for Eisenhower started from 1935 and lasted till 1952. It was during Mercury Dasa that Eisenhower, an almost unknown hard-working colonel, as late as in the autumn of 1941, was honoured as a strategist, diplomat and leader. Mark the position and strength of Mercury. As lord of the 4th and 7th, he is exalted in the 7th, aspected powerfully by a neechabhanga Jupiter who is lord of Lagna and the 10th. In Navamsa, Mercury is equally well placed. It is no wonder therefore that it was during Mercury (in 1941) that General Marshall recommended Eisenhower to President Roosevelt for an important assignment because Eisenhower had demonstrated unusual planning and leadership abilities—abilities largely due to exalted Mercury aspecting Lagna. His remarkable success in planning, co-ordinating and executing the military and diplomatic phases of the liberation of Europe was due as much to his understanding of people as it was to his broad grasp of the military requirements, which in their turn are clearly the result of the dignified positions of Mercury and Mars respectively. The Sun, Moon and Mars Bhuktis in Mercury Dasa saw him U.S. Commander in Europe (1942), as Supreme Commander,

Allied Expeditionary Force (1943) and winning victory in Europe (1945). As Supreme Allied Commander, using foresight and great executive ability he kept more than a dozen nationalities serving under him in harmonious relations and led all to victory. After the Nazi surrender, he commanded the U.S. occupation forces in Germany and was recalled to Washington in November of that year to become Army Chief of Staff. He resigned the post in 1948 to become President of Columbia University and he resigned his latest assignment as Supreme Allied Commander in Europe, effective, June 1, 1952, to participate actively in the election campaign. This happened just at the fag end of Murcury Dasa. He became President in Ketu Dasa. It is fitting that Ketu gave the results of Mars in whose sign Ketu is placed. It will be seen that Mars is in a highly dominant position. Rahu in Venus proved fatal.

Remarks.—The significant features in the horoscope are the presence of *Bhadra Yoga*, the disposition of the lords of the 2nd and 9th in the 10th, Sagittarius, a war-like sign, and the neechabhanga of Lagna lord Jupiter, having reference to the 11th from Lagna and the 4th from Chandra Lagna. He was chosen by the American people in the most keenly contested election in U.S. history to lead them and because of the ideal position of Mercury in the 7th, he managed to get on with Russia in spite of differences of opinion.

No. 6l.—GENERAL FRANCO

Birth Details.—Born on 4th December 1892 at about 4-9 a.m. (L.M.T.) (Lat. 42° 30′ N., Long. 8° W.)

Planetary Positions.— The Sun 231° 39′; the Moon 53° 3′; Mars 323° 54′; Mercury 247° 21′; Jupiter 354° 9′; Venus 196° 9′; Saturn 169° 55′; Rahu 15° 8′; Ketu 195° 8′; and Lagna 194° 36′. Ayanamsa 20° 54′.

Jupiter	Rahu	Moon			Mars	Mercury Saturn
Mars			Lagna Jupit. Venus Ketu			Moon
	RASI			NAVAMSA		
			Sun			Rahu
Mercury	Sun	Lagna Venus Ketu	Sat.			

Balance of the Moon Dasa at birth : Year 0-2-17.

Special Features.— In the above chart, we find that Saturn is an extremely favourable planet both from Lagna and the Moon. His situation in the 12th from Lagna is also favourable. This statement may look paradoxical but it is deliberately made and is full of meaning. The ascendant is hemmed inbetween two malefics, the Sun and Saturn, causing *Papakarthari Yoga.*

This is highly significant. The Moon being aspected by Mars is indicative of natural hastiness of temper and impetuosity. Mars, lord of the 2nd and 7th, is in the 5th from Lagna and the 10th from the Moon. This denotes Franco's connection with the military ever since his longing for adventure and military prowess began in 1912. A noteworthy combination is the complete absence of malefic aspects either on Mars or on the 10th from Lagna. On the other hand, the horoscope gets fortified by the powerful aspect of Jupiter on the 10th, Saturn (yogakaraka) on the 9th and Mercury (lord of 9th) on the 9th. The horoscope is somewhat baffling and eludes superficial analysis. Mars aspecting the Moon denotes also much hidden enmity. Ketu in Lagna with Venus cannot make him frank and outspoken. Although inclined to be somewhat 'ruthless' as a soldier, Jupiter's position in the 11th from the Moon denotes an innate respect for religion. Mars gives him executive ability, firmness and an attractive personality.

Important Events.— The commencement of Jupiter Dasa had already seen Franco a general. In fact he was the youngest general in west Europe and had received Spanish and even French decorations. However, it was only after Satrun's Dasa commenced that Franco was appointed Chief of Staff and acting President of the Supreme War Council. The dictum of *Bhavartha Ratnakara*, with a slight modification, is eminently applicable in this case. The combination suggests that 'one born in Libra becomes forunate during Saturn Dasa, provided Jupiter is in the 6th or 12th and the Moon is in Lagna'. Here, Jupiter is in the 6th, the Lagna is Libra but the Moon is exalted in the 8th in the sign of Lagna lord. Saturn is a yogakaraka both from Lagna and the Chandra Lagna and from the latter occupies the 5th, the lord of which has caused an *Adhi Yoga*. Even in Navamsa Saturn

being lord of Lagna is in the 5th with Mercury. Saturn is devoid
of malefic aspects, except that of Mars, and is further subjected
to Jupiter's powerful vision. Just at the close of Saturn Bhukti
in Saturn Dasa, Franco was sent to the Canary Islands (as a result
of the victory of the Popular Front in February 1936). It was
from here that he participated in the organisation of the milita-
rist rebellion. The leadership of the movement actually concentrated in the hands of Franco in September 1936, Later on a
'Nationalist Government' was officially proclaimed at Burgos
on February 7, 1938. Interestingly enough this occurred during
Mercury's sub-period. Mercury is lord of the 9th and is in the
3rd in Sagittarius—ruling Spain. This cannot certainly be a
more coincidence. About this date, Mars almost in conjunction
with Saturn in Pisces—the 11th from Franco's Janma Rasi and
Jupiter and Venus were transiting the 9th. From Chandra
Lagna, the disposition of the major lord (who is also yogakaraka
in the 5th, and in a kendra from the sub-lord Mercury, who
owns the 2nd and 5th, must be clearly noted. Mercury gave the
results due to *Adhi Yoga* in his Dasa. Saturn also enabled
General Franco to preserve Spain's neutrality in the course of
the II World War. He died in Saturn's sub-period in Ketu Dasa.

Remarks.— Franco's horoscope is notable for the manner
in which yogakaraka Saturn conferred the Rajayoga results in
his Dasa. Saturn is no doubt a yogakaraka both from Lagna
and Chandra Lagna, but from the latter he is more ideally disposed. Saturn is in the nakshatra of the Moon who in his turn
is exalted. He is further aspected by the war lord Mars, lord of
the 7th (defence, foreign relations, etc). It is remarkable therefore
thet it was only after the commencement of Saturn Dasa that
fortune began to dawn on Franco especially after Mercury
Bhukti set in. Mars occupying the 10th from the Moon and

aspecting Saturn conferred on the native qualities of a dictator, which found visible expression in the course of Saturn Dasa. it will be seen that Franco, ''as the author of the new historic era in which Spain acquires the possibility of realising her destiny'' assumed the positions of the head of the state, Generalissimo of the armed forces, national Chief of the Phalange Party and Candillo (leader) of the empire in Saturn Dasa Mercury Bhukti. According to a decree signed by him on 3-8-1939, Franco was ''responsible only to God and history''. This is a somewhat perverted assumption but nonetheless justifiable due to the aspect of Jupiter, as lord of a dusthana, on Saturn.

No. 62.—RAMAKRISHNA DALMIA

Birth Details.—Born on 7th April 1893 at 9-31 a.m (L.M.T.) (Lat. 20° 56′ N., Long. 75° 55′ E.)

Planetary Positions.—The Sun 356° 39′; the Moon 241° 15′; Mars 45° 14′; Mercury 346° 2′; Jupiter 12° 3′; Venus 350° 7′; Saturn 167° 54′; Rahu 8° 30′; and Lagna 60° 49′. Ayanamsa 20° 55′.

Sun Venus Mercury	Rahu Jupiter	Mars	Lagna		Moon	Mars	Saturn Rahu
—				Sun			Jupiter
	RASI				NAVAMSA		
				Venus			
Moon		Ketu	Sat.	Ketu	Mercury	Lagna	

Balance of Ketu Dasa at birth : Years 6–4–4.

Special Features.—Gemini Lagna rising aspected by Saturn confers a personality that is ambitious, aspiring, active, and given to enquiry. The native will be sympathetic and sensitive. The karaka of the mind, *viz.*, the Moon is in a common and war-like sign Sagittarius the result being, at times, a restless, high-stung and diffusive, indecisive, and timid personality.

Saturn aspects not only Lagna, but also Lagna lord who is in debility in the 10th but has obtained neechabhanga. Consequently, the native would be endowed with a nature that is industrious, steady, persevering, practical and secretive also. It will be seen that both the Lagna and The Chandra Lagna have been rendered strong by the Lagna lord being in association with Venus, lord of the 5th (and 12th) and causing a Rajayoga and by Chandra Lagna being aspected by the lord Jupiter. The vitality of Lagna lord is further heightened because he is free from combustion.

So far as this horoscope is concerned, emphasis must be laid on the wealth-giving combinations. The native was a big industrialist and was one of the wealthiest Indians. Finance has to do with not only the 2nd house, but also the 9th (fortune), 10th (profession) and the 11th (gains), apart from the fact that Lagna must be strong. Here we see a curious blending of the influences emanating from almost all these significations or Bhavas. Lagna lord Mercury is in the 10th and in a kendra from lord of the 2nd, and in association with the lord of the 5th who is exalted and aspected by Saturn lord of the 9th or house of fortune. The 10th lord Jupiter, who is the natural Dhanakaraka, is in the 11th with Rahu, a planet that rules over industries. The planet of trade Mercury's disposition is ideal while Venus exalted in the 10th in a kendra produces Malavya Yoga, the blessings of which are : "strength of mind, wealth, happiness from wife and children, possession of vehicles, renown and learning and clean sense-organs". If you view from Chandra Lagna, you will again find that the Lagna, the 2nd, 9th, 10th and 11th are all highly fortified and Chandra Lagna is aspected by the lord Jupiter and Mars, owner of the 5th house. The 2nd lord Saturn is in the 10th aspected by the

Sun, lord of the 9th, Mercury lord of the 10th and Venus lord of the 11th—all ideal combinations denoting "immense wealth".

The Sun in the 10th as lord of the 3rd is not desirable as it often brings the person into conflict and misunderstanding with authority. The position of two first-rate malefics, *viz.*, Mars and Ketu, in the 6th and 11th respectively from the Moon is a desirable feature indicating obstruction and opposition but ultimate success in his efforts to earn wealth. Lord of lagna in aspect with Saturn confers simple and austere habits, while Venus, as Mokshasthanadhipati (12th) exalted in the 10th makes the person not only religious and conservative but also spiritually inclined. Because of the absence of mutual aspects between first-rate malefics (Mars, Saturn and Rahu), he was a nationalist. The variety of influences centered on the Dhana (2nd), Bhagya (9th), Labha (11th) and Karma (10th) Bhavas gives a clue to the wide range of his industrial acquisitions.

Mark the affliction of the Kalatra Bhave. 7th lord Jupiter is in the 11th with Rahu. The 7th is occupied by the Moon, and aspected by Mars. Venus is in a common sign, in association with two malefics and aspected by Saturn These combinations lend credence to the romour that the native married five wives.

Important Events.—In 1931 he started sugar mills in Bihar and acquired a big insurance company, these events happening in Chandra Dasa. The position of Chandra as lord of the 2nd in the 7th, aspected by Jupiter lord of the 10th, should be noted. In Mars Dasa he started Dalmia Cements, the first Indian enterprise, for manufacturing cement. Mars is no doubt lord of the 6th and placed in the 12th, but as he is in the constellation of the Moon, he is qualified to give industrial and financial prosperity. The beginning of Rahu Dasa coincided with the starting of Bharat Bank. Rahu is well placed in the 11th or house of gains. In Jupiter Bhukti Rahu Dasa, he purchased another organisation—a big managing agency comprising of such industries as Indian National Airways, as also several coal mines. Under the same directional influences some of the biggest newspapers like *The Times of India* came under his control. Mark the Dasa lord Rahu is with Saturn in the 9th in Navamsa. The sub-lord Jupiter enabled him to acquire other substantial business interests such as the Swadesi Cotton Mills of Kanpur, Gwalior State Bank Ltd , etc. The Rahu Dasa not only gave him considerable wealth but an equal measure of responsibility and uneasiness which very few could ever dream of acquiring and also coping with. In Jupiter's major and sub-periods, the native was convicted. Jupiter is subject to Papakarthari Yoga, hemmed in as he is between Mars, lord of the 6th and Venus lord of the 12th and the Sun lord of the 3rd. He died in Saturn sub-period in his own major period. Saturn is not only a natural maraka for longevity but here he owns the 8th from the Lagna and the 2nd form the Moon.

Remarks.—Without any rich inheritance, to become a businessman with such colossal commitments, is no easy joke. This remarkable achievement was rendered possible by the unique disposition of Saturn, the Moon, Mercury, Venus and Jupiter, causing a formidable set of Dhana and Rajayogas of a dynamic nature. In the Navamsa, Jupiter's exaltation in the 10th house causing Hamsa Yoga is of immense significance in further enhancing the worth of the horoscope. Though he is exalted in the 10th in Navamsa, he could not save the native from suffering incarceration because perhaps of his quadrangular ownership, association with Rahu and being subject to Karthari Yoga by lords of the 6th and the 12th.

No. 63.—MEHER BABA

Birth Details.—Born on 25th February 1894 at about 4-30 a.m. (L.M.T) (Lat, 18° 31′ N., Long. 73° 52′ E.)

Planetary Positions.—The Sun 315° 26′ ; the Moon 196° 24′ ; Mars 256° 18′ ; Mercury 332° 20′ ; Jupiter 33° 7′ ; Venus 301° 51′ ; Saturn 183° 49′ ; Rahu 351° 19′ ; Ketu 171° 19′ ; and Lagna 284° 9′. Ayanamsa 20° 55′.

Mercury Rahu	Jupiter			Lagna	
Sun Venus	RASI		Sun Moon	NAVAMSA	Mercury Ketu
Lagna			Jupit. Rahu		
Mars	Moon Saturn	Ketu	Saturn	Venus	Mars

Balance of Rahu Dasa at birth: Years 5-3-21.

Special Features.—Lagna is Capricorn, a movable sign, and it is aspected by Jupiter lord of the 3rd and 12th, denoting an ambitious, persevering and plodding disposition; the lord Saturn is exalted in the 10th and is associated with the Moon in the visible hemisphere so that this clearly indicates increased ambition. In the Navamsa, lord of Lagna is in the 6th but subject to a powerful *Papakarthari Yoga* being hemmed inbetween Saturn and Venus. This does not make the Lagna quite strong. The Moon is approaching debilitation and is associated with Saturn while in the Navamsa, the Moon is equally devoid of any beneficial aspect. The 'ego' planet Sun is in the house of an enemy in conjunction with the sensual planet Venus. These positions of the luminaries suggest the psychological straws that show which way the Baba's mind would be moving. The Moon's position and association coupled with the fact that Mercury is neecha and posited with Rahu aspected of course by Mars reveals a man subject to constantly changing moods. Mercury, debilitated in the 3rd and associated with Rahu (besides being aspected by Mars), reveals an inward nervousness that acts on the native. The association of Venus, yogakaraka for Capricorn Lagna, with the Sun, lord of the 8th, is not conducive to domestic happiness and indicates a man of impulsiveness and emotions. The *Dhana Yoga* is well marked by the fact of Saturn's exaltation in the 10th house but this does not add the qualities needed to make one spiritually elevated. Jupiter's disposition in the 8th from the Moon constitutes a powerful *Adhi Yoga* but its significance is felt in making him rich, collect funds in the name of noble causes and proclaim himself a Messiah who has come to save the world from sins. Despite these negative factors Jupiter's aspect on Lagna (both in Rasi and Navamsa) is a silver lining facilitating, the tearing away of the veil of Prarabdhakarma before the native shuffles off his mortal coil.

The horoscope will be interesting to us in estimating whether Meher Bada was what he claimed either wholly or within certain limits. The disposition of the Sun and Saturn in

Rasi coupled with the presence of the Sun and the Moon in Navamsa brought him to the glare of considerable publicity.

Important Events.—We do not have manyimportant events to give. Before the end of Jupiter Dasa, he is supposed to have met Hazrat Babajan and Upasani Maharaj who 'unlocked' the door to him. Jupiter is in the 5th from Lagna in a Dharmatrikona and debilitated in the 9th in Navamsa and associated with Rahu. The spiritual episodes which Meher Baba is supposed to have undergone during this period and in the beginning of Saturn Dasa cannot be considered as mere proofs of plain mental unbalance though neither Jupiter nor Saturn has the requisite power to elevate his mind nor get him initiation into the secrets of Brahma Vidya. Jupiter is fortified by occupying his own nakshatra. Meher Baba considers his Guru Upasani Maharaj as a great spiritual personality of his times. In 1921, Meher Baba was made spiritual successor to Upasani Maharaj. This occurred in Ketu Bhukti of Saturn Dasa. Saturn is in the 10th and Ketu is in the 9th justifying his being made "spiritual" successor. It seems that Baba's preceptor had once been prosecuted under Bombay Brothels Act and that he used to see God in faeces and that his habits were so dirty and unhygienic that even lice would not be removed from his clothes. Meher Baba sailed for Europe and America in Rahu Bhukti in Saturn Dasa. Saturn is in a movable sign and Rahu in a common and aquatic sign. In the Navamsa sgain Rahu is in a Chara Rasi indicating a voyage. He is supposed to have observed silence since 1925, that not even Venus Dasa proved fatal.

Remarks.— Here we shall examine the trends in the light of astrological factors and see if there is any truth in the claims of Meher Baba being a perfect 'Master' and a 'Messiah'. The presence of Jupiter and Ketu in Dharmatrikona is no doubt an indication of his spiritual inclinations but Jupiter, being in the house of Venus, reveals that he had actually gone through no training and no discipline to fit him to what might be tantamount to a yogic initiation. The natural Atmakaraka (Sun) is not only in the house of an enemy but associated with the sensual planet Venus who is subject to a powerful *Papakarthari Yoga* in Navamsa. This gives strong sensual instincts but because of Jupiter's position in the 5th, he tried to sublimate them.

The 9th from Karakamsa being occupied by Mars is not favourable for spiritual attainments. There could be an element of exaggeration in his claims to spiritual greatness. Jupiter in the Navamsa no doubt gave him an element of Gnana but as Jupiter is neecha and neechabhanga is caused by a malefic planet Saturn, Meher Baba could not have been an infallible authority. He was subject to constantly changing moods demanding enslavement on the part of his stupefied followers. Karakamsa is aspected by Ketu, Mercury and Saturn. This is not a combination conducive to pure spiritual attainments. Meher Baba claimed to be the 'perfect Master' and prided himself as 'His Divine Majesty'. If he were the Messiah who had come to herald the dawn of the millennium then he should have been a prophet also. The Vaksthana (2nd house) is devoid of Jupiter's aspect and he must therefore have been a 'prophet' whose predictions were seldom verified. Some years ago, he predicted a World War without mentioning even the probable period and said that it would last *for only a few months* and passed himself as the instrument in bringing the conflict to a close. On each occasion he had to give a different date for this calamitous event because, as each date arrived, no event occurred. Summing up, the horoscope contains no powerful combinations of *Pravrajya* or renunciation. The position of Saturn made him rich and emphasizes his fondness for spectacular demonstration. His Messiahship consisted in what psychologists would call 'paranoia'. He exaggerated everything pertaining to himself and this is denoted in the horoscope by the absence of harmonious blending of rays between the Sun, the Moon, Venus and Jupiter. Much ado was made about the time when he would break his silence. The horoscope does not reveal any distinguishing marks of Messiahhood. On the contrary, it reveals a man sincere in his objectives, but ignorant of real spiritual values, expecting his followers to spread his message and always interested in talking of his own personal greatness.

No. 64.— EDWARD, DUKE OF WINDSOR

Birth Details.— Born on 23rd June 1894 at 10 p.m. (L.M.T.) (Long. 0° 5′ W., Lat. 51° 30′ N.)

Planetary Positions.— The Sun 71° 24′; the Moon 313°; Mars 339° 27′; Mercury 96° 42′; Jupiter 57° 27′; Venus 32° 4′; Saturn 177° 29′; Rahu 344° 57′; Ketu 164° 57′; and Lagna 283° 4′. Ayanamsa 20° 56′.

Mars Rahu		Jupiter Venus	Sun	Lagna	Ketu
Moon	**RASI**		Merc.	**NAVAMSA**	
Lagna			Sun Moon Venus		Mercury
			Sat. Ketu	Rahu	Saturn Mars Jupiter

Balance of Rahu Dasa at birth : Years 9–5–12.

Special Features.— The ascendant is Capricorn and the lord Saturn is in the 9th house in association with Ketu and aspected by Jupiter, Mars and Rahu. Lagna is aspected by both Mercury and Jupiter. Capricorn rising and the lord subject to a number of evil influences has rendered the foundation of the horoscope somewhat weak. But Lagna being aspected by the two benefics balances the otherwise weak disposition—weak considering the environment in which the native was born. The Sun being placed in a common sign denotes that the native is generally reserved, firm, self-reliant. Capricorn quickens the mental and intellectual qualifications. Administrative ability is marked by the situation of three planets in Navamsa in Capricorn. The Moon's position in a mystic sign like Aquarius is always indicative of some trouble connected with parents. Two malefics in the 2nd from the Moon make him careful with money matters, calculating and cautious. The situation of Marcury in the 6th is suggestive of the presence of a trace of *Adhi Yoga* while Jupiter and the Moon in mutual kendras have given rise to *Gajakesari Yoga*. Mars in Karakamsa has frequently led him to dangerous places but the presence of Jupiter has always protected his body. The common people had made him an international hero and this is indicative of the insignificant position of the Sun and his being powerfully aspected by both Mars and Saturn. That he had to forego many of the hazardous pleasures—pleasures he might have derived from solar or royal sources is evident from the strong aspect Mars casts on the Sun situated in the 5th from Chandra Lagna. The 9th indicating distant and foreign travels is here a common sign aspected by Mars and occupied by Saturn and Ketu. The lord of this is in a Chara Rasi. This probably accounts for his extensive travelling. It will be seen that considerable stress has been laid on the 8th, 9th and 10th houses in the Navamsa and by way of location and aspect. Saturn, Mars, Rahu and Ketu have all focussed their influences on the 8th and 9th. The 2nd lord from Chandra Lagna is in the 4th in conjunction with the 4th lord while the 2nd lord from the ascendant is in the 9th aspected by Jupiter. Venus yogakaraka for both Capricorn and Aquarius Lagnas is in association with Jupiter, lord of wealth. This made the Duke very rich; while not exceedingly rich according to world standards, he was always assured of a greater than "comfortable income". The Sun in the 6th gives good health and vitality and success over opponents and enemies. The presence of *Malavya Yoga* from Chandra Lagna may also be noted in explaining the exalted birth.

   Important Events.—The greatest and the most important event was his father's death on 8th January 1936 just at the fag end of Rahu Bhukti in Saturn Dasa. The major lord Saturn is in the 9th, house of father, in conjunction with Ketu and aspected by Mars and Rahu (ignoring for the moment Jupiter's aspect). The major lord, in his turn, aspects powerfully the Sun (Pitrukaraka), while the sub-lord is associated with Mars and aspects powerfully the 9th. The major lord is in the 9th from Pitrukaraka and the Moon (in Navamsa) in conjunction with Mars. Moreover, the subject was undergoing *sadesati* so that father's death was inevitable. It will be seen that Jupiter (whose results Rahu should give) is in association with Venus, lord of the 9th from the Moon. Both Rahu and Saturn are afflicted. The second important event is his accession to the throne on 21st January 1936. The same directional influences were present: Saturn, the major lord, occupying the house of fortune and very strongly disposed by virtue of having attained Vargottamamsa and Rahu occupying the 3rd from Lagna in association with Mars Saturn is the Atmakaraka and Rahu (who should give Jupiter's results) is the Amatyakaraka. Their conjunction in Navamsa fortified them considerably and rendered them capable of making the native taste power, even of only temporarily. It will be seen that Rahu is in the constellation of Saturn and Saturn in that of Mars, while Mars is in the constellation of

Saturn. The last and the most important of all events is his abdication on 10th December 1936, as soon as Jupiter's sub-period had commenced. Firstly, this marks *Dasa Chidra*; secondly, Saturn Dasa is the one presided over by "vipat" constellation and hence extremely unfavourable. Added to all this, the Prince was installed on the throne at an inauspicious moment, when he was undergoing *sadesati*. From the Sun, both Saturn and Jupiter are in the house of fortune (in the amsa) in conjunction with Mars. Again in the Rasi all the malefic Influences have been centered on the house of fortune with the result he was deprived of the fortune of ruling an empire.

Remarks.—The horoscope is interesting in two ways, *viz.*, (1) though born as heir to a kingdom, he chose to abdicate, and (2) he married a common woman for whose sake he renounced his throne. It should occur to us at once that the most salient astrological element is the complete absence of jupiterian and solar influences on the 9th and 10th houses. The 9th from Karakamsa being occupied by a malefic is suggestive of the dangerous conflict in which he was involved. Mars, Rahu. Saturn, Ketu concentration on the 8th from Chandra Lagna suggests his love marriage and how a native such as him met with many obstacles from a personal standpoint. The 2nd from Upapada Lagna having beneficial aspects will also explain to some extent his 'love marriage'.

The potentiality of the 10th house which would have made him a great monarch has been completely shattered by the fact that the lord of the 10th is placed in the 8th from the 10th, and the 10th being aspected by Mars. Though *Rekha Yoga* (an unfortunate and wretched combination) cannot strictly be applied to such a case, we can still feel its presence here. Malefic planets in 1, 2, 9, 10, 11, 4, 5, 7, 3 produce *Rekha Yoga* in respect of Bhavas affected. In other words, malefic influences concentrated in a particular Bhava weaken it to such an extent that it becomes almost defunct. The house of fortune subjected to the influence of *Rekha* is suggestive that kingly power could not be wielded. Saturn–Ketu conjunction opposed by Mars–Rahu conjunction and the kingly planet Sun receiving the combined aspect of Mars and Saturn were all detrimental factors, which forced the king to execute an Instrument of Abdication which was read in Parliament after the announcement of his irrevocable decision. As heir to the throne, in youth, he was of necessity hedged round with saturnine prohibition. Perhaps these were the true originating causes of the drama in which the attention of the world was focussed, a drama culminating in a great sacrifice.

No. 65.—AN EXAMPLE FOR RAJA YOGA

Birth Details.—Born on 20th September 1897 at 6–21 a.m. (L.M.T.) (Lat. 13° N., Long. 5h. 10m. 20s. E.)

Planetary Positions.—The Sun 156° 19′; the Moon 76° 32′; Mars 175° 50′; Mercury 156° 35′; Jupiter 151° 15′; Venus 121° 37′; Saturn 215° 20′; Rahu 282° 18′; Ketu 102° 18′ and Lagna 166°. Ayanamsa 20° 58′.

			Moon		Rahu Venus	Lagna
			Ketu	Sun Moon Merc.		
	RASI				NAVAMSA	
Rahu			Venus	Jupit.		Mars Saturn
	Saturn		Sun Mars Merc Jupiter Lagna		Ketu	

Balance of Rahu Dasa at birth: Years 4–8–5.

Special Features.—The ascendant is Virgo, an earthy and common sign, and the lord Mercury is exalted in Lagna itself thus fortifying the foundation of the horoscope considerably. The Lagna is occupied by the Sun (lord of the 12th), Mars (lord of the 3rd and 8th) and Jupiter (lord of the 4th and 7th). In the Navamsa again, the Lagna is Taurus aspectad powerfully by

Jupiter who has obtained neechabhanga. The lord of Navamsa Lagna Venus is however afflicted by association with Rahu. These indicate the prominence of earthly elements inasmuch as in Rasi both the Lagna and the Moon are in common signs while in the Lagna is located a satellitium of four planets. Note the predominance of Mars, Jupiter and Mercury making the native quiet, self-possessed and persevering. The Moon is in a common sign unaspected by malefics but in the Navamsa he is subjected to the combined aspect of Mars and Saturn. The Sun is also in a common sign so that while in the Rasi the three important factors, *viz.*, the Sun, the Moon and Lagna are in common signs, in the Navamsa all the three have occupied fixed signs. This is significant inasmuch as the native becomes what may be called 'Worldly minded'. The Sun's disposition blends the ideal and the practical in the native, makes him discriminative and critical. The Moon's position gives a pure and fertile mind, not spiteful but somewhat vindictive, sensitive and discriminative and also worldly success. Virgo rising with Mars in Lagna makes the native somewhat domineering, passionate, somewhat reserved, orderly, critical, optimisitic, polite and helpful to others. The combination of Mars and lord of Lagna is again important inasmuch as the native becomes a victim of communal bickerings on the part of others and the pace of progress is temporarily obstructed. The *Gajakesari Yoga* (centering primarily on Lagna and 10th) is powerful enough to overcome the minor afflictions. The 2nd lord Venus is in the 12th aspected by Saturn while in the Navamsa the situation of the 2nd lord is good. From the Moon the 2nd house is not well situated so that for a superficial observer the Dhanabhava is not at all strong. Dhanakaraka Jupiter in Lagna with Mercury and Rajyakaraka Sun—and all placed in a kendra from the other Rajyakaraka Moon should be sufficient to confer wealth. The 7th lord Jupiter is no doubt in a benefic sign but Kalatrakaraka Venus is not only in the house of an enemy aspected by Saturn but hemmed inbetween Ketu and Mars ; the 7th from the Moon in Rasi, Venus in Navamsa and the 7th from the Moon in Navamsa are equally afflicted so that the married life cannot be as happy as one would wish. The position of Venus must make the wife extremely sensitive. The disposition of the 10th house is of considerable significance in this horoscope.

Important Events.—The subject's marriage took place in the sub-period of Mars within the Dasa of Jupiter—the major lord owning the 7th and the sub-lord owning the 8th from Lagna in Rasi, the 7th from Lagna in Navamsa and posited in Lagna. The first appointment was secured at the fag end of Jupiter Dasa. A son was born in Saturn's sub-period within the Dasa of Saturn. Mark Saturn is lord of the 5th and is in an upachaya. Two more sons were born in Mercury's sub-period —Mercury owning the 5th from Lagna in the Navamsa and occupying the 10th. Venus as owning the 5th from the Moon and occupying the 3rd from the Moon gave another son in his sub-period while in the remaining period of Saturn four more female issues were born. Saturn Dasa is specially important inasmuch as the family expanded by the birth of children consistent with the position of Saturn in his relation to the 5th house in the horoscope.

Remarks.—This is a fascinating horoscope because we are here dealing with a person who has occupied eminent positions. To a student of astrology the 10th Bhava is very significant. Mark, that when viewed from the Moon—the 10th house is immensely fortified by being aspected by exalted Mercury,

Jupiter, Sun and Mars. The Sun and Mars are strong enough to give political power while Mercury's situation is unique. Jupiter's presence adds dignity inasmuch as he makes the subject important, honest and principled and invests him with high character. Corruption is a concomitant of power and where Saturn is the investing deity, the politician or statesman concerned will be sinister, mean and selfish. Such a combination here is conspicuous by its absence. In this particular case, Jupiter and Mercury in combination in Lagna—aspecting the 10th from the Moon—render the native selfless.

It was in Mercury Dasa that he occupied various high offices —as Minister in a South Indian State, as a Prime Minister in a Central Indian State and after this as director of very big business organisation. Mark again the conjunction of three planets in the 10th in Navamsa—the Sun (lord of 4), the Moon (lord of 3) and Mercury (lord of 5), aspected by Mars and Saturn a yoga-karaka for Taurus Lagna. Allowing due margin to the inherent evil nature of the malefics concerned, one cannot deny that the five planets concentrating their influences on the 10th house have their functions to manifest. These maleflcs cause opposition and act as brakes for the smooth-running of fortunate currents. Jupiter is neecha in the 9th but has obtained a distinct neechabhanga thus rendering the house of fortune highly powerful.

Mercury Dasa which terminated in 1954 was of utmost importance inasmuch as it was during his Dasa that the native occupied very high positions. The Moon's sub-period in Mercury's major period continued till about the end of 1945. The major lord Mercury is of course lord of Lagna and the 10th and is in Lagna exalted while the sub-lord Moon is in the 10th from the major lord. The sub-lord gets vitiated by owning the 3rd in Navamsa and 11th in Rasi. Added to these, the native was undergoing elarata influences for the second time and the conjunction of Rahu and Saturn in his Janma Rasi was least conducive to a happy state of mind. Saturn gave him lot of mental worry, obstruction, annoyance and suspense and frustration of hopes and following Saturn-Rahu conjunction the native had a change for good. Jupiter's sub-period in Mercury Dasa gave him a change of career from an administrator to that of a businessman.

Saturn's presence in the 6th indicates that he had a number of smooth faced villains posing themselves as friends and well-wishers. He had the knack to overcome opposition because Mars in Lagna gave him strong will-power, rendering him at the same time somewhat aggressive.

The house of profession is peculiarly disposed indicating rise by merit. All the benefics including the commander-in-chief Mars and the royal planets are in some way or other connected with Lagna, the 9th and 10th. Astrological forces have been blended in such a way that money, influence, power and opposition are shown. The aesthetic Venus in the royal sign Leo makes him fashionable, artistic and love order and romance and makes him practical-minded.

The native is intellectually analytical and grave, thorough, self-reliant and of independent mind, persevering, moulded by principles and due appreciation of responsibility.

No. 66.—GEORGE VI

Birth Details.—Born on 14th December 1895 at 3-5 a.m. (L.M.T.). (Lat. 52° 51' N., Long. 0° 30' E.)

Planetary Positions.—The Sun 239° 56'; the Moon 213° 56'; Mars 220° 25'; Mercury 237° 18'; Jupiter 107° 38'; Venus 194° 58'; Saturn 203° 49'; Rahu 316° 28'; Ketu 136° 28'; and Lagna 187° 3'. Ayanamsa 20° 57'.

			Merc. Sun		Saturn	
Rahu			Jupit.	Rahu Venus		
	RASI			NAVAMSA		Ketu Moon
		Ketu				
	Moon Sun Mercury Mars	Lagna Saturn Venus	Jupit. Lagna		Mars	

Balance of Saturn Dasa at birth : Years 18-1-22.

Special Features.—Libra rising with Venus within 7° from the ascending degree inclined the native to liberal tendencies, an amiable, sympathetic and affectionate disposition and a refined, generous and just nature. The Moon is debilitated and in association with malefics, but aspected by Jupiter, lord of the 3rd and 6th. This is not good for mental peace and health, showing liability of trouble to the throat, speech and blood vessels. Mercury with Mars and the Sun made him rather critical at times and liable to suffer from nervous strain. Venus, lord of Lagna in Lagna with Saturn, the planet of solitude, indicates that the pattern of his life followed a certain swing of habit as was the case with his father. Strongly rooted in his own existence he tended to be withdrawn from the hurly-burly of life. He was a devoted family-man, a quality that goes a long way for a king in a constitutional monarchy. George VI found himself in possession of an empire under circumstances rarely witnessed before in the annals of English History. The political planet, who happens to be in the 10th from Chandra Lagna, is with Mars, Bhratrukaraka, while the 10th lord Moon is aspected by exalted Jupiter, lord of the 3rd and in assoication with Mars. These dispositions explain the fact that the native got the kingdom not from his father but from his brother. The horoscope has three important Raja Yogas, justifying the exalted position of the native. Jupiter's exaltation in the 10th from Lagna constitutes *Hamsa Yoga*. Saturn's exaltation in Lagna causes *Sasa Yoga*. The location of Venus in Lagna which he happens to own gives rise to *Malavya Yoga*. These *Panchamahapurusha Yogas*, having reference to the Lagna and the 10th, are indeed a unique feature rendering the horoscope highly fortunate.

Important Events.—In the first World War, he served on the western front in October 1918 when he was having Mercury Dasa Venus Bhukti. Consistent with the Raja Yoga nature of both the sub and major lords, the native was made Duke of York under the same directional influences. He married during Mercury Dasa Mars Bhukti. Note that both Mercury and Mars are in the 2nd, while the sub-lord owns the 7th or house of marriage. Elizabeth, the present Queen, was born in Mercury Dasa Rahu Bhukti. Mark the fact that Rahu is in the 5th while Mercury is aspected by Jupiter lord of the 5th from the Moon. The other daughter Margaret was born in Saturn Bhukti. Saturn, it will be seen, owns the 5th house and is in Lagna with Venus, lord of Lagna. Father's death took place in January 1936, when the sub-period of Saturn in the major period of Ketu was operating. Ketu is posited in the 10th house from the Moon in the sign of the Sun and, therefore, Ketu, being a shadowy planet, must necessarily give the results of the Sun, who is also Pitrukaraka. The Sun, lord of father, is with the Moon, lord of the house of father and in the 2nd (maraka place) from the sub-lord. The relation between the Sun and Saturn is that of *dwirdwadasa*. Saturn himself being yogakaraka, the results of this yoga could be realised only by the death of the native's father. Saturn in the 10th from the Moon in Navamsa gives the King the right to perform his father's obsequies. He ascended the throne in the inter-period of Mercury in Ketu's major period. The Sun represents political power. As lord of the 10th (from the Moon) and being posited in the ascendant (Moon's) itself in the Rasi and in the 4th house in the Navamsa, and aspected by exalted Jupiter who is in the 10th from the ascendant, the Sun gets every astrological "qualification" to bestow an empire. The coronation took place in Ketu Dara Mercury Bhukti. Ketu's position in the 11th is good while that of Mercury, as lord of the 9th in the 2nd with lords of the 10th and 11th is also favourable. The Dasa of Venus was the most momentous in the life of King George. Venus has no doubt caused *Malavya Yoga* and his strength is *par excellence*, especially that he is Lagna lord ; but because he is in the constellation of Rahu and somewhat afficted in Navamsa, during Venus Dasa, the empire faced a crisis of the first magnitude. Heavy burdens were imposed on the King due to the outbreak of II World War, as soon as Venus Bhukti in Venus Dasa started. During the Moon's sub-period, he visited the land-fronts in N. Africa and Italy. In the sub-period of Mars, the war ended with the victory of the Allies.

Mark the strong position of Mars in the 2nd in his own sign. In Rahu's sub-period, India became independent and the greater part of the British Empire was liquidated. Rahu is in the 5th aspected by Mars lord of the 7th; and hence the disintegration of the empire. The King died in Saturn Dasa Venus Bhukti, as Ayushkaraka Saturn aspects the 7th, a maraka house. From Chandra Lagna, Venus is a maraka and he is joined by Saturn. Thus both Saturn and Venus have become powerful marakas.

Remarks.—What is of significance in this horoscope to a student of astrology is the highly fortunate combination of planets favouring the inheritance of an empire without expectation of succeeding to the throne, victory against the most abnormal difficulties and peaceful liquidation of the major part of the empire. The situation of Jupiter in the 10th from the ascendant was no doubt the most sustaining factor which stood the native in good stead when Hitler was striking England at vital spots at vital moments, and when he was the master, practically of the whole of Europe. The three *Panchamahapurusha yogas* already referred to above *plus* the existence of two more powerful Raja yogas, *viz.*, Mercury occupying a Rasi other than Capricorn identical with Chandra Lagna; and the occupation of a kendra position from the Moon, by the lords of the 2nd, 9th (and 11th) are outstanding features which rendered the reign of this monarch colourful and unique.

No 67.—AN EXAMPLE FOR DHANA YOGA

Birth Details.—Born on 30th/31st January 1896 at 4-30 a.m. (L.M.T.) (Lat. 22° 20' N., Long. 73° E.)

Planetary Positions.—The Sun 289° 39'; the Moon 116°; Mars 253° 19'; Mercury 304° 54'; Jupiter 102° 20'; Venus 249° 49'; Saturn 207° 27'; Rahu 313° 14'; Ketu 133° 14'; and Lagna 257° 27'. Ayanamsa 20° 58'.

		Mandi	Mandi		Sun Venus Saturn
Mercury Rahu	RASI	Moon Jupit.	Moon	NAVAMSA	Mars Ketu
Sun		Ketu	Rahu		
Lagna Mars Venus	Saturn			Mercury	Jupiter	Lagna

Balance of Mercury Dasa at birth: Years 5-1-16.

Special Features.—Lagna is Sagittarius or Dhanus and the lord Jupiter is exalted and in conjunction with the Moon in his own house. This is a highly favourable combination adding great vitality to the inherent strength of the horoscope. Mars in Lagna coupled with the fact that the Sun in the Navamsa is associated with Saturn and Venus makes the native independent and detest being dictated to. The same combination indicates a distinct conflict between ideals and practices and the spiritual life will remain clouded in material attachments. Jupiter aspecting the Sun is an example of the soul asserting its individuality. Mars in Lagna suggests that the personal life would be marked by strong passions. The Moon's situation in a movable sign makes the mind wavering and somewhat unsteady. But Jupiter's association (partially blemished by Saturn's aspect) is of very great importance emphasising mental purity and making the native just, impartial, accurate, striving to be precise, persistent, cheerful, diligent and self-conscious of what he is. Saturn's aspect renders the person sometimes melancholic, doubtful and sceptical but Jupiter restores the equilibrium. Sagittarius rising gives an exaggerated faith in human nature. The influences of the Sun, the Moon and Lagna summed up reveal that the subject would be sincere, generous, magnanimous, somewhat ambitious, not fond of show or pomp. Emotion plays a large part. The Lagna and the lord of Lagna are disposed so strongly in this horoscope that they are capable of lifting the native by his own efforts to a position of considerable honour and celebrity. The 4th lord Jupiter is exalted in the 8th and is placed with the Moon. From Chandra Lagna the 4th is occupied by exalted Saturn. Both the 4th house and the 4th lord are aspected by Mars. The Jupiter–Mars influence denotes property, wealth and prosperity, a happy home and peaceful and successful domestic surroundings—though the martian aspect has got its own evil effect to produce. The karaka for 4th house in Lagna is suggestive of substantial landed and house properties. The 5th from Lagna is aspected by exalted Saturn while the 5th from the Moon receives the aspect of exalted Jupiter. In either case the 5th lord is Mars and he is aspected by Saturn. The native's fifth Bhava is fairly well disposed while the hand of Mars may cause an abortion or two to the wife. Mars aspecting the 7th and the 7th lord in conjunction with Rahu gave two marriages. The presence of *Obhayachari Yoga*, *Kesari Yoga*, *Adhi Yoga*, *Adhama Yoga*, *Lakshmi Yoga*, and *Dhana Yoga* are very important. *Adhama Yoga* indicates humble beginnings.

Important Events.—The marriage of the native took place in 1923 in Saturn's sub-period within the Dasa of Venus. The major lord Venus is the Kalatrakaraka and he is in Lagna aspecting the 7th while Saturn the sub-lord owns the 2nd or house of family. The first wife's death (October 1926) took place just before the close of Mercury Bhukti in Venus Dasa. The sub-lord Mercury is with Rahu. The death occurred when Saturn (lord of the 2nd) was transiting Scorpio Navamsa in which Mercury is placed. The second marriage occurred in May 1927 in the course of Ketu Bhukti within the Dasa of Venus. Ketu who is in the 9th is to give the results of the Sun and the Sun is in the house of family. Father's death occurred in 1930 in the sub-period of Jupiter within the Dasa of the Sun. The major lord owns the 9th besides being karaka for father. The sub-lord owning the 9th from the Moon is in a house of death from the major lord ; Saturn was about to leave Gemini by transit and the Sun is placed in Gemini Navamsa. The eldest boy was born in January 1936 in Rahu Bhukti of Moon Dasa. The major lord is in conjunction with Jupiter, Putrakaraka, besides being aspected by the 5th lord Rahu the sub-lord should give the results of Saturn who in his turn aspects the 5th house. In the Navamsa, Saturn rules the 5th from Lagna and occupies the 5th from the Moon. All these dispositions enabled Rahu to give birth to a son in his sub-period. Mother's death took place in Saturn's sub-period within the Moon Dasa. The Moon is the natural karaka for mother while Saturn is in the 4th from the karaka. In the Navamsa the sub-lord Saturn aspects the 4th while from the Moon he is in the 5th with the 4th lord. The native's death took place in Sun's sub-period in Rahu Dasa. Both are powerful marakas.

Remarks.—We are concerned with the financial and professional aspects of the horoscope. The strength of the Lagna is of supreme importance whatever be the Bhava in consideration. We have already seen how the Lagna and the lord are very powerful. The native rose to eminence and wealth as a great industrialist from humble beginnings. He was the head of an important organisation, which he joined at first as an ordinary clerk in 1921. What are the conspicuous combinations for wealth and position in this case? Money matters are judged largely, but not exclusively by the 2nd house while the 2nd house indicates wealth, the source of earning it comes from the 10th and whether one becomes wealthy or not is judged from the 9th and 11th. The 2nd lord (wealth) Saturn is exalted in the 11th (gains). In the 2nd are placed the Sun and Mercury lords of the 9th and 10th respectively, forming a powerful Raja yoga. The whole combination derives the aspect of Jupiter and the Moon forming *Gajakesari*. Jupiter (Dhanakaraka and lord of Lagna) is being aspected by Saturn lord of the 2nd. Thus it will be seen that on the house is brought to bear the combined influences of exalted Jupiter, Saturn and lord of the 9th and 10th. Dhanakaraka in this case happens to be lord of Lagna which is a force to reckon with. Viewing from the Moon we find that the 2nd lord Sun is in the 7th while the 9th lord Jupiter is exalted in Chandra Lagna. The 2nd from the Moon again receives the aspect of Mercury and Rahu. The native is an industrialist having to do with labour, iron, steel, aluminium, factories and so on.

Mark the interrelations between 1st, 2nd, 9th, 10th and 11th houses. The natural tendency is to gain through the lord of the 2nd. The 2nd lord in the 11th promises gain through co-operation. Since Saturn is powerful, gain by labour, responsibility, heavy trading in dark or white metals, investments and minerals is indicated. Saturn has predominantly to do with labour and as he is in the 11th, gain through employing labour on a large scale will be the important source of wealth. Since Jupiter is equally powerful, acquisition of wealth through managements, trusts and banking are also possible. The Moon's favourable disposition in his own house aspecting the 2nd signifies earnings from factories and business where a large number of hands are employed. Some of the more important combinations for much wealth, present in the horoscope, are (a) The lord of Lagna in (or aspecting) the 2nd, the 2nd lord in the 11th and the 11th lord in Lagna make one very wealthy. (b) Much gain of wealth is shown through various means if the planet owning the Rasi occupied by the lord of the Navamsa in which Lagna lord is placed, is exalted or is in his own house. (c) The exchange or *parivarthana* in its subtle aspect between Jupiter and Saturn— Jupiter occupying Pushyami, Saturn's constellation and the latter occupying Visakha, Jupiter's constellation. This inter-change of constellations between 1st and 2nd lords is of much importance. When a point of contact is established between the lords of the 1st and 9th, fortune in general seems to receive an impetus. This goes under the name of *Lakshmi Yoga*. Jupiter, lord of Lagna, powerfully aspects the Sun, lord of the 9th and *Lakshmi Yoga* is given rise to. Moreover, one of the planets causing the yoga has obtained the special distinction of exaltation and hence the native enjoyed the benefits of this yoga fully.

Here is the horoscope of a person who has risen to eminence as an industrialist by sheer merit coupled, of course, with good luck. In the horoscope of an industrialist always look for a connection between Mars, Mercury, Saturn, Jupiter and the 10th, the 2nd, 11th, 9th and 1st houses. Mercury gives business talents, Saturn—control over labour, Mars—connection with factories, the 9th—promotion of fortune through these means, the 2nd—source of wealth, the 10th—activity in the above spheres, the 11th—gain and the Lagna, general vitality.

No. 68.—SUBASH CHANDRA BOSE

Birth Details.—*Born on 23rd January 1897 at about 12 noon (L.M.T.) (Long. 5° 44′ E.,) Lat. 20° 38 N.)

Planetary Positions.—The Sun 282° 23′ ; the Moon 159° 16′ ; Mars 50° 55′ ; Mercury 279° 56′ ; Jupiter 137′ 55 ; Venus 327° 59′ ; Saturn 218° 5′ ; Rahu 295° ; Ketu 115° ; Lagna 8° 24′ ; and Hora Lagna 171°. Ayanamsa 20° 59′ .

	Lagna	Mars	Moon Merc.	Sun		Venus Lagna
Venus			Ketu	Ketu		Mars
Sun Rahu Mercury	RASI			NAVAMSA		Rahu
			Jupit.			
	Saturn		Hora Lagna Moon			Jupiter Saturn

Balance of Sun Dasa at birth : Years 0-4-15.

Special Features.—The Lagna is Aries or Mesha, a positive and fiery sign and the lord of Lagna Mars, an

---

* We cannot vouchsafe for the accuracy of the birth time nor can we doubt the authenticity of the source of this information. We have been able to rectify the time as 11-24 a.m. (L.M.T.) by a consideration of the life events of the subject.

aggressive planet, is in the second aspected powerfully by Saturn. The Lagna is again powerfully aspected by Jupiter from a fiery and royal sign Leo. Hence the Lagna is strong with considerable martian and saturnine influences being blended. This denotes a frank, open, outspoken and free-handed disposition, qualities which to a large extent shaped the career of Subash Chandra Bose. Aries or Mesha resembles the ram. We have thus at once a clue to the nature of Bose. Being positive and fiery, it made Subash act independently and assert his force. The cardinal nature of the sign coupled with the presence of Mars in the 2nd indicates that Bose was a pioneer of dauntless courage and fiery enthusiasm. No wonder he assaulted Prof. Oaten who was alleged to have vilified Indians. Even in Navamsa, Mars is in the 2nd while Lagna as well as the lord receives the malefic aspect of Saturn indicating suffering. Gemini rising in Navamsa indicates a well-developed body while the disposition of a malefic in the 3rd from Karakamsa is suggestive of extreme bravery. The Moon's situation in a double-bodied sign makes the mind somewhat wavering but since the Moon is in a benefic sign devoid of malefic aspects, it gave Subash a fertile mind, and made him accurate, just and precise. Jupiter in the house of intelligence is a good combination but being aspected by Mars and Saturn clouds his vision now and then. His 'mistaken enthusiasm' is perhaps due, in a large measure, to this combined malefic influence over the 5th house, coupled with the fact that Mercury, the planet of intelligence, is in a malefic sign in association with Rahu and the Sun. Jupiter is the planet of wisdom as different from intelligence. The situation of Jupiter and the fact that the Karakamsa is aspected by Saturn are indices that whilst he was moved by the highest impulses of patriotism there was a sense of frustration also. *Anapha, Suvesi* and *Adhi yogas* are all strong and pure. Mars does not aspect the 7th; the 7th lord is also free from martian and saturnine influences. These clearly reveal that Subash was not a fascist but that he was a true servant of humanity. Fascist tendencies can be present only when there is an inter-mingling of saturnine and martian vibrations in relation to the 7th house. Because this intermingling has reference in this particular case to the 2nd and 8th houses, he could have been somewhat of a dictator, not in the sense of Hitler or Mussolini, but for the sake of discipline in his ranks. The conjunction of the Sun, Rahu and Mercury is noteworthy because it indicates the enormous suffering of the man. If there were no Rahu in the 10th, Subash would perhaps have been in the place of Nehru or Prasad. Rahu eclipsing the Sun in the 10th in a sign owned by Saturn is significant inasmuch as his entire life constituted one long battle against British Imperialism. Ketu in the 4th gives changeable views. That Subash bore arms and that he, may be even if only for a short time, was head of his 'army' and 'State' is borne out by the disposition of Saturn in the 4th from Karakamsa. His spiritual inclinations are well brought out by Mercury aspecting the 4th from Kara-kamsa and Jupiter and Saturn occupying the 5th and 8th respectively in the Rasi. The 8th lord Mars happens to be Lagna lord and he is in the 2nd. The 8th is occupied by Saturn, the Ayushkaraka. These and other combinations no doubt indicate a fairly long life but because lord of Lagna and lord of 8th are in fixed signs, because Lagna and the Moon are in Chara and Dwiswabhava Rasis respectively and because Lagna and Hora Lagna are also disposed respectively in Chara and Dwiswabhava signs only Madhyayu is indicated which according to Jaimini would vary from 33 to 66. The 8th house indicating the marriage thread is subject to a series of malefic influences while the 7th lord, who is also Kalatrakaraka, is in the 11th aspected by Jupiter. Hence his unconventional marriage with an Austrian lady. The 5th house so far as children are concerned is spoiled by the presence of Putra-karaka *plus* the influence of Mars and Saturn. Certain elements of *Parivraja* are also present. Bhratrukaraka Mars is afflicted but the 11th is well fortified. Hence he was the youngest son of his father.

Important Events.—The beginning of Rahu Dasa synchronised with his spiritual thirst. In 1914 he stole away from home in search of a Guru but returned home disgusted with the luxury of the Mahants. Rahu, being placed in Karmasthana, must have given Bose a clear insight into spiritual values. He left for England in Saturn Bhukti of Rahu Dasa, the Dasa lord occupying a watery sign. Mercury's sub-period in Rahu Dasa made Subash fot the first time the guest of His Majesty. He was arrested in 1921 December. Mercury is lord of the 3rd and 6th while Rahu the major lord is in the 10th with the political planet Sun. The sub-period of Mars in Rahu Dasa reveals signs of tuberculosis in Subash Bose. Mars aspecting the 5th from Karakamsa was responsible for affecting the health of the native. The father's death occurred in Jupiter Dasa Saturn Bhukti, Jupiter owning and aspecting the 9th while Saturn powerfully aspects both the lord of the 9th and Pitrukaraka, the Sun. The greatest honour that the country could confer befell on Subash Bose in 1938 when he was elected to the Presidentship of the Congress. This occurred in Mercury's sub-period in Jupiter Dasa. Mercury is in the 10th with the Sun but subject to the evil association of Rahu. Consequently, Subash had to resign, even when he was again elected as President, just because Gandhi wanted someone else to ascend the presidential gadi. Mercury is lord of the 6th as well, ruling enemies and hence Subash had to come out of the Congress being 'expelled' for he was declared unfit by the 'old guard' of the Working Committee of the Congress. During Mercury Bhukti he had to suffer from the machinations of his enemies, all of which he faced bravely. He mysteriously disappeared in Venus Bhukti Venus being placed in the mystical sign of Aquarius. Venus as lord of the 2nd and 7th is in the 11th and in Karakamsa having Samasaptaka relations with Jupiter Hence during Venus period Subash enjoyed in the hands of the Axis all the honour due to the head of a State and also got married. The mutual aspects between the lords of the 9th and the 7th both being placed in friendly houses, the major lord Jupiter causing strong *Anapha* and the sub-lord Venus giving rise to strong *Adhi Yoga* rendered operative the Raja yoga due to their horoscope dispositions. He is reported to have died in an air crash on 22nd August 1945 in the sub-period of Mars within the Dasa of Jupiter, Mars being placed in maraka house both in Rasi and Navamsa.

Remarks.— As we have said above, it is Rahu's position in the 10th with the Sun that gave Subash such a checkered political career. Rahu and Ketu are incendiary in nature. As Rahu is with Mercury, the patriotism of Bose in the last few years was, of course, misguided. It was a grievous mistake to think that Japan would help India out of any higher motives. But a careful study of the horoscope, especially the position of the Moon and the absence of martian and saturnine influence on the 7th house, reveals that Subash was neither a quisling nor a traitor. Jupiter in the 5th suggests that lofty motives guided Subash, but he was misled into thinking, on account of Mars and Saturn aspecting Jupiter, that with Japanese aid he would be able to liberate India. Lord of Lagna has a strong element of jupiterian influence. This coupled with the fact that the Lagna is free from affliction made him a man of action first. His daring, his energy, his uncompromising nature and his dynamic personality are all qualities of Aries, the first sign of the zodiac. The Sun–Rahu combination in the 10th whilst afflicting the political career conferred on him the capacity for supreme sacrifice of all that is dear and precious to a human being. His horoscope also reveals that, being primarily an Arian, Subash must have firmly resisted the Axis attempts to make him their tool.

So far as longevity is concerned, one or two observations seem to be necessary. According to general canons of astrology Saturn in the 8th confers good longevity. Besides this the Lagna is powerful by being aspected by Jupiter. In 1945 he was having Mars Bhukti Jupiter Dasa. Jupiter is no doubt in the constellation of Venus and aspected by Saturn. But his location and ownership would not have invested him with power to kill the native, especially that Gochara or transiting positions were not adverse. But Jupiter presides over *Pratyak* or a constellation indicating danger. The fact that Saturn is in the 8th and lord of the 4th is in the 6th indicates death while journeying and therefore the sub-period of Mars (Mars ruling the 3rd or a dangerous constellation) which ruled till about the middle of January 1946 was critical for Bose's life.

No. 69.—SUDDHANANDA BHARATHI

Birth Details.—Born on 12th May 1897 at 10–19 a.m. (L.M.T.) (Lat. 9° 51′ N., Long. 78° 37′ E.)

Planetary Positions.—The Sun 30° 43′ ; the Moon 149° 50′ ; Mars 95° 28′ ; Mercury 43° 25′ ; Jupiter 129° 36′ ; Venus 10° 46′ ; Saturn 216° 58′ ; Rahu 289° 13′ ; Ketu 19° 13′ ; and Lagna 95° 50′. Ayanamsa 20° 59′.

	Venus	Sun Mercury			Mercury	Jupiter Rahu
			Ketu Lagna Mars			Venus
Rahu	RASI			NAVAMSA		Lagna Mars
			Jupit. Moon	Sun		
	Saturn			Ketu Moon		Saturn

Balance of Sun Dasa at birth :   Years 4–6–27.

The Lagna being Cancer, a movable sign occupied by Mars and Ketu confers imagination and delighting in strange scenes and adventures, power of adaptation and the faculty of absorbing other people's ideas. Mars in Lagna indicates a restless, active mind while Ketu, the planet of spirituality, makes the native, not stick to any one particular locality for

long. The Moon, karaka for the mind, is in Leo in association
with Jupiter lord of the 9th and aspected by Saturn, lord of
the 7th. This is the most important combination in the horoscope round which the entire life of the native revolved.
Besides causing *Gajakesari Yoga*, this combination is capable
of producing a certain sensitiveness (a lunar trait) which always
finds expression in sublimal ways. Venus, the planet of poetry,
who happens to be lord of the 4th, is in the 10th in the house
of the practical Mars and aspected by the Gnanakaraka Jupiter
from Chandra Lagna.   This confers poetical talents of an
extraordinary nature. It must be noted that he was considered
to be the greatest Tamil poet of his times. He could easily
versify in English and French. The 10th house is not afflicted.
Mars yogakaraka is in Lagna but his association with Ketu is
not desirable for political success.   But it gives him a real
sense of political values enabling him to work for the sake of
the country and not for the sake of position. From Chandra
Lagna, the lord Sun (Atmakaraka) is in the 10th with the
intellectual planet Mercury causing *Budha-Aditya Yoga*, aspected
by Saturn.   According to classical astrology, the Sun stands
for *Vanaprastha* (high intellectual and spiritual development,
simple living and high thinking), Mercury stands for *Jeevitha*
(form of Vishnu worship) and Saturn stands for *Nirgrastha* or
some sort of a *digambara* sanyasin. The disposition of these
three planets denotes renunciation, service, yogic sadhana and
attainment of inner peace. It will be seen that the Manahkaraka
Moon and Kamakaraka Venus are not afflicted. Both these
are subject to the influence of Jupiter. On the contrary, the
7th house has the influences of all the malefics—Saturn, Rahu,
Ketu and Mars centered on them. This is a very significant
combination making the native a real Brahmachari and enabling him to observe celibacy, physically and mentally. Such a
combination is unique by its rare occurrence. Most of the

planets are disposed in *dwirdwadasa* positions. Obviously this denotes intense struggle within the mind between spiritual forces that are real and enduring and those material that are fleeting and transitory. Ultimate triumph of the Divine is evident in view of the disposition of the Moon, Jupiter and Venus in Dharmatrikonas.

Suddhananda Bharathi's horoscope is important to students of astrology in regard to three aspects. First and foremost, he was essentially an ardent and a fiery nationalist as indicated by the conjunction of yogakaraka Mars with the rising degree in Lagna. Since Ketu is nearly 14° away from Mars he hated political opportunism and had no charm for the trappings of office. Secondly, the intellectual planet Mercury in the 10th from the Moon and in the 2nd from the planet of poetry, *viz.*, Venus, who in his turn is aspected by Jupiter has made the native a great poet and author. As this biographer mentions "there is not one aspect or department of literature in which he has not written and which he has not adorned". Saturn's aspect suggests that his "national songs are sparks of spiritual heroism, simple in diction, direct in expression, deep in meaning, clear in sentiment and sweet to sing and hear". The result of Jupiter's aspect on Venus is that his poems are an expression of the spirit of the Upanishads, Bhagavad Geeta and all that ancient Indian culture stands for. And lastly, the presence of both the Atmakaraka and the Manahkaraka (the Sun and the Moon respectively) in the constellation of the Atmakaraka, situation of the Sun in the 10th from the Moon, and the lord of the 10th being aspected by Jupiter from Chandra Lagna indicate high spiritual and yogic attainments especially in Saturn Dasa.

No. 70.—AN EXAMPLE FOR SCIENTIFIC EMINENCE

Birth Details.—Born on 23rd/22nd November 1902 at 5-16 a.m. (L.M.T.) (Lat. 23° 6′ N., Long. 72° 40′ E.)

Planetary Positions.—The Sun 218° 44′; the Moon 137° 22′; Mars 145° 37′; Mercury 207° 51′; Jupiter 290° 11′; Venus 217° 14′; Saturn 272° 45′; Rahu 182° 10′; Ketu 2° 10′; and Lagna 204° 17′. Ayanamsa 21° 0′.

	Ketu				Ketu	Lagna	Mercury
							Jupiter
	RASI		Moon Mars	Sat.	NAVAMSA		
Saturn Jupiter							
	Venus Sun	Mercury Lagna Rahu			Mars	Rahu	Moon Sun Venus

Balance of Venus Dasa at birth: Years 13–11–12.

Special Features.—The Lagna is Libra, the sign of the balance and the lord of Lagna Venus is in the 2nd in conjunction with the Sun lord of the 11th and aspected by Mars. Chandra Lagna is rendered very strong due to the presence of yogakaraka Mars there. Mercury the karaka for the rational and intellectual faculties in conjunction with Lagna shows the bent of mind towards science from early life and confers versatility of talent, ability, readiness of resource and a pretty wit. Mercury in Lagna is aspected by Saturn in the 4th and this disposition confers solidity of intellect, patience, candour and generosity. Mercury rising in Lagna confers moderate stature and fair complexion. The disposition is extermely good in that the person loves justice, virtue and morality in all its forms.

The house of education and intellectual acquisitions is pretty strong. With the 4th lord Saturn posited in the 4th having attained Vargottama and in association with Jupiter who has obtained neechabhanga, the native possesses amazing intellectual versatility peculiar to Libra. We have heard him converse knowledgeably on a dozen and one different subjects.

The *Chandra Mangala Yoga* caused in the 11th house is highly significant involving as it does the 2nd (finance), 7th (marriage and foreign travels) and the 10th (occupation) lords. It makes the native free, open-hearted and liberal-minded, causing him to be courageous and high spirited. It gives him wide and frequent travels in connection with his profession. As Mars is *Vaksthanadhipati* and the Moon karaka of mind, the person will be a very fluent, eloquent and agreeable speaker. Despite the strength of the *Chandra Mangala Yoga*, as the sign involved is Leo, and as Mars is one of the Netrakarakas, the native is liable to defective vision and occasional eye troubles. But as the 12th lord Mercury is unafflicted, he will have no permanent eye trouble. Due to the Moon's affliction by Mars the native is liable to frequent mental worry. *Sasa Yoga* caused by the presence of Saturn in his own house in a kendra from Lagna is highly significant. Though Saturn is a natural malefic, the evil is minimised considerably by Jupiter's association with Saturn and the yoga having reference to the 6th from Chandra Lagna. The 10th house highly fortified by being aspected by *Sasa Yoga* causing Saturn puts the native in positions of great responsibility and prominence giving him authority over others. He is rendered honourable, high-minded, candid and warm-hearted. The yoga also favours intuition and genius Lord of the 6th Jupiter is neechabhanga. This means secret foes trying to work against the subject in his own field of study, and that he had to encounter a lot of opposition from other scientists. But Mercury's position in Lagna enables him to cultivate that strength of mind and detachment which are so very essential for achieving great things. Mark the concentration of Rahu–Ketu influences on the 7th or house of marriage, 7th lord Mars having no aspect of a benefic and Venus Kalatrakaraka being aspected by Mars. This denotes a "peculiar and exceptional union" and a marriage that is out of the common. So far as health is concerned, it will be seen that Lagna lord Venus as well as the Sun (indicator of vitality) are in the constellation of Mars—a maraka, but otherwise unafflicted. The Sun ruler of the heart is in the 4th house (ruling heart) from the Moon aspected by Mars. Whilst the general health will no doubt be good, it also shows a liability to suffer from debility and nervous weakness and occasional pains in the chest region. There are no indications of his being disabled by any serious or chronic diseases. Jupiter–Saturn's position in the 6th from Chandra Lagna can affect the blood and the liver.

There are several important Dhana yogas, the most significant ones being the *parivarthana* between the 2nd and 11th lords, the position of lord of the 9th in Lagna and Lagna lord in the 2nd, and the association of the 2nd and 10th lords in the 11th. Here, it must be noted that the dominant position of

Mars as lord of the 2nd (money) and 7th (wife) and as an associate of the Moon (10th) in the 11th (gains) is a general indication of not only good fortune throughout life but also legacy through marriage.

In this astrological sketch we are concerned more with the scientific eminence of the native than with any other aspect of his life, the strong disposition of the intellectual planet Mercury in Lagna in association with the mystic planet Rahu confers on the native pointed wit, ingenuity and inventive genius. According to a famous classical work, when Mercury is strongly placed in Lagna, the person will possess ''strong imagination and retentive memory. He is an excellent orator and logician. He will be given to the attainment of learning, of sharp witty and pleasant conversation, curious in pursuit of natural knowledge (science) with an inclination to travel in foreign countries''.

Important Events.—The first and the most important happening in the life of the native was his trip to England for studies. This took place in the Dasa of the Sun and Bhukti of Jupiter. Mark the position of Jupiter in the 4th with the 4th lord from Lagna and that of the Sun, the major lord in the 2nd from Lagna. Jupiter has obtained neechabhanga and occupies a Chara Rasi. In the Navamsa again the sign positions of the Sun and Jupiter especially from Chandra Lagna are noteworthy justifying the trip overseas for purposes of education. The disposition of the Moon as lord of the 10th in the 11th with Mars lord of the 2nd or house of finance explain the native getting his first job in England in the Moon Dasa and subsequently another important job in India, under the same directional influences, which paved the way for his future phenomenal rise in life. Rahu's position deserves to be carefully studied. He is in Lagna, in the house of Venus, and therefere capable of giving rise to the results of Venus as lord and sub-lord of a Dasa. Rahu is in the constellation of Mars, a yogakaraka from Chandra Lagna. Ketu's occupation of the third from the Moon is an ideal position. Again from Lagna, Mars, whose results should be given by Rahu (as he is in the constellation of Mars), is in the 11th, as lord of the 2nd, in association with the Moon lord of the 10th ; while Venus whose results should also be given by Rahu (as he is in the sign of Venus) is in the 2nd in association with the Sun, lord of the 11th, and aspected by Mars the 2nd lord, there is a certain conglomeration of Raja and Dhana yogas which Rahu is empowered to confer during his Dasa. It must be noted that it was only during Rahu Dasa that the official position of the native was built up until he reached the present enviable position of all-India importance, Rahu and Mars are associated with engineering. Rahu conferred on the native great name and fame as a scientist of international repute and gave wide travelling all over the world, great distinction, respect and responsibility. The native's marriage took place in Rahu Dasa Saturn Bhukti. Mark the fact that Saturn owns the 7th from Chandra Lagna. Mercury saw him as head of a great Research Institution, which he expanded and built up enormously. Again the Moon's sub-period consistent with his rulership and disposition gave the native further elevation, distinction and responsibility which required tact and skill, all of which the native possessed abundantly.

The Dasa of Jupiter which commenced in 1958 and ended in 1973 brought the native further laurels. He became connected with a number of organisations in different parts of the world and served as a member of the Planning Commission. The 3rd and 6th lordship of Jupiter worked adversely, leading him to conflict between conscience and expedience. The conscience asserted and he came out unscathed to maintain a reputation not only as a scientist but also as a man of clean public life. Saturn, whose Dasa was next though Yogakaraka occupying his own place is blemished because of his occupation of the constellation of the Sun. As lord of the 7th from Chandra Lagna and placed in the 6th, Saturn caused the death of the native's wife. In the sub-period of Mercury, the native gifted his property worth nearly six lakhs to a hospital for running a cancer-research center. His death came about in the same Bhukti of Mercury. Dasa lord Saturn is a powerful maraka from Chandra Lagna. The Bhukti lord owning the 12th is in the 2nd Bhava from Lagna and is the 2nd lord from the Moon.

Remarks.—The subject of the horoscope was a leading scientist and a world figure. With staunch patriotic leanings, he occupied a top position in the world of science. Pride of place should be given to *Sasa Yoga* caused by Saturn, especially that Saturn is in Vargottamamsa. Saturn who has caused neechabanga for Jupiter is in association with Jupiter. Consequently, most of the results due to *Sasa Yoga* happened during the Dasa of Jupiter. The native occupied a high position of world-wide importance which enabled him, as an outstanding scientist, to work for the peace of the world. Owing to the 6th lordship of Jupiter, he no doubt encountered considerable opposition from other scientists who did not relish his achievements but he was able to overcome them as Jupiter is situated in the 6th from the Moon.

Summing up, Libra rising and unafflicted, conferred a strong and forceful nature with pronounced likes and dislikes. The mental attitude was somewhat fatalistic but courageous, self-confident and ambitious. Gifted with splendid vitality, the health was good. But due to the martian aspect on the Sun, he was inclined to overdo both in work and in the pleasures. Health in this case largely depended upon the native's mental state and the way he lived.

The disposition of the Sun, the Moon and Mars and Lagna lord in mutual kendras, is a testimony for a life of self-expression, a creative growth of character and a command of destiny.

A common-place person has several complexes of planetary aspects unrelated to one another and so his energies are scattered into various fields. A well-integrated chart, like the one under discussion, indicates a person of achievement and prominence.

No. 71.—MADHAVRAO SADASIVRAO GOLWALKAR

Birth Details.—Born on 19th/18th February 1906 at 4–34 a.m. (L.M.T.) (Lat. 21° 8' N., Long. 79° 5' E.)

Planetary Positions.—The Sun 308° 15' ; the Moon 254° 30' ; Mars 349° 21' ; Mercury 306° 37' ; Jupiter 36° 42' ; Venus 309° 22' ; Saturn 313° 37' ; Rahu 119° 27' ; Ketu 299° 27' ; and Lagna 274° 57'. Ayanamsa 21° 6'.

			Rahu Jupit.		
Mars	Jupiter				
Mercury Sun Venus Saturn		Rahu	Sat. Lagna		
	RASI			NAVAMSA	
Lagna Ketu					Moon
Moon			Venus Sun Mars	Mercury	Ketu

Balance of Venus Dasa at birth: Years 18–3–0.

Special Features.—Of the three important constituents of the horoscope, *viz.*, the Lagna, the Sun and the Moon, it is only the Sun that is subjected to certain afflictions. The Lagna lord is in his own sign and Lagna is aspected powerfully by Jupiter. The Moon is in a benefic sign and is free from affliction. Capricorn or Makara rising endows the native with a quiet, persevering and persistent spirit. He will be capable of enormous efforts towards the realisation of a cherished object. The desire for power will be strong but Jupiter's aspect sublimates the desire for nobler ends. The Moon, karaka for the mind, is in a dual sign but free from any evil aspect or association. In the Navamsa, however, he is powerfully aspected by Saturn. Consequently he will have a strong, forceful and enduring temper. The 9th house from Chandra Lagna has some of the most powerful influences focussed on it, notably the combined aspect of the Sun (lord of the 9th), and Mercury lord of the 10th and 7th. Such dispositions frequently result in great achievements but as Venus lord of the 6th and 11th also aspects the 9th, the life is often unhappy. The influences due to the Lagna may be summed up in the following words:—subtle disposition, collected, calm, witty and yet melancholic. The intellectul planet Mercury is in conjunction with the Sun and Saturn. The Sun–Mercury conjunction confers great mental abilities, while Mercury-Saturn conjunction gives patience, solidity of intellect, a love for antiquarian studies and a tendency to asceticism. The array of four planets in the 2nd house from Lagna and the 3rd from the Moon, involving lords of Lagna, the 9th and 10th, denotes humble parentage, but dawn of prosperity to the poverty-stricken parents after his birth. Mark Bhratrukaraka Mars in the 3rd and Bhratrusthana from the Moon afflicted. In the Navamsa again, the 3rd house is aspected by Saturn while the karaka Mars is afflicted due to association with the Sun and Mandi. Golwalkar was the sole surviving son of the nine children of his parents. Saturn and the Sun in the 2nd make the subject obstinate and self-willed. The Sun, in conjunction with Mercury indicates pride and conscientiousness while the Venus–Mercury conjunction confers taste, elegance, love of music, amiability and noble motives. The *Budha-Adhitya Yoga* and even *Budha-Sani Yoga* in the mystic sign of Aquarius, contrary to views held in some quarters, have made the man a curious mixture of zoologist, lawyer and philosopher. In whatever he does, he will be generally confronted with obstacles and delay but as Lagna is strongly disposed, the ultimate objects will be realised. Though both the Moon and Mercury have sway over the mind, different kinds of results will manifest when they are in association with Saturn. The Moon–Saturn conjunction makes one melancholic. The native's good name will be in danger at some time of life. He will suffer from slander or public attack or open opposition. He meets with frequent reversals and rebuffs. He will be in danger of imprisonment. But Mercury, though he may give more or less similar results, will considerably temper the evil. In the case of Mr. Golwalkar, Mercury and Saturn are almost in exact conjunction. But the evil is considerably lessened because of the sign being Aquarius Saturn's Moolatrikona place. This gives a great degree of mental control, good power of observation quick perception, and excellent faculties of reflection reasoning and analysis. Moreover, the presence of Venus, in between Mercury and Saturn, enables him to arrive at an accurate, truthful and impersonal judgment, especially in such matters in which the feelings and emotions are involved. Note the powerful afflictions to the lord of the 7th and Venus—the Kalatrakaraka. He is a bachelor. That the Chief does possess considerable humanitarian ideals is shown by Jupiter's presene in the 5th, in the house of the planet of reality, *viz.*, Venus. This makes him practical, idealistic and imaginative. The house of intelligence is well fortified.

Important Events.—Golwalkar's active interest in Hindu culture appears to have really begun with the advent of Moon Dasa. The Moon is lord of the 7th and occupies the 12th, a sign of Jupiter. The Moon Dasa gave him lot of activity. He became connected with the Sangh, and his meeting with the founder changed the whole course of his life. He spurned all offers of marriage (Moon lord of the 7th in the 12th); he took his Degree in Law, started practice, left it, joined the Ramakrishna Ashram, came back to Nagpur, became a Training Camp officer of the Sangh in 1936, Chief Secretary in 1937 and Sar Sang Chalak in 1940, just about the beginning of Mars Dasa. Mars is favourably disposed. He is lord of the 4th from Lagna and 5th from the Moon and aspects the 10th from the Moon which is also aspected by Jupiter, lord of Chandra Lagna. This curious mixture of martian and jupiterian influences on the 10th house is highly significant. It explains how his organisation is marked out for its efficiency, discipline and concerted work. Golwalkar was arrested in Rahu Dasa Rahu Bhukti, exactly when Gochara Saturn was passing through the radical Rahu who occupies the 8th Bhava. Rahu is in the constellation of Mercury and Mercury, we have seen, has caused a powerful Raja yoga in the 2nd house from Lagna by his association with Venus. From Chandra Lagna the yoga has reference to the 3rd house, the planets involved being the Sun and Mercury. The latter part of Rahu Dasa, consistent with the fact that Rahu is in the nakshatra of Mercury lord of the 9th, resulted in the Chief's, *i.e.*, Guruji's name and fame greatly increasing.

The native suffered from cancer which was detected in the sub-period of Mercury in Jupiter's major period. The major lord owning the 3rd and 12th is in Krittika ruled by the

Sun lord of the 8th while the sub-lord Mercury owning the sixth (disease) is in Dhanishta ruled by Mars.* He died in Venus sub-period. Venus though Yogakaraka is in a maraka place in the constellation of Rahu who occupies a death-inflicting place.

Remarks.—There are no visible outstanding Rajayogas in the horoscope. But the importance of the four-planet combination in the 2nd from Lagna and the 3rd from the Moon cannot be ignored. The intellectual planet Mercury, the political planet Sun, and the planet of the masses Saturn are all brought together within an arc of 5 degrees. Four planets in a single sign may be considered as a *Sanyasa Yoga*. But in the present context, it will not be renunciation of the world but renunciation of his self-interests. A great Sanskrit work suggests that one born under such a combination "will be surrounded by friends, be pure-hearted, fortunate and learned". The combination happening in the mystic sign of Aquarius and in a kendra from Jupiter denotes substantial achievements on the part of Golwalkar.

The 7th lord has no conjunction with or aspect of Mars and Rahu. The 7th as well as the 10th (from the Moon) are of course aspected by Mars. This gave him dynamic energy, fiery enthusiasm and made him bold. But there is no conjunction at all between Mars and Saturn or Mars and Rahu. Therefore his capacities could not be directed in destructive channels. There may be an instinctive sense of domination but that does not make him a 'Fuehrer' unless the three first-

---

* His ascendant was fixed as *Dhruvamsa* and according to Sathya-nadi : "the native gets *Vrunarogam* (Cancer ?) in Mercury in Jupiter and dies in Venus Sub-period in Jupiter's Dasa, when he is aged 68 and the Sun transits through Libra."

rate malefics, *viz.*, Rahu, Saturn and Mars are in mutual conjunction and aspects involving the 7th and 8th houses. The horoscope relates to the head of an organisation who was committed to the awakening of the conscience of the Indian youth to their moral rights and guiding the minds of the younger community from the morasses of the mischievous, materialistic, political and social doctrines of the West to the idealism of benevolence and spirituality of Indian culture. The association of the lord of Lagna, the 5th, 9th and 10th in the 2nd should be carefully noted.

No. 72.—NATHURAM VINAYAK GODSE

Birth Details.—Born on 19th May 1910 at 8–29 a.m. (I.S.T.) (Long 73° 52′ E., Lat. 18° 31 N.)

Planetary Positions.—The Sun 36° 41′ ; the Moon 160° 43′ ; Mars 79° 16′ ; Mercury 45° 39′ ; Jupiter 163° 44′ ; Venus 351° 42′ ; Saturn 9° 4′ ; Rahu 37° 17′ ; Ketu 217° 17′ ; and Lagna 79° 16′. Ayanamsa 21° 1′.

Venus	Saturn	Mercury Sun Ketu	Lagna Mars	Mars Lagna Rahu	Moon	Jupiter Mercury	Saturn
				Sun			
	RASI				NAVAMSA		
				Venus			
	Ketu		Moon Jupit				Ketu

Balance of Moon's Dasa at birth : Years 9–5–16.

Special Features.—Just as a doctor is concerned with an objective diagnosis of the case he handles, similarly an astrologer must analyse the horoscope objectively and with detachment. Here is the horoscope of a person who committed the most brutal and inhuman crime of killing Mahatma Gandhi, the greatest embodiment of *ahimsa*. The horoscope has certain peculiar traits. The Lagna being Gemini is in exact conjunction with Mars who is in the constellation of Rahu. Saturn aspects Mars in Lagna. These combinations indicate restlessness, a nature contemptuous of danger and quick to anger. Lagna lord Mercury is with Rahu and the Sun. This again tends to express an ungrateful, quarrelsome, revengeful overbearing and selfish nature with scant regard for the rights and feelings of others. The most destructive influences have been centered on Lagna and the lord of Lagna, the planets causing such an affliction being Rahu, Mars and Saturn, three first-rate malefics. Atmakaraka Sun, in exact conjunction with Rahu and thus eclipsed, is in the 9th from the Moon ruling the mind. This disposition inclined the native to inversion of the better qualities due to the Moon–Jupiter association in the 4th house, resulting in lack of conscience, indecency, disrespect for law and criminal proclivities. It will be seen that the 4th and 10th are occupied by two first-rate benefics. But Jupiter's beneficent effects are neutralised by his being Kendradhipati and by his being aspected by the 6th and 11th lord Mars, whose affliction is further augmented by his situation in Rahu's constellation. It may be argued that exaltation of Venus in the 10th might suggest that in resorting to this dastardly crime, his motives, though perverse, might have been good. But the fact that Venus himself is in the constellation of Mercury, the ruler of the mind, who in his turn is violently afflicted, clearly brings to light that the native was impulsive, erratic, reckless and visionary.

Important Events.—In dealing with such horoscopes, one should carefully study the disposition of Lagna, the Moon and the Sun. As in this case, Mercury the lord of Lagna and the indicator of the mind is subject to *Papakarthari Yoga* and is with Rahu, and as the Sun, Atmakaraka, is also similarly afflicted, it indicates a rupture between the mind and the spirit : with the result the cunning and craftiness of the mind exerted themselves to take charge of the lower personality and therefore he must have gone about for years plotting and scheming with such consummate cunning that no one could have suspected his diabolical plot which brought the death of India's greatest man of this age. He committed the dastardly act of murdering Gandhi in Saturn Bhukti of Jupiter Dasa. He was hanged under the same directional influences. It will be seen that Jupiter is a definite maraka both from Lagna and the Moon while Saturn is in the 8th from Lagna as well as Dasanatha in Rasi while they are in *dwirdwadasa* in *Navamsa* occupying the 2nd and 3rd respectively from Chandra Lagna. The nature of the death, *viz.*, by hanging is shown by Saturn lord of the 8th occupying Ayudha Drekkana. According to Jaimini, when the 3rd house from Atmakaraka (here Venus) is occupied by the Sun, death will be due to political offences. Astrological students must mark the concentration of the influences of the worst malefics, *viz.*, Rahu, Saturn and Mars, both on Lagna and Lagna lord, both in the Rasi and the Navamsa. Deeds, which offend public opinion, or meet with punishment at the hands of the State are generally the indications of misdirected energy shown in the horoscope by Rahu, Saturn and Mars not only by their mutual adverse relationships but also in the affliction they cause to Lagna and Lagna lord as lords of the 6th and 8th. Note Mars as lord of the 6th and Saturn as lord of the 8th both afflicting Lagna point out the direction of his destiny—incarceration and death by hanging.

No. 73.—AN EXAMPLE FOR POVERTY

Birth Details.—Born on 31st October 1910 at 1–37 p.m. (I.S.T.) (Lat. 13° N., Long. 77° 35′ E.)

Planetary Positions.—The Sun 196° 2′ ; the Moon 175° 31′ ; Mars 184° 48′ ; Mercury 186° 26′ ; Jupiter 186° 42′ ; Venus 189° 33′ ; Saturn 9° 55′ ; Rahu 28° 33′ ; Ketu 208° 33′ ; and Lagna 299°. Ayanamsa 21° 9′.

	Rahu Saturn				Saturn Ketu
			Sun		
	RASI			**NAVAMSA**	Moon
Lagna					
	Sun, Jupit. Mercury Ketu, Mars Venus	Moon	Rahu Jupit. Venus	Mars Mercury	Lagna

Balance of Mars Dasa at birth: Years 5–10–7.

Special Features.—Lagna or the ascendant is Capricorn, a movable sign and the lord of Lagna Saturn is debilitated in Aries and is in conjunction with Rahu—a combination that is most undesirable in a horoscope. The lord of Lagna is powerfully aspected by a conglomeration of good and evil forces—the latter predominating. Even in the Navamsa, the Lagna lord is subjected to the association of Mars and occupies Scorpio, an insect sign. The Lagna is therefore weak rendering the general structure of the horoscope shaky. Capricorn rising and lords of Lagna and the 8th—both debilitated and mutually aspecting—renders the native tall, lean, reddish brown in colour, the body being thin and bony. Rahu joining the scene suggests that the native is somewhat crafty and poses superior airs. Lack of self-confidence, nervousness and weak-mindedness are all concomitants of the affliction of the ascendant lord—an affliction somewhat rare and conspicuous inasmuch as even the benefics aspecting Saturn are rendered weak by their lordships, etc. The Moon being placed in a common and benefic sign and unaspected by malefics is a good feature in an otherwise unfortunate horoscope. This makes the native somewhat sympathetic and generous, the instincts being limited by the stress and strain of poverty. The presence of a powerful *Papadhi Yoga* in the shape of the disposition of Saturn in the 8th from the Moon has considerably sapped the vitality of the horoscope. Rahu and Saturn in the 4th is typical example of 'unhappiness' throughout life. Six planets in the 10th from Lagna and the 2nd from the Moon have lot of astrological significance. Ketu, Mars and Sun in conjunction give a false sense of prestige though the native possesses none.

Important Events.—The house of mother being afflicted considerably by Rahu indicates protection under a foster-mother during the period of Rahu. The beginning of Jupiter Dasa was significant as causing the greatest mental strain to the native in the shape of misunderstandings with brothers, relatives and cousins. Mark the presence of Jupiter, lord of the 3rd with Mars, Gnatikaraka—both being subjected to extremely evil influences. The same combination gave separation and estrangement.

Steady financial improvement was noticed in Jupiter Dasa,
though in the sub-period of Venus there was an appreciable
rise in money and professional matters. Venus, a Yogakaraka,
is situated in the 10th in his own house and is in the 2nd from
Chandra Lagna. His presence in Karakamsa is also a 'favourable'
combination. The major lord Jupiter occupies the 10th from
Lagna and the 2nd from the Moon, though by lordship he
becomes malefic.

Remarks.—In the horoscope under discussion, the Moon
is in the 9th house, the 2nd lord has obtained neechabhanga
and six planets are placed in the 10th house, suggesting indeed
strong elements. Study the horoscope carefully and you will
find the whole structure is rotten. The mutual aspect of two
debilitatad planets, lord of Lagna and the 2nd in conjunction
with Rahu and aspected by other evil forces, the *mutual aspects
between all the evil planets, viz.*, the Sun, Saturn, Mars, Rahu and
Ketu, suggest poverty, dissatisfaction and suffering. Venus is the
strongest planet in the horoscope and even he is afflicted by
being aspected, apart from malefics, by lords of 3rd, 6th and 12th.

The 10th Bhava is powerfully subject to *Rekha Yoga*
because the lord of Lagna has no strength, is aspected by the
8th lord, and Jupiter is obscured by the Sun. The result has
been, the person has neither knowledge nor wealth, he is
penurious, wrathful ; his mind is always distressed ; he is crafty,
disagreeable and miserable. The situation of five planets in a
single sign may be construed as a *Parivraja Yoga* (ascetic combination) but in the light of the planetary fight between Mercury
and Jupiter and other afflictions, it has lost its significance. The
native has a leaning for piety and religiousness. The 10th house
in any horoscope being the centre of gravity, even afflictions
in it cannot be altogether ignored. All the planets being

concentrated in the house of Karma has given the native great aspirations and he is capable of much endeavour and is intellectually inclined. Note the house of wealth from Chandra Lagna ; whilst it should have made the subject a millionaire it has been so spoiled by the evil combinations mentioned above that the person was a common man, hardly getting 100 chips a month. Rahu being the Atmakaraka, and the 10th being aspected by Saturn and Rahu, and occupied by Ketu and Mars (apart from the Sun, Mars, Mercury, Jupiter and Venus) made the press compositor.

The readers will do well to note the concentration of six planets in one sign and how the lords of 8, 12, 6 and 11 have all contributed, not a little, for the poverty, low social position and mental frustration of the native.

No. 74.—AN EXAMPLE FOR RAJA YOGA

Birth Details. —Born on 16th October 1918 at 2–25 p.m. (I.S.T.) (Lat. 13° N., Long. 77° 35′ E.)

Planetary Positions. —The Sun 180° 54′; the Moon 34°17′; Mars 229° 31′; Mercury 180° 32′; Jupiter 84° 1′; Venus 171° 10′; Saturn 124° 23′; Rahu 224° 24′; Ketu 44° 24′; and Lagna 298° 27′. Ayanamsa 21° 16′.

		Ketu	Jupit.			Jupiter Saturn	
Moon	RASI			Rahu	NAVAMSA		Venus Lagna
Lagna			Sat.	Moon			Ketu
	Mars Rahu	Mercury	Sun Venus	Mars		Mercury	Sun

Balance of Rahu Dasa at birth : Years 10–7–13.

Special Features. —Saturn lord of Lagna as well as Chandra Lagna aspects Chandra Lagna while in the Navamsa the Lagna is fairly strong by the occupation of Venus and the aspect of Lagna lord Moon. The native is handsome, fair-complexioned and of slender build. The qualities of the Moon and Venus, *viz.*, delicacy of figure and softness are well pronounced.

The 2nd is occupied by the Moon lord of the 7th and lord of the 2nd aspects the 2nd, as also Jupiter. This makes the native discriminative and gives large reasoning powers. As two malefics, one of them Mars, aspect the 2nd occupied by the emotional planet Moon, the native, somewhat quick-tempered, emotional and seemingly vindictive has been able to overcome the negative traits, thanks to the jupitarian aspect which restores equilibrium and self-possession. The position of the Sun makes the native careful, cautious and methodical. Precise in details, industrious and presistent, practical yet idealistic, sensitive, God-fearing and introspective, the native is endowed with all the blessings due to the strength of Lagna lord Saturn and the Lagna Capricorn, especially that Saturn has digbala and is free from the aspect or association of Mars or Rahu. Lord of the 4th or house of education is in the 8th from the 4th in association with Rahu. Lord of the 4th from Chandra Lagna is neecha but has neechabhanga. Vidyakaraka Jupiter aspects the 2nd or house of intelligence. The native is not much educated in the sense of school-going, but she has the capacity of quick comprehension, is well informed and cultured. Jupiter's disposition confers some sort of a psychic sense and the ability to intuitively study character. Matrukaraka Moon is afflicted by Saturn–Mars aspect, while Pitrukaraka Sun's position in Pitrusthana is not generally favoured. But as Saturn and Mars happen to be lords of Chandra Lagna and the 10th therefrom and as the Sun happens to be in a friendly sign, the parents were well placed in life. Superficially the 5th house seems to be afflicted because of the presence of Ketu and the aspect of Mars and Rahu. As however both Mars and Rahu are in the constellation of Mercury and the 5th lord Venus is neechabhanga and otherwise unblemished, the 5th house is well disposed. The 5th lord Venus and Putrakaraka Jupiter have gained 7 and 8 Navamsas respectively. Consequently, the number of surviving children are 7. The 7th lord Moon is well placed and Kalatrakaraka is neechabhanga, so that married life would be fairly happy. Mark the absence of influences of Rahu or Mars either on the 7th or on the Kalatrakaraka. The native's wifely qualities approximate almost to the ideal of Indian womanhood. The husband is of good social and financial standing, patient, scholarly, faithful and deeply attached, not demonstrative or emotional. Saturn's presence in the 7th from the Moon always favours affections that are stable and lasting. The Sun–Venus association in the 9th makes the native sociable, cultured, independent, artistic and gives high ideals.

Important Events.—Marriage took place in Jupiter Dasa own Bhukti, by virtue of the fact that Irom Kalatrakaraka-Jupiter happens to be the 7th lord. In the Navamsa, Jupiter joins the 7th lord from Lagna. Mercury, in the 2nd from Kalatra, karaka, gave during the sub-period (in the Dasa of Jupiter) independent life with husband, As lord of the 5th from the Moon is placed in the 5th from Putrakaraka Jupiter, the first issue was born in the same sub-period. Ketu and Jupiter are *dwirdwa-dasa*. Ketu is in the constellation of Mars. Consequently during this sub-period, the native's family broke up and she had to pass through great mental distress due to husband's misfortunes and financial upsets and the constant nagging of relatives which she bore with remarkable restraint and resignation. In the sub-period of Venus a daughter was born ; and the family was again set up. Mark the fact that Venus owns the 5th from Lagna. As the Sun is with Venus, another male issue was born during Sun's sub-period. Mars aspects the 5th Bhava. During the sub-periods of Mars and Rahu, two more sons were born.   It will be seen that both Mars and Rahu aspect the 5th and are in the constellation of the 5th lord from the Moon. In Sarurn Dasa Saturn Bhukti, there was loss of an issue and birth of another son.   Saturn aspects the 5th lord from the Moon in Rasi, while in Navamsa he has joined Putrakaraka. Saturn as Lagna lord is dignified.   In Mercury's sub-period, a daughter was born and there was acquisition of house pro- perty. In the sub-periods of Ketu and Venus (in Saturn Dasa) there was birth of two more male issues·   Jupiter and Saturn are lords of the 2nd from Lagna and Chandra Lagna respectively and both aspect the 2nd Bhava, thus causing fairly powerful Dhana Yogas which found expression in the Dasas of the two planets. Saturn Dasa favoured the native with fame, name and honour to husband.

The end of Saturn Dasa was of a poignant nature. Saturn occupies the constellation of Ketu who is in the 6th house and aspects Mercury lord of the 5th from the Moon. Jupiter is in a maraka (from 5th house) aspected by Mars, lord of the 12th (from 5th).   The native lost her eldest son and had to pass through a period of intense distress and mental affliction.

Saturn in spite of being lord of Lagna gave much worry and bodily suffering, at the same time conferring good name and financial stability.

The period of Mercury which commenced in 1965 is full of significance. As lord of the 9th Mercury is in the 10th having exchanged place with Venus lord of the 10th thus generating *Dharma-Karmadhipa Yoga.* Immediately after the commence- ment of this Dasa the native took to a most humanitarian and social activity, *viz.*, teaching Yoga to women thereby ena- bling them to get back their health, mental peace and equani- mity. She has been rendering yeoman service to her sisters.

Mercury has given her the capacity arising out of inner promptings to tackle complicated health problems and has given and been giving relief to innumerable ladies.   Being the planet of intellect and intuition Mercury has also enabled her to master the theory and practice of advanced yogic techniques.

Thanks to the strong yoga caused by Mercury, and his being aspected by Saturn, lord of Lagna and planet of philosophy and Jupiter planet of wisdom, there is perceptible an inner change in her thinking and values on the lines of our ancient scriptures.   Mercury has mellowed her personality.   She loses no opportunity to remove misunderstandings and bring together individuals and families when they have fallen out.

Mercury in the 10th in the constellation of Mars has given her considerable reputation as an exponent and teacher of Yoga.

Venus sub-period was highly significant.   The major lord owning the 9th and the sub-lord posited in the 10th gave her a world tour.   She gave talks in different parts of Europe and America and created in the minds of foreign ladies a keen interest in Yoga and the Hindu way of life.   During Venus, her sons were married and there were other auspicious happenings.

Remarks.—The horoscope becomes notable because of the presence of a powerful *Dharma-Karmadhipathi* Yoga.   Mercury lord of the 9th is in the 10th while Venus lord of the 10th is in the 9th.   Venus is a yogakaraka for Capricorn Lagna.   Mercury, who is in the 10th from Lagna is aspected powerfully by Saturn lord of Lagna and the 2nd and Dhanakaraka Jupiter.   Mercury becomes almost glorified when viewed from Chandra Lagna, as, happening to be lord of 5th, he occupies the 9th, aspected by Jupiter, lord of the 2nd and 11th and Saturn, lord of Chandra Lagna.   These combinations have immense potentiality in producing Dhana yogas and Raja yogas.   Born in a middle-class family, married at 12 to a person with hardly any pretensions to education or property, and faced with the tough problems of life, the native, by dint of luck and determination overcame all troubles and earned the affection and admiration of her kith and kin. The native's husband's financial prosperity is largely due to the neechabhanga of Kalatrakaraka Venus and the dig-bala of Chandra Lagna lord Saturn in the 7th therefrom. It is not enough if yogas are merely present. Dasas of planets causing such yogas must operate in appropriate time. The present horoscope is an illustrotion of the dawn of prosperity and afflu-ence in accordance with the presence of typical yogas and the operation of the Dasas of planets causing such yogas.

No. 75.—EX-KING FAROUK

Birth Details.—Born on 11-2-1920 at 10-18 p·m. (L.M.T.) (Lat 30° 2' N., Long. 31° 15' W.)

Planetary Positions.—The Sun 300° 32'; the Moon 210° 19'; Mars 192° 14'; Mercury 305° 17'; Jupiter 110° 46'; Venus 264° 56'; Saturn 138° 18'; Rahu 208° 53'; Ketu 28° 53'; and Lagna 180° 33'; 10th house 92° 1'. Ayanamsa 21° 18'.

	Ketu					Rahu
Mercury Sun	RASI		Jupit.	NAVAMSA		Moon
			Sat.	Jupit, Mars		
Venus	Moon	Mars Lagna Rahu	Ketu	Mercury Venus	Sun Lagna	Saturn

Balance of Jupiter Dasa at birth: Years 3-7-13.

Special Features.—Lagna is Libra or Thula. Lord of Lagna Venus is in the 3rd, Sagittarius, a war-like and inimical sign. In the Navamsa again, Lagna is Libra and Venus is in the second, aspected by Saturn and subjected to *Papakarthari Yoga*. Lagna is occupied by Mars and Rahu and aspected by Saturn. The focussing of the influences of the three first-rate malefics on Lagna is highly significant suggesting Farouk's instinctive sense of dominion and an insistent, determined energy. His personality expression is aggressive because of martian influences. Mars gives him dynamic energy and fiery enthusiasm and makes him penetrative. But the association of Rahu directs his capacities and energies in perverse channels. If Mars were alone, he would have perhaps been a benevolent Dictator-Monarch, owing to the presence of exalted Jupiter in the 10th. But Saturn and Rahu, lending their influences, have sapped up all the vitality so that he brought ruin not only upon himself but also to his country. The position of Mars alone would have given intellectual courage and optimism, positive thought and critical abilities but Rahu and Saturn take away much of the good with the result, Farouk, weak and ineffectual, had the misfortune of being an ambitious man more addicted to the guilded pleasures of a royal life than to its responsibilities. Such a combination renders the native to lose his balance of mind at the last moment in a crisis. This inference gains added strength because the Moon representing the mind is *neecha* and is aspected by Saturn (in the sense, the aspect angle between the Moon and Saturn is $72° 1'$). A little relief is of course lent by Jupiter's aspect. Jupiter's exaltation in the 10th, constituting *Hamsa Yoga*, endows him with a regal consciousness. And he feels the right of rulership by Divine endowment. But Saturn and the Sun aspecting each other make him too selfish. It will be seen that Egypt's tragedy was heightened by the fact that the King played for purely personal stakes. The situation of Saturn in the Sun's house and *vice versa* explains the traditional struggle between the Wafd and Farouk which more or less dominated the political scene. The Rahu–Mars association in Lagna is noteworthy. This reveals that the king was weak and ineffective and at crucial moments unable to strike hard at opposition and corruption. Some astrological writers think that Jupiter's exaltation in the 10th is a most fortunate position indicating for all-time uninterrupted prosperity. Such a position of Jupiter, according to them, affords a powerful protective influence. We have to differ a little and observe that whilst Jupiter's exaltation in the 10th would no doubt constitute a formidable strength, yet consistent with the malefic nature of directional influences, changes of fortune must occur. The heavy aspect, involving the 7th and 8th houses, emphasises the unhappiness in Farouk's demostic life and increases his desire for position and status in life. The Sun's disposition in a mystical sign gives him remarkable ability for the study of human nature, while the Sun and Mercury being aspected by Saturn suggests nervous and heart troubles. The horoscope is also distinguished by the presence of certain important yogas like *Hamsa*, *Amala*, *Damini* but *Hamsa Yoga* has lost some of its strength by virtue of Jupiter being Neecha in Navamsa. In Farouk's horoscope, except Jupiter and Saturn, the rest of the planets are located below the horizon. This has its own significance.

Important Events.—Farouk ascended the throne in his 17th year, in the course of Saturn Dasa. Saturn is a Yogakaraka and occupies the 11th aspected by Mercury lord of the 9th and the Sun lord of the 11th. Saturn is in the constellation of Venus, Lagna lord. He ascended the throne, adored by the people. It will be noted that four months after Farouk ascended the throne he set himself to break the power of the formidable Wafd which seriously threatened his rights. When he opened the Egyptian Parliament, the Wafd attempted to introduce a bill depriving the king of the right to dismiss a Cabinet or choose a Premier. Farouk acted fast. He dismissed Nahas Pasha on December 30, 1937. There were disorderly scenes in Parliament but Farouk carried off the situation. *Hamsa Yoga* is not without its blessings. He was strongly a nationalist. Though he observed to the letter Egypt's treaty obligation to Britain, he fought throughout the second world war to keep Egypt out of the fighting and he left little doubt of his desire to see Egypt's connection with Britain finally broken.

Beginning with the latter part of Mercury Dasa, his prestige faded so rapidly that he became the centre of a national and personal controversy. Besides, lord of the 9th is spoilt by his association, rather combustion with the Sun. Moreover he occupies the constellation of Mars and as we know, Mars is considerably afflicted by his association with Rahu and aspect of Saturn. Venus Bhukti in Mercury Dasa saw the dissolution of Farouk's marriage with Farida. Venus is the Kalatrakaraka and occupies a common sign which happens to be the 2nd from Chandra Lagna. The Moon Bhukti saw his marriage with Narriman Sadek, daughter of a commoner. The Moon's disposition in Kutumbasthana from Lagna and in a kendra from Dasanatha was responsible for Farouk's second marriage. And in Mars Bhukti Prince Ahmed Fuad was born. Mark the position of Mercury in the 5th from Lagna. Farouk was thrown out of power in Mars Bhukti in Mercury Dasa. Mercury Dasa commenced in 1943. Mercury is lord of the 9th and is in the 6th in combustion with the Sun, lord of the 11th, and aspected by Saturn the Yogakaraka. From Chandra Lagna, Mercury becomes bad by ownership but has the distinction of association with the 10th lord Sun. Saturn's aspect again

adds blemish to the combination. Mercury is in the constellation of Mars, who, it must be noted, is not only a maraka but
is considerably afflicted owing to his association with Rahu
and aspected by Saturn. Farouk's fall took place at the fag
end of Mars Bhukti in Mercury Dasa. He died in the sub-
period of the Moon in Venus Dasa.

Remarks.—The horoscope brings into relief certain specific
features or combinations indicating loss of power or Raja
Bhanga Here the planets involved in causing this misfortune
are Mercury, lord of the 9th or house of fortune, and Mars,
lord of the 2nd and 7th, a maraka. Mercury's situation in the
constellation of Mars *plus* the affliction of Mars in Lagna,
rendered him so powerful as to make the native fall from power
in his sub-period despite the general strength of the major lord.
It will also be seen that Saturn as a Yogakaraka, placed in the
11th from Lagna and the 10th from the Moon, conferred Raja
Yoga in his Dasa. His Dasa expired in 1943 and throughout
this period, while retaining Farouk in power Saturn give rise
to endless troubles which made Farouk's position unenviable.
Saturn is in the 2nd half of Leo. Consequently during the first
half of Saturn Dasa Farouk began is reign as a popular prince
and that popularity continued for long. In the second half of
Saturn, his position became a bed of thorns and he decided to
act more or less autocratic. All the same Saturn saw to it that
he did not get dethroned.

No. 76.—BANGALORE VENKATA RAMAN

[It may be asked whether our own horoscope merits inclusion along with the other notable horoscopes dealt with in this book. It will be difficult to answer such a question. The indulgent reader will nevertheless concede that if not for any other outstanding virtues, at least for the single circumstance of having brought together such a variety of horoscopes in book form, the author's horoscope should find a place. Because of the awareness that an objective assessment of our own horoscope may be quite beyond our capacity we are giving below the analysis of our chart as made by our esteemed colleague, Mr. S. Rajagopala Iyer, in the December 1957 issue of THE ASTROLOGICAL MAGAZINE.]

*Planetary Positions.—The Sun 113° 0'; the Moon 56° 38'; Mars 141° 23'; Mercury 133° 59'; Jupiter 222° 59'; Venus 122° 16'; Saturn 40° 11'; Rahu 352° 49'; Ketu 172° 49'; and Lagna 308° 16'; M.C. 222° 49'; Asterism—Mrigasira 1.

Rahu	Moon Saturn			Saturn Venus		
Lagna		Sun				Ketu
	RASI		Mars Merc. Venus	Rahu Sun	NAVAMSA	Moon Mercury
	Jupiter		Ketu	Lagna	Jupiter Mars	

Balance of Mars Dasa: 6 years, 10 months and 3 days.

°The casting is made by Mr. S. Rajagopala Iyer adopting an Ayanamsa of 22° 38'.

General.—The figure that stands out like a colossus in the history of modern Hindu Astrology is that of Prof. B. Suryanarain Rao the paternal grandfather of the native whose horoscope is the subject-matter of the present delineation. The great man made Astrology 'respectable' and rescued it from the cheap jeers of ignoramuses whose only qualification to criticise astrology was that they knew nothing about it.

The place of the Sun in the horoscope of Prof. Rao is occupied by Lagna in the subject's case and the Lagna sign in the lattar becomes the Moon-sign here. Both have Jupiter in the 10th, Jupiter aspecting Saturn and Mars aspecting the Lagna also. Yogakaraka Saturn in B. S. Rao's nativity becomes the ruler of Lagna in the others. The ruler of the 9th and 10th houses is Saturn and in Raman's horoscope there is a combination of rulers of the 9th and 10th houses also. B. Suryanarain Rao's horoscope is unique in having no *dwirdwadasa* or *shashtashta* positions of planets both in the Rasi and Navamsa. In Raman's horoscope this feature is present except for the Sun. But this horoscope excels in one respect. Six out of seven planets are in angles which is a very unusual feature and present generally in horoscopes that are destined to achieve something remarkable in this incarnation. But a fundamental difference exists between the two horoscopes in the fact that in the older horoscope, the sign of a benefic rises but in the other horoscope the sign of a malefic is on the Ascendant. B. S. Rao while doing a tremendous lot of work in the cause of astrology that would well-nigh have been impossible for any other, had congenial surroundings and the times propitious; people were ready and willing to be taught and he had a congenial social order to deal with. But now the times are different. Atheism and agnosticism prevail; not only that, but people have become militant and aggressive. Surely this is not conducive to the spread of astrology. What is worse is that there is opposition from higher circles and great people who think their greatness is due to their own remarkable wisdom and is not, and cannot be due to the planets. So Astrology is decried. To carry on a campaign on a wide front against all this is indeed a very difficult and unenviable task.

As typical of the greater difficulties to be encountered, we have the fact that Jupiter is also aspected by Saturn in this horoscope whereas in Prof. Rao's Jupiter alone aspects Saturn and not *vice versa*. This mutual aspect of Jupiter and Saturn implies that any success the native may achieve comes only after much opposition and effort and after having been worked for strenuously. With all this we have a horoscope that is well equipped for ultimate success. Jupiter on the meridian is the key planet of the horoscope and he is an outright benefic and the index of success. Though the inherent strength of the Moon is greater, being nearly 9 rupas, his residential strength is poor. Jupiter has got both, with nearly 7 rupas and 90 per cent in residential strength. He occupies a friendly sign and by reason of their being in kendras from each other, both Jupiter and Mars have also become intimate friends. Jupiter is in lunar Hora ($\frac{1}{2}$ sign), his own Drekkana (decanate) and Trimsamsa (1/30th division) and Navamsa of Venus—four benefic vargas in all—Gopuramsa. All the other planets except the Sun are in kendras from him and so connected; and the Sun is aspected by Jupiter and so is in a trine from Jupiter. This is also another mode of connection recognised in the texts.

Important Combinations.—*Gajakesari Yoga* is the one that prominently strikes the eye at the outset, Jupiter being in the 7th from the Moon. That the Moon is exalted adds to the efficacy of the yoga, and the strength of Jupiter will lead to its fulfilment. *Rajalakshana Yoga*: All the benefics, *i.e.*, Jupiter, Venus, Mercury and the Moon, should all be in kendras or in Lagna. Depending upon the strength of the yoga the native will have an attractive personality and will be endowed with all the good qualities of high personages. The effects of this yoga tend more to contribute *Adrishta* or luck. In fact this yoga is looked upon very highly even by such great Western astrologers as Cyril Fagan and others who interpret Sidereal Astrology to the West. This yoga is mentioned as "all benefics in the foreground" which means the same thing. Jupiter being in kendra or quadrant from Lagna itself gives rise to *Amala Yoga*, the effects of which are that the native will achieve lasting fame and reputation. The life too is rendered generally prosperous. A contribution towards the same end is also made by *Vesi Yoga* as the two benefics Mercury and Venus are placed in the 2nd from the Sun. Of course Vesi Yoga can arise from any planet, benefic or malefic in the 2nd from the Sun, except the Moon. Special significance is given to even one benefic occupying 2nd from the Sun by Varaha Mihira, who in his *Brihat Jataka*, Chapter XXII, Verse 4, says :

"A person born when the rising Navamsa is on Vargottama or when the Moon occupies a Vargottama position will be happy and prosperous. The same remark applies to a person at the time of whose birth the 2nd house from the Sun may be occupied by benefic planets or the kendra houses may happen to be occupied by planets. Also a person at the time of whose birth there are karaka planets occupying the signs of the zodiac will be happy and prosperous."

It may be pointed out here that the other combinations mentioned in the above verse are also present. It has already been mentioned that kendras are occupied by planets. But this will not by itself make the planets karakas. Planets in Lagna, 4th and 10th become karakas as also planets in exaltation, own sign and friendly signs.

Tungasuhritswa grihaamshe sthitaa grahaha karakaha samakhyataha
(Verse 3, Chap. VI, *Saravali*)
Lagnasthaha sakhasamsthaa dasamasthaaschaapi karakaha sarve
(Verse 4, Chap. VI, *Saravali*)

"Planets in exaltation, own sign or friendly signs, become karaka planets." In this horoscope Moon is in exaltation and Jupiter is in friendly sign. So they become karaka planets.

"All planets placed in Lagna, 4th and 10th become karaka planets." (7th is excluded.) Therefore in this horoscope, Saturn, Moon and Jupiter become karaka planets. These karaka yogas are often ingnored without reason by the rank and file of astrologers.

Sankha Yoga.—This yoga arises when the lord of 5th and 6th houses are in mutual kendras and the lord of Lagna is powerful. Both ingredients are present in this horoscope. Mercury, ruler of 5th house, and the Moon, ruler of the 6th, are in the 4th and 10th from each other and hence in mutual kendras. Saturn, ruler of Lagna, is one of the strongest planets in the horoscope having attained nearly 7 rupas and in point of residential strength, has the greatest percentage, namely 95 per cent. The principal effects are "that the native will be humanitarian, blessed with wife, children and lands, he will be righteously inclined, doing good deeds, learned in the sciences and living upto a good old age" (81 years).

Bheri Yoga.—This yoga is not common as its requirements are rigorous. Venus as well as lord of Lagna should occupy a kendra position with respect to Jupiter and the lord of the 9th

Bhava should be strongly disposed. Venus is ruler of the 9th and he is in kendra from Lagna which in itself is a position of strength. As both Jupiter and Saturn are in kendras from Venus, the requirements of the yoga are fully complied with. Verse 141 of Chapter VII of *Jataka Parijata* gives the effects as follows :

"Those born in Bheri Yoga are lordly men, of good birth, long-lived, exempt from diseases and danger, possessed of much wealth, lands, sons, wife, of great renown, enjoying much happiness out of their virtuous lives, eminently heroic and of great experience in the affairs of the world."

Parijatha Yoga.—The lord of the Navamsa in which the lord of the house occupied by the ascendant lord is placed should join a quadrant, a trine, or his own or exaltation place. Saturn ruler of ascendant occupies Taurus ruled by Venus. Venus occupies the Navamsa of Aries ruled by Mars who is in kendra from Lagna. Hence this yoga too is present. The effects of the yoga may be held to be equivalent to a powerful Rajayoga.

Brahma Yoga.—The yoga is only rarely found and the requirements are even more rigorous than for *Bheri Yoga.* Jupiter should be in a kendra from lord of the 9th house. Venus should be in a kendra from lord of the 11th house. Mercury too should be in kendra from lord of Lagna or the 10th house. As Jupiter is in a kendra from Venus and Venus is in a kendra from Jupiter necessarily and as Mercury is in kendra from Saturn, ruler of Lagna, the requirements of this yoga are fully complied with. The native will be respected by Brahmins and learned men, will be himself learned, long-lived, will be charitable and always bent on doing good deeds.

Rajayogas.—This class of yogas arises in two ways : (1) by combination, exchange, mutual aspect as between lords of kendras and konas, (2) in other ways. Rajayogas of both types are present in this horoscope. We have a conjunction of Venus, Mercury and Mars in the 7th in Leo. For purposes of Rajayoga, these have to be grouped as Venus conjunction Mercury (Venus, ruler of the 4th a kendra, with Mercury, ruler of the 5th), Mercury conjunction Mars (ruler of the 5th, a kona with ruler of the 10th, a kendra), Venus conjunction Mars (Venus, lord of the 9th with Mars, lord of the 10th Dharma-karmadhipati Yoga) and all these three combinations for Rajayogas occur in a kendra from Lagna as well as the Moon and it may be said that this feature is highly noteworthy.

Other Ways.—(1) Rajayoga arises when the Moon occupies a kendra other than Lagna and is aspected by Jupiter and otherwise powerful. The definition is taken from *Three Hundred Important Combinations* but *Jataka Parijata* requires that the Moon should be aspected by Venus as well (*vide* Verse 47 of Chapter VII).

Lagnam vidya kendrasthe chandre poornabalanvite ;
Gurubhargavasamdrishte jaatho rajaja bhavennaraha.

But in this horoscope, though the other elements are present, Venus does not aspect the Moon. Rajayoga according to Verse 53 of Chapter VII of *Jataka Parijata* is caused if the Moon in conjunction with Saturn be in the 11th, 4th or 10th. The person born, if of a royal family, will become a king.

Out of the lords of the 11th, 9th and 2nd houses, at least one planet must be in a kendra from the Moon and Jupiter must be lord of the 2nd, 5th or 11th house. In this horoscope Jupiter is ruler of the 2nd house. Jupiter, also ruler of the 11th, is in a kendra from the Moon. Venus ruler of the 9th is also in kendra from the Moon. Thus the yoga is amply borne out.

The above yogas take the horoscope high above average levels. But their effects will be only nominal if the planets concerned are not strong. But we have seen that the principal planets Jupiter and Saturn are endowed with great strength, inherent as well as residential. Thus far we have proceeded analytically and sympathetically in a general way but have not fully brought out the unique features present in the horoscope.

Special Features.—We have already pointed out that all the planets are connected with each other, i e., being either in kendras or in trines from each other. Excepting the Sun all planets are in kendras, a feature of great strength. According to Jaimini Astrology, Karakamsa, that is, the Navamsa occupied by the Atmakaraka planet is a centre for reckoning. In this horoscope, the Moon is the Atmakaraka as no other planet has advanced as much in its sign as the Moon has in the sign occupied by it. The Moon occupies the Navamsa of Leo and so Leo is Karakamsa. He is in conjunction with Mercury. According to the system of aspects in Jaimini, where all immovable signs are aspected by all other movable signs (except the one adjacent), Leo is aspected by all the other planets, as they are located only in movable signs including Rahu. This no doubt is an unusual feature and found only in exceptional horoscopes.

Aquarius is the sign that ascends at birth and this sign is powerfully aspected by its own lord Saturn. It is also aspected by two benefics Venus and Mercury. Though aspected by Mars also, this aspect is nearly out of orbs. Even this aspect will be an aspect by the ruler of the 3rd and 10th houses.

Western text-books have given the characteristics of Acquarius rising at birth but they refer to tropical signs. Yet the following taken from Llewellyn George, a standard American writer on Astrology, shows how truly they apply to the Sidereal Zodiac, incidentally testifying to the validity of this zodiac. "Determined, quiet, patient, unobtrusive and of faithful nature as a rule, Aquarians are philosophical, very humanitarian, usually refined, fond of art, music, scenery, literature. In disposition reasonable, thoughtful, discriminative. Have good memory, are clear reasoners, and very capable of dealing with facts. Everything in the mental world appeals to them and they are sincere and practical, fond of honour and dignity, active in reforms, progressive in ideas and possess a sympathetic, good-hearted, pleasant, generous nature. Have strong likes and dislikes, usually sociable and of large acquaintance ; intuitive, fond of occult research, peculiar, radical or eccentric in some ways. They succeed in pursuits where steady application of mind and concentration of thought are necessary, or where sociability and friends are required. They have inventive genius and literary ability. Uranus is the planetary significator." One need not even know the native in person except through his writings and works to judge how the above description fits like a glove. According to tropical longitudes, the ascendant would be Pisces.

Next in importance to Ascendant is the Moon-sign which is Taurus where it is in exaltation. This sign is the best sign for the Moon. It tends to bring out the quiet and reflective side of the Moon and at the same time to steady its changeful nature. Their memory is good and even tenacious and so once an impression is made, they "mould their actions for a long period on the original die". It is very difficult to make such people change their minds and this makes the native therefore conservative and conventional. **It is perhaps to this influence, that even holding an exalted position in the field of modern Astrology the native, in spite of irrefutable proofs that the trans-saturnine planets do act upon men and things, has not yet recognised them and boldly aligns himself with traditional astrology in this respect, and confines himself to the nine planets alone.** The conjunction of Saturn with the Moon may also have a good deal to do with it. If even the single planet Uranus is considered in connection with this nativity, the aspect Uranus sextile Jupiter and trine Saturn would very nicely sum up the life and work of the native.

Another impotrant and unignorable feature of the horoscope is the presence of all planets (except the Sun as well as Lagna) in fixed signs. This gives determination, firmness and self-reliance. The native will be either proud or dignified, inclined to be austere or autocratic but will always be dependable and reliable. He will be capable of patience and will rise in life through fixity of purpose and persistent effort. It confers the capacity to push a matter through thick and thin to a successful conclusion with a sort of missionary zeal before which no obstacles can hold out for long. We know that but for these qualities, THE ASTROLOGICAL MAGAZINE would not be in a position to serve its thousands of readers at the present moment ; in fact, it would have been non-existent long ago. Its present assured position has before it a long period of trials and tribulations.

Karma (Sphere of Work).—The 10th house is called the house of Karma and the 9th house is said to be the house of fortune. The sum of a native's past Karma is indicated by the 9th house, the assets and liabilities with which he incarnates.

The 10th which indicates his actual work will show how this is modified in the course of the present life. This fact has been well grasped by the more enlightened among the Western astrologers. Cartter in that very excellent work of his *Zodiac and the Soul* says: "Between its lives on earth the soul probably returns to a condition more similar to its own nature…having thus recuperated itself the spiritual impulse towards fresh experience and unfoldment becomes patent once more; then it will descend into a body at a time when the celestial conditions, resemble itself, its wishes, choice and aspirations. It therefore would follow that the nativity indicates the general destiny of life, for the soul, once incarnate, cannot reverse its choice…it is in fact the record of its past successes and failures in its attempts to adapt itself to an alien condition." Sepharial says thus in his *Cosmic Symbolism*: "In this connection, Astrology affirms that persons are born with particular horoscopes because when the heavens are so disposed as to admit of and indeed to favour the expression of certain forms of genius and faculty, the soul requiring those conditions is born into earth life." It has been defined by the ancient seers that the principal activities of this reincarnating ego in this life are indicated by the tenth house and the Sun which give its specific field of work, social and professional. A more general idea can be gleaned from the distribution of benefic and malefic planets in the horoscope. According to the doctrine of change of nature by rulership, malefics can become converted into benefics. As Lagna is both a kendra and kona, ruler of Lagna is always the most benefic planet for the horoscope. Thus Saturn becomes the best planet of this horoscope though usually the worst malefic. The Sun another 'malefic' by ruling the 7th, a kendra, also becomes benefic. Mars the only other malefic rules the 3rd and

10th and he also becomes benefic. On the other hand, the only benefic who rules an angle is Venus and by also ruling the ninth he becomes Yogakaraka These observations hold good for most natives who are born in Aquarius in these latitudes and so perhaps not so very individualistic as may be supposed. But it is not so common if not rare that all the malefics *also occupy asterisms that are ruled by only benefics*. It will be readily seen that Saturn is in Rohini an asterism ruled by the Moon, the Sun in Aslesha ruled by Mercury, Mars in Poorvaphalguni ruled by Venus ; Ketu in Hasta ruled by the Moon and Rahu in Revati ruled by Mercury. The principal malefics Mars and Saturn have also attained each, a minimum of four benefic vargas. All these generally indicate that the native will be the author of good Karma and the special field of work will be indicated by the 10th house and the Sun. *I will make bold to assert here that destiny as indicated by both these factors unmistakably points to Astrology as the special field of work for the native ;* not merely astrology, but I will go still further and demonstrate that the native is and will be the discoverer and disseminator of the truths of Astrology, not by forced reasoning or strained efforts but by the application of simple, straight textbook rules.

What are the elements in the horoscope from which the field of work is to be determined ? All authorities agree that it is the tenth house and that the karaka is the Sun. It may be tenth house from Lagna, Moon or Sun. But the greatest significance is attached to the planet occupying the 10th house. Only when the tenth from any of the above three centres is unoccupied by the planet, other factors are to be looked to. This Varaha Mihira enumerates tersely in a single verse, which is variously interpreted by other text writers. Prithuyasas exemplifies this in three verses in his own book *Horasara* thus in Chapter XXII :

1. "A person gets wealth in various ways suited to his inner nature. Wealth is acquired through planets posited in the 10th house reckoned from Lagna, the Moon or the Sun or their Navamsas.

2. There is acquisition of wealth from the father, mother, brother, relative, elder, wife or an inferior according as the Sun or any other planet taken in order occupies the 10th place from Lagna, the Sun or the Moon ; or other kinds of relatives.

3. If the 10th house be planetless, then the livelihood will be through that prescribed from the ruler of that house (or the ruler of the Navamsa occupied by the planet owning the 10th house) reckoned from the Lagna, the Moon or the Sun whichever is stronger or that prescribed for the lord of the sign in which the lord of the above 10th house is posited."

It may be noted that Prithuyasas makes two significant changes in Varaha Mihira's specification which others have not dared to do. For Mars he boldly puts brother, whereas Varaha Mihira says foe and for Jupiter he puts 'elder' whereas Varaha Mihira and others put 'brother'."

Thus Prithuyasas makes it abundantly clear that when the 10th from Lagna, the Moon or the Sun is occupied by a planet, that becomes the key planet for profession. In the nativity on hand, Jupiter occupies the tenth from Lagna in great strength. The scope of Jupiter has also been defined by the same author thus in verse 8 of the same chapter :

"When the Navamsa in question belongs to Jupiter, the native will obtain his livelihood by the chanting of the Vedas, worshipping Gods, chanting mantras, exposition of mantras, *by astrology* and by royal favour."

Astrology is one of the matters ruled by Jnpiter. Now we have to look to the karaka, also the Sun, as to the indications furnished thereby. The Sun occupies Cancer, the sign that is known as the sign of the prophet or the teacher the keynote of which is patience, watchword, sympathy and its rular is the Moon. The Sun is aspected by both Jupiter and Saturn. It is significant how Saturn comes to be inextricably connected with both Jupiter and the Sun. Both Jupiter and the Sun are aspected by Saturn in the Rasi and in the Navamsa. The Sun occupies the Navamsa of Saturn and Jupiter, the asterism ruled by Saturn. The dispositor of the Sun in the Rasi is associated with Saturn. Western astrologers have found after an extensive statistical analysis that Saturn is the most strongly aspected planet in the figure in 40 per cent of the horoscopes examined. The degree influences occupied by both Saturn and the Sun are very significant and point to astrology. Maurice Wemyss in dealing with professions and occupations says:
"Astrologers are as a rule mathematicians and exhibit a combination of Cancer–Capricornus 13-15 with Gemini–Sagittarius 3. The peculiar faculty however which distinguishes them is their power of scientific prediction. Cancer–Capricornus 22-23 degrees connected with forethought and their rules are specially prominent. Taurus–Scorpio 11 connected with "forethought" are specially prominent indicating understanding of human nature. Is it an accident that Saturn occupies the eleventh degree of Taurus and the Sun the twenty-third degree of Cancer in the horoscope of the native whose life-long work is devoted entirely to the cause of Astrology? It is no object to state that the above degrees are found in a work devoted to the Tropical and not Sidereal Zodiac. Even in the West something is being accomplished with the Tropical longitudes because only of a

symbolic validity which stems from their sidereal counterparts. Sepharial, an astrologer of the Tropical School, has made it clear that the degree influences can relate only to "the specific degrees of the Fixed Zodiac".

There is also a special Yoga for proficiency in the science of astrology.

"When the lord of the 2nd house is strong and Mercury is posited in a kendra or kona or the 11th house, the native will be one of the foremost astrologers."

The next important planet whose bearing on the question of profession we have to take note of is Mars. Mars is the ruler of the tenth house from Lagna as well as the Sun. Mars is the ruler of the Navamsa in which the lord of the 10th house from the Moon is located. Verse 6 of Chapter XXII of *Horasara* attributes to Mars the following means of livelihood :

"If the Navamsa in question belongs to Mars, the person gains a livelihood by teaching, by proficiency in the mantras, an aggressive bold act, weapon, fire or drug, trading things in the market and from Kshatriyas."

The native is a teather of astrology, an expounder of the truths of astrology and also author and publisher of works on Astrology. Note Mars is the ruler of the 3rd and the 10th houses and the third house represents writings and publications. Mars is also in conjunction with the ruler of the 9th house (also publications). Saturn is also the ruler of the 9th and the 10th houses from the Moon and aspects Jupiter in the 10th from Lagna. Mars ruler of the 3rd and the 10th from Lagna aspects Jupiter in the 10th. In the Navamsa, Mars ruler of the 9th from the Moon is in conjunction with Jupiter ruler of Navamsa Lagna. Jupiter, ruler of the 9th from the Sun, is aspected by Mars, ruler of the 10th from the Sun. Thus the function of teaching astrology is carried on by writings, publications and also as a professional astrologer. This is the logical result of blending all the influences bearing on the tenth house or Karma Bhava of the nativity in accordance with the standard texts.

Principal Events.—If anybody had gathered the impression that because of the above discussions the native's life should be a prosperous one with uniform progress in all such matters, he would be very much mistaken. Almost the entire period of Mars remained at birth and then Rahu and Jupiter followed. Rahu occupies the second, a maraka house and is aspected by Mars and Jupiter. Being in the sign of Jupiter and aspected by him, it is Jupiter's influence that he would imbibe and reflect. However well-placed Jupiter is, it cannot be ignored, that he is the ruler of the 2nd and the 11th houses from Lagna, the 8th and the 11th from the Moon who is more powerful than the Lagna. Life should have been difficult and the native may have had to face several periods of crisis. The close of the major period of Rahu and the beginning of that of Jupiter should have proved most critical indeed in more respects than one. Even the sub-period of Jupiter in the major period of Jupiter (11-6-1937 to 29-7-1939) should have been very trying and relief seen only in the sub-period of Saturn (29-7-1939 to 11-2-1942). For in the mutual aspect between Jupiter and Saturn, it is Jupiter that suffers from the aspect of a malefic while the malefic gains by the aspect of a benefic. This also furnishes a clue to the fact that the major period of Saturn beginning from 11-6-1953 should have proved helpful and prosperous.

The native lost his mother quite early in his life.

Sukhe Shanou Matrunashameti.

Saturn in the 4th along with the Moon the karaka posited therein is not conducive for long life of mother.

"Ascertain the Navamsa occupied by lord of the 4th. Look to what Navamsa is occupied by him. The lord of this Navamsa will indicate, by his rays, the time of demise of mother." Venus lord of the 4th occupies the Navamsa of Aries ruled by Mars. Mars occupies Navamsa ruled by Venus (Libra). So the rays of Venus will give clue. Venus has 8 rays, that is, this is the full quota when in exaltation. It will be zero at debilitation point which is Virgo 27. Longitude of Venus is Leo 2° 16'. There are yet 55 degrees. $55/180 \times 8$ will give the number of years $= 2\frac{1}{2}$ years. Some reduction is due for his occupation of inimical Dwadasamsa, Leo (one-twelfth). Having regard to all this, the mother's death is due when the native was about two years old. In 1914 the mother died. Death of father took place in the sub-period of Mercury in the major period of Jupiter. Both planets are marakas for the horoscope and Mercury ruler of the 8th in the 7th is especially so. He is associated with ruler of the 9th as well as ruler of the 10th—father and father's death (10th being 2nd from the 9th). In the Navamsa, he rules the 7th and the 10th from Lagna. The profession of the native began as early as 1936 when he started RAMAN PUBLICATIONS for publishing books on Indian Culture and Astrology and in the same year restarted THE ASTROLOGICAL MAGAZINE as a Quarterly. It was in the sub-period of Mars in the major period of Rahu—what a combination ! Rahu is no doubt aspected by Jupiter and Mars is ruler of the 3rd and the 10th and the time quite appropriate for restarting an enterprise which had been discontinued and had ceased to exist. But Mars in the 6th from Dasanatha implies

stupendous difficulties and it was no easy task to overcome
opposition, external and internal. Mars being angular alone
saved the situation from disaster as also the dogged persistence evidenced by nearly all the planets being in fixed signs.
In the face of odds, the magazine made slow headway until it
could be made into a monthly characteristically enough in the
sub-period of Saturn in the major period of Jupiter. The time
now was most propitious as borne out by the steady upward
progress it has maintained till now. The popularity and
success of THE ASTROLOGICAL MAGAZINE is not a little due to
the remarkable editorials in which critical world situations are
judged to a nicety and events foretold long before anybody can
even conceive of them as being likely from the trends of political
events. It is only proper that such merits should receive
recognition. He was conferred the dignity of Doctor of
Science (*Honoris Causa*) by the "Academie et Universite
Internationale" in the sub-period of Venus in the major period
of Jupiter. The only auspicious planet for Aquarius is Venus.
His conjunction with Mercury and Mars gives rise to Raja Yoga.
He is in kendra from Lagna as well as Dasa lord and in the
second from the Sun. His rulership of the 4th is responsible
for such honours and in the Navamsa he is aspected by Jupiter,
ruler of the 4th from Lagna as also by Mars, ruler of the 4th
from the Moon.

The native married early and has a large family of seven
children. The native is happily married, lords of 1 and 7 being in
the 3rd and the 11th from each other and lord of the 7th being
aspected by Jupiter powerfully. The seventh itself is occupied
by three planets, two benefics and a malefic. Lord of the 5th
Mercury is in the 7th. According to *Saravali* "When lord of the
5th occupies the 7th house, his wife will bear good sons, will be

devoted to her kinsmen, of sweet speech, of good conduct and graceful hip.'' The fith falls in a benefic sign ruled by Mercury from Lagna as well as from the Moon. Mercury is Vargottama. Both Mercury and Jupiter (Putrakaraka) have attained good shadbala strength and are posited in kendras, the strength being slightly greater for the karaka who is posited in a prolific sign. The seventh from the Moon is occupied by Jupiter in full strength. The seventh from Lagna, as well the Moon in the Navamsa, is also aspected by Jupiter.

The native had a successful tour of United States and Europe in October and November 1959, another blessing of Saturn Dasa.

It is not difficult now to guess at the future in store for the couple. The native is engaged in research work in his favourite field of astrology and we can expect the results of such rasearch in the pages of the magazine. In this connection we cannot but be struck with the significance of the effects attributed to the combination of Saturn and the Moon in the 4th house given in *Saravali* though in a figurative sense. Verse 43, Chapter XXI says:

Jalamutkramanipoutairjavinti.

''The native is a trader in pearls, a pearl-diver. And we get pearls of wisdom as the result of his deep researches into astrological lore of the past, and to trade these pearls for the benefit and edification of his readers, whose number must be very large, in his profession.

Postscript by Agastya

The end of Saturn's period (Jupiter's sub-period) was highly significant. Under these directional influences the native had a world tour and delivered innumerable lectures in Europe and America. He had the unique honour of giving a lecture on astrology at the United Nations in October 1970. Again in April 1971, he visited U.S.A. to inaugurate an international congress of astrology. Jupiter and Saturn conferred honours, reputation and financial prosperity.

Mercury's major period has been equally outstanding— another world tour for lectures, creation of interest in astrology in several places of learning and raising the status of astrology to academic levels, presiding over innumerable conferences and frequent visits from persons in high walks of life. Mercury has caused a powerful Raja Yoga in the 7th from Lagna and the 4th from Chandra Lagna, which means the 10th from Chandra Lagna is influenced. Mercury is in conjunction with Venus, a Yogakaraka. As lord of the 5th, his conjunction with Mars, lord of the 10th, has strengthened the Yoga further. Besides this, Mercury is Vargottama and occupies the constellation of Yoga-karaka Venus. Thus the period of Mercury could confer further reputation and honour and the fulfilment of the native's objective —putting astrology on a level with other so-called respectable sciences—an objective, for which the native has been striving for over four decades.

Venus is a potential Yogakaraka. Consequently in his sub-period (in Mercury's major period), the native received high distinctions—an honorary D.Litt. degree from the Kumaon University and the titles of *Abhinava Varahamihira*, *Jyotirvidya Marthanda* and *Abhinava Bhaskara* from the Varahamihira Memorial Celebrations Committee, Jyotirvidya Mandal and Saraswat Mahaviswa Vidyalaya respectively.

There is the other side of the coin. Mercury as lord of the 8th in association with Mars lord of the 3rd subject to Papakarthari Yoga has its own malefic influences to exercise —opposition, unhealthy rivalry, and attempts by ill-intentioned persons to indulge in character-assassination to harm the native. But Jupiter in the 10th aspecting the ascendant lord, the Sun and the Moon could rescue the native from all troubles and give him triumph in his desire to find an honorable place for astrology in the comity of other sciences.

Mars Bhukti in Mercury Dasa proved highly troublesome. Mercury as the 8th lord and Mars as the 3rd and 10th lord are hemmed in between malefics, the Sun and Ketu. Mars aspects the 2nd house adversely. As a result, the native had to face a severe crisis in his domestic life and heavy expenditure. However, Jupiter, strong in the 10th, enabled him to tide over the difficulties in the face of many odds and maintain mental equilibrium. But the Rajayoga effects also continued. To him pleasure and pain are the same and this attitude. has stood him in good stead and enabled him to come out of the ordeals he had to face during a distinguished career of over 45 years.

Rahu in Mercury gave him another trip to Europe and America in May 1981.

INDEX OF HOROSCOPES

TABLE OF

H.No.	Sun		Moon		Mars		Mercury		Jupiter	
1	2		3		4		5		6	
	°	′	°	′	°	′	°	′	°	′
1	139	48	47	42	91	6	152	48	148	54
2	29	3	200	45	26	54	53	6	11	0
3	123	35	208	31	86	18	105	31	185	54
4	183	25	303	55	39	25	173	25	111	25
5	8	12	69	12	332	36	24	6	303	36
6	247	59	336	41	314	29	255	58	353	17
7	267	30	139	2	271	2	245	2	229	32
8	28	45	136	0	90	35	2	24	209	50
9	11	32	73	50	121	24	24	42	63	0
10	53	12	79	54	28	36	57	36	297	0
11	169	23	198	12	179	38	154	33	170	0
12	16	30	100	7	317	0	358	48	260	6
13	220	30	38	18	211	24	232	24	164	30
14	323	52	142	52	282	56	342	0	261	40
15	235	12	70	0	294	42	251	30	187	18
16	251	48	42	18	336	48	267	48	19	18
17	203	50	35	14	144	0	199	0	310	0
18	323	56	178	48	76	37	338	10	307	19
19	237	24	227	42	222	5	216	42	238	12
20	136	0	323	0	254	30	130	0	337	0
21	229	54	24	24	318	0	227	42	47	30
22	201	0	182	0	87	0	224	0	169	0
23	23	9	96	40	64	9	0	21	143	14
24	304	6	275	20	185	46	312	44	332	16
25	113	45	53	45	196	45	95	45	4	45

PLANETARY POSITIONS

Venus		Saturn		Rahu		Ascendant			Ayanamsa	
7		8		9		10			11	
°	′	°	′	°	′	°	′		°	′
102	54	224	42	106	24	50	0	+	50	40
6	12	24	36	86	54	116	45	+	14	16
126	20	59	54	314	2	19	31	+	10	32
230	25	36	55	39	25	180	30	+	6	25
3	0	265	30	41	18	99	22	+	6	10
233	1	351	47	210	35	165	29	+	5	27
298	2	182	2	278	50	267	32	+	5	2
39	29	211	46	35	31	304	47		2	26
16	36	260	18	43	42	102	2		8	40
67	0	278	48	161	6	49	1		9	6
155	24	174	18	3	10	100	40		11	2
346	24	64	0	42	30	262	29		12	34
186	0	39	6	263	48	136	28		15	0
6	7	236	2	328	10	184	24		15	14
200	2	209	12	309	36	203	22		16	1
271	40	281	48	111	24	226	18		16	56
259	0	48	0	280	0	313	45		17	4
10	1	197	37	60	49	149	9		17	14
281	41	239	58	65	12	182	28		18	32
157	30	206	0	267	0	208	0		18	54
194	6	236	24	225	0	258	0		18	56
202	0	274	0	156	0	74	1		18	57
50	57	59	3	284	17	115	0		19	9
347	46	223	16	197	44	316	39		19	40
67	45	217	45	187	36	55	0		19	45

TABLE OF

H. No.	Sun		Moon		Mars		Mercury		Jupiter	
1	2		3		4		5		6	
	°	'	°	'	°	'	°	'	°	'
26	24	18	24	8	90	58	40	12	263	5
27	42	13	43	40	357	42	19	2	297	4
28	308	19	323	15	293	9	316	33	76	0
29	301	12	18	29	180	53	308	27	321	38
30	99	55	349	15	185	10	82	32	348	44
31	103	36	44	36	186	36	88	36	348	36
32	330	23	283	45	216	55	317	53	22	58
33	227	1	170	0	291	52	243	48	56	39
34	292	34	285	4	340	34	270	34	51	4
35	25	48	351	59	61	36	9	18	117	24
36	270	52	168	54	7	46	283	13	185	28
37	329	30	228	31	40	56	302	40	186	42
38	106	34	290	12	127	35	102	32	179	56
39	76	50	16	19	2	39	57	50	207	36
40	157	52	300	3	76	0	148	25	271	54
41	168	22	120	10	207	39	193	9	30	25
42	201	48	345	47	133	14	191	8	65	36
43	121	47	247	11	96	50	144	57	113	2
44	321	6	32	42	11	29	295	36	221	5
45	332	46	233	48	276	12	342	25	306	44
46	257	4	89	58	23	26	234	36	317	57
47	290	20	75	5	66	15	306	23	26	10
48	342	17	165	20	317	33	321	50	62	43
49	46	10	304	28	8	5	60	26	74	0
50	105	13	48	21	52	13	104	43	87	43

PLANETARY POSITIONS (Contd.)

Venus		Saturn		Rahu		Ascendant		Ayanamsa	
7		8		9		10		11	
°	'	°	'	°	'	°	'	°	'
39	12	325	59	18	39	302	56	19	52
6	45	338	53	358	17	41	19	19	53
339	29	195	10	214	20	304	53	20	6
260	33	63	20	6	9	43	9	20	24
100	24	76	53	358	57	110	23	20	24
105	36	77	36	358	14	44	36	20	24
333	7	91	6	327	21	192	50	20	26
247	38	111	17	312	49	32	0	20	26
247	34	108	4	310	4	307	4	20	26
24	32	132	37	266	17	336	9	20	28
278	32	165	2	233	41	267	31	20	30
351	17	162	31	230	38	258	40	20	30
151	44	160	32	223	5	211	52	20	30
71	26	170	59	205	24	56	43	20	30
204	9	199	11	162	15	273	16	20	32
205	53	229	57	103	36	193	14	20	35
193	36	245	1	82	35	210	13	20	36
129	59	265	2	48	4	116	42	20	37
358	33	309	29	339	33	221	6	20	33
356	16	343	28	280	46	81	47	20	43
211	57	348	22	265	23	182	18	20	43
285	16	15	20	224	55	143	32	20	46
298	38	31	51	202	49	340	37	20	47
15	51	39	45	199	20	266	45	20	43
90	43	46	43	196	4	211	43	20	47

TABLE OF

H.No.	Sun		Moon		Mars		Mercury		Jupiter	
1	2		3		4		5		6	
	°	'	°	'	°	'	°	'	°	'
51	27	54	194	27	116	27	40	29	97	19
52	53	9	182	56	128	54	32	44	101	28
53	230	47	55	28	247	30	246	7	134	33
54	171	58	140	9	110	24	164	2	151	19
55	355	50	19	10	135	45	0	20	158	18
56	113	38	332	46	86	21	100	16	188	0
57	144	8	24	13	106	41	141	32	192	46
58	9	56	255	46	25	31	4	48	257	23
59	211	43	109	20	161	25	198	35	256	38
60	180	2	192	44	263	13	162	40	281	54
61	231	39	53	3	323	54	247	28	354	9
62	356	39	241	15	45	14	346	2	12	3
63	315	26	196	24	256	18	332	20	33	7
64	71	24	313	0	339	27	96	42	57	27
65	156	19	76	32	175	50	156	35	151	15
66	239	56	213	56	220	25	237	18	107	38
67	289	39	116	0	253	19	304	54	102	20
68	282	23	159	16	50	55	279	56	137	55
69	30	43	149	50	95	28	43	25	129	36
70	218	44	137	22	145	37	237	51	290	11
71	308	15	254	30	349	21	306	37	36	42
72	36	41	160	43	79	16	45	39	163	44
73	196	2	175	31	184	48	186	26	186	42
74	179	8	312	8	229	45	180	33	83	35
75	300	32	210	19	192	14	305	17	110	46
76	113	0	56	38	141	23	133	59	222	59

PLANETARY POSITIONS (Contd.)

Venus		Saturn		Rahu		Ascendant		Ayanamsa	
7		8		9		10		11	
°	′	°	′	°	′	°	′	°	′
73	13	49	30	181	1	178	15	20	47
92	54	52	52	179	37	117	40	20	47
194	35	60	42	169	59	260	10	20	47
211	11	77	24	153	43	112	4	20	48
312	8	71	42	144	2	181	50	20	49
156	0	97	44	118	12	222	42	20	50
164	18	101	28	116	30	119	0	20	50
25	50	112	35	86	6	185	54	20	52
188	48	132	15	74	10	114	25	20	52
225	14	141	51	56	27	357	2	20	52
196	9	169	55	15	8	194	36	20	54
350	7	167	54	8	30	60	49	20	55
301	51	183	49	351	19	284	9	20	55
32	4	177	29	344	57	283	4	20	56
121	37	215	20	282	18	166	0	20	58
194	58	203	49	316	28	187	3	20	57
249	49	207	27	313	14	257	27	20	58
327	59	218	5	295	0	8	24	20	59
10	46	216	58	289	13	95	50	20	59
217	14	272	45	182	10	204	17	21	0
309	22	313	37	119	27	274	57	21	6
351	42	9	4	37	17	79	16	21	1
189	33	9	55	28	33	299	0	21	9
170	4	124	58	233	25	293	18	21	16
264	56	138	18	208	53	180	33	21	18
122	16	40	11	352	49	308	16	21	38

INDEX OF TECHNICAL TERMS

Acharyas ... Teachers, Preceptors.

Adhi Yoga ... Benefics in 6, 7 and 8 from the Moon.

Adhi Mitra ... Intimate friend.

Ahimsa ... Non-violence.

Alpayu ... Short life.

Amala Yoga ... Benefic in the 10th.

Anapha Yoga ... Planets in the 12th from the Moon.

Aputra Yoga ... Combination for childlessness.

Arishta ... Misfortune.

Aryavartha ... Part of India from Himalayas to Vindhyas.

Asura Yoga ... A malefic combination.

Aswatha ... *Ficus religiousae* tree

Atma Gnana ... Knowledge of Self.

Atmakaraka ... Significator of the Ego, the Sun.

Atmasakti ... The subtle and spiritual force of the soul.

Ayudha Drekkana ... Middle ones of Virgo and Gemini.

Ayushkaraka ... Indicator of Longevity, Saturn.

Bahukalatra Yoga ... Combination for more than one wife.

Bandhana Yoga ... Combination for incarceration.

Bhagawad Gita ... The Song Celestial.

Bhagavata ... The sacred book dealing with Sri Krishna's life.

Bhaktas ... Devotees.

Bhakti ... Devotion to God.

Bharani ... 2nd constellation from Aswini.

Bhava ... A 'house' in Astrology.

Bhratrukaraka	...	Indicator of brothers, Mars.
Bhukti	....	Sub-period.
Brahma	...	Creator, first of the Hindu Trinity.
Brahmacharya	...	Continence.
Brahma Sutras	...	Philosophical treatise by Vyasa.
Budha	...	Mercury.
Chaitra	...	The first lunar month.
Chara Rasi	...	Movable sign, Aries, Cancer, Libra and Capricorn.
Chandra	...	The Moon.
Chamara Yoga	...	Lord of Lagna occupying own or exaltation house.
Chandalas	...	Depraved people.
Chandra Mangala Yoga		Moon–Mars combination.
Damini	...	A special combination of planets.
Dasa	...	Directional measure, period.
Dasanatha	...	Lord of Dasa or period.
Dhanakaraka	...	Indicator of wealth, Jupiter.
Dhana Yoga	...	Combination for wealth.
Dhanus	...	Sagittarius.
Dharma	...	Righteousness, moral order.
Dharmasthana	...	9th house.
Dharmatrikona	...	1st, 5th and 9th houses.
Digbala	...	Directional strength.
Dwirdwadasa	...	Planets in the 2nd and 12th from each other.
Dwiswabhava	...	Common sign. *e.g.*, Gemini.
Elarata	...	The period of Saturn's transit of the 12th, 1st and 2nd places from the radical Moon.
Eswara	...	Lord.

Gajakesari Yoga	...	Moon–Jupiter in mutual angles.
Gayatri Japams	...	Recitation of the name of Goddess Gayatri.
Gnanakaraka	...	Indicator of wisdom.
Gocahara	...	Transit results.
Gola Yoga	....	Seven planets in one sign.
Gowdapada	...	Preceptor of Sankara.
Guru	...	Jupiter.
Harsha Yoga	...	Lord of the 6th in the 6th.
Hatha Yoga	...	A system of physical and mental discipline.
Jyotisha	..	Astrology.
Janma Lagna	...	Birth Ascendant.
Kahala Yoga	...	An important combination.
Kaladi	...	Birthplace of Sankara.
Kalatrabhava	...	The 7th house.
Kalatrakaraka	...	Indicator of wife, Venus.
Kali Yuga	...	The fourth of the Time-cycles according to Hindus.
Kamsa	...	A king of Mathura, maternal uncle of Lord Krishna.
Kanya	...	Virgo.
Karaka	...	Significator, Indicator.
Karakamsa	...	Navamsa held by Atmakaraka.
Karkataka	...	Cancer.
Karma	...	Action, profession, law of cause and effect.
Karmasthana	...	The 10th house.
Karma Yoga	...	One wedded to action.
Kauravas	...	Cousins and enemies of Pandavas.
Kendra	...	An angular house.

Ketu	...	Cauda, Dragon's tail.
Kshatriya	...	The warrior caste.
Kuja	...	Mars.
Kumbha	...	Aquarius.
Kundali	...	Horoscopic chart.
Lagnadhipathi	...	Lord of Ascendant.
Lakshmi Yoga	...	Association or aspect between lord of 1 and 9.
Madhyayu	...	Middle term of life.
Mahants	...	Priests.
Maharshis		Great Sages of India.
Malavya Yoga	...	Venus in an angle identical with own or exaltation house.
Maha Yuga	...	Great Cycle of Time comprising of one each of Krita, Treta, Dwapara and Kaliyugas.
Makara	...	Capricorn.
Maraka	...	Death, Death-inflicting planet.
Marakasthana	...	House of death.
Matrukaraka	...	Indicator of mother, the Moon.
Maya	...	Illusion.
Mesha	...	Aries.
Mimamsakas	...	Expounders of the ritualistic thought.
Mithuna	...	Gemini.
Meena	...	Pisces.
Moksha	...	Emancipation, Liberation.
Mokshasthana	...	The 12th house.
Mrityu Yoga	...	An evil combination.
Nakshatra	...	Constellation.
Naidhana	...	Destruction.
Navamsa	...	One-ninth division of a sign.